COMMUNISM AND SOCIAL DEMOCRACY

PART II

By the same author

AN INTRODUCTION TO ECONOMIC HISTORY,

1750–1950

CHARTIST PORTRAITS

THE CASE FOR INDUSTRIAL PARTNERSHIP

With A. W. Filson

BRITISH WORKING CLASS MOVEMENTS:

Select Documents, 1789–1875

COMMUNISM AND SOCIAL DEMOCRACY

1914–1931

BY

G. D. H. COLE

MACMILLAN

London · Melbourne · Toronto

ST MARTIN'S PRESS

New York

1969

© Margaret Cole 1960

First Edition 1958
Reprinted 1961, 1965, 1969

Published by
MACMILLAN AND CO LTD
Little Essex Street London W C 2
and also at Bombay Calcutta and Madras
Macmillan South Africa (Publishers) Pty Ltd Johannesburg
The Macmillan Company of Australia Pty Ltd Melbourne
The Macmillan Company of Canada Ltd Toronto
St Martin's Press Inc New York

Printed in Great Britain by
REDWOOD PRESS LIMITED
Trowbridge, Wiltshire

CONTENTS

PART II

THE PRINCIPAL CHARACTERS

[1] Discussed also in Volume II.
[2] Discussed also in Volume III.

[1] Discussed also in Volume II.
[2] Discussed also in Volume III.

CHAPTER XIII

FRANCE, 1914-1931

FROM 1905 up to the break between Communists and anti-Communists in 1920, the French Socialists were organised in a single Unified Party which described itself as the Section Française de l'Internationale Ouvrière (S.F.I.O.). This description was in part a tribute to the pressure which the Second International had brought to bear on the contending factions. Without this pressure it is more than doubtful whether any sort of unification could have come about ; and the behaviour of the French delegations at International Congresses after 1905 plainly showed that the differences had by no means disappeared. The old leaders, Jean Jaurès (1859-1914) and Jules Guesde (1845-1922) found themselves on opposite sides on more than one occasion, especially in relation to the critical issue of international action to prevent war. They differed also about the correct attitude towards anti-militarist campaigns, towards joint action with the bourgeois left, and, not least, towards the Trade Unions. Guesde continued to insist on the necessity of bringing the Trade Unions under the control of the Socialist Party ; whereas Jaurès, whatever he would have preferred, was ready to accept the doctrine of Trade Union independence of party commitments laid down in 1906 by the Confédération Générale du Travail in the Charter of Amiens and was thus able to keep on good terms with the main body of the C.G.T.

French delegations at International Congresses continued on critical occasions to cancel their vote by dividing it, in contrast to the solid voting of the German Social Democratic Party. Moreover, the Trade Unions, even after the great Syndicalist wave had begun to subside, stuck firmly to the Amiens Charter and refused to be drawn into any formal association with Socialist parliamentary politics.

Nevertheless, the unification had some meaning, and Jaurès

did, from 1905 onwards, hold a position of undisputed primacy in the French Socialist movement. The question of Socialist participation in a predominantly bourgeois Government had been settled mainly against him by the terms of the Kautsky resolution of 1904 ;[1] but he had accepted the decision as a necessary condition of unity, and the issue had not arisen again, up to 1914, in such a way as to precipitate a fresh crisis. Millerand, Viviani, and their immediate supporters had passed right out of the Party ; and the Socialists had formed a united opposition to the Ministries of the critical pre-war years.

Then came, at the very moment when the die had been cast for war but the actual fighting had still to begin, the assassination of Jaurès by a Royalist fanatic — a tragic loss to the Socialist cause not only in France but throughout the world. At any other time the removal of Jaurès would have led to a stiff faction fight for the succession ; but in August 1914 the Socialists were in no mood to fall out among themselves. To practically all of them it seemed entirely clear that Germany was the aggressor and that the German Socialists, in voting for the war credits, had been guilty of betraying the international Socialist cause. On this issue there was no difference of view either among the Socialist deputies or among the leaders of the C.G.T. Even such professed anti-militarists as Gustave Hervé turned in an instant into patriots : indeed some of them, including Hervé, became the most intransigent advocates of war to the bitter end. Even to the less excitable Socialists, it appeared perfectly plain that France had not wanted war, even if her Russian ally must share with Austria-Hungary and Germany the blame for bringing it on. Jaurès had always proclaimed at the International the right and duty of national defence ; and in August 1914 even those who had opposed him were converted as the Germans swept on through Belgium to their lightning attack on France. When, within a few days, the question arose of Socialist participation in a broadly based Ministry of National Defence, there was no articulate opposition. The French Socialists, with unwonted unanimity, not only agreed to support the war but also consented to the entry of two of their leaders into the Cabinet ; and these two, Marcel Sembat (1862–1922) and Jules Guesde,

[1] See Vol. III, Part I, p. 45.

included in the latter the principal pre-war opponent of all forms of Socialist-bourgeois collaboration. Guesde, the doyen of French Marxism, was already 69 years old when he became a Minister and reversed the policy of a lifetime in the great emergency of 1914. Sembat, in his early fifties, was able to play a more active part. They were presently joined, in the spring of 1915, by a much younger man, Albert Thomas (1878-1932), who, as Minister of Munitions, played an important part in the organisation of war production and was, after the war, to pass out of activity in the Socialist movement by becoming the first Director of the International Labour Organisation.

This unanimity in high places — among the Socialist deputies and in the leadership of the C.G.T. — must not be taken as meaning that every French Socialist favoured Socialist participation in the Government of the 'Union Sacrée'. For the moment, however, opposition was dramatically silenced. Many of the younger militants, both of the Party and of the Trade Unions, were called up for military service ; and the local organisations were for the moment paralysed and needed time before they could again find their voices. While the Germans were making their swift advance towards Paris no voice critical of the leadership made itself heard : only after this advance had been checked and the possibility of a long war of attrition had begun to be faced ; only when rising prices and economic dislocation had confronted the working classes with a serious immediate situation, did protests become audible against the suspension of the class-struggle and against the subordination of the Socialist Ministers to the will of their bourgeois colleagues. Then, in May 1915, the Union of Metal Workers, under the forceful leadership of Alphonse Merrheim (1871-1925), appeared as the champion of an opposition not afraid to claim that 'This war is not our war' and to denounce the imperialist, annexationist aims of the French and other Allied Governments ; while Pierre Monatte (b. 1881), editor of *La Vie ouvrière*, and a small group of left-wing Syndicalists began to urge that the French Socialists should have followed the example of the Italians by proclaiming that, while they would do nothing to hamper the war effort, they would on no account enter into any form of collaboration with the bourgeoisie in supporting it.[1] We have already seen that Merrheim, together with Albert Bourderon (1859–1930) of the Coopers' Union and the Socialist Executive, attended the Zimmerwald Conference of September 1915 and there joined the German minority delegates in a common declaration of working-class unity.[2] But at that stage they represented no general organised opposition, though they set to work to create one after their return. There can be no doubt that in 1914 and 1915 the French working-class movement was almost solid in support of the war effort, even if it was more doubtful about the rightness and expediency of Socialist participation in a predominantly anti-Socialist Government.

Immediately after the outbreak of war the Socialist Party and the C.G.T. had so far broken with precedent as to set up a joint Committee of Action for the defence, *inter alia*, of working-class interests. But this joint body was established, in its own words, for 'the maximum development of the support which, in the present circumstances, they must give to the public authorities in all questions concerning the workers' rights (provisioning, unemployment, free meals, allowances, etc.), and in the work of national defence'. This collaborative attitude, though increasingly challenged, lasted on the whole up to the latter part of 1917 and was brought decisively to an end only when Clemenceau became Prime Minister in November of that year and inaugurated a policy which brought him into sharp conflict with all those who questioned the need for carrying on the war to the bitter end.

At Zimmerwald Alphonse Merrheim met Lenin and had a long discussion with him concerning the attitude which the working-class movement ought to take up towards the war. Lenin called on Merrheim to return to France and lead a mass anti-war movement. Merrheim announced that he had come to Zimmerwald for the purpose, not of founding a new revolutionary International, but of relieving his troubled conscience by calling upon the workers of all countries to take immediate steps by international action to bring the slaughter to an end. He was well aware that, as the spokesman of a still small and unorganised minority, he had no power, even if he had had the will, to lead a mass revolt. Merrheim belonged, as events were

---

[1] See p. 30 for the Italian attitude.   [2] See p. 33.

soon to show, not to the Leninist left, but to the more moderate pacifist opposition which prevailed over Lenin at the Zimmerwald Conference. When he and Bourderon got back, they set to work to organise the opposition by setting up a Committee for the Resumption of International Relations, which advocated working-class action for a negotiated peace; and the Metal Workers' Federation continued to play a leading part in this movement in face of violent denunciations both from the bourgeois press and from the patriotic majority in the Socialist Party and the Trade Unions. When the Kienthal Conference met in April 1916, Merrheim and his group were unable to attend because the Government refused them passports; but Alexandre Blanc (1874–?) of Vaucluse, and two other Socialist deputies, defying the ban imposed by the Party, took part in the Conference and were duly censured for their action.

By this time, indeed, a minority group was already beginning to appear inside the Socialist Party. Led by Marx's grandson, Jean Longuet (1876–1938), it was even less extreme than Merrheim and his supporters in the C.G.T. It agreed with the Majority in putting on the Germans the principal blame for the war and in maintaining the right of national defence, but disagreed in holding that a peace 'without victors or vanquished' should be demanded by the workers as a basis for united international working-class action. In 1916 this minority was still weak: it became strong only the following year, when the military reverses of the spring combined with the changed attitudes, brought about by the first Russian Revolution and, by increasing economic pressures, greatly to strengthen the desire for peace.

The Russian Revolution was, indeed, in France as in many other countries, a turning-point. The fall of Czarism was acclaimed not only by revolutionaries and opponents of Allied war policies but also by practically all Socialists, even the most patriotic and the most reformist. As we have seen, it gave an immense impetus to the demand for an International Socialist Conference that would bring the war to an end and proclaim the terms of a just and durable peace. But although Majority and Minority both acclaimed the Revolution, its effect was not to lessen their differences but to intensify them. The Majority hoped that revolutionary Russia would continue the war with enthusiasm renewed, and sent its delegates to Russia to help in bringing this about ; whereas the Minority, for the most part, saw in the Revolution a powerful new force making for a negotiated peace in the determination of which the working-class movement would be able to play a large constructive part. The Minority gained within both the Party and the Trade Unions a great accession of strength ; but it also became increasingly divided into rival factions, of which one put its hopes on an early negotiated peace, while the other took up a revolutionary line and called on the workers to follow the Russian example by overthrowing the Government and taking power into their own hands. This second group had little or no following among the Socialist deputies : its strength was in the Trade Unions and in some of the local party Federations.

Then came the Bolshevik Revolution, followed immediately by the advent of the Clemenceau Government. During the preceding months the feeling for peace had been gaining ground fast, not only among the workers but also among a section of the Radicals, headed by Joseph Caillaux and by the Minister of the interior, Louis Malvy, against whom a great agitation had been worked up by the advocates of war to the bitter end. Clemenceau, by taking a strong line against the pacifists, attacking Malvy for his undue complaisance to the working-class movement, and adopting a policy of rigorous repression against the more militant workers, speedily drove leftwards a large proportion of those Socialists and Trade Unionists who had hitherto given full support to the war effort, and at the same time the Bolshevik Revolution moved the more extreme left to a much more revolutionary frame of mind. The moderate left felt serious misgivings when the new rulers of Russia proceeded to make a separate Peace and thus allowed the Germans to launch the great offensive of early 1918 ; but most of them saw that the Russians had been compelled to act in this way and regarded the collapse of the Eastern Front as an additional reason for intensifying their propaganda for a general pacification.

Already, in the spring of 1917, there had been extensive strikes, mainly on economic issues but serving also as an occasion for the manifestation of high enthusiasm for the Russian Revolution and of growing anti-war feeling. The Trade

Union extreme left, organised in a Trade Union Defence Committee, had been attacking the C.G.T. leadership with growing vehemence. Towards the end of 1917, however, at a C.G.T. Conference held at Clermont-Ferrand, an acrimonious debate between right and left ended in an agreed resolution approving President Wilson's peace proposals, acclaiming the peace policy of revolutionary Russia, and calling on the Clemenceau Government immediately to publish the conditions on which it was prepared to make peace. The coming to power of Clemenceau had, indeed, for the moment united Majority and Minority in the Trade Unions in common opposition to the Government's *jusquauboutisme*. The Clermont-Ferrand Conference further called for the summoning of a full C.G.T. Congress to test the opinion of the Trade Unions on the question of war and peace.

This agreement, based on large concessions by both left and right in the interests of Trade Union unity, provoked violent protests on the extreme left. Merrheim and Bourderon were accused of betraying the cause of revolution and of surrendering to the 'patriots'; and the Trade Union Defence Committee, led by Pierre Monatte, redoubled its efforts to win the Trade Unions over to a thoroughgoing revolutionary policy. In May 1918, following the big further call-up arising out of the German offensive, there was a widespread strike movement in Paris, Lyons, Saint-Étienne, and other industrial centres; and this movement was much more political and anti-war than that of the previous year. The C.G.T. having failed, so far, to summon the full Congress demanded at Clermont-Ferrand, the Trade Union Defence Committee called together a left-wing Congress of its own and threatened to secede from the C.G.T. — a policy which Merrheim and his followers strongly opposed. The full C.G.T. Congress at length met in Paris in July 1918, and provided the occasion for a violent attack, led by Monatte and Gaston Monmousseau (b. 1883), the railwaymen's leader, on Léon Jouhaux (1879–1953) and the C.G.T. leadership. An attempt was made to oust Jouhaux from his position as C.G.T. secretary; but he was re-elected by a large majority. The main resolution reaffirmed the decision of the Clermont-Ferrand Conference, calling for a peace based on the principles of President Wilson, the Russian Revolution, and the Zimmerwald

Conference — no contradiction being seen, or at any rate admitted, in this triple affirmation by the sponsors, who included Merrheim as well as Jouhaux in opposition to the extreme left.

Meanwhile opinion within the Socialist Party had been moving rapidly away from unqualified support of the war. After the Zimmerwald Conference the Administrative Committee had issued a special warning to the local Federations against 'even the appearance of participation in any propaganda contrary to the interests of national defence', but had been unable to prevent the spread of peace propaganda and of minority opinion. The national Socialist Congress of December 1915 was still able to pass almost unanimously a resolution favouring the continued prosecution of the war, calling on the Germans to establish a democratic Government, and refusing to resume international relations until German Social Democracy had restored life to its long-established principles. The Congress also declared in favour of continued support for the war credits and for the continuance in office of the three Socialist Ministers, and called for Socialist unity in the pursuance of this policy. But early in 1916 the position began to change, and at the meeting of the Party's National Council in April more than one-third of the delegates voted against a motion made by Pierre Renaudel (1871–1934) declaring that conditions were not yet ripe for the meeting of an International Socialist Conference. By this time the moderate Minority, headed by Jean Longuet, had formed a Committee for the Defence of International Socialism, which soon fell foul of Merrheim's Committee for the Resumption of International Relations and, of course, much more so, of the extreme Syndicalist left led by Pierre Monatte. Through the remainder of 1916 the strength of the moderate Minority continued to grow, and at the full Party Congress held in Paris at the end of December the Minority resolution, moved by Longuet and Paul Mistral (1872–1932), and declaring for a policy based exclusively on proletarian interests and in accordance with the pre-war policies of the International, was only narrowly defeated. A second resolution, calling for a total resumption of international relations, was beaten by an even smaller majority.

In 1917 came the struggle over the issue of participation in the Stockholm Conference. When the Administrative Committee rejected outright the appeal to take part, the Minority decided to call a Conference of its own. This met in May 1917, and declared unanimously in favour of sending delegates to Stockholm. Later in the same month the Party's National Council met in Paris at a moment when the big strikes already referred to were in progress and, after receiving the report of Marcel Cachin (1869–1958) and Marius Moutet (b. 1876) on the visit to Russia from which they had just returned, voted unanimously in favour of sending delegates to Stockholm, while declaring also in favour of a prior Inter-Allied Conference at which the Socialists of the Allied countries were to formulate a common policy dealing both with the terms on which peace should be made and with the question of responsibility for the war. This apparent unanimity, however, covered up big differences ; for whereas the Minority favoured an unqualified acceptance of the Stockholm invitation, the Majority remained firmly against attendance until an agreed Inter-Allied Socialist policy had been reached.

In September 1917 the fall of the Ribot Ministry and the succession of Painlevé to office again produced an apparent agreement when the Socialist Ministers were refused permission to enter the new Government, to the composition of which the Majority objected, whereas the Minority opposed participation in principle. But the basic disagreement became apparent again at the full party Congress of December 1917, held at Bordeaux soon after the Bolshevik Revolution. The Majority there won a substantial victory over a moderate Minority motion. This motion gave unqualified adhesion to the Stockholm project and condemned participation in the Government, but recommended that the Party should continue to support the war credits until the Government had definitely rejected the terms of peace which the Socialist movement had approved. A motion of the extreme left, against voting for the war credits, received only a handful of votes. At the same time, the group of Socialist deputies declared in favour of sending a delegation of their own to Russia to ask the Russians not to make a separate peace ; but Clemenceau, newly seated in office, refused to grant the necessary passports.

Thus the matter remained until February 1918, when the

refusal of the Government to make any response to the Bolsheviks' demand for general peace negotiations caused an
abrupt shift to the left in the Socialist National Council.
Adrien Pressemane's (1879-1929) resolution, calling on the
Socialists to cease voting for the war credits, was defeated only
by a very narrow margin. During the next few months the
great German offensive ran its course and was finally checked ;
and by July, when the Socialist National Council met again,
the Minority had become the Majority. Renaudel's resolution,
upholding the war policy of the old Majority and even defending Allied intervention in Russia in the interests 'both of the
struggle against Germany and of the destruction of the Brest-
Litovsk Treaty', received only 1172 votes against 1544 for
Longuet's, which demanded of the Government a declaration
of peace terms in conformity with those of President Wilson
and of the Russian Revolution, condemned all forms of intervention against the Soviets, and called on the Socialist Party
to go to the length of voting against the war credits unless the
Clemenceau Ministry granted passports for the Stockholm
Conference.

This decisive change of party policy was confirmed by
1528 votes to 1212 when the full party Congress met at Paris
early in October 1918. Renaudel, who had already resigned
his position as political director of *Humanité*, was replaced by
Marcel Cachin, and Louis Oscar Frossard (1889-1946) succeeded Louis Dubreuilh (1862-1924) as secretary of the Party.
The former Minority also gained majority control of the
Party's Administrative Committee ; but the former Majoritaires
were not excluded, and their leading personages kept their seats
on the Committee. The victory had gone, in the main, to
Longuet and his moderate followers and not to the extreme
left, though a few of the latter's nominees were among those
chosen for the Committee. This reversal of positions was
accomplished only as the military power of Germany and
Austria-Hungary was evidently beginning to crack. Within a
month of the Paris Congress came the armistice and, with the
end of the fighting, the Revolutions in Germany and Austria-
Hungary.

It is important at this stage to be clear about the policy for
which Jean Longuet and his supporters stood in 1918. They

were certainly not revolutionaries, in any sense of the word that has any clear meaning. They had no thought of a new French Revolution that would violently overthrow the bourgeoisie and place the proletariat in dictatorial power. Fully as much as their antagonists of the late Majority they thought in terms of parliamentary government and of the democratic conquest of political power through electoral success. At most, they wanted only a more rapid evolutionary advance towards Socialism than would have satisfied the right wing of the Party and were more reluctant to enter, even in war-time, into any coalition with the bourgeois left — though most of them were not prepared to say that such coalitions could *never* be justified. They were strong opponents of imperialism and of secret diplomacy, and exceedingly distrustful of the bourgeois politicians who controlled the Governments of France and its Allies. They blamed these things — imperialism and its concomitant militarism, bad and perfidious diplomacy, and unscrupulous politicians — for bringing the war about ; and therewith they blamed capitalism itself, as the underlying cause of international quarrels. But the conclusion they drew was not that the proletariat must be induced to levy war — civil war — in every country against the ruling classes and the bourgeois State, but rather that these evil things must be tamed and brought under democratic control by a great popular movement of opinion among the oppressed. Immediately they looked, not for World Revolution as a means of ending war and capitalism together, but for a negotiated peace the terms of which would involve the general acceptance of arbitration as a way of resolving international disputes, the abolition of secret diplomacy and of partial alliances and agreements, and the inauguration of some form of international government strong enough to deter would-be aggressors and to initiate real processes of international co-operation. Most of them were no less convinced than the late Majority that the Germans were chiefly to blame for the war, though they also put some blame on Allied imperialism and diplomacy. On this account, they were not opponents of national defence and had been prepared to vote in favour of the war credits throughout the struggle, albeit with increasing reluctance. They took, in other words, much the same view as Branting in neutral Sweden or Ramsay

MacDonald in Great Britain ; and, because this view was easily misrepresented, they gained the reputation of being a great deal further to the left than actually they ever were, and were denounced, while the war lasted, as roundly as if they had accepted the entire Leninist gospel.

What has been said holds good, of course, only of the moderate section of the war-time Minority — the section led by Jean Longuet within the Socialist Party. It does not apply either to the small group of Kienthaliens within the Socialist Party or to the Trade Union extreme left led by Monatte and Monmousseau or to the less extreme Trade Union group that followed Merrheim and Bourderon. These last, indeed, found themselves very awkwardly placed ; for they were neither parliamentarians who believed in evolutionary, ballot-box Socialism nor out-and-out revolutionaries in the Leninist sense, but Syndicalist upholders of the doctrine of Direct Action and of the cause of Trade Union independence of party politics in accordance with the Amiens Charter. Revolutionaries in a sense they were ; for they believed in the need in due course to destroy the bourgeois State ; but they had no wish to replace it by a new State based on proletarian dictatorship, or to carry on the work of revolution under the auspices of a highly disciplined and centralised Party. On the contrary, they believed in decentralisation and in reliance on the spontaneous capacity of the workers in their own local groups, and looked for the coming of the Revolution, not as a sudden *coup*, but rather as the culmination of a continuous process of working-class action and self-education for power and responsibility. That was why, when they saw the advocates of Revolution after the Bolshevik manner gaining control of the left, they were first forced back into co-operation with the Trade Union right in an attempt to maintain working-class unity, and then pushed out altogether when the main body of the C.G.T. went over, after the end of the war, to a completely reformist policy.

The extreme left, as it developed during the war, was badly lacking in leaders. It had in its ranks a number of able Trade Unionists bred up in the school of revolutionary Syndicalism, such as Pierre Monatte and Alfred Rosmer (b. 1877) ; but politically it found no outstanding spokesman. The handful of deputies who attended or supported the Kienthal Conference of 1916, headed by Alexandre Blanc, were minor figures, without wide popular appeal. After the Bolshevik Revolution it took time to build up a new leadership of the political left ; and not much could be done about this until the war was over and the non-revolutionary outlook of the Longuet New Majority had become fully apparent.

Thus, in the France of the closing months of 1918 and the early part of 1919, there was no real question of immediate Revolution, or even of any revolutionary attempt. The revolutionary elements in the pre-war Labour movement had been associated much more with the C.G.T. than with the Socialist Party ; for the Guesdists, though, like the German Social Democrats, they used revolutionary phraseology, were in practice no more revolutionary than the followers of Jaurès. Even in the C.G.T. the wave of Revolutionary Syndicalism had been ebbing for some time before the war ; [1] and there, as well as in the Socialist Party, the collaboration practised under war conditions brought about a substantial transformation of attitude among the leaders. The Russian Revolution had caused a recrudescence of revolutionary feeling among both Socialists and Trade Unionists ; and the reactionary policies of the Clemenceau Government had to some extent reinforced this. But hardly anyone, at the end of 1918, was thinking in practical terms of any attempt to overthrow the Government by force, though many were contemplating forthright agitation for far-reaching measures of social and economic reorganisation.

Thus the C.G.T., when it issued its post-war programme in December 1918, made large demands ranging over a wide field, but none which contemplated either the destruction of the existing State or that 'abolition of the wage system' which had taken so large a place in pre-war Syndicalist propaganda. What the C.G.T. demanded in the first instance was, first, a peace treaty based on Wilsonian principles and drawn up with working-class participation in its making ; secondly, a series of social and industrial reforms beginning with the eight hours' day and including full recognition of Trade Union rights for public employees (*fonctionnaires*) as well as for employees of private concerns, and also old-age pensions and other forms of social security legislation ; thirdly, reconstruction of the

[1] See Vol. III, Part I, p. 361.

devastated areas by producers' and consumers' Co-operative Societies ; fourthly, the paying-off of war debts by means of taxes on profits and inheritance ; fifthly, the establishment of a representative National Economic Council to devise plans for national reconstruction, and sixthly, 'the return of all essential resources to the nation and their exploitation under national control through the instrumentality of autonomous societies representing producers and consumers'. With the possible exception of the last, these were all demands capable of being met without violent revolution, and were indeed put in a way that implied its absence. Moreover, the final demand was one for extensive socialisation of industry with a measure of workers' and consumers' control rather than for outright revolution requiring the destruction of the existing structure of government. True, these demands were embodied in what was described as a Minimum Programme, which 'must be realised immediately' ; and there was no explicit withdrawal of earlier revolutionary propositions. It was, however, sufficiently clear that the C.G.T. was not contemplating any immediate resort to the methods which Lenin and the Kienthaliens had been pressing upon the workers in all countries. Moreover, Léon Jouhaux was authorised to accept a seat at the Peace Conference, as a colleague of Clemenceau.

This C.G.T. concession to reformism did not, of course, go unchallenged ; but there was no doubt that Jouhaux had the majority behind him. This, however, did not in the circumstances mean very much ; for at the end of 1918 total effective Trade Union membership was very low. The C.G.T. had never been a very large body : up to 1914 it had never had more than about half a million members, and many of these had been irregular in paying their contributions. It had always relied rather on a 'conscious minority' of activists — who, when the occasion arose, could draw the less conscious majority along behind them — than on a mass membership ; and, except in the war industries, its organisation had been greatly affected by the heavy call-up for the armed forces and by the dislocation of normal production. No-one, I think, knows how many members the C.G.T. really had when the war ended, though it is known that the Metal Workers' Federation had expanded during the war from 40,000 to 200,000. Despite this growth, the C.G.T. probably had in all fewer than the half-million of its great pre-war days ; but from the beginning of 1919 it expanded very rapidly, reaching by late 1920 a total of about 2½ million, in which the pre-war militants were thoroughly submerged. This is not meant to imply that the new recruits necessarily accepted the reformist policy which the C.G.T. had adopted during the war. Many of them did not ; but the new revolutionary elements were not so much Syndicalists as admirers of revolutionary Russia and did not, for the most part, take over the Syndicalist tradition of complete Trade Union independence of political Parties. They tended to rally to Communism rather than to Syndicalism of the pre-war type : so that, despite the continued efforts of the autonomists who stood by the Charter of Amiens, the struggle inside the Trade Unions came to be more and more part and parcel of the struggle that was proceeding between Communists and Social Democrats inside the Socialist Party.

In 1919 the Metal Workers were still the spearhead of French Trade Unionism, though their power was being rapidly undermined by the cessation of war production. In April the C.G.T. set out to conduct a nation-wide campaign of preparation for a series of mass demonstrations on May Day, in support of its new Programme. At the same time difficulties over demobilisation and reinstatement and sharply rising prices were causing a wave of economic discontent. Outside Paris the May Day demonstrations passed off quietly ; but in Paris, where such demonstrations were forbidden under police orders, there were serious clashes with the police, involving two deaths and many injured, and feelings rose high. There was a wave of strikes throughout the industrial areas, mainly for wage-increases or for the enforcement of the new Eight Hours' Law, which the Parliament had hurriedly enacted in April 1919. The left wing made some attempt to give these strikes a political colour, but not with much success. In most cases the strikers secured substantial concessions ; but in Paris, where the left was strong, the Metal Workers, in the course of a dispute over the application of the Eight Hours' Law, struck, against the advice of their Federation, under the auspices of an unofficial joint committee of factory delegates, and were thoroughly beaten — a serious set-back to the biggest of the C.G.T. Unions.

The miners, on the other hand, consolidated their separate Unions into a single bargaining body and won an outstanding victory. As an outcome of the Metal Workers' defeat a bitter contest developed in the C.G.T. between revolutionaries and reformists. When the C.G.T. held its first post-war Congress at Lyons in September 1919 the battle was immediately joined. The C.G.T. leaders, anxious to win the support of the old Syndicalists as well as of the reformists, took refuge in a re-affirmation of the Amiens Charter, with its assertion of the predominance of Direct Action and of the need for complete Trade Union independence of political Parties ; and, by taking this line, they were able to rout the extremists when it came to a vote, though these latter had largely dominated the debates.

Meanwhile, a parallel struggle was in progress in the Socialist Party, now under the control of the new Majority under Longuet's leadership. Here, the main immediate issue was that of international affiliations. Was the French Socialist Party to co-operate in the attempt set on foot at the Berne Conference of February 1919 [1] to rebuild the Second International, or was it to throw in its lot with the new International set up at the hastily improvised Moscow Congress of the following month ? [2] Or, alternatively, had it better stand aside for the time being from both Internationals and watch out for a chance of helping to create a new International wide enough to include the main working-class organisations of all countries, revolutionary and reformist alike ? The old Majoritaires, headed by Renaudel, were wholly in favour of the first of these courses, having quite given up their refusal to meet the German Majority on friendly terms — though not their determination to compel their late enemies to eat humble pie.[3] The extreme left, for whom the Russian-born Boris Souvarine and Fernand Loriot (?-1932) were for the time being the most prominent spokesmen, naturally wished to bring the French Party bodily into the Third International, which had not yet formulated the inconvenient 'Twenty-one' conditions that were to cause so much trouble the following year. But the controlling group, Longuet's, did not like the look of either of these courses. Before joining the Third International they wanted to know a good deal more about it ; and they also disliked the temper

[1] See p. 290.   [2] See p. 298.   [3] See p. 293.

of the Berne Conference, which seemed to be altogether too much under the right-wing influence of the British Labour-Party and the German Majority. They therefore preferred to wait and see, but not for the time being to sever relations with the International Socialist Bureau, which remained in existence as the representative of the Second International. When the Socialist Party Congress met in Paris in April 1919 it was confronted with three rival resolutions. One, proposing immediate adhesion to the Third International, received only 270 votes ; a second, in favour of unqualified adhesion to the Second, received 757 ; while the successful resolution, with 894 votes, proposed that the French Party should maintain for the time being its connection with the International Socialist Bureau, but should invite the Parties and groups which had not been represented at Berne to send delegates to the further Conference which the Berne Commission was proposing to call, and should there take steps to purge the International and to reaffirm the full acceptance of 'the principles of the class struggle and of unqualified opposition to bourgeois Parties and Governments, so as to reorient the International immediately and really towards the social Revolution, after the example set by Russia, Hungary and Germany'. The action of the French Socialist Party, at this early stage, thus plainly foreshadowed the policy which led later to the setting up of the Vienna Union, or 'Two-and-a-Half' International.[1]

The voting at this Paris Congress showed clearly that the old war-time Majority, though beaten, had by no means been eclipsed. In the Chamber its members continued to vote for the war credits for some time after the actual fighting had ended. Even when the main body of the right had ceased to do this, some deputies persisted : 11 of them voted for the credits in July 1919, and were censured for doing so. The Seine Federation, a stronghold of the left, thereupon refused to readopt the offenders as Socialist candidates for the coming General Election ; and the dissidents thereupon resigned and, a little later, formed a separate 'French Socialist Party' which worked in closely with the Radicals but had no substantial popular following. The main body of the right wing, however, stayed inside the old Party.

[1] See p. 337.

In November 1919 came the first post-war General Election, fought under a system of Proportional Representation which was highly unfavourable to minority groups unless they were prepared to enter into electoral alliances. In the election, the Socialists, fighting as an entirely independent Party, were confronted by a National Bloc, based on an attempt to carry on the 'Union Sacrée' under Clemenceau's leadership. They fared badly : Socialist representation in the Chamber fell from 104 to 68, despite a substantially increased Socialist vote and a sharp rise in Party membership, which had shrunk to about 35,000 at the time of the armistice.

As soon as the election was over, the French Socialists returned to their battle over the question of their international affiliation. By this time the partisans of the Second International had lost nearly all their support ; and the main struggle was between the out-and-out partisans of the Third International and those who considered that an attempt should be made to set up a broader International on a basis to be agreed upon between the Moscow body and the Western Parties, including those which had already broken away from the Second International. When the national Congress of the Party met at Strasbourg in February 1920, the remaining partisans of the Second International were defeated by a majority of more than 13 to 1, and the Kienthaliens got about a third of the votes against the delaying resolution of the Longuet Majority. The successful resolution declared the effective reunion of the forces of revolutionary Socialism to be an urgent need, and saw no incompatibility between the programme of the Moscow International and the 'traditional principles of Socialism', but held that it was necessary to take full account of the existing state of working-class organisation and opinion in Western and Central Europe, and laid down that the Parties of these regions should confer with representatives of the Moscow International concerning the terms on which a new unified International should be set up. Following this decision, the party Administrative Committee decided to send Marcel Cachin and Jean Longuet to Russia on a mission of enquiry and discussion with the Moscow International. Louis Frossard, the Party's secretary, replaced Longuet ; and after some delay over getting passports the mission arrived in Moscow, whence, in June, its members wired asking for authorisation to attend, in a consultative capacity, the coming Second Congress of the Third International — at which the Twenty-one Points took their definitive form. Permission being given by the National Council of the French Party, Cachin and Frossard participated in the Moscow Congress, from which they returned to France to advocate the acceptance of the conditions and the immediate adherence of French Socialism to the Third International.

By the time the Party met again in Congress, in December 1920, on this occasion at Tours, the German Independents had already met at Halle, and had decided by a majority to join the Moscow International.[1] The French Party, in the meantime, had grown enormously in numbers, from the 35,000 of two years before to 180,000 : so that at Tours the decision was in the hands mainly of delegates representing newly enrolled members, and the balance of power between the old Majority and Minority had ceased to be of much account. Most of the newcomers were supporters of the left and were strongly in favour of adhesion to the new International, which seemed to them to embody the spirit of the Russian Revolution ; but some of them had qualms about accepting the Twenty-one Points as they stood, less because this involved not only the expulsion of the reformist right wing, but also the repudiation of the Centre, than because the proposed subordination of the Trade Unions to control by the Party ran counter to the still cherished doctrine of Trade Union independence. At Tours the central group, which had hitherto favoured an attempt to construct a broader International on negotiated terms, split : the larger fraction joined the extreme left in supporting adhesion to Moscow subject only to certain limited reservations, whereas the smaller, though it also favoured adhesion on terms, wished to accompany it by a refusal either to expel the reformists from the Party or to endorse the proposed subordination of the Trade Unions to party control. The right wing, without hope of success, was opposed to adhesion to the Third International on any terms. When the vote was taken, the left wing was found to have an overwhelming majority against the combined strength of the right and the Centre. The delegates of the two minorities

[1] See p. 168.

475

thereupon left the Congress, and the victorious left wing proceeded to take over the control of the Party and to transform
it from a Socialist into a Communist Party, while the two
minorities set to work to refound the Socialist Party as a
separate body, with the support of a majority of the Socialist
deputies, but with the loss of the old party machine and its
official press, including *Humanité*, which under Cachin's
editorship became the organ of the new French Communist
Party. 'Moscow' had succeeded in capturing one of the great
Socialist Parties of Western Europe which it had denounced
as the most dangerous enemies of the revolutionary cause.

This was indeed a most signal victory; for it enabled the
French Communists, instead of having to build up from the
foundations a new Party of their own, to take over the entire
apparatus of one of the main Parties of the pre-war Second
International and to throw on their opponents the burden of
building up a new organisation. There were, however, flies in
the ointment. In the first place, the great majority of the
Socialist deputies in the Chamber refused to accept the decision
of the Tours Congress and remained faithful to the old Socialist
Party, which they were in a position to play a leading part in
building up anew; and in the second place some of the traditions of the old Party remained very much alive in its Communist successor, so that the latter at once got involved in a
faction fight between the out-and-out supporters of Moscow
and those who argued that the workers in each country were
the best judges of the methods of organisation and of the
immediate policies to be followed by each national Party.
Thus, the anti-Communist minority was able fairly rapidly to
re-create a tolerably effective organisation, though not, of
course, without serious gaps and defects; whereas the French
Communists became involved in a series of clashes with the
Comintern that led to a succession of purges and defections
and brought the Communist Party to a low ebb before it succeeded in reconstructing itself on the foundations demanded
by the Comintern.

In the new Socialist Party, too, there were serious internal
differences. It was not easy for Longuet and his followers to
forget their past quarrel with the 'social patriots' led by Pierre
Renaudel, or for the Renaudel group to come to terms with

them in matters of either national or international policy. The old Majoritaires were whole-hearted supporters of the new right-wing International, whereas the old Minoritaires were still hoping for a wider International that would somehow bring the rival bodies together in the cause of working-class unity ; and in relation to home affairs the Renaudel group favoured collaboration with the bourgeois Radicals, whereas the Longuet group stood for Socialist independence and refusal to participate in bourgeois Governments. For the time being these differences were overshadowed by common hostility to the Moscow policy of subordinating everything else to the cause of World Revolution and to defence of the Soviet Union against its enemies ; but they could not be kept altogether in the background. The old Majoritaires, however, had so little support outside the Chamber of Deputies that they had, for the time being, either to fall in with the views of the Longuet group or leave the Party altogether ; and before long the followers of Longuet, in face of the bitter hostility of the Communists, were driven step by step into a position well to the right of their earlier attitude. Little more than two years were to pass before the Centre, organised round the 'Two-and-a-Half' Vienna International Union, came to terms with the right and joined forces with it in the new Labour and Socialist International set up at Hamburg in May 1923.[1] As the war receded, the matters which had divided the old Majority and the old Minority counted for less and less, and there was accordingly less and less room for a centre faction in between the reformists and the Communists, even if there was a great deal to be said in favour of a middle course and of unity in the pursuit of Socialist objectives. Parliamentarism and Sovietism were both clear points of view capable of exerting a strong popular appeal. Centrism, under the prevailing conditions of popular excitement, unhappily was not. Nor, if a choice had to be made between parliamentarism and Sovietism, was there any doubt about the side of the fence on which the followers of Longuet would come down. They had been prepared, under stress of the excitement caused by the Revolution in Russia, to make considerable concessions to the idea of a World Revolution that might involve, in some countries, the use of dictatorial

[1] See p. 684.

methods and a resort to civil war. But they had never really thought of such methods as applicable to French conditions. They were parliamentarians in respect of French politics, even if they did not agree with the Berne Conference's proclamation that Socialism and parliamentary democracy were inseparable under all circumstances ; [1] and in practice this attitude lined them up with the right against Moscow the more decisively because Moscow itself was in no mood to make any concessions to the Centre, which it was actually denouncing even more bitterly than it was the right.

Thus, as an outcome of the Tours Congress of 1920, the French Socialist movement relapsed into disunity after fifteen years of formal, but by no means untroubled, unification. The new line of division was, however, essentially different both from the differences between Guesde and Jaurès over the Dreyfus affair and over Millerand's acceptance of office and from those which had divided Majority and Minority during the war. The dispute was now between parliamentarians and Sovietists, so that Longuet found himself in alliance with Renaudel, whereas Cachin, formerly a moderate Centrist, went over wholly to the opposite camp, and Frossard, compelled to choose between the two, for the moment chose Moscow, though he was by no means prepared to accept the full rigour of centralised control which the Comintern proceeded to enforce. The Syndicalist militants also for the most part rallied to the Comintern, with similar mental reservations about Trade Union independence. It should indeed be noticed that the left had won its great victory at Tours only at the cost of substantial concessions to the strong feeling against complete acceptance of the Twenty-one Points. The Tours resolution had laid down that the full rigour of the Moscow conditions should apply only to the future and should not involve the expulsion of anyone who was prepared to accept the Tours verdict and behave in future in accordance with it. This reservation was soon to land the new French Communist Party in serious trouble with the Moscow International. Zinoviev had addressed to the Tours Congress a message vehemently attacking the French Centrists and declaring that the Third International could have nothing in common with them ; but many who

[1] See p. 294.

voted for the left resolution were by no means prepared to accept the claims of the Third International to give orders to the French Party about whom it should expel or to endorse a complete subordination of French policy to the will of the Moscow leadership. For the moment this difficulty was glossed over ; but it was bound, in view of Moscow's uncompromising attitude, soon to give rise to trouble.

In the meantime the new Communist Party fell heir to the organisation of the Socialist Party, including its structure of local branches and Federations which had been built up mainly with a view to electoral and parliamentary action. With Frossard as secretary, the Party made no sharp break with the past in its general structure and methods of work, though it did lose most of its parliamentary representation. The immediate question was one of competitive struggle between Communists and Socialists to secure the support of the local organisations ; and in this, though the Communists for the time being came off best, what took place most of all was a great drop in total membership of both Parties taken together. In order to explain this drop it is necessary to consider what had been going on in the industrial field while the great debate was raging over the issue of the International.

During the early months of 1920 the cost of living rose more sharply than ever, and there was a fresh outburst of strikes. The main trouble began in February with a strike of the Paris railway workers of the P.L.M. Railway, called in the first instance without the endorsement either of the national Federation of Railway Workers or of the C.G.T. The strike, led by Monmousseau, spread rapidly to other railways, and both the Railwaymen's Federation and the C.G.T. were compelled to give it their support. It was settled after Briand had made promises which appeared to meet most of the workers' claims ; but when the men had returned to work nothing was done to realise these promises, and the agitation set in afresh. At the beginning of April the Railway Workers' national Congress declared for a renewed strike, to be called after consultation with the C.G.T., and included in its demands the immediate nationalisation of the entire railway system. On the occasion of the February dispute the C.G.T. had instructed the Economic Council of Labour, which it had established to serve as its adviser on matters of post-war reconstruction,[1] to prepare a scheme of railway nationalisation ; and this report was in course of preparation when the second dispute broke out. The C.G.T. leaders would have much preferred to be given a respite until the report had been published and presented to the Government ; but in the prevailing temper of working-class feeling they agreed to support the Railway Workers. A national railway strike was declared and, when the Government refused to give way, the C.G.T. proceeded to call out, first the dockers and seamen, and then the rest of the transport workers, the miners, the metal workers and the builders in a sympathetic movement which approached the dimensions of a general strike. The Government retaliated by arresting the Railway Workers' Executive and many of the left-wing leaders of the C.G.T., and by announcing that it would refuse to enter into any negotiations for a settlement until the strikers had returned to work. The C.G.T., which had been on the point of extending the strike to still more industries, thereupon took alarm and called off the sympathetic strikes, leaving the railway workers to fight on alone with financial help from those at work. The railway workers, despite the arrest of their leaders, did continue on strike till nearly the end of May, when they were forced to admit defeat in view of an increasing drift back to work. The Government took vengeance both by wholesale dismissals of railway workers and by proclaiming the C.G.T. itself dissolved, though nothing was actually done to enforce the dissolution. The effect, however, was disastrous for the Trade Union movement. C.G.T. membership shrank abruptly from about $2\frac{1}{2}$ millions to about 600,000 — not much above the pre-war total. The great wave of militant Trade Unionism had been decisively repelled some months before the Communists won their victory at the Tours Socialist Congress.

The great strike had, indeed, been from the first seriously incomplete. On two important lines the railway workers had refused to come out ; and the sympathetic stoppages in other industries had been from the beginning no more than partial. The Government had been able, with the aid of those who remained at work and by extensive use of blacklegs, to keep

[1] See p. 470.

up a skeleton railway service and to maintain necessary supplies ; and there had been a tendency almost from the first for a considerable number of strikers to drift back to work. The middle classes had been effectively mobilised as strike-breakers ; and among the Trade Unionists there had been a persistent quarrel between the right and left wings. The C.G.T. had found an excuse for calling off the sympathetic strikes when the Government promised a Railway Bill, which failed at all to satisfy the left-wing advocates of Direct Action, but accentuated the quarrel between parliamentarians and Direct Actionists on the working-class side. In May 1920 left-wing Trade Unionism shot its bolt and ceased to constitute, even in appearance, a revolutionary menace ; and though working-class political opinion continued to move leftwards up to its victory at the Tours Socialist Congress, the peak of working-class action was reached and passed, and the Bloc National and the bourgeois Republic were confirmed in authority. When the C.G.T. Congress met at Orléans in September 1920, the left wing, undeterred by their defeat, demanded that the C.G.T. should join the Red International of Labour Unions — the Trade Union subsidiary of the Comintern.[1] But the C.G.T. leaders easily defeated this proposal, which, while affirming their admiration for the Russian Revolution, they denounced as contrary to the Charter of Amiens and to the entire tradition of Trade Union independence of party politics. The C.G.T. rejected the R.I.L.U. and reaffirmed its loyalty to the Amsterdam International Federation of Trade Unions,[2] of which Jouhaux was a Vice-President ; and at the same time the programme drawn up at Lyons was reaffirmed and the reformist policy of 1918-19 endorsed. The Minority thereupon withdrew and held a separate Conference, at which, without actually seceding from the C.G.T., they set up a Revolutionary Syndicalist Centre and instituted a policy of 'boring from within' the C.G.T. Unions and Federations, in the hope of bringing them over to support the R.I.L.U.

There followed a confused period of struggle inside the Trade Unions. The Minority which had set up the new Centre was made up of a number of elements — Anarchist and

[1] For the R.I.L.U., see p. 335.
[2] See p. 332.

Syndicalist as well as Communist — and was by no means ready as a whole to accept the subordinate rôle assigned to the Trade Unions by the Third International. Indeed, at the outset, the Anarchists and Syndicalists were predominant over the orthodox Communists, and an Anarchist, Pierre Besnard, held the position of general secretary. In the summer of 1921 the C.S.R. (Centre Syndicaliste Révolutionnaire) sent two delegates, Temmasi and Alfred Rosmer, as delegates to the R.I.L.U. Congress ; but when they came back after accepting the R.I.L.U. principle of subordination to the Comintern, the C.S.R. repudiated them and insisted on maintaining its position of independence. At the same period — July 1921 — the left-wing delegates at the C.G.T. Congress were again decisively defeated and again held a separate Conference at which they decided to strengthen the C.S.R., still without actually seceding from the C.G.T. They then proceeded on their own authority to invite all Trade Unions to send delegates to a new Congress, at which they put forward proposals for a complete reconstruction of the C.G.T. As a result of this meeting, an attempt was made to negotiate with the C.G.T. leadership ; but the discussions broke down practically at once, and the C.S.R. thereupon took the further step of turning itself into an open rival to the C.G.T. under the title 'C.G.T. Unitaire', but was still careful to proclaim the new body as only provisional and to hold the door open for further negotiations.

At this point the conflict inside the Trade Union left wing came to a head. The Anarchists, with some Syndicalist support, succeeded in inserting into the constitution of the C.G.T.U. a clause denouncing not merely the bourgeois State but States in all their forms, and in persuading the C.G.T.U. to send observers to an International Anarchist-Syndicalist Conference that had been summoned to meet in Berlin for the purpose of setting up yet another International. Not much came of this, though the proposed International was actually founded ; but in the following May (1922) the Anarchists and Syndicalists were strong enough to take the lead in a substantial strike movement in Paris and other centres. This failed ; and when, a month later, the C.G.T.U. Congress met at Saint-Étienne, there was a big struggle between Anarchist-Syndicalists and Communists for the control of the movement, with the Italian

Anarchist A. Borghi arguing vehemently with Arnold Losovsky, the Russian protagonist of the R.I.L.U. At this Congress the Communists were able to wrest the control of the C.G.T.U. from their rivals ; but they could not persuade it immediately to join the R.I.L.U., on the ground that the rules of that body included provisions inconsistent with the Charter of Amiens and with Trade Union independence.

It might have been expected that the R.I.L.U. would have received this evidence of insubordination in an uncompromising spirit. But, having little effective backing outside Russia, the R.I.L.U. was exceedingly eager to secure the adhesion even of a fraction of the French Trade Union movement ; and at its Congress of November 1922 it agreed to expunge the offending clause from its rules, without therewith promising to modify its practice. On this basis the C.G.T.U. at length became reconciled to joining the R.I.L.U., and at its Bourges Congress of 1923 the Communists consolidated their control. Their victory, however, was followed by a further split. The following year a Syndicalist group broke away to form a Federal Union of Autonomous Trade Unions, which two years later became the C.G.T. Syndicaliste Révolutionnaire in opposition to both the old C.G.T. and the C.G.T.U. The C.G.T.U. was from this point an entirely Communist body, closely related to the French Communist Party and accepting the regulative authority of the R.I.L.U. and of the Comintern.

The Socialist Party, before the Tours split of 1920, claimed a membership of 180,000 — largely recent recruits. After the new Communist Party had taken over the old party machine, the rebuilding of a Socialist machine had to be begun afresh. By 1922 the re-established Socialist Party had about 49,000 members. It included on its first Administrative Committee after the split such veterans of the old Majority as Jules Guesde (d. 1922), Marcel Sembat (d. 1923), and J. Paul-Boncour (b. 1875), together with the leaders of the old Minority — Jean Longuet and Paul Faure (b. 1878), and other outstanding personalities such as Pierre Renaudel, Vincent Auriol (b. 1884), and Alexandre Bracke (1861–1955), the classical scholar who had been actively connected with the Second International before 1914, and was one of the outstanding French interpreters of Marxism. Its principal organ, now that *Humanité* had passed into Communist hands, was *Le Populaire*. The Socialist Party at its Congress of 1921 reaffirmed the charter of 1905, drawn up at the time of unification of the rival Parties, and issued a programme which included extensive plans of socialisation on the lines advocated by the C.G.T. At the outset it had to engage in a bitter struggle with the Communist Party, which accused it of betraying the workers' cause and of being a defender of the capitalist régime ; and it had also to make up its mind what attitude to adopt in relation to the Parties of the bourgeois left, especially in view of the electoral law, which made its prospects of electoral success dependent on finding allies against the candidates of the Bloc National. In 1922 the Communists, changing their tactics, began an agitation for a United Front of the working-class Parties ; but this proposal was rejected by the Socialist Congress of February 1923. At its next Congress, held in Marseilles in January 1924, the Socialist Party declared in favour of a policy of local electoral pacts with the Radicals. In authorising such pacts at the forthcoming elections, the Socialist Party announced that it would enter into them 'with all its doctrine' and that no joint action with the Radicals in Parliament and no participation in a possible Radical Cabinet were involved. On this basis the Socialists, in most areas, fought the General Election of 1924 in alliance with the Radicals and won no fewer than 103 seats, whereas the Communists, fighting alone, won only 27. This electoral success, in conjunction with the Radical victories, made possible the formation of a Radical Cabinet under Édouard Herriot, on condition of his getting Socialist support. The Socialists did in fact give their support, but refused to enter the Government, though a substantial minority among them favoured full participation. In effect, a *de facto* 'Cartel des Gauches' came into being as the only workable alternative to the 'Front Unique' demanded by the Communist Party.

As we have seen,[1] the Herriot Radical Government came to power a few months after MacDonald had formed the first Labour Government in Great Britain ; and the two worked closely together during the ensuing months in the field of international policy. The most urgent task was that of liquidating the French occupation of the Ruhr and of coming to terms

[1] See p. 434.

with Germany on the basis of a more realistic attituae to the problem of Reparations. The outcome was the Dawes Plan issued in April 1924 and accepted in August at an inter-Allied Reparations Conference, which German delegates were invited to attend. This agreement was followed by the evacuation of the Ruhr, which was completed in November ; and the Dawes Loan was made the basis for ending the German inflation and stabilising the mark.[1] At the same time MacDonald and Herriot were attempting to strengthen the League of Nations by getting arbitration accepted as the means of settling future international disputes ; and on their joint motion the League unanimously adopted in September a resolution in favour of progressive disarmament. Early in October the League Assembly approved the proposed Protocol on arbitration and requested the Council to call a Disarmament Conference to meet the following year. But, only a week later, the MacDonald Government was defeated in the British House of Commons on a Liberal motion dealing with the Campbell prosecution,[2] and by the end of the month the Labour Party had lost the 'Red Letter' General Election.[3] At the beginning of November the British Conservatives came back to office ; and the brief period of close co-operation between the two 'left' Governments came to an abrupt end. In France Herriot remained in office until October 1925 ; but with the fall of the British Labour Government the prospect of success in promoting international action for the maintenance of peace had in effect disappeared, though the Locarno Treaty was signed in London in December of that year.

The Communists, meanwhile, had suffered a split, forced on them by the policy of the Comintern. That body, at its 1922 Congress, vehemently attacked the French Communist Party for keeping in leading positions persons who were tainted with reformism and were attempting to carry on the traditions of the old Socialist Party. The Comintern went to the length of insisting that these persons, including Frossard, the general secretary of the Party, should be displaced, and its own nominees installed in the leading positions. As a result Frossard, the well-known Socialist writer, Paul Louis (1873–1955), and a number of others left the Communist Party and formed a new

[1] See p. 647.   [2] See p. 434.   [3] See p. 435.

body, the Union Socialiste-Communiste, in the hope of bringing about reunion between the rival Parties. The Frossard-
Louis group, while opposed to the parliamentary reformism of
the Socialist Party, denounced the 'autocratic centralisation'
of the Comintern and demanded a return to the 'principles of
1905'. Reform, it declared, should not be neglected, but
should be subordinated to the aim of preparing for the coming
Revolution, in which the general strike and the Trade Unions
should play a most important part. The group was opposed
in especial to Moscow's insistence on the subordination of the
Trade Unions to the Communist Party : it was prepared to
accept the dictatorship of the proletariat only as a short-lived
temporary measure that might be necessary during the Revolution in its early phases, but must be prevented from degenerat-
ing into 'irresponsible oligarchy' or being made a cloak for
'proletarian militarism', of which the Red Army of the Soviet
Union seemed to be regarded as at least a potential example.
The Union Socialiste-Communiste, not surprisingly, met with
no success in its attempt to reunite the Socialist forces. In
1924 Frossard and a good many of the group rejoined the
Socialist Party, and others followed their example during the
next few years. The Union remained in existence, but ceased
to count for much after 1924. By 1926 the membership of the
Socialist Party had risen to 111,000, whereas the Communist
Party, which had claimed 130,000 at the time of its foundation,
had shrunk to 48,000 in 1924 and to a mere 15,000, after an
orgy of heresy-hunting, in 1926, though it rose again to about
50,000 in 1928, after its reorganisation under orders from
Moscow on a basis of party 'cells' in factories and workplaces
as well as on a residential foundation.

In the French Communist movement, from the moment of
its victory over the Social Democrats in 1920, there was, as we
have seen, perpetual dispute between the faithful supporters
of Moscow, who were prepared to do whatever the Comintern
commanded, and the dissidents, who upheld the claim of the
French movement to shape its own course without external
dictation. The dissidents, however, did not form at all a
homogeneous body. One section, consisting of Revolutionary
Syndicalists rather than of Communists, held fast to the traditional insistence on complete independence of political Parties

and was as little prepared to be dictated to by the Comintern as by the French Socialist or the French Communist Party. Many of those in this section were altogether hostile to parliamentary action ; and, even those who were not, assigned to it only a subordinate function and kept their belief in Direct Action as the main instrument for achieving proletarian victory. These were the old advocates of the revolutionary general strike, still hoping to bring back the great days of the pre-war C.G.T. They went into the Red International of Labour Unions with high hopes, at a time when that body was extending a welcome to Revolutionary Syndicalists, Industrial Unionists, and shop stewards without enquiring into the orthodoxy of their Communist beliefs ; and it was not long before they found the company they were keeping distasteful, as it was made clear to them that the R.I.L.U. was meant to be, not an independent International with a right to shape its own policy, but a docile instrument of the Comintern. Men such as Alfred Rosmer, who had played a very active rôle in the R.I.L.U. in its early days, drew back disillusioned, and renewed their attempt to revive the old Syndicalist agitation, but found themselves, like the Centrists in the political movement, caught between two fires and unable to come to terms with either the now reformist C.G.T. or the Communist-controlled C.G.T.U. They had still a following ; but they found that there was no room for a third mass movement different from both.

Distinct from this Syndicalist opposition to both reformism and Moscow Cominternism was the political opposition that grew up inside the French Communist Party, though there were a good many persons who in fact adhered to both. What this political opposition objected to was not so much the subordination of the Trade Unions to the Comintern as the subordination of the French Communist Party. Those who took this view objected strongly to having their policy and strategy dictated to them from Moscow, and to being told by Moscow who their leaders were to be. They swallowed the Comintern's Twenty-one Points without any real intention of enforcing them more than they wished ; and each fresh order from Moscow and each fresh heresy-hunt provoked angry resistance. When the struggle between Stalin and Trotsky spread from the Russian to the international field, there were many in

France who were disposed to side with Trotsky, and to echo his denunciations of the increasing bureaucratisation of the Communist Party of the Soviet Union. Even before this, there were many who were seriously disquieted by the suppression of the Kronsdadt Rising of 1921, by the repudiation of 'workers' control' in the factories, and by the partial return to private enterprise under the New Economic Policy. The unquestioning acceptance of whatever the Bolsheviks did as right and proper revolutionary conduct came to be challenged more and more ; and with it the whole conception of a single, centralised and centrally disciplined world Communist movement came under hostile scrutiny. The French are not a people who readily accept the notion that anyone else knows better then they do ; and Moscow was kept busy suppressing tendencies among the French Communists to insist on a 'Gallican' independence of the Comintern. Boris Souvarine, who had been one of the chief propagandists in France on behalf of the Soviet Revolution, was among the earlier victims of the purges by means of which the party leadership, under orders from the Comintern, set out to maintain party discipline ; and many others accompanied or followed him into disgrace under the charge of 'Trotskyism'. As we saw, the French Communist Party, as an outcome of these faction fights, had sunk in 1926 to a very low level indeed, retaining only a fraction of the membership it had previously enrolled. It did, however, as a body, cleave to the Comintern, even at this high cost in influence ; and the dissidents who were driven out failed to cohere into any effective alternative grouping — partly because they were divided into Syndicalists and advocates of left-wing political action based on French conditions. The French Communist Party was therefore able to outlive its set-backs, and to develop as a body signalised by its devotion to whatever policies the Comintern might call upon it to pursue.

When the world depression of the years after 1929 set in, it hit France later than the other great capitalist countries, largely because the terms on which Poincaré had stabilised the franc in 1926–7 made French goods cheap in the world market and thus rendered deflation unnecessary for the time being. Accordingly, unemployment and labour troubles came later in France than elsewhere ; and the ferment of the 1930s, which led to the formation of the Front Populaire of 1936, was so timed as to fit in with the changed Comintern policy that ensued on the Nazis' victory in Germany.

It is unnecessary to set out here the numerous exclusions and secessions from the French Communist Party during the 1920s. It suffices to say that most of the political dissidents who remained active — as many did not — presently grouped themselves in a Socialist-Communist Union, called later the Socialist-Communist Party, which rejected both the reformism of the Socialist Party and the centralised discipline of Moscow, and attempted to maintain within its limited membership a régime of free discussion and democratic decision. Formed originally in 1923, this group recruited its members as a result of further secessions and exclusions from the Communist Party, including a considerable secession in 1930. It was, however, unable ever to gather round it more than a small popular following, or to elect more than an occasional deputy to Parliament.

Meanwhile the Socialist Party was having its own troubles. Included in its ranks were many, especially among its representatives in Parliament, who, keenly hostile to Communism and seeing no prospect of winning a parliamentary majority, wanted to come to terms with the bourgeois Radicals, at any rate to the extent of electoral pacts for mutual support at the second ballot used in French elections when no candidate got a clear majority at the first voting. A good many, indeed, wished to go beyond this, and were prepared to enter a coalition Government with the Radicals should their combined strength be enough to enable the two Parties to form such a Government. As against this, the more left-wing Socialists desired an electoral pact with the Communists, who came forward with various proposals for the 'Front Unique' when the offer of such 'Fronts' had secured the Comintern's ambiguous approval.[1] The majority of the Socialist Party, however, rejected the 'Front Unique' both when it was first put forward in 1923 and on many subsequent occasions. At the elections of the following year, as we saw, the Socialist Party authorised local electoral arrangements with the Radicals and derived great advantage from them in securing the election of 103 Socialist

[1] See p. 703.

deputies, whereas the Communists, fighting alone, won only 27 seats. The Socialists, however, while they supported the Herriot Government of that year, refused to take office in it ; and after its fall the dissensions between 'participationists' and 'anti-participationists' continued unabated. At the Party Congress of January 1926 Renaudel, Vincent Auriol, and Paul-Boncour vainly argued for participation against Paul Faure, Léon Blum (1873–1950), and Alexandre Bracke. The following year the Party rejected participation in Poincaré's Government of National Union, which was joined by a number of Radicals and proceeded to carry through the stabilisation of the franc.

At the General Election of 1928 the Communists, under the new Comintern slogan, 'Class against Class', recommended their followers not to support Socialist candidates at the second ballot ; but despite this the Socialists won 104 seats, with Radical aid, and the Communist Party a mere 12, though it polled over a million votes at the first ballot, compared with the Socialists' 1,700,000. Violent recriminations between the two Parties followed, the Communists accusing the Socialists of becoming stooges of Poincaré, and the Socialists retorting that the Communists, by their action at the second ballot, had handed many seats over to the right.

On the fall of the Briand Cabinet in October 1929, the Radical leader, Daladier, approached the Socialists with an offer of coalition. The Socialist parliamentary group voted in favour of acceptance ; but the proposal was rejected by a very small majority at the meeting of the National Council of the Party, and this decision was confirmed by a bigger majority at a special Congress. The conflict of views, however, remained sharp. In the elections of 1932 the Socialists and Radicals again supported one another at the second ballot ; and the Socialist vote rose to over 2 million and the number of Socialist deputies to 112, whereas the Communists suffered a further decline. At this point began the series of short-lived Radical Ministries, without Socialist participation but with Socialist support, that prepared the way for the 'Front Populaire' of a few years later. In 1932 projects of coalition broke down because the Radicals refused to accept the minimum programme laid down by the Socialists as a condition of participating in the Government. This included, besides reduction of armaments and prohibition of the traffic in arms, the enactment of a general system of social security, and the introduction of the forty-hour week. The insistence on these terms antagonised the participationists in the Party, and prepared the way for the subsequent secession of the Néo-Socialistes headed by Renaudel and Adrien Marquet (1884–?). This episode, however, belongs to a later period.

Throughout the period discussed in this chapter the French working-class movement was in a ferment of ideological discussion ; but it is not easy to discover any really significant contribution that the warring factions made to Socialist thought. Revolutionary Syndicalism, the outstanding French contribution of the years before 1914, underwent no important fresh development as a theory : the post-war C.G.T. had ceased to be revolutionary, though it continued to affirm its loyalty to the pre-war Amiens Charter, and the C.G.T.U. soon turned into little more than an adjunct to the Communist Party, shedding from its leadership those who had hoped to make it a means of carrying on the Revolutionary Syndicalist tradition. French Socialism, rent first by war-time dissensions and later by the struggle between Communists and anti-Communists, conducted its battles in the realm of theory mainly in connection with issues of international policy and in terms which were not distinctively French. The French Communists, though in continuous trouble with the Comintern, produced no distinctive ideas of their own ; and the non-Communists, though they argued a great deal first about the claims of 'la patrie' and then about the attitude they should take up towards the bourgeois Radicals, found nothing particularly novel to say on either of these matters. Neither Renaudel nor Longuet was in any respect an original thinker, and no really significant theorist emerged to take the place of Jean Jaurès, or even of Jules Guesde.

Indeed, the only new idea that emerged in French Socialism during these years was the outcome of the C.G.T.'s abandonment of Revolutionary Syndicalism in favour of a non-revolutionary programme of economic reconstruction. As we saw,[1] the C.G.T. included in the reconstruction programme which it drew up in 1918 a demand for a National Economic Council

[1] See p. 470.

and the outline of a project of 'nationalisation industrialisée' under which nationalised services were to be put under joint control by producers' and consumers' representatives. When the Government refused to set up an Economic Council with the wide powers demanded, the C.G.T. proceeded to establish an advisory body of its own, a Conseil Économique du Travail, representing, in addition to the Trade Unions, the National Federation of Consumers' Co-operative Societies, the Union Syndicale des Techniciens de l'Industrie, du Commerce, et de l'Agriculture, and the Fédération Nationale des Fonctionnaires. This body was given the task of working out plans for the reconstruction of French economic life, in such a way as to 'disarm the State and cause it to evolve towards the time when it will represent nothing more than the collective organs of production and distribution; to eradicate the coercive elements which it at present contains; to deprive capital of its control over the national economy; and to grant to Labour the rights to which it aspires and the responsibilities it is fit to assume'. The Council, working through nine sub-commissions, proceeded during the year after its appointment to work out a series of proposals covering not only the restoration of the war-devastated areas, chiefly by means of Co-operative enterprise, but also the replacement of capitalist control by a form of nationalised ownership and administration designed to reconcile the claims of producers and consumers and to take due account of the technical requirements of efficient management. In the industries to be taken over under this scheme — railways and other transport undertakings, mining, and public utility services — ownership was to pass to the public, either nationally or locally, but in the words of the Council's report, 'we do not intend either to extend or strengthen the influence of the State, or above all to have recourse to any system that would put the essential resources of the nation under the control of an irresponsible bureaucracy'. The administration of the nationalised enterprises was accordingly to be placed in the hands of representatives of the producers and of the consumers, the former including technicians and managerial as well as manual workers, and the latter state or municipal, as well as Co-operative, nominees. The public authorities were to become financially responsible for these undertakings, but the managing bodies were to enjoy complete autonomy in relation to the state machine.

In another report, the Council of Labour made parallel proposals for the conduct of industries that were not to be nationalised, at any rate at once. It proposed that in each such industry all the firms involved should be compulsorily grouped into a syndicate, which would not only act as a sole buyer of raw materials for the entire industry but would also determine the total volume of output and allocate a quota to each firm or establishment, and would be responsible for guiding the course of investment and technical development. For co-ordination between industries, both nationalised and 'syndicated', there was to be a Council of Industrial Syndicates ; and over the whole economy was to preside a central Directing Committee which was to be responsible for the drawing up and execution of a comprehensive national economic plan.

These C.G.T. projects of 1919 and 1920 were, of course, in part a continuation of the old Syndicalist projects, shorn of their complete anti-parliamentarism and of their revolutionary character. Much that Jouhaux and other advocates of them said harked back to Fernand Pelloutier and the early days of the C.G.T. But Jouhaux had discarded the old insistence that the workers were fully capable of managing the entire economy for themselves without either invoking the State or needing to give special consideration to the place of consumers or technicians in the structure of the new society. The Council of Labour's plan was based on the idea of bringing into collaboration every factor except the capitalist investor and on making use of State and municipality while keeping them out of the actual management. The new version of 'workers' control' differed greatly in spirit from the old Syndicalist conception, but was recognisably derived from it under the influence of war-time experience of a 'directed' economy in which the workers had achieved some measure of participation.

Nothing came of these plans. There was, of course, never any question of their being adopted by any Government the French people was likely to have in the near future ; and the C.G.T. itself speedily became so deeply involved in its own internal disputes that they dropped right into the background. The Council of Labour, after working at top speed for a few months, relapsed into inaction ; and all that remained was the inclusion of the C.G.T.'s conception of 'industrial nationalisation' in the programme of the French Socialist Party after the split. From the beginning, the Trade Union left, Communists and Revolutionary Syndicalists alike, denounced the Council of Labour's plan as a lapse into reformism, involving class-collaboration with middle-class managerial elements and with the bourgeois State — as indeed it did. The Co-operative Societies, which Jouhaux had hoped to draw into close alliance with the Trade Unions, dropped away in the *débâcle* of 1920 ; and the C.G.T. lost so much of its strength even before the breakaway of the C.G.T.U. as to destroy all prospect of getting even a part of its way. Nevertheless, in drawing up these projects of 1919 and 1920, the C.G.T. did make the one constructive contribution of French Socialism to the stock of Socialist thinking during the years just after the war. The only practical outcome, however, was the establishment by the Herriot Radical Government of 1924 of a new National Economic Council, made up of representatives of employers' associations, Trade Unions, Co-operative Societies, and a number of other bodies. But, whereas the C.G.T. had demanded an Economic Parliament, invested with real powers parallel to those of the political Parliament, the National Economic Council was a merely consultative body, authorised only to study economic problems and to issue recommendations which the Government was free to accept or reject, or to ignore. Its establishment made no real difference to the economic structure of French society.

Why was French Socialist thought, during the years after 1914, on the whole so poor in quality and so devoid of new ideas ? Maybe, it was sheer accident — simply that no outstanding French thinker happened to arrive. But I am inclined to believe that in the conditions which existed in post-war France it was exceptionally difficult for any realistic thinker to see his way clearly. France had suffered terrible war losses not only in the devastation of the northern departments, but, much more, in the sacrifice of young lives and in the dislocation of cultural relations. Socialism is essentially a form of optimism, resting on a belief that society can and should be improved by deliberate planning ; and France, as far back as 1918, was already to a great extent a country of pessimists mistrustful of old creeds and made fearful, rather than uplifted, by new winds of doctrine. A small, very vocal minority was deeply stirred by the events in Russia, and the readier to accept Russian leadership because Bolshevism offered them a call to action that did not require much intellectual effort. The majority, however, even of the Socialist and Trade Union activists did not respond at all fully to this stimulus or, if they did, before long found it unsatisfying and, failing to meet with any powerful alternative stimulus, relapsed into sceptical inactivity. There were other factors — notably the long-standing French reluctance to pay regular contributions for the support of any cause — that help to account for the quite exceptional rate at which both party and Trade Union membership ebbed and flowed almost from moment to moment ; but undoubtedly one very important reason for this instability was that, in the absence of any clear sense of direction, men alternated rapidly between a mood of high excitement and a feeling of futility, and flowed into and out of movements and campaigns as the mood took them. Nowhere in Europe did the Russian Revolution engender so much enthusiastic acclaim as in France ; but nowhere was the enthusiasm less to be relied on as a basis for sustained activity.

To be sure, these characteristics of the French working-class movement were not new : they were only aggravated and not engendered by the war and by the events in Russia. They had been present markedly in the pre-war C.G.T. and, to a smaller extent, in the Socialist Party as well. In both the Guesdists, who admired and envied the solidity and high organisation of the German movement, had represented the most solid element ; and it is significant that the Guesdist strongholds were chiefly in Northern France, which was overrun and experienced the largest share in the destruction. In comparison with the Guesdists the Socialist followers of Jaurès and the Revolutionary Syndicalists who repudiated party leadership had both been unstable groups, though the causes of their instability had been different. The Syndicalists had been essentially rebels against the entire tradition of the bourgeois Republic and had been always eager to seize on any rebellious tendency among the masses, relying rather on their capacity to lead the masses when the right moment came than on any sustained effort at mass organisation. Jaurès, on the other handhad, been deeply devoted to the Republican tradition, as he had shown at the time of the Dreyfus affair. He had been in essence a Radical politician turned Socialist because he looked on Socialism as the completion of what had been begun in 1789. As a Socialist he had accepted the verdict of the Second International against Socialist participation in bourgeois Governments save under highly exceptional circumstances — the Kautsky resolution of 1904 ; [1] and he, more than any other Socialist leader, had seen the necessity of bowing to the claims of the Trade Unions embodied in the Amiens Charter of 1906. But this acceptance had not caused him to be in spirit less a Radical or a less ardent upholder of the duty of all good men to rally to the defence of the Republic against enemies within or without. He had been ardent also in his internationalism and in his hatred of war ; but there is not a shadow of doubt that, had he lived on into the war years, he would have rallied strongly to the national cause — although, I think, he would have kept his head and would have taken the first opportunity of adhering to the cause of a negotiated peace. Longuet, I feel sure, was more faithful than Renaudel to the spirit of Jaurès, though far below him in capacity and imaginative understanding. Jaurès's political Radicalism, however, had been a cause of instability in his wing of the Socialist Party ; for it had encouraged Frenchmen of the left to swing to and fro between Socialism and Radicalism, or at all events between Socialist self-sufficiency and alliance with the bourgeois left. I am not suggesting that Jaurès was wrong in taking up this attitude, though both Guesdists and Syndicalists attacked him for it. I feel sure that it was a necessary condition of the rapid growth of Socialism as a parliamentary force. Nevertheless, it tended to render Socialism unstable because it made against the sharp separation, social as well as political, between Socialists and non-Socialists that characterised both French Guesdism and German Social Democracy and, in a very different way, Revolutionary Syndicalism as well.

During and immediately after the war, the situation was quite different. The working-class movement was no longer a third-party intruder into the conflict between bourgeois right

---

[1] See Vol. III, Part I, p. 45.

and bourgeois left, but the principal antagonist of a bourgeois Bloc National in which Radicals as well as reactionaries were enmeshed. Electorally the Socialists, even united, were not nearly strong enough to defeat this Bloc ; but, aided by the Trade Unions, they were powerful enough to make things awkward for it, though not to overthrow it by revolutionary means. As in post-war Italy, there was a large mass of revolutionary feeling, but not nearly enough to serve as a foundation for a successful Revolution. Moreover, whereas before the war the centre of revolutionism had been in the Trade Unions, in 1919 this was no longer the case. Events in Russia and the establishment of the Comintern had shifted the centre of revolutionary feeling into the Socialist Party. The C.G.T. leadership had discarded its old revolutionism and had become reformist ; and, though there were considerable revolutionary elements left in the Trade Unions, especially among the Metal Workers and the Railwaymen, these elements were quickly defeated when they attempted to challenge the authority of the bourgeois State — for they could look neither to the C.G.T. nor to the Socialist Party for united or sustained support. The C.G.T. was busy with its projects of industrialised nationalisation and its demands for a National Economic Council with the powers of an Industrial Parliament ; and the new Majority which had ousted the old one from control of the Socialist Party was hardly more revolutionary, at any rate in its leadership, than the fraction it had ousted. There was, no doubt, among those who had voted for Longuet against Renaudel a substantial and growing revolutionary element ; but it took two years for this element to become strong enough to defeat Renaudel and Longuet combined and to turn the majority fraction of the Socialist Party into a Communist Party — and a good deal longer to hammer the new Party into the pattern required by the Comintern. By the time the first of these things had been done, the wave of revolutionary feeling had ebbed away and the time for revolutionary action — if there had ever been one — had evidently gone by. In truth, there had been no such moment, and everybody except a few fanatics knew this. But neither the Trade Unions nor the Socialist Party nor the Communists were ready with any practicable alternative. Like the Italians, they had been too busy fighting one another to give much thought to devising new policies to fit the conditions of post-war France.

Nor should it be left out of account that in post-war France, exhausted by its heavy war losses, there existed, side by side with other impulses, a strong current of feeling against war in all its forms. This sentiment, which could take various shapes, was particularly marked among such groups as the teachers and lesser *fonctionnaires*, which were both strongly represented in the Socialist Party. It could find expression either in pacifism or in sympathy with Communism as a way to peace through revolution. The two outstanding literary exponents of these attitudes were Henri Barbusse (1873-1935) and Romain Rolland (1866-1944). Barbusse, who served in the French army as a common soldier, published in 1916 his vivid description of the horrors of warfare, *Le Feu*. Despite its fierce anti-militarism it was awarded the Prix Goncourt ; and its author followed it up with other anti-militarist writings, including *Clarté* (1919) and *Paroles d'un combattant* (1920). After the war he joined the Communists and finally settled in Russia where he died. Rolland, first known as a writer on music and as an art critic and a leading contributor to Péguy's *Cahiers de la Quinzaine*, reached the height of his fame before the war with his discursive ten-volume novel, *Jean Christophe* (1904-12), for which he was awarded the Nobel Prize for Literature in 1915. He was already a pacifist, and published his *Vie de Tolstoi* in 1911. During the war he took refuge in Switzerland, where he issued his pacifist *Au dessus de la mêlée* (1915) and a second study of Tolstoi two years later. After the war he became deeply interested in India, and above all in Mahatma Gandhi, of whom he published a study in 1924. In his later years he modified his pacifism and attached himself to the cause of Communism as the way to peace. (See his *Par la révolution la paix* (1935).) In 1939, however, he rallied to the Allied cause against Nazism in an impassioned letter addressed to Daladier.

Barbusse and Rolland were both important figures, but neither was primarily a Socialist, and neither can be held to have made any distinctive contribution to Socialist thought. What led them both towards Communism was the horror they felt at the insensate inhumanity of modern warfare, and therewith an entire disillusionment with the politicians of all the older parties. France had indeed lost in killed and mutilated so many of its sons that this mood of disillusionment was very strong. It helped the Communists to win control of the Socialist Party ; but many of those who adhered in this mood to Communism subsequently dropped away and in many cases gave up all forms of political activity, while others presently rejoined the Socialist Party and became supporters of its pacifist wing. The Socialists, however, though they recovered in some degree from the low point to which they fell at the time of the break with the Communists, were never able to win back the allegiance of the main body of industrial workers. Throughout the 1920s and right up to the formation of the Front Populaire as a reaction to the Nazi danger in the middle 'thirties, the French Labour movement, both politically and industrially, was too deeply divided either to exert any considerable influence on the general course of affairs or even to give effective protection to the workers' interests through collective bargaining.

CHAPTER XIV

BELGIUM AND SWITZERLAND

BELGIUM

THE violation of Belgian neutrality in August 1914 ranged the Belgian Labour Party solidly behind the Government in support of the war. Émile Vandervelde (1866-1938), its leader, joined the Government as Minister of State, thus inaugurating a policy of ministerial participation which was to continue after the war. The Party issued a manifesto calling upon all its members to rally to the cause of national defence. In face of the German invasion, the Government moved into exile and presently established itself on French soil, at Le Havre. Vandervelde had long been Chairman of the International Socialist Bureau, which had its headquarters in Brussels, with another Belgian, Camille Huysmans (b. 1871), as Secretary. The question at once arose whether Vandervelde, having become a Minister, could keep his position at the head of the International. His fellow-leader in the Belgian Labour Party, Louis de Brouckère (1870-1951), was among those who expressed doubts about the propriety of his doing so ; but Vandervelde insisted on his right to retain both offices. The International Socialist Bureau, headed by Huysmans, moved to neutral territory in Holland, and was thus cut off from close contact with its President and also with the Belgians who had constituted its Administrative Committee. These, too, kept their official positions, but were replaced by Dutch delegates for the carrying on of the day-to-day work of the Bureau. Édouard Anseele (1856-1938), next to Vandervelde the outstanding leader, stayed on in Belgium under the German occupation and did what he could to keep the Labour and Socialist organisation in being.

Belgian industry suffered severely under the occupation, and there was also an acute shortage of food. The Labour organisations set to work to organise a system of relief for the unemployed, in face of many difficulties both with the occupation authorities, who imposed a military dictatorship, and with employers who sought to exclude the Trade Unions from representation on the official bodies in charge of unemployment relief. In dealing with the food problem, rendered very difficult by German requisitions as well as by the Allied blockade, the Socialist, Joseph Wauters (1875–1929), played an outstanding part inside Belgium, while the Government in exile did its best to procure the admittance of imported supplies. The Allies at first refused to raise or limit the blockade ; but in view of the danger of mass starvation an arrangement was at length made under which a Commission for Belgian Relief was set up, supervised by the embassies of the United States and of Spain, and foodstuffs provided by the Commission were allowed to pass through the blockade. Up to the entry of the United States into the war Herbert Hoover was in charge of this work, which was then taken over by a Spanish-Dutch Committee.

Economically, under German pressure, the situation in Belgium grew worse and worse. Not only were raw materials for industry unobtainable : before long the Germans began to dismantle Belgian factories and to remove to Germany any plant that could be put to war use, and even wantonly to destroy plant, while seeking to coerce the Belgian workers into working under German orders in the service of the occupation forces. This provoked much resistance, especially in the French-speaking areas ; but matters became a great deal worse when, in 1917, the Germans instituted a new policy of mass deportations of Belgians for work in Germany. Nearly 60,000 were thus deported, and another 60,000 were sent to work at the front in France, digging trenches, building emergency railways, and doing other work for the German armies. In Germany the deportees were kept in concentration camps, whence they were sent out in batches to work in factories or in labour battalions, under conditions of great hardship. There were strong protests, from neutral as well as from Allied countries, against these violations of international law ; but the Germans disregarded them and steadily intensified their pressure, especially during 1918.

It was the policy of the German Government to do all it could to drive a wedge between the Flemish- and the French-speaking parts of Belgium and to favour the Flemings in the bilingual areas. Among the Belgian Flemings there arose a party of Activists who were prepared to collaborate with the Germans in return for the favours shown them and wished to organise a separate Flemish State under German protection. The Germans encouraged this movement, but were deterred both by neutral protests and by the strength of the feeling against separation in the central bilingual areas from giving definite recognition to the proposed Flemish State. In Brussels, on February 11th, 1918, a great demonstration against separation was violently dispersed by German troops, but had some deterrent effect on German policy.

Meanwhile, outside Belgium, Vandervelde and his colleagues at Le Havre and in London continued to give full support to the Allied war effort and, in the affairs of the International, took a strong line against any meeting with the German Socialists so long as the German armies continued to occupy Belgian territory. The Belgian Socialist leaders in exile took an active part in the series of Allied Socialist Conferences on War Aims, and ranged themselves with those who were most insistent on the need for a fight to a finish. They could hardly have been expected to take up any other attitude while the Germans were not only occupying their country and oppressing the Belgian people, but also refusing to give any assurance that Belgian independence would be restored after the war and laying plans, if not for outright annexation, at any rate for turning Belgium permanently into a satellite country under German control. This attitude gave rise to difficulties when in 1917 the Dutch-Scandinavian Committee, in collaboration with Camille Huysmans, began to plan for the proposed International Socialist Conference at Stockholm. Belgian Socialists who had remained in the country and had suffered the increasing oppression of the German authorities, were in many cases naturally eager to see the war brought to a speedy conclusion if this could be achieved on terms that would restore the independence of their country ; and some of them, including Anseele, were more disposed than the leaders in exile to look with favour on the Stockholm project. They had, however, no effective means of bringing pressure to bear either on their exiled Government or on Vandervelde and the party leaders outside Belgium, who had the ear of the other Allied Socialists.

A few days before the armistice of November 1918 the Socialist Ministers resigned from the exiled Belgian Government. This action arose out of a strike that had broken out among Belgian workers employed in France under the Belgian Government's auspices. The strikers demanded the same rates of pay as were allowed to French workers employed on similar work ; but the Government not only rejected this demand but threatened the strikers with condign punishment under military discipline. In view of the armistice, the proposed action was not taken ; but the resignations were not withdrawn. The Belgian Government, however, was reconstituted almost at once on the return of the King and the exiled authorities to Belgian soil ; and the Socialists obtained permission from the Belgian Labour Party to enter a new broadly based coalition Government charged with the pressing tasks of reconstruction. In the new Ministry Vandervelde took office as Minister of Justice, and Jules Destrée (1863-1936) and Joseph Wauters held other Cabinet posts. Édouard Anseele joined them a little later.

From 1884 to the General Election of 1919 the Catholic Party was continuously in a majority in the Belgian Parliament, which was elected first on a restricted franchise and later on a basis of manhood suffrage vitiated by plural voting for the wealthier classes. In the first post-war election, held on a basis of real manhood suffrage, the Catholics lost their majority but still remained the largest Party. The three main Parties — Catholic, Labour, and Liberal — were all represented in the first post-war Government, which enacted a large body of progressive social legislation. The Trade Unions, which had had only about 200,000 members in 1914, rose sharply to about 600,000 soon after the war ; and by 1921 the Central Trade Union Commission had risen to 720,000, apart from the Unions organised under Catholic auspices. In the post-war situation the Socialists, aided in most matters by the progressive wing of the Catholics, were able to bring strong pressure to bear. At the election of 1919 the Labour Party won 70 seats, as against 34 held by it in 1914. In 1919, in face of strong employer opposition, the eight hours' day was made law, and large changes were made in the tax system by the introduction of a graduated income tax and death duties. A system of old-age pensions was also brought into force. But, as the fears of the bourgeoisie subsided, resistance to such measures stiffened, and in the Labour Party growing opposition made itself felt to the continued participation of Socialists in a Government dominated by the bourgeois Parties. At the Party Conference of 1920 one-third of the votes were cast against participation, and the following year more than two-fifths. The left wing set to work to organise its own groups inside the Party under the name 'Friends of the Exploited' ; and when the Party ordered these groups to dissolve, the dissidents, reinforced by a section of the Party's Youth Movement, seceded and established a Belgian Communist Party as a section of the Comintern. Under pressure of these developments, in 1921, the Socialists resigned from the Government. At the ensuing General Election the Labour Party fell to 68 in the Chamber, but rose from 13 to 52 in the Senate, which was elected under a reformed constitution ; and there were also very large gains in the local elections for the provincial and communal councils. During the next few years the Catholic-Liberal Coalition reduced unemployment pay, altered the pension law, and in a number of ways attacked the Trade Union rights conceded in 1919. These reactionary measures strengthened the position of the Labour Party, which at the Election of 1925 raised its representation in the Chamber to 78 and thus became for the first time the largest Party, though still a long way short of a majority of its own. The Socialists then refused to form a Government of their own, but agreed to enter a Coalition with the Catholics with the object of stabilising the currency, which had been depreciating heavily on account of the high costs of economic reconstruction. The first attempt at stabilisation failed and, to the accompaniment of a 'flight from the franc', the Belgian currency suffered a further catastrophic fall. The Catholic-Socialist Ministry was then replaced by an all-party Coalition under Henri Jaspar ; and the new Government at length succeeded in stabilising the currency with Socialist support. But immediately afterwards the Socialists fell foul of the bourgeois Parties over the question of military service, which the Socialists wished to reduce to six months ; and in 1927 the Labour Party left the Government, which was reconstituted without them as a Catholic-Liberal Coalition. From 1927 to 1935 the Socialists were in opposition.

During the years after 1918 Belgian Communism, though always active, was never able to rally any large body of support. It became important only in the later 1920s, during the stabilisation crisis, in view of heavy unemployment and of policies of national economy which included severe restrictions on unemployment relief. The Communists then adopted an energetic policy of boring from within the Trade Unions and put themselves at the head of an unofficial strike movement which led to serious disturbances and to sharp divisions in the Socialist and Trade Union ranks. Politically, however, the Communists made little headway, returning only 2 members at the General Election of 1929 and falling into sharp conflict among themselves between the orthodox supporters of the Comintern and a large Trotskyist minority, which was duly expelled in 1928.

During the 1920s the Belgian Socialist movement remained for the most part under the same leaders as had stood at its head before the war. Émile Vandervelde continued to hold an unquestioned position as party leader ; and with him were Louis de Brouckère, who had already made important theoretical contributions to the work of the Second International,[1] Joseph Wauters, who had greatly increased his stature as a consequence of his leadership of the movement inside Belgium during the war, the veteran Co-operator Édouard Anseele, Corneille Mertens (1880–1951), the Trade Union leader, who became Vice-President of the Amsterdam I.F.T.U., and Henri de Man (1885–1953), who had emerged into prominence before the war as the organiser of the Socialist Youth and was to become the outstanding theoretical influence during the 1930s, when he formulated his celebrated *Plan du travail* and succeeded to the presidency of the Party. This period of his activity, however, falls outside the scope of the present volume ; and so do his later adventures when, during the second world war, he remained in Belgium as adviser to the King under the German occupation and was accused of collaborating with the Nazis.

[1] See Vol. III, Part I, p. 72.

His own account of the matter was that, believing the Nazis to have won the war, he remained in Belgium in the hope of protecting his fellow-Socialists against German excesses. It is clear that up to a point he did become a collaborator, being convinced of the need to come to terms with the Nazi 'New Order'. This cost him his position in the working-class movement; and he spent the post-war years in exile in Switzerland, issuing defences of his attitude, such as his *Cavalier seul*, and continuing to write quite impressively about the crisis confronting the post-war world. De Man was a remarkable person, whatever may be thought of his later doings. He spoke French, Flemish, German, and English with equal facility and, in addition to his political career, held professorships in both Germany and America as well as in Belgium. His most remarkable book is his *Psychology of Socialism* (1927). The *Plan du travail* (1933), in which he incidentally attacked the Marxian notion of capitalism as advancing towards its 'final crisis', was also an important contribution to the policy of economic planning.

Already, in the 1920s, de Man was often at loggerheads with Vandervelde and the older political leaders of his Party, whom he accused of having no constructive economic policy. The gist of his argument was that the proletariat, as long as it attempted to act alone, stood no chance of being in a position to establish Socialism, at all events in the countries governed under democratic parliamentary régimes. As long as it worked in isolation, its success was limited to advances towards the 'Welfare State'; and even these could be made only in times of economic prosperity, and were always liable to be undermined in times of depression. Therefore, he argued, the proletariat must seek allies among all sections of the people that suffered under capitalist oppression; and among these he named especially the small business men and the peasants, who were at the mercy both of the great financiers and of the monopolists who controlled a number of essential industries. These groups, however, would certainly not support any programme of comprehensive socialisation, which they would regard as directed against themselves. It was therefore necessary for the Socialists to draw up a clear plan limiting socialisation to the banks and other credit institutions and to those industries which were subject to monopolistic control, and to give an assurance to the lesser entrepreneurs, not only that they would be immune from socialisation, but also that under the reformed public credit system they would be treated a great deal better than under monopoly capitalism. De Man hoped, by putting forward a policy of this kind, to end the stalemate in Belgian politics by winning over the main body of adherents of the Catholic Party, which rested largely on the support of the Catholic Trade Unions and, as long as this support continued, would be able to block the Belgian Labour Party's road to power. His arguments gained additional force when the depression of 1931 and the ensuing years struck hard at the Belgian economy, and led to widespread hostility to the deflationary measures by which the Government met the crisis. In 1933 he succeeded in persuading the Belgian Labour Party to endorse the *Plan du travail*, which involved a large change in the nature of its appeal. Many Socialist stalwarts feared, not without cause, that in seeking to broaden its appeal the Party would be led away from Socialism to a form of class-collaboration that would undermine its working-class influence ; and these fears were increased as it became plain that de Man had considerable sympathy with the Neo-Socialist movement that was developing at the same time in France. Nevertheless there was some sound thinking in the *Plan du travail* ; for undoubtedly the Belgian Socialists had got into a position in which they took almost for granted the continual division of the working class between the Labour Party and the Catholics and the consequent need for coalition Governments incapable of achieving any real advance in a Socialist direction. The stale-mate which, as we saw,[1] had existed in Belgium well before 1914 had continued, despite constitutional reforms, into the post-war period ; and de Man's was a significant attempt to escape from it, though at a possible high cost in endangering the loyalty of its traditional following. In practice, this cost was not incurred, but neither was the deadlock broken ; for the Catholics did not allow themselves to be weaned away from their Party. The stalemate continued : indeed it has continued up to the present time.

The theories of Vandervelde and de Brouckère were discussed

[1] See Vol. III, Part II, p. 617.

in the preceding volume [1] and need not be considered again here, except to mention that Vandervelde, after visiting Russia in 1917 in order to urge the Russian Government to continue the war, became one of the most vehement antagonists of Bolshevism. We have seen how he returned to Russia in 1923 for the purpose of acting as defence counsel to the Social Revolutionaries accused of counter-revolutionary activities, only to throw up his brief in protest against the unfair conduct of the case. [2] Vandervelde was also active in the cause of the Georgian Mensheviks [3] in their struggle against the Bolsheviks after 1918. He took an active part in the Berne International Socialist Conference of February 1919 and in the revived Second International. In the realm of ideas, however, he added little to his pre-war contributions to Socialist thinking, though, as Minister of Justice, he was able, between 1919 and 1921, to make substantial practical contributions to the cause of penal and prison reform. In general, the Belgian Socialists acted during the post-war period as a moderate, constitutional Party, ready to co-operate with the bourgeois Parties in the exacting tasks of national reconstruction and well aware that they were not strong enough to be able to carry through any programme of constructive Socialism beyond a limited advance towards the Welfare State. Their acceptance of these limitations constantly exposed them to left-wing criticism ; but they managed always to hold the allegiance of the great majority of the Belgian Socialists and to prevent Belgian Communism from developing into a really formidable movement. There was, indeed, in post-war Belgium little or no room for any sort of revolutionary activity, both because the national situation clearly called for a common effort towards economic reconstruction and because the presence of a separatist or autonomist Flemish agitation tended to consolidate the support of the main part of the people behind the existing State. The Belgian Communists lessened their own chances by quarrelling vigorously among themselves ; but even if they had been united it is unlikely that they could have made any large political impact. Industrially, because of unemployment and wage troubles arising first out of currency depreciation and then out of the deflationary measures adopted

---

[1] See Vol. III, Part II, pp. 646 and 653.
[2] See p. 187.   [3] See p. 207.

in the interests of stabilisation, they were better placed to make trouble ; but even there they never managed to become more than a nuisance. The Belgian working-class movement, both politically and industrially, found more serious antagonists in the Catholics than in the Communist Party and its various 'front' organisations. It never looked like winning a parliamentary majority of its own ; but it held its own, within its reformist assumptions, with no little tenacity and organising skill.

SWITZERLAND

We have seen already how the Swiss Socialist Party cooperated with the Italians in attempting to bring about a meeting of the Socialists of the warring countries, in the hope of putting an end to the fighting, and how Robert Grimm (b. 1881) and Charles Naine (1874–1926), the one from German and the other from French Switzerland, were mainly responsible for the arrangements for the Zimmerwald Conference of 1915.[1] Both that Conference and the Kienthal Conference of the following year were held on Swiss soil, which had been a notable international meeting-place from the days of the First International. Up to 1914 the Swiss Social Democratic Party, led by Otto Lang (1863–1936), had been regarded as standing well on the right wing of the international Socialist movement ; but during the war a large section of it moved sharply leftwards, especially after the Russian Revolution, and early in 1919 the party Congress voted in favour not only of secession from the Second International but also of adhesion to the newly formed Comintern. This vote was the sequel to the growth of unrest which had led, the previous year, to the formation of a joint committee by the Trade Unions and the Social Democratic Party to formulate demands to be laid before the Government for the redress of an accumulation of grievances that had been piling up as wages lagged behind the rising cost of living. The joint committee called an emergency Trade Union and Socialist Congress, which met at Olten in July 1918 and decided to call a nation-wide general strike unless the Government agreed to meet its claims. The Government did not make the required concessions ; and, fuel having been

[1] See p. 32.

added to the flames by the calling out of soldiers to act against strikers at Zürich and by the banning of a proposed demonstration to celebrate the anniversary of the Bolshevik Revolution, a general strike was actually called for three days in November 1918 and met with great success, the railways in particular being thoroughly held up. The evidence furnished by the strike convinced the Government and the employers that the workers were in a militant mood and thus helped to win the concession of the eight hours' day in 1919.

As we saw earlier, the vote of 1919 in favour of joining the Third International was not the end of the matter. The issue was referred to a referendum of the Social Democratic Party, and the majority voted against affiliation.[1] This rejection of the Comintern was followed by a split. An extreme group, headed by Fritz Platten (1883–1942), had broken away earlier to form a Communist Party, and, in 1921, this group joined forces with the new secessionists. Meanwhile, the Social Democratic Party, clear of its Moscow commitments, became a member of the 'Two-and-a-Half' Vienna International Union;[2] but when that body merged with the right-wing Berne-Geneva International to form the Labour and Socialist International at the Hamburg Congress of 1923, the Swiss Party remained outside, fearful that adhesion might cause fresh dissensions in its ranks. Not until 1927 did it finally make up its mind to throw in its lot with the Labour and Socialist International. By that time the Communists, who had never been able to win more than 2 or 3 seats on the Federal National Council, had lost nearly all their support, whereas by 1928 the Socialists held 50 seats, as compared with 41 in 1919, and polled more than a quarter of the total vote. They were not, however, able to secure the election of any of their members to the Federal Executive Council, which is the nearest Swiss equivalent to the Cabinet in other countries. Not until 1935 did the Socialists even become the largest Party in the National Council ; and they were never anywhere near becoming a majority.

In effect the Swiss Socialists, after a short-lived leftward move in 1918 and 1919, went back to their older policy of moderate reformism and showed no further sign of reverting

[1] See p. 321.   [2] See p. 338.

to any sort of revolutionism. The chief member of the Party, Hermann Greulich (b. 1842), died in 1925, well stricken in years ; and no outstanding personality emerged to take his place. Robert Grimm, who had been the most active left-wing figure during and after the war, remained as the best-known leader of the Party and became its principal representative when it joined the L.S.I.

CHAPTER XV

HOLLAND, SCANDINAVIA, AND FINLAND

WHILE war raged over most of Europe from 1914 to 1918, Holland and the Scandinavian countries were able to maintain their neutrality. It thus fell to their lot both to provide a temporary home for the International Socialist Bureau when it was driven out of Belgium and to take a leading part in the attempt to bring together an International Conference representing the working-class movements of both sides as well as of the neutral countries. Camille Huysmans, the secretary of the International, transferred his office from Brussels to Amsterdam in 1914, and Dutch delegates temporarily replaced Belgians as members of the administrative committee of the I.S.B. As we saw, in April 1917, after the outbreak of the Russian Revolution, the Dutch members of the I.S.B., having consulted the Scandinavians and the Americans, sent out an invitation to all the affiliated bodies to attend an International Socialist Conference to be held at Stockholm the following month. It was also decided to set up at Stockholm a joint Dutch-Scandinavian Committee to take charge of the arrangements with the co-operation of Huysmans and of the I.S.B. The subsequent history of this project has been outlined in a previous chapter : [1] in this chapter we are concerned with the course of events inside Holland and the Scandinavian countries during and after the war.

HOLLAND

The Dutch Socialist movement, led by Pieter Troelstra (1860–1930), had been, up to 1914, greatly under the influence of German Social Democracy, but had within it both a strong pacifist and anti-militarist group, greatly influenced by the Anarchist-pacifist Domela Nieuwenhuis (1876–1919), and a Syndicalist wing, in which Christiaan Cornelissen (1864–1942)

[1] See p. 45.

was the principal figure. It had also a left-wing Marxist group, gathered round a journal, the *Tribune* ; and this group, expelled in 1908 from the Socialist Party, had set up the following year an Independent Socialist Party with an uncompromising revolutionary programme. This independent Party, in which the outstanding figures were David Wijnkoop (1876–1941), the astronomer Anton Pannekoek (b. 1873), and the poet Herman Gorter (1864–1927), developed after 1918 into the Dutch Communist Party. The *Tribune* group consisted mainly of intellectuals and had no large popular following ; but after the split it entered into friendly relations with the Syndicalist fraction of the Trade Union movement, which grew considerably during the war years under stress of the prevailing shortage of food and other supplies. Indeed, war conditions in Holland had been productive of considerable unrest. There, as elsewhere, the Russian Revolution had ministered to the growth of revolutionary feeling, though the main body of the Socialist Party and of the Trade Unions had remained steadily reformist. Russia was too far away for events there to have much practical influence on policy, save among the extreme left. Germany was another matter ; and when the German Revolution broke out in November 1918 there was a sudden excitation of revolutionary feeling. The usually moderate Troelstra, leader of the right-wing Socialist Party, underwent a sudden conversion to the cause of revolution and called on the Dutch workers to follow the German example. There were tumultuous strikes, especially at Rotterdam — always the chief centre of disturbance — and for some days the city was virtually in the hands of the workers. Troelstra, however, was disavowed by most of the Socialist leaders ; and the Government took energetic action to quell the disturbances. Holland returned to its habitual calm : only the small minority which followed Wijnkoop and Gorter maintained its revolutionary line and took part in the formative Congress of the Third International in March 1919. The engineer S. Rutgers (b. 1879), its delegate to the Congress, remained in Moscow till the autumn, when he returned to Holland with a mandate from Lenin to set up a West European Bureau of the Comintern at Amsterdam, almost at the same moment as that body was establishing a West European Secretariat in Berlin under the auspices of the

German Communist Party. This duplication was soon to lead to trouble. The Amsterdam Bureau got together, in February 1920, an international conference attended by delegates from groups in Holland, Belgium, France, Germany, Italy, the Scandinavian countries, Great Britain, and the United States, with Michael Borodin (1890–1954) representing the Comintern. The police, however, broke up the proceedings on the second day ; and the affair had no practical outcome except that almost immediately after it Moscow wound up the Amsterdam Bureau and transferred its functions to Berlin.

At the root of this action lay a doctrinal dispute. The Dutch group, as we saw, had entered into close relations with the Syndicalist Union, representing the anti-parliamentary element in the Dutch Trade Union movement, and had been considerably influenced by Syndicalist ideas. The Comintern, at the time of its formation, was appealing to revolutionary Syndicalists for support, and had not yet made plain its intention of subordinating the Trade Unions firmly to Communist Party control or of centralising authority in its own hands. By 1920, however, the situation had changed, and there was no longer a place for independent revolutionary Trade Unionism in the Communist fold, or for the acceptance of groups which rejected parliamentary action, as many of the Gorter group did. When Lenin published in 1920 his attack on such deviations — in his *Left-wing Communism : an Infantile Disorder* — Gorter immediately replied to him in *An Open Letter to Comrade Lenin*. Gorter had been to Moscow, where he had talked to Lenin ; and he had come back deeply disillusioned. As he told Pannekoek after his return, 'I expected this man to be and to feel himself the *generalissimo* of the world revolution ; but I had to realise that Lenin thought constantly of Russia and saw all things exclusively from the Russian point of view'. In saying this, Gorter was not accusing Lenin of nationalism, or of putting Russian interests above those of World Revolution. What he meant was that Lenin was obsessed by the notion that whatever had been done by the Bolsheviks in making the Revolution must be right not only for Russia but for every country, and that he had no real understanding of conditions or of the state of working-class feeling in the West.

Lenin, in his *Left-wing Communism*, was arguing, against

those Communists who rejected parliamentary action as 'reformist' and scorned working inside the Trade Unions as involving compromise with reaction, that it was 'infantile' to suppose that the Revolution could be made without winning over the masses or without pressing every available instrument into its service. Gorter's answer, in his *Open Letter*, was that, whereas in Russia it had been practicable to base the Revolution on an alliance of workers, soldiers, and peasants, with the Bolsheviks guiding and leading the masses, in Western Europe no such thing was possible. In the West, Gorter argued, the peasants, the lower middle classes, and the intellectuals were all bourgeois-minded and opposed to revolution : so that the proletariat would have to act without their aid, and indeed against them. Therefore, he contended, in the West the essential task of the revolutionaries was to create a revolutionary proletariat, powerful enough and conscious enough to act on its own account ; and this could be done only by concentrating on revolutionary propaganda among the workers, and not by compromising with parliamentarians or reformist Trade Union leaders. This amounted to saying that there could be no Revolution in the West until this task of proletarian education had been carried out — in other words, that the immediate Western Revolution Lenin was asking for could not in fact happen — a view which the Comintern was naturally not prepared to accept, or even to tolerate. As a sequel to this dispute, which raised the fundamental issue between Syndicalism and Communism, Gorter and his close associates passed out of the Communist movement and, at the second Comintern Congress, the other groups which had expressed similar doctrines, such as Sylvia Pankhurst's in England and others in France, Italy, and the United States, were made either to recant their heresies or to understand that there was no place for them in the Moscow International. This did not prevent a residue of the Dutch Communists, under Wijnkoop's leadership, from remaining within the Communist fold ; but they were unable to gain any really substantial support. Wijnkoop himself was to be excluded in 1927, as a result of his opposition to the sectarianism of Comintern policy at that time.

Meanwhile the Dutch Socialist Party, having shed its left wing, followed its reformist course. It emerged from the war years substantially stronger than it had been in 1914, with a parliamentary vote of 568,000 in 1922 as compared with 144,000 in 1912 before the Reform Act of 1917 had introduced manhood suffrage. In 1912 it had 19 seats out of 100 in the Lower House, in 1918 it had 22, and by 1929 it had risen to 24 — just under a quarter of the whole. It maintained its pre-war policy of refusal to enter a Coalition Government, but gave its support to the bourgeois Parties when they were prepared to introduce measures of social reform. In 1920 it adopted a programme of socialisation by stages, beginning with monopolised or highly concentrated industries and providing for full compensation to the owners ; but it had no chance of putting this part of its policy into effect. Internationally, it took part in the Berne Conference of February 1919 and supported the Second International. Industrially, it was hampered by the division of Trade Unionism among a number of rival movements — Socialist, Syndicalist, Catholic, and neutral — all competing for members, though they co-operated occasionally in the industrial field. The veteran Anarchist leader, Domela Nieuwenhuis, died in 1919 ; but his influence survived in a small but active Anarchist movement which served as a rallying point for international Anarchist effort. ·

The outstanding figure in the Dutch working-class movement in the 1920s was Edo Fimmen (1881–1942), the Secretary of the International Transport Workers' Federation — the strongest and most vigorous of the so-called 'Trade Secretariats' loosely attached to the Amsterdam I.F.T.U. From 1915 to 1919 Fimmen was secretary of the Dutch Federation of Trade Unions : in the latter year he helped to set up the International Transport Workers' Federation and became its honorary secretary. On its behalf he took a large part in 1920 in organising the international Trade Union boycott of Hungary, then the victim of the 'White Terror', and also the boycott put on the transport of arms to Poland during the Soviet-Polish war. In 1922 he played a leading part in the International Peace Conference at The Hague, summoned by the I.F.T.U. ; and for part of the following year he was acting secretary of the I.F.T.U. He then fell out with that body, but continued in office as full-time secretary of the I.T.F. The trouble arose mainly because Fimmen, acting without prior consultation with the I.F.T.U., had headed an international transport workers' delegation which met the Russian Transport Workers and Losovsky in Berlin and set up a joint committee. This led to strong protests both from the I.F.T.U. leaders and from some of the I.T.F. leaders as well. Fimmen, offering to resign his official positions, defended himself by claiming that it was much better to collaborate with Russian Communists than with Western capitalists ; but he failed to carry the day, and the joint committee came to nothing. He was able, none the less, to remain at the head of the I.T.F., but was before long in trouble again on account of his association with a left-wing international Trade Union periodical, published in Belgium, which violently attacked the Amsterdam Trade Union leadership. He was forced to give up his connection with this paper, but retained his strong left-wing sympathies. When a left-wing split occurred in the Dutch Labour Party in 1932 and a separate left-wing Party was set up, Fimmen agreed to become its President, but was forced by pressure from his I.T.F. colleagues to give up this office in order to keep his hold on the transport workers' movement. In the repeated disputes between the I.F.T.U. and the 'Trade Secretariats', which the I.F.T.U. wished to make wholly subject to its control, he stood consistently for the independence of the Secretariats and was largely successful in carrying his point. He succeeded in building up the I.T.F. as by far the most lively of the 'Trade Internationals' and won for himself a devoted personal following in many countries. In the 1920s he laid the greatest stress on the need for working-class unity as a means of preserving peace ; but after the rise of Nazism his foremost idea was that of building up working-class resistance to it in every country in which this remained possible. He actively supported the Austrians in their long-drawn-out struggle against Seipel and the Heimwehr, and later threw himself into the cause of the Spanish Republicans during the Civil War. In 1938 serious illness overtook him, and thereafter he worked on under growing difficulties. In 1939, when war threatened, he transferred the I.T.F. headquarters to London ; but two years later he accepted an invitation from the Mexican Confederation of Workers to become their guest until he was well again. Finally, at the end of 1942, he died in Mexico of a cerebral seizure.

Fimmen was not only an outstanding Trade Union leader, but also a Socialist thinker of distinction. His book, *Labour's Alternative : the United States of Europe or Europe Limited* (1924), was a forcible attack on international capitalism and a plea for united working-class action against it. In many speeches and pamphlets he vigorously stated the case for working-class unity as the only way to build up a secure and peaceful world system and to check the growing power of large-scale capitalism as an international force. Even those with whom he quarrelled respected his sincerity and devotion and approved his untiring effort to establish the I.T.F. as a solid international force. But Fimmen was no more able than other leaders who took up a Centrist position between the right wing and the Communists to bring about the unity he desired and worked for. He remained, in the international Trade Union movement, rather a lonely figure, plunging from one trouble to another in his efforts to stand out against the paralysis that seemed to him to be afflicting the Trade Unions of the West.

DENMARK

In Denmark, even more than in Holland, Socialism, both before and after the war, was essentially a reformist movement. At the outbreak of war the Social Democrats had 32 seats in the Lower Chamber out of a total of 149 ; but together with the Radicals, with whom they had been co-operating closely in an endeavour to break the power of the reactionary Upper Chamber, they had a substantial majority in the Lower House and had just succeeded, for the first time, in getting a majority in the Upper Chamber as well. Partly in deference to the views of the Second International, they had stopped short of entering bourgeois Governments ; but that had not prevented them from giving such Governments full support against the right. The electoral victory of 1913 provided the opportunity for amending the Constitution ; and in 1915 a new electoral law provided for universal suffrage for men and women alike and for a system of proportional representation. This law did not come into force until 1918. In the meantime, under stress of war conditions, the Socialists had modified their previous policy by allowing their leader Thorvald Stauning (1873-1942) to enter a Radical Cabinet, in which he remained as a Minister until 1920. In Denmark neither the Russian nor the German Revolution led to any substantial manifestation of left-wing sentiment, though a small, uninfluential Communist Party duly made its appearance. At the elections of 1920, the Socialists raised their representation in the Lower House to 48. Four years later, they won 55 seats and, though lacking a majority, formed a Social Democratic Government with Stauning as Prime Minister. This Government remained in office for two years. It was then evicted by a coalition of its opponents ; but three years later, in 1929, the Socialists, having raised their representation to 61, again formed a Government, this time with three Radicals among the Ministers. They were able, with the aid of the Radicals, to enact a substantial amount of industrial, agricultural, and social legislation and to stay continuously in power until the Germans occupied Denmark in 1940. They made, however, no attempt to introduce Socialism, or even to advance in a clearly Socialist direction, unless it be regarded as socialistic to defend the 'small man' against the exactions of landowners and monopolists, to uphold the right to strike and to keep on good terms with the Trade Unions, and to make substantial advances in social legislation towards the Welfare State. For more than this there doubtless seemed, in a mainly agricultural country with a high standard of living and a very well-organised rural Co-operative movement, no prospect of a popular mandate. The most marked characteristic of Danish Socialist policy was pacifism, extending as far as opposition to the maintenance of any armed forces beyond a small body of frontier guards. The attempt to put this policy into effect falls, however, well beyond the period with which I am dealing in this chapter. During the years immediately after 1918 the Danes went their own untroubled way in a troubled world, though they did not escape the world depression that set in towards the end of 1920. Internationally, they took part in the Berne Conference of 1919 and rallied without hesitation to the Second International.

SWEDEN

Sweden, internally, went through much more troublous times. As we saw, up to 1914 Swedish Socialism had made no great mark in the world, though Hjalmar Branting (1860-1925), its leader, had already emerged as a considerable figure at International Socialist Congresses. In 1914 the Swedish Labour movement had been still only in process of recovering from the serious setback caused by the general strike of 1909, which had involved a big loss of members to Party and Trade Unions alike.[1] Politically, however, this loss had been more than offset by the electoral reform law of 1909, which had introduced manhood (but not women's) suffrage, and had enabled the Social Democrats to become for the first time a powerful parliamentary party, with 87 seats out of 230 in the Lower Chamber. They had been, and remained, a moderate, constitutional Party ; and in November 1914, after the outbreak of war, they declared their willingness, when it was over, to enter a Coalition Cabinet for purposes of reconstruction. A left wing within the Party strongly opposed this decision ; and tension continued until in 1917, well before the Bolshevik Revolution, the critics broke away and formed an Independent Socialist Party. Branting, meanwhile, had been playing an active part in the attempt to convene the Stockholm Conference of 1917. Though strongly in favour, like the rest of the Party — and, indeed, practically the entire nation — of Swedish neutrality in the war, Branting was generally regarded as a strong supporter of the Allies, whereas the Parties of the right were on the whole pro-German. Branting's pro-Ally sympathies were a factor in alienating the left wing, which took a Zimmerwaldian and, subsequently, a Kienthalian line and rejected all forms of co-operation with the bourgeois Liberals, either during or after the war. The question of coalition actually came up while the war was still in progress. The Conservative Government fell in the spring of 1917 and, after a few months of uncertainty, the General Election of the autumn brought the Liberals, under Nils Edén, to office, after the King's attempt to form an all-party coalition had failed. Edén offered four Social Democrats, including Branting and Baron Erik Palmstierna (b. 1877), seats in his Cabinet ; and the offer was accepted, though Branting resigned soon afterwards for reasons of health. Thus, during the critical years from 1917 to 1920, Sweden had a Government which included a minority

[1] See Vol. III, Part II, p. 690.

of Socialists ; and this Government completed the process of electoral reform by enfranchising women and establishing universal suffrage for both Chambers.

By the time of the 1917 election the Socialist Party had already split. In the election the Social Democratic Party increased its representation to 86, and the Independent Socialists secured another 12. Headed by Carl Lindhagen (1876–1950), the Mayor of Stockholm, and by Zeth Höglund (1884–1956), the former leader of the Socialist Youth, about one-fifth of the members of the S.D.P. seceded to form the new Party, which at once established close links with the Russian Bolsheviks and especially with Bucharin, who had been living in Stockholm. Following the Russian lead, the Independent Socialists presently took the name 'Communist Party' and were among the first adherents to the Comintern. Höglund remained at the head of the Swedish Communist Party until 1924 and seems at first to have had no fault to find with the policies of the Comintern. But before long he became convinced that the possibility of early revolution in Western Europe had gone by, and grew more and more restive under the centralised directions of the Comintern. The trouble came to a head at the Fifth Congress of the Comintern in 1924, when Höglund flatly refused to obey orders, saying that the new policy there laid down for the struggle against 'opportunism' within the Communist movement would, if it were accepted, speedily reduce every Western Communist Party to an impotent rump. Höglund's rebellion, which followed on that of the Norwegians under Martin Tranmael in 1923,[1] was met by excluding him from the Party ; but he took with him about a third of its membership. The remainder carried on under new leaders, with Karl Kilbom (b. 1885) as the principal figure ; and, rather surprisingly, the Party actually increased its strength till the new leaders in turn fell foul of the Comintern and seceded from it in 1930, leaving only a minority group under Hugo Sillen (b. 1892) faithful to the Moscow body. This time, the majority of the members, having followed their leaders out of the official Communist Party, set up a new Independent Communist Party of their own. This situation lasted right on to 1937, when most of the dissident Communists at length rejoined the Socialist Party.

[1] See p. 527.

The split of 1917, though it checked the growth of the main Social Democratic Party, did not prevent it from increasing its strength quite rapidly during the next few years. Branting presided over the Berne International Conference of February 1919 and played a leading part in the reconstruction of the right-wing International. Then, in March 1920, the Liberal and Socialist members of the Ministry fell out over the question of tax reform. The Edén Government resigned ; and Branting, though he was a long way short of a clear majority, formed his first entirely Socialist Cabinet, which held office for only a few months. The Conservatives then came back to power, and were in office when the post-war slump set in. The effect of this was an electoral swing to the left ; and after the General Election, held in the autumn of 1921, Branting was able to form his second all-Socialist minority Cabinet, again dependent on Liberal support. The main question that had to be faced was that of unemployment relief, for which very large sums were paid out, mainly in wages for relief works set on foot by the Government. In April 1923 the Branting Ministry fell foul of the Riksdag majority over the terms on which relief was to be allowed, and the Conservatives returned to office. The following year they in turn suffered defeat in the Riksdag over their defence policy, and in October Branting formed yet another Socialist Cabinet. His health, however, was failing, and he died in February 1925, Richard Sandler (b. 1884), also a Social Democrat, taking his place as Prime Minister.

Hjalmar Branting had been the outstanding figure in the Swedish Socialist movement almost from the beginning.[1] Throughout his career he had been a moderate — a convinced believer in gradualism and in orderly development by parliamentary methods. He was among those who, in connection with the rebuilding of the International after the war, insisted most strongly on the inseparability of Socialism and parliamentary democracy and emphatically denounced all forms of dictatorship. During the war, as we saw, he had been a strong supporter of the Allies against Germany, though he had not wished Sweden to become an actual belligerent. The son of a well-to-do Professor, Branting had entered the Socialist movement as a successful Radical journalist with an active interest

[1] See Vol. III, Part II, p. 681.

in social reform ; and in this capacity he played an important part in winning the support of the Trade Unions for the Social Democratic Party. Elected to the Riksdag in 1897 as its first parliamentary representative, he was securely installed as leader well before the Party gained any substantial importance as a political force. Though a Social Democrat, he was no Marxist : he remained throughout his life primarily a reforming Radical, with little or no interest in Socialist theory or in any aspect of Socialism going beyond the Welfare State. Within these limits he was a forcible advocate of social and industrial legislation, well able to hold his own in any company ; but he neither contributed nor attempted to contribute anything original to Socialist thought or doctrine. He was indeed the quintessential exponent of that 'middle way', for finding which Swedish Socialism won so much praise in reformist circles between the wars.

The Sandler Government fell from power in June 1926, after a year and a half in office. The cause of its defeat was a combination of the other Parties against it on the question of the terms governing receipt of unemployment benefit. The Liberals in their turn then formed a minority Government, which proclaimed a policy of industrial peace and, in 1928, passed into law an Act providing for compulsory arbitration in industrial disputes. There was, however, no drastic change in policy, especially in international affairs ; and B. O. Unden (b. 1886), who had been Foreign Minister under Branting, continued to represent Sweden at the League of Nations. At the elections of 1928 the Social Democrats lost heavily, falling from the 105 seats of 1924 in the Second Chamber (out of 230) to 90, whereas the Communists, fighting on this occasion under the name 'Labour Party', rose from 4 to 8. The Conservatives took office with yet another minority Government, but fell from power in mid-1930, when yet another minority, the People's Party, accepted office. In the autumn of 1930 the Socialists won substantial gains in the local elections ; and two years later at the General Election of 1932 they regained their strength, with 104 members in the Second Chamber, the Communists again securing 8 seats. In these circumstances, the Socialists agreed to form a Government, with Per Alvin Hansson (1880-1946) as Prime Minister, thus resuming office at a time when the world economic depression was at its lowest point. Then began the long period of much-applauded moderate Socialist rule which lasted up to the second world war and enabled the Socialist Party, with Ernst Wigforss (b. 1881) at the Ministry of Finance, to give an impressive demonstration of financial capacity in handling the economic crisis without resorting to the traditional deflationary policies. The account of these developments, however, must be left over to a future volume.

NORWAY

Norway provides the one example in Western Europe of a Labour movement which, after the Russian Revolution, went over *en bloc* to the Third International as soon as it was set up, only to secede no less solidly as soon as it had found out the consequences of subjecting itself to the centralised discipline of that body. In Norway, theretofore predominantly an agricultural, or foresting, and seafaring country, industrial development had been proceeding very fast during the years before 1914, to the accompaniment of strong feeling against control of the developing enterprises by foreign capital. Up to 1905 the Labour movement had been inchoate, and the struggle for national independence had taken pride of place ; but thereafter it had grown fast and, while increasing its parliamentary representation from 10 in 1906 to 23 in 1912, had taken to a considerable extent a Syndicalistic direction, with a tendency to regard the general strike as the best weapon for achieving social revolution. But the Norwegian Syndicalists, instead of refusing to associate themselves with the Socialist Party, had set out to capture it and convert it into an auxiliary instrument of revolutionary social changes, in which the Trade Union movement was cast for the principal part.

In the Norwegian Labour movement the outstanding figure was the house-painter Martin Tranmael (b. 1879), who stood head and shoulders above all his colleagues in both personal quality and popular influence. Tranmael had lived for a time in the United States, where he had been associated with the groups that went to the making of the Industrial Workers of the World. Returning to Norway in 1905, he speedily established himself as journalist and orator and also showed remarkable organising capacity. Settling at Bergen, he made himself the leader of a left-wing movement, which in 1912 constituted itself as a distinct group within the Labour Party, and set out to capture the Party for its views. During the war, Tranmael built up a position of almost unquestioned ascendancy as a strike-leader and organiser of popular discontent, not only among the industrial workers but also among the army reservists who had been called to the colours and deeply resented being taken away from their normal way of life. He succeeded in establishing Soldiers' Councils, which co-operated with the Councils set up by the workers ; and after the Bolshevik Revolution Norway appeared to be moving fast towards a social revolution of its own under stress of war-time economic hardships, which had engendered a widespread mood of working-class revolt. By 1918 Tranmael's group was able to win control of the Labour Party, of which he then became Secretary. The war, however, ended before this threatening crisis had come to a head ; and the consequent relaxation of Norway's internal tension averted a revolutionary outbreak, but did not prevent Tranmael and his followers from consolidating their hold on the main body of Norwegian Labour.

When the Bolsheviks summoned the left-wing Socialist Parties and other revolutionary groups to the constituent Congress of the Communist International at Moscow early in 1919, the Norwegian Labour Party, which had taken an active part in the Zimmerwald Conference of 1915, responded to the invitation and thus became one of the original constituents of the new International. Tranmael and his associates, however, were at no time Bolsheviks : they were revolutionary Socialists with a mainly Syndicalist attitude, though they did not, like most Syndicalists, reject parliamentary political action, provided that it was subjected to revolutionary industrial control. It must be borne in mind that Moscow, at this stage, was appealing for support against the 'social patriots' and reformists not only to left-wing elements in the Socialist Parties but also to the adherents of revolutionary industrial movements such as the I.W.W. and the 'revolutionary shop stewards', though these latter were for the most part strong opponents of the doctrine of 'democratic centralism' upheld by Lenin and of any sort of party dictatorship. In the conditions of 1918 and 1919 these fundamental antagonisms had not yet come to the front. Up to the Brest-Litovsk Treaty the Left Social Revolutionaries in Russia, who had much in common with Tranmael's ideas, were the partners of the Bolsheviks in the Soviet Government, and Lenin, while firmly insistent on his own conception of revolutionary strategy, wanted to get the support of every left-wing group for the cause of World Revolution. The Norwegian Socialists were therefore able to go to Moscow without being in any way committed to Leninism: they went as whole-hearted sympathisers with the cause of proletarian Revolution, but interpreted it in their own way, and did not regard it as involving, at any rate in Norway, either civil war in arms or acceptance of centralised control of their strategy by any authoritarian international body. Nor did they in practice, as members of the Communist International, accept that body's orders or agree to expel their own right wing so as to convert their broadly based Labour Party into a firmly disciplined Communist Party under Moscow's direction. They were, nevertheless, tolerated by the Comintern, which was reluctant to drive out the one Socialist movement in the West that had come over solidly to its side against the Reformists.

Naturally, there was in Norway itself a substantial minority opposed to Tranmael's policy and standing for the old Social Democratic orthodoxy ; and this minority had its adherents in the Trade Unions as well as in the Labour Party. At the outset, however, Tranmael's opponents did not break away from the left-wing majority. There was deep reluctance on the right as well as on the left to split the movement either industrially or politically ; and for a while the defeated minority remained within the Labour Party and the Trade Unions and bided its time. Before long, however, the more convinced Social Democratic politicians found the strain of acquiescence in Tranmael's left-wing policy too great to be borne, and in 1920 a substantial parliamentary group broke away and established a separate Social Democratic Labour Party, led by Magnus Nilssen (1871–1947). At the ensuing General Election the Labour Party won 29 seats and the Social Democrats 8. Some, however, of the old leaders, especially in the Trade Unions, refused to follow the seceders and remained inside the

Labour Party, in the well-founded hope that its adherence to the Comintern would not endure. Among those who took this line was the veteran of the Second International, Christian Holtermann Knudsen (1845–1929), who retired from active participation but refused to follow the Social Democratic secession.

Tranmael's Party, however, soon became involved in a serious quarrel with the Moscow controllers of the Comintern. At the beginning the main point at issue arose out of the action of the Norwegian Labour Party in expelling certain Communists who were accused of violating party discipline — *i.e.* the discipline of the Norwegian Party and not of the Comintern. The latter body thereupon declared that no expulsions could be made without its consent, and ordered the Norwegians to reinstate the excluded members. This the Norwegian Labour Party, by a Congress vote of 169 to 103, refused to do, thus rejecting the central authority of the Comintern. The delegates who had been sent from Moscow to attend the Norwegian Congress thereupon declared that the Comintern would no longer recognise the Norwegian Labour Party as a constituent body, but would transfer its recognition to the minority, who seceded from the Labour Party and set up a separate Communist Party.

By this time Tranmael had been thoroughly disillusioned by the course of events in Russia — above all, by the suppression of the Kronstadt Rising of March 1921 — and had ceased to believe that the Russian Bolsheviks and their supporters had any longer a valid claim to stand for the cause of proletarian Socialism in any sense which he as a convinced upholder of proletarian democracy could accept. It took, however, two years from the time of the Rising for the quarrel with Moscow to result in a final break. Only at the beginning of 1923 had Tranmael succeeded in ousting the supporters of the Comintern from their positions of authority and influence within the Labour Party, and in inducing the party executive to offer uncompromising opposition to Moscow's claim that it had an overriding right to interfere in the Party's affairs. Tranmael strongly affirmed the view that the Norwegian Party must be full master in its own house, and thus rejected the entire centralising doctrine of the Comintern. Finally in

November 1923, the Party, by a large majority, decided to leave the Comintern. The pro-Communist minority thereupon set up a Communist Party, which in 1924 was strong enough to win 6 seats at the Norwegian General Election. But thereafter its influence waned rapidly, and at the following election it could hold only a single seat. Meanwhile, in 1927, the Social Democrats who had left the Labour Party in 1920 and had thereafter joined the Labour and Socialist International returned to the Labour Party fold, leaving the Norwegians unrepresented in either of the rival Internationals. Not until 1938 did the reunited Labour Party join the Labour and Socialist International, having by that time shed most of its Syndicalistic tendencies as well as its revolutionary outlook.

Long before that, in 1928, the Party, having won 59 seats out of 159 at the General Election of the preceding year, had formed its first, minority Government, under Christian Hornsrud (1859–?), and had at once introduced a challenging Bill for the redistribution of wealth. The other Parties had thereupon united to throw the Government out ; but it came back to office three years later, in 1932, with the former railway worker, Johan Nygaardsvold (1879–1952), as Prime Minister. This new Government, formed in alliance, though not in coalition, with the Agrarian Party, contented itself with useful social reform legislation and was able to consolidate its position and increase its hold on the electorate. The story of its achievements belongs, however, to a later section of this narrative.

The case of Norway illustrates very clearly the difficulties of that part of the Socialist left wing which sympathised deeply with the Russian Revolution and was utterly dissatisfied with the reformist parliamentarism of the right wing, but was not prepared to travel the Moscow road or to accept the overriding authority of the Comintern. The Norwegian Socialists under Tranmael's leadership were revolutionaries in the sense that they stood for the overthrow of capitalism not by gradualist parliamentary methods but by a mass uprising of the workers ; but they never conceived of their Revolution in terms of an armed rebellion against the bourgeois State. They remained throughout strong anti-militarists, opposed to the use of armed force, and they offered vigorous opposition to all forms of military expenditure and advocated universal arbitration as the means of resolving all international disputes. This attitude affected their conception of revolution. They relied for revolutionary success, not on civil war, but on the weapon of the mass strike, for which they needed to keep the working-class movement united : so that they were entirely unwilling to adopt the Moscow strategy of intense struggle against the Centre, or even of exclusion of the reformist right wing from the ranks of the Labour Party. Their position, however, differed from that of the Socialist left in other countries because they were already in firm control of the Party and the Trade Unions when the Comintern was set up, so that they became original members and could not be confronted with the Twenty-one Points as a condition of admittance to it. This enabled them to stand out against the Comintern's attempts to brow-beat them into obedience to its policy of war against the Centre, and allowed them to withdraw their forces intact when their differences with Moscow could no longer be glossed over. They were not, however, an important enough group in the world Socialist movement to be in a position to carry on a revolutionary policy in isolation, after their break with Moscow ; and accordingly they relapsed in due course into a reformist policy not different in essentials from that of the other Scandinavian countries.

Tranmael, who led the Norwegian movement during the critical years of war and revolution, is still living as I write and, though he has passed out of active politics, is still looked up to as the 'grand old man' of Norwegian Socialism. In addition to being a remarkable organiser and leader of popular quasi-revolutionary movements, he was an ardent social reformer in many fields, including that of temperance ; and his Socialism was always strongly ethical. This helped him to win support among men and women who stood far to the right of him in economic and political affairs, and allowed his influence to persist after the rupture with the out-and-out Communists. These qualities, however, also prevented him from exerting any effective influence in the Comintern, while his association with that body cut him off from contact, during the post-war years, with the non-Communist left-wing Socialists in other Western countries. By the time the Norwegian Labour Party came out of the Third International, the attempt to build a Socialist middle way by means of the Vienna 'Two-and-a-Half' International had already been abandoned, so as to leave the Norwegians isolated from the international movement, even after they had lost all sympathy with the Comintern.

FINLAND

Up to the Bolshevik Revolution Finland formed part of the Russian empire, but had its own Diet, which was in constant dispute with the Russian authorities over the question of Finnish autonomy. There was a Russian Governor, and Russian troops were stationed in the country side by side with the Finnish regiments which formed part of the Russian army but could not, the Finns claimed, be called upon to serve outside their own country. Up to 1906 the Finnish Diet had been elected on a class system which gave the workers and small farmers little chance of securing representation ; but in the course of the Russian Revolution of 1905–6 even this Diet had been induced to reform itself by introducing universal suffrage, including women, and single-chamber government ; and the Czar, under heavy pressure from the Revolution, had been compelled to accept the change. At the first election under the new system the Socialists, leaping into sudden prominence, won 80 out of the 200 seats ; and the new Diet included 19 women — the first to be elected to any Parliament — of whom 9 were Socialists. The reformed Diet proceeded at once to enact a large body of highly progressive social legislation ; but hardly any of it was allowed to come into force. The Czarist autocracy, having got the better of the Revolution in Russia, disallowed it, and was supported by the reactionary Duma chosen after the Revolution had been beaten back. The Russian Government in 1909 and again in 1910 dissolved the Finnish Diet and ruled Finland under laws and *ukases* of its own. The Socialist and Trade Union organisations established during the Revolution were suppressed, and many of their leaders sent to prison or exiled. From 1910 onwards Finnish autonomy was finally abrogated and the resistance driven underground.

The war, however, restored to the Finns a measure of freedom because of Czarism's increasing difficulties. It also brought with it a rapid development of the war industries and a revival of Labour and Socialist activity. But at the same time it created a new serious cause of trouble when the Czarist Government attempted to enforce conscription into Russian military units and to compel the Finnish conscripts to serve outside Finland. In 1916 elections were held for a new Diet and the Socialists won a clear majority — 103 out of the 200 seats. Then came the first Russian Revolution of 1917. Up to this point the Finnish Diet had not demanded complete independence of Russia — only full self-government in internal affairs. But on the outbreak of the Revolution the Social Democrats declared for complete independence, and the Socialist Prime Minister, Oskar Tokoi (b. 1873), pressed the new Russian Provisional Government to recognise Finland's national claims. Kerensky, instead of granting independence, dissolved the Finnish Diet and attempted to maintain Russian rule. At the ensuing election, in October 1917, the Socialists lost their clear majority, falling from 103 seats to 96, and the other Parties formed a Government without them. At this point the Bolsheviks, came to power in Russia. In December 1917 the Diet proclaimed Finland's independence, and Lenin immediately accepted the right of the country to secede. In January 1918 the Soviet Government formally recognised Finland as an independent State ; and this recognition was duly embodied in the Brest-Litovsk Treaty. By this time, however, Finland was itself moving rapidly towards civil war ; for, although there had been a general demand for autonomy, there were acute differences of opinion about the character of the policy to be followed after the liberation. In general, the working classes were in strong sympathy with the Russian Revolution ; but the upper classes and most of the considerable Swedish minority were pro-German as well as hostile to working-class and popular agrarian claims. Well before the end of 1917 the urban workers had begun to form Red Guards to carry on the Revolution, while the anti-Socialists, under the leadership of General Mannerheim, had set to work to establish a counter-revolutionary force of Defence Guards, commonly known as 'White Guards', mainly in the country districts. These rival forces soon came to blows. In January 1918 the White Guards launched an attack and the Helsinki workers set up a revolutionary Government in opposition to the Diet Government, and took possession of the city. In the ensuing struggle the Reds were defeated ; but the Whites, conscious of their inability to rule the country by their own strength, called in the Germans, who sent an army to occupy Helsinki. The revolutionary Government fled from the capital ; and the Whites embarked on a reign of terror in which 15,000 of their opponents are said to have perished. This massacre was said to be a reprisal for acts of terror committed by the Reds during their brief tenure of power. Such acts had certainly been committed, but only on a relatively small scale. It was the Whites, not the Reds, who embarked on mass terror, including not only those killed but also much greater numbers shut up in concentration camps under very bad conditions. At the same time the Socialists — that is, almost half the total member-ship — were excluded from the Diet, which had made a treaty with Germany in March and now proceeded to draw up a new Constitution making Finland a monarchy and inviting a German prince, Frederick Charles of Hesse, brother-in-law of the German Kaiser, to assume the throne. Frederick Charles accepted ; but before he had made up his mind to go to Finland, the European war ended in the defeat of Germany, and he never actually became king. Instead, in December 1918, Mannerheim assumed supreme power as Regent and formed a Government made up equally of Royalists and Republicans. Meanwhile, in June 1918, a new Diet had been elected on a register from which the working-classes were excluded ; and it was this new Diet which had invited Frederick Charles of Hesse to accept the throne.

In face of the German defeat, the Finnish reactionaries had rapidly to readjust their policy, in order to curry favour with the Allies. The German forces, under van der Goltz, were sent away, and Mannerheim organised his White Guards into a regular force for the maintenance of order. Some measure of constitutional right was restored ; and in March 1919 the workers — except those who were still in concentration camps — were allowed to vote in the election for a new Diet. The Socialists won 80 seats, with the Agrarians, numbering 42, as the next largest Party. The Diet, abandoning monarchism, voted in June 1919 for making Finland a Republic and for single-chamber government resting on universal suffrage ; but an anti-Socialist coalition remained in power. Mannerheim made repeated offers to the Allied Powers to join them in their attempts to intervene in Russia, first by supporting the British forces in Murmansk and then by reinforcing General Yudenich in his march on Petrograd towards the end of 1919 ; but these offers were not accepted. Not till October 1920 did the Finnish Government make a Treaty of Peace with Bolshevik Russia ; and in the following year the rebellion in Karelia against Soviet Russia again endangered relations. The Finnish Government carried the question before the .Council of the League of Nations, after the Permanent Court of International Justice had refused to deal with it on the ground that Russia was not a member of the League. But the Russians remained firm in insisting that Karelia was part of Soviet Russia and succeeded in quelling the rebellion.

Since the disturbances of 1918 the Finnish Communists had been separate from the Social Democrats. The Communist Party had been dissolved by law in 1919 ; but thereafter it returned to life, after the Armistice Act passed by the Vinnola Government in 1921, and was able to win 27 seats at the General Election of 1922, when the Social Democrats were reduced to 53. The following year the Government again dissolved the Communist Party, suppressed its newspapers, and gaoled most of its leaders, including 25 out of its 27 M.P.s. The Communists nevertheless fought in the Election of 1924, and retained 18 seats, while the Social Democrats increased to 60. The following year the coalition anti-Socialist Government fell from power, and Väinö Tanner (b. 1881), the Social Democrat and Co-operative leader, formed an all-Socialist minority Government, which managed to pass a second Amnesty Act, securing the release of those still incarcerated for their part in the civil war. After a further Election in 1927 had left the Socialist and Communist representation practically unchanged, the Socialist Government was defeated in the Diet, and resigned. The Socialists thereafter remained in opposition right up to 1937, and had, from 1929 onwards, to face the rise of the so-called 'Lappo' anti-Communist movement ; but this later story of the antagonisms within Finnish society falls beyond the scope of the present chapter.

What does concern us at this stage is the persistent sharp division within the Finnish working-class and Socialist movement between those who looked towards Soviet Russia and those who, hostile to Bolshevism, looked rather to the West for guidance. The outstanding Communist figure was Otto Kuusinen (b. 1881), who, after leading the Socialist Party during the war years, became the leader of the Communists in 1918 and, after the defeat of the Finnish revolutionary Government, settled down in Russia and became an important figure in the Comintern, to reappear in 1939 at the head of the Russian-sponsored Finnish People's Government during the Russo-Finnish War. On the Social Democratic side the leading personality was Väinö Alfred Tanner (b. 1881), who was also at the head of the Finnish Progressive Co-operative movement. Tanner first became a member of the Diet in 1907 and was for a time Minister of Finance in 1917 and Prime Minister in 1927. He became an outstanding figure in the International Co-operative Alliance. Always on the right wing of Finnish Socialism, and strongly hostile to Communism, he exerted between the wars a commanding influence in the Socialist Party and in the Co-operative Movement.

CHAPTER XVI

SPAIN AND PORTUGAL

SPAIN was in a state of intense internal ferment when the European War broke out in August 1914. Such a condition was, of course, nothing new ; but the tension had been aggravated both by the reign of violence in Catalonia that had come to a head in the 'bloody year' 1909 and by the struggles connected with the repeated callings up of reservists for service in the Moroccan War.[1] Both the rival Trade Union movements — the Anarcho-Syndicalist Confederation of Labour (C.N.T.) and the Socialist General Union of Labour (U.G.T.) — had been growing fast ; and in July 1914 the C.N.T., previously in the main an underground organisation, had for the first time come into the open by holding a public National Congress.

When war broke out it became immediately apparent that Spanish sympathies were sharply divided. The left, in general, was favourable to the Allies, whereas the Conservatives and the upper classes were almost solidly pro-German. There were few, however, who wished Spain to take part in the war on either side. Under the Cartagena Agreement of 1907 it had been laid down that, should circumstances arise to threaten the territorial *status quo* in the Mediterranean or in North-west Africa, there should be consultations between Spain, France, and Great Britain with a view to the taking of agreed measures. But no such consultations occurred, or were even asked for, when the time came. Spain stayed neutral and soon began to profit considerably by war orders, especially from France but also from Great Britain and other countries. Later, as submarine warfare developed, the Spaniards suffered considerable shipping losses ; but Spanish neutrality was never seriously questioned. What did occur was a very sharp rise in internal prices, resulting in great hardships for the poorer classes and

[1] See Vol. III, Part II, p. 761.

in a rapid spread of strikes, especially in 1916 and 1917. In the spring of 1916 both the C.N.T. and the U.G.T. launched national campaigns to demand a reduction in the cost of living : there were disorderly strikes in May over this question in Madrid and elsewhere, and in July the railwaymen declared a national strike, in which they were joined by the miners of the Asturias. The Government met this movement by declaring a state of siege, suspending constitutional guarantees, and calling the railway strikers to the colours. In November the C.N.T. and the U.G.T., under pressure of the popular feeling, temporarily sank their differences and entered into a 'revolutionary pact', under which they agreed to join in calling a general strike to protest against the high cost of living. A 24-hours' general strike took place the following month.

The Government tried to meet the growing unrest by intensified measures of police repression ; but the unrest continued to develop, and in March 1917 there was a renewed and widespread burst of strikes and disturbances. The C.N.T. and U.G.T. again met jointly to protest against the Government's arbitrary measures, but obtained no satisfaction. In July 1917 there was a further outbreak of strikes on a larger scale than ever ; and in August the U.G.T., supported by the C.N.T., proclaimed a revolutionary general strike throughout the country. The Government retorted in October by arresting most of the strike leaders and by launching numerous prosecutions against persons held responsible for promoting the unrest.

During this period the Socialists and Syndicalists were by no means the only disturbers of the Government's authority. From about the middle of 1916 increasing unrest among the officers of the army led to the formation of the so-called 'Committees of Defence', which displayed an increasing propensity to interfere in political affairs, demanding a structural reform of the system of government. As one feeble Cabinet succeeded another without any firm majority in the Cortes behind it, as the traditional Parties broke up more and more into warring factions, and as the King manifested an increasing tendency to throw out any Cabinet that showed signs of asserting its independence, the entire system of government fell into deeper disrepute. Elections offered no remedy ; for, as we saw,[1] the

[1] See Vol. III, Part II, p. 754.

whole electoral system was utterly corrupt and, though the Government's power to rig the elections at will had broken down, the only effect of this had been to produce a political stalemate. In Catalonia, the most highly organised centre of discontent, the long-standing pressure for autonomy was threatening to turn into a demand for complete separation and independence, and there was a continual struggle for power between the military and the civil authorities as well as between the middle classes and the workers, most of whom accepted the Syndicalist leadership of the C.N.T. In face of this complex pattern of contending groups and factions, a complete breakdown of government seemed to be imminent. Near the end of 1916 the Liberal Cabinet of Count Romanones attempted to dissolve the officers' juntas and even ordered the arrest of their leaders ; but the King intervened and the arrested officers were released and were allowed to resume their agitation. Romanones resigned in April 1917 ; and his Conservative successor, Dato, virtually capitulated to the juntas. This action provoked a series of manifestoes of protest from Socialists, left-wing Radicals and Republicans, and Catalonian nationalists ; and in July the Catalonian deputies held at Barcelona a meeting at which they threatened to call an unofficial assembly of all members of the Cortes unless the Government agreed to summon it at once. The Government replied by stating that any such meeting would be treated as an act of rebellion ; but the assembly none the less met in July, with 68 Socialist and left-wing deputies and senators attending, demanded a revision of the Constitution, and set up three commissions to prepare reports to be laid before a further Assembly.

This was the point at which the C.N.T. and the U.G.T. proclaimed the revolutionary general strike of August 1917. There were thus, in effect, three revolutions in progress at the same time — the military revolution of the officers' juntas, the parliamentary revolution of the left-wing political Parties, and the Syndicalist revolution of the combined Trade Unions. These three revolutions, however, were at cross purposes and could by no means join forces to overthrow the existing structure of government. The military were quite prepared to play their part in suppressing the strikers and quite unprepared to put power into the hands of either Catalonian autonomists or left-wing politicians. The left-wing politicians were hostile both to the military juntas and to the Syndicalists and Anarchists who dominated the C.N.T. ; and the Trade Unions, or at any rate the C.N.T. — the strongest body among them — were extremely hostile to the military and despised the left-wing political Parties. In this situation the real power was in the hands of the army, which, having ruthlessly put down the strike, forced the Conservative Government to resign. A stop-gap Coalition Cabinet came in on a promise to hold free elections for a new Cortes.

The General Election of February 1918, however, achieved only a continuance of the political stalemate. A 'Ministry of All the Talents', made up mainly of former Prime Ministers, took office in March and lasted till the beginning of November, when it was brought down by internal dissensions at the very moment when the Germans were capitulating to the Allies. The German collapse naturally had its effect on the Spanish political situation, as it seemed to foreshadow a peace based on Wilsonian principles and a strengthening of the forces of democracy in Europe. After a brief interval, Count Romanones came back to office as Prime Minister and hastened to Paris, where he met President Wilson, and returned to find himself faced with a new political crisis arising out of a bitter industrial conflict in·Barcelona. Already in January 1918 there had been a wave of strikes covering the greater part of Spain ; and in February a strike of the workers in the power services at Barcelona (the 'La Canadienne' strike) first spread to a number of other trades and then, in March, developed into a general strike throughout Catalonia. The civil authorities at Barcelona came to terms with the strikers, granting most of their demands ; but the military then stepped in, expelled the civil authorities, and took control of the city. These events led to the fall of the Romanones Cabinet, and during the ensuing months one Government after another took office only to be forced to resign under military pressure. A General Election held in the spring of 1919 under conditions of strict censorship failed, despite the utmost resort to measures of corruption, to produce a workable parliamentary majority. Widespread strikes continued, and employers, who had formed a strong combination of their own to resist the Trade Unions, declared a series of lock-outs which led to extensive disturbances and further military intervention. In the midst of these troubles the eight-hours' day was proclaimed by royal decree in April 1919 and came into force in October ; and at the same time the coal-miners won the seven-hours' day. Also in October, a royal decree set up in Catalonia a Mixed Commission for the settlement of labour disputes. But these measures did nothing to quell the troubles : strikes and lock-outs followed one another in rapid succession both in Catalonia and elsewhere, and were accompanied increasingly by acts of violence, including not a few assassinations.

In December 1919 the C.N.T., by now representing over 700,000 members, held a National Conference at Madrid, and decided to reorganise itself on a new basis. Instead of distinct Unions, each representing a particular trade or industry, there was to be in future in each locality a single Union, or Sindicato Único, including all trades and subdivided into trade or industrial sections ; and the C.N.T. itself was to become a federation of these inclusive local Unions, which had already been established in some areas. The same C.N.T. Conference adopted a declaration of principles embodying Anarchist Communism, and voted provisionally in favour of adherence to the newly founded Communist International — which, it must be remembered, had appealed at its foundation Congress earlier in the year to revolutionary industrialists as well as to supporters of revolutionary Communism of the Soviet type. The C.N.T., in connection with these decisions, called for the establishment in Spain of 'One Big Union' including all workers, and appealed to the U.G.T. Unions to join forces in such a body.

Even while the Madrid Conference was in session, a further general strike was being called in Barcelona as a protest against the employers' attempts to discriminate against Trade Union activists at the conclusion of the lock-out. In response to this outbreak, on 6th January 1920 the military Governor declared all Trade Unions in the city to be dissolved, and arrested more than a hundred active Unionists. Almost at the same moment, a revolt under Anarchist leadership broke out in the military barracks at Saragossa and was ruthlessly put down, seven of the leaders being shot. During the next few months there were more strikes than ever, both general and in particular trades ; and in Barcelona and some other towns the employers began to organise counter-Unions of their own in the hope of dividing the workers' forces. In June the Socialist Party, hitherto moderate and reformist, held an Extraordinary Congress at Madrid and decided by 8000 votes to 5000, with 2000 abstentions, in favour of joining the Third International, provided that satisfactory conditions of admission could be got. Two delegates were appointed to go to Moscow for the purpose of negotiating about the terms. But, only a few days later, the Congress of the U.G.T., which usually followed the Socialist Party's line, rejected the Comintern and decided by an overwhelming majority to join the Amsterdam International Federation of Trade Unions. This did not prevent the C.N.T. from signing in September 1920 a new pact of alliance with the U.G.T. ; but this alliance did not last long. There were further violent struggles in Barcelona between the Syndicalists and the so-called 'Free' Unions formed by the employers ; and the former set up a new organisation of Syndicalist Youth for the purpose of meeting the violence of the 'Free' Union detachments. Martinez Anido, the newly appointed Civil Governor of Barcelona, responded by arresting a large number of the Syndicalist leaders, many of whom were deported to Mahón, in the Balearic Islands, and by suppressing the activities of the C.N.T. That body thereupon declared a general strike, which at the end of November spread to Madrid, Bilbao, Saragossa, and other centres, and thereafter all over Spain The U.G.T. at first collaborated with the C.N.T., but on 4th December called off the strike in Madrid and Bilbao and thus caused its collapse in those areas. The C.N.T. then denounced the pact with the U.G.T., which it accused of betrayal ; and the general strike gradually petered out.

This defeat brought the period of intensive strike action to a halt. In face of severely repressive measures against the C.N.T., the year 1921 was relatively free from large-scale strikes, though numerous fracas between the Syndicalists and Anarchists and their adversaries continued to occur. Angel Pestaña, the C.N.T. leader, was arrested at Barcelona on his return from Russia in December 1920 ; but the following month the Socialists, Fernando de Los Rios and David Anguiano, were able to report to the National Council of the Socialist Party on their Russian mission of negotiation concerning the conditions for admission to the Comintern, with the result that the Council rejected the 'Twenty-one Points' by a vote of 9 to 3. In April 1921 this decision was confirmed at an Extraordinary Congress of the Party, which decided against joining the Comintern by a vote of 8808 to 6025. The Party thereupon split, the minority seceding to form a Communist Party under the leadership of Anguiano, Antonio García Quejido, and E. Toralba Beci. During the same month the C.N.T., in the absence of the members of its National Committee and of others who were in gaol, held at Lerida a Conference of regional delegates, which, under the influence of Andreas Nin (1892–1937), Joaquín Maurin (1897–1937), and others, decided to send a delegation to Moscow for the forthcoming Congress of the Third International; but in August a further Conference held at Logroño disavowed this action, and finally, in June 1922, after the state of siege had been ended and constitutional guarantees restored, the full Congress of the C.N.T. voted for withdrawal from the Comintern, reaffirmed its opposition to political action, and decided to join the new Anarcho-Syndicalist International that was on the point of being set up in Berlin under the leadership of Rudolf Rocker. Thus, the Syndicalists as well as the majority of the Socialist Party and the U.G.T. repudiated the policies of Moscow, which were thereafter supported only by the small Communist Party and by a few Trade Union groups, especially among the miners, which it was able to detach from their allegiance to the U.G.T.

Meanwhile, in July 1921, the Spanish forces in Morocco had met with military disaster at Anual and had been compelled to withdraw from the entire zone of Melilla. This severe defeat provoked an internal crisis. A new Cabinet under Antonio Maura succeeded in getting together and dispatching to Morocco a relief army of 140,000 men; but the call-up for this army was met by widespread resistance, and a great clamour went up for a full enquiry into the causes of the disaster, which was said to have been the result of gross mismanagement and corruption in high quarters. On the other hand, the officers' juntas threw the blame for the disaster on the Parliament and bitterly resented the Government's action in appointing General Picasso to make an official report on the affair. Faced with their resistance, the Government attempted to disband them and to replace them by official juntas under the control of the Minister of War ; but the unofficial juntas resisted and compelled the Cabinet to resign. A new Conservative Government under Sanchez Guerra then took office in March 1922, and the Picasso Report was submitted to an all-party Commission, which in due course produced three rival reports. Guerra made some attempt at pacification by restoring the constitutional guarantees and recalling the unpopular Anido from the governorship of Barcelona ; but when the rival reports were debated in Parliament the discussions ended in such scenes of violence that the Government collapsed and the Liberals, who had temporarily made up their differences, came back to office and conducted, in April 1923, a General Election in which the Socialists increased their representation from 2 to 6, winning 5 seats in Madrid, mainly as a result of their vigorous campaign against the Moroccan war.

The Liberal Government speedily found itself in difficulties, not only over Morocco but also with the Church. It proposed to amend the Constitution so as to extend toleration to other religions besides Roman Catholicism. This aroused the Church to vehement protests, and the Government hastily withdrew its proposals. Meanwhile, the debates on the Moroccan question had been resumed and had led to serious charges against a number of leading politicians and also against the King, for unwarrantable intervention in military and political affairs. The financial situation, in view of steeply rising war expenditure, which the new Government made some attempt to cut down, was also increasingly grave ; and the officers' juntas were more and more resentful of criticisms levelled against the military authorities. Just as the Parliament was on the point of drawing up its conclusions on the long debate, the Captain-General of Catalonia, Miguel Primo de Rivera, acting in collusion with the Catalonian Conservatives, rose in arms against the Spanish Government and announced the constitution of a military directorate to take over the government of the country. The Liberal Prime Minister, the Marqués of Alcuhemas, wished to resist ; but the King refused to support him and he was forced to resign. The King thereupon accepted the authority of Primo's military directorate and called upon Primo himself to form a new Government. Primo then appointed a new, enlarged military directorate, which declared the country to be in a state of war, put the press under strict censorship, and forbade all political meetings and demonstrations. All provincial governors were dismissed and replaced by soldiers, and all local authorities were severely purged and placed under military control. At the same time, Primo issued a manifesto addressed to the working classes, announcing measures of public regulation of wages and hours of work. The Presidents of the two Chambers of the Spanish Parliament went to the King and demanded the calling of a new Cortes in accordance with the Constitution ; but the King merely referred their request to the military directorate, which rejected it as an attempt to revive a decayed parliamentary system that had become obsolete.

Thus Spain, in September 1923, had its Revolution, but this time from the army and not from the workers, and resulting in the establishment of a complete military dictatorship. The C.N.T. endeavoured to counter the *coup* by declaring a general strike ; but the U.G.T. refused to join in. Up to the spring of 1924 the C.N.T., despite the defeat of the strike, was able to maintain a shadow of open organisation. On 4th May of that year it held an Extraordinary Delegate Assembly at Sabadell, attended by 237 delegates ; but that was its last public act under the Directory. During the same month the Government ordered the arrest of all its leading personalities, to the number of more than 200, and ordered its local organisations, the Unique Syndicates of each area, to be closed. What was left of it went underground, maintaining a precarious existence mainly under Anarchist leadership. A number of its activists escaped to France, where they formed a group called the 'Thirty' and attempted to organise an armed incursion into Spain. They actually marched upon Vera, in Navarre, in November 1924, but were easily defeated — partly by means of *agents provocateurs* who had infiltrated into their group and given away their plans. There were also a number of small local risings inside Spain ; but no concerted resistance was offered to the dictatorship.

The U.G.T., as we saw, refused to co-operate with the C.N.T. in the general strike of September 1923, and was largely exempt from the persecution which fell upon the Syndicalists and Anarchists of the latter body. For the time being the U.G.T. and Socialist leaders thought discretion the better part of valour, and bowed to the storm. Parliament having been set aside, the Socialists had lost their representation in it ; but they knew themselves to be much too weak for an appeal to arms to have any prospect of success. Primo de Rivera was anxious to avoid solid working-class opposition to his régime, and began before long to make overtures to the moderate leaders of the U.G.T. In December 1924 the National Committee of the Socialist Party publicly announced its approval of the acceptance by Francisco Largo Caballero (1870–1946), the leader of the U.G.T., of the office of Councillor of State under the military directory ; and thereafter the U.G.T followed a policy of making the best of such freedom as the dictatorship allowed it. In May 1925 the state of siege was ended and some measure of Trade Union, though not of political, liberty was restored for such Unions as were prepared to co-operate with the dictatorship and to abstain from any sort of revolutionary activity. This toleration did not, of course, extend to the C.N.T. Unions, which continued their clandestine existence and took part in a number of unsuccessful conspiracies against the dictatorship. Meanwhile, the military Government was carrying through a number of measures designed to regulate labour conditions and prevent industrial conflict. In August 1926 it published a new Labour Code ; and in November of that year it issued a decree-law setting up a national corporative organisation of labour with provision for the adjustment of disputes through a system of joint committees of employers and workers. At about the same time the Spanish Anarchists got together a Congress at Lyons and decided to set up an Iberian Anarchist Federation among the exiles living in France. This was followed by a secret Anarchist Congress held in Spain itself, at Valencia, in July 1927, at which the Iberian Anarchist Federation (F.A.I.) was definitely constituted as an underground, revolutionary organisation.

At about this time Primo de Rivera was endeavouring to establish, not a Parliament, but a purely consultative National Assembly of 400 members to act as a civilian auxiliary to the military Government. He offered the Socialists six seats in this Assembly, but the Socialist Party, at a Congress held in October 1927, refused to allow any of its members to serve, and those who were invited declined the invitation. The following September, however, the U.G.T. at its Madrid Congress decided in favour of its affiliated Unions' representation on the corporate public bodies set up by the Government, on condition that the representatives should be freely elected and should obey the instructions of the Trade Unions concerned. So things continued until, in January 1930, Primo de Rivera renounced his dictatorial powers and was replaced at the head of the Government by General Bérenguer, who at first restored the constitutional guarantees and proclaimed a general amnesty for persons imprisoned for political or social offences, but speedily made it clear that in practice he intended, in all essentials, to maintain the system of military dictatorship which Primo had instituted seven years before.

In these circumstances even the right-wing leaders who had been prepared to come to terms with Primo were driven into revolt. Before 1930 ended, Largo Caballero, together with Fernando de Los Rios and Indalecio Prieto, had lent themselves to a conspiracy which had for its object the overthrow of Bérenguer and of the monarchy and the establishment of a Republic. Their plans having come to light, they were thrown into prison — except Prieto, who escaped abroad. But the forces needed for a revolutionary upheaval were rapidly gathering strength ; and the following year, after Admiral Aznar had succeeded Bérenguer, municipal elections were held throughout Spain. As usual, it was claimed that the Government Parties had won most of the seats ; but the fact that the Republicans and Socialists had captured all the big cities could not be concealed. These victories led the Republican Committee under Alcalá Zamora, which had previously come to an agreement with the Catalonian autonomists, to come out openly with a demand for the King's abdication and the formation of a Republican Government. The King refused to abdicate ; but, seeing resistance to be futile, he agreed to cease to exercise his powers and to leave the country while its fortunes were being decided. Elections were then held under free conditions, and resulted in the return of a predominantly Republican Cortes. Zamora, himself a conservative Catholic, then formed an all-party Government, but resigned office a year later because he was opposed to the anti-Church policy of most of his colleagues. The Radical leader, Manuel Azaña, succeeded him as Prime Minister in October 1931 ; but the Lerroux Radicals soon afterwards seceded from the Government, leaving it mainly in Socialist hands. Its subsequent fortunes in drafting the new Spanish Constitution, and the course of events which led up to the military revolt in Morocco in 1936 and to the Civil War of the following years, fall outside the period covered in the present volume. We leave the Spaniards, set free for the time being both from the monarchy and from the rule of the army, attempting to establish Republican unity over a country which had again and again shown its incapacity for working together for a common end.

The Spanish record during the troubled years from 1918 to the *coup d'état* of September 1923 is that of a country almost without a Government ; for though Cabinet succeeded Cabinet in swift succession, none of them was able to exercise effective power either against the military or the Catholic Church or against the constant outbursts of working-class and peasant revolt or the violent measures used by employers and land-owners for its suppression. Catalonia, and above all Barcelona, were the scene of almost continuous violence, as in the years before 1914.[1] Many murders and attacks on persons and property were committed year after year by both sides ; and there were many organised gangs of sheer thugs who were prepared to carry out murders for payment from any source. The Barcelona police continued to be implicated in these disorders and to make extensive use of the services of *agents provocateurs* ; and the military garrison intervened from time to time to quell disorders and to levy war on the Syndicalist and Anarchist groups, which they were never able wholly to suppress. Catalonian nationalism, divided sharply into right and left wings, played an ambiguous part. The right-wing Catalonian autonomists, while opposed to the centralised

[1] See Vol. III, Part II, p. 761.

system and demanding the re-establishment of an autonomous Catalonian Parliament, were usually ready to invoke the help of the Government in suppressing Syndicalist disorders and for their attempts to build up tame 'free' Unions in opposition to the C.N.T. Primo de Rivera, when he launched his *coup d'état* as Captain-General of Catalonia, acted with the support of the right-wing Catalonian autonomists, who hoped that he would use his power to meet their claims. But the army authorities were, in general, strongly in favour of centralisation, and Primo was speedily forced to change his tune and insist on the maintenance of centralised rule. A Catalan Socialist Party had been founded at Barcelona in 1923, shortly before the *coup d'état*, under the leadership of Gabriel Alomar, but did not achieve any large following in face of the strength of Anarcho-Syndicalism in Catalonia and of the centralising policy of the Spanish Socialist Party. After 1923 the centre of left-wing Catalonian autonomism shifted to France, where Colonel Francisco Macia (1859–1933) set to work to build up the Esquerra as a Party of the bourgeois left. In November 1926 Macia attempted a rising, which was put down ; and thereafter the Catalonian autonomists had to await the fall of the dictatorship before they were able to re-create a powerful movement.

From 1918 to 1923 Spain was continually on the verge of revolution ; but no force except that of the military was strong enough or well enough organised to overthrow the existing State, despite its evident and even despicable rottenness. There were altogether too many rival contestants for power, unable and unwilling to join forces on any constructive programme. The rival political Parties, based on an utterly corrupt and meaningless electoral system, had no real power and stood for no clear or consistent principles : so that the King was able to turn out Cabinets almost at will, and actually used his authority in such a way as to make effective civil government impossible. The army, dominated by the regimental juntas of officers, utterly despised the politicians, resented all civilian criticism, and made itself a 'state within the State' which the Government was entirely unable to control. The Church, securely entrenched in monopolistic authority, would brook no political move to diminish its power and was able to overthrow any Government that ventured to dispute its monopoly. The working-class forces were divided between Socialist centralisers, who were also moderate reformists, and Anarcho-Syndicalists, who were revolutionary advocates of regional autonomy and rejected every form of centralised power, even in their own organisation. Trade Unionism was divided between the C.N.T., which they controlled, and the U.G.T., which was in effect an annex of the Socialist Party. Although these rival factions now and again joined forces against the Government and the employers, each alliance they made fell apart almost at once because their entire conceptions of Trade Unionism were different. The U.G.T. held to the principle of separate *national* Trade Unions for the various trades and industries, whereas the C.N.T. went over to the principle of complete *local* solidarity through the Sindicato Unico.

In face of these differences there was no real possibility of a united Spanish working-class movement, either politically or in the industrial field. The antagonisms between the rival movements were doubtless mitigated in some degree in practice by the fact that the C.N.T. and the U.G.T., the Anarcho-Syndicalists and the Social Democrats, had their principal strongholds largely in different parts of the country, the C.N.T. and the Anarcho-Syndicalists being by far the stronger in Catalonia and the south-east, and the U.G.T. and the Social Democrats in Madrid. There were, however, areas of serious local conflict — for example, Bilbao — as well as wide regions where neither party commanded any continuous organised following. Spain, it must always be borne in mind, was predominantly an agricultural country, with widely varying systems of land-tenure and cultivation ranging from huge, barely cultivated estates owned by the landlord families to the exiguous peasant holdings of Galicia, with oases of fertile land and relatively prosperous farming in the coastal regions of the north and east. Industrially, the only large developed region was in Catalonia : elsewhere there were only patches — the mining areas of the north and the south-west, the metal district centred on Bilbao, and a few more local concentrations. Madrid itself was not a great industrial centre. There was a considerable artisan population in the towns, practising small-scale crafts ; but Catalonia, which had attracted much immigrant labour from other areas, was the undisputed centre of developed industrialism, dependent on all Spain for its market and serving as the main source of domestic capital for investment. If there was to be a Spanish proletarian Revolution, Catalonia, and above all, Barcelona, was bound to play the leading part. There were, however, many difficulties in the way of Catalonian leadership of a nation-wide revolutionary uprising. For one thing, the Catalans were by no means united about the kind of revolution they wanted to make. One group among them put first the demand for autonomy — for a Catalonian Parliament that should establish regional self-government ; but even on this issue the autonomists were not united. The industrialists who dominated the right wing wanted autonomy, but by no means separation from the rest of Spain — for this might cost them both their preferential market and their position as the foremost providers of investment in Spanish economic development as a whole. The more radical autonomists were less moved by such economic considerations ; but even they, for the most part, wanted regional self-government rather than complete independence. They were federalists, rather than out-and-out nationalists taking their stand on the full right to self-determination.

This federalist outlook of the left-wing autonomists was shared in by the leaders of the Catalonian workers attached to the C.N.T. and to its regional representative — the 'Solidarity' of the Catalonian Trade Union movement. The C.N.T., however, was dominated by Anarcho-Syndicalists, who were opposed to all forms of State and parliamentary government, and accordingly were hardly less hostile to a purely Catalonian than to an all-Spanish Parliament and apparatus of civil and military government. The C.N.T. leaders wanted autonomy for Catalonia ; but they wanted it to be exercised, not through a Parliament, but through a structure of local communes based on the free association of the workers and peasants, without any authoritarian State set over them in a posture of command. They envisaged the Revolution that would set Catalonia free in this sense as an all-Spanish Revolution, in which the workers and peasants throughout Spain would make common cause against their oppressors, and were hostile to any purely Catalonian nationalism that would cut them off from their fellow-rebels in other parts of Spain. There was, for this reason, no possibility of unity between the bourgeois autonomists of Catalonia and the workers who accepted the Anarcho-Syndicalist gospel — the more so because the right-wing autonomists were their most direct antagonists in the local class war which made Barcelona the most turbulent city in all Europe. There were, moreover, cross-currents even among the workers of Catalonia ; for many of them were not Catalans but immigrants from other parts of the country and were unmoved by the purely Catalan cultural influences which played a large part in the Catalonian autonomist movement.

Even if the industrial workers had been united, not merely in Catalonia, but over all Spain, there could have been no successful social revolution without the support of the peasants. The peasants, no doubt, were in many parts of the country ready enough to revolt at any sign of opportunity ; but their readiness was for purely local revolts, arising out of local grievances, rather than for revolution on a national scale. They could be roused to such revolts again and again by travelling Anarchist orators and organisers ; but no way was found of organising them for common action over wide areas or of linking their local movements in any lasting way to the movements of the urban proletariat. Moreover, the areas least ready for revolt were those in which agricultural conditions were better than elsewhere, both for economic reasons and because the influence of the Church was greatest among the more prosperous peasants.

In these circumstances, proletarian revolution stood little or no chance of success. It could, in the period under review in this chapter, have been only an Anarcho-Syndicalist revolution ; for the Social Democrats were not really revolutionaries at all, and the Communists who broke away from them were at this time an almost negligible faction. But the Anarcho-Syndicalists, despite their hold in Barcelona and in other areas of Spain, chiefly in the east and south, were never in a position to put themselves at the head of an effective all-Spanish civil war. Their very hostility to all forms of centralised control stood seriously in the way of this ; and their relative powerlessness in Madrid was also a formidable obstacle. They were strong enough to reduce Spain to a state of lawlessness, but not to overthrow either of the two great centralised forces that barred their way — the army and the Church. The army was indeed, as the event showed, the only power capable of imposing any rule of law on the whole country when once its leaders had made up their minds to take power into their own hands ; and in Spain the army meant the officers and not the private soldiers. There were, no doubt, occasions on which the private soldiers did make some attempt, in particular places, to assert themselves as a revolutionary force — for example, at Saragossa in January 1920 ; but such uprisings were purely local and were easily suppressed. The continuous action of the army was in the hands of the regimental 'Defence Juntas', which gave so much trouble to successive Governments during the long-drawn-out Moroccan crisis. These juntas, however, were in themselves a disturbing rather than a constructively revolutionary force : only when Primo de Rivera and most of the higher ranks of the military command put themselves at the head of the movement was the civil Government finally overturned and the alternative revolutionary movement of the Anarcho-Syndicalists summarily repressed.

Thus, though in 1919 the Spanish proletariat seemed to be on the point of rallying to the side of the Comintern and accepting Russian leadership in the cause of World Revolution, no such conversion was ever really on the cards. The feeling against every sort of centralised authoritarian leadership was far too strong to be overborne ; and the C.N.T. recoiled as soon as it found itself face to face with Moscow's claim to determine policy and organisation over the heads of the Spanish revolutionaries. Indeed, the Comintern found more friends among the non-revolutionary Social Democrats than among the Anarchists and Syndicalists ; for the Social Democrats favoured centralisation and were immune from the 'infantile disorders of leftism' which Lenin so roundly denounced. But though Spanish Social Democracy rather than Anarchism provided the members for the new Spanish Communist Party, it found far too few followers along this line to constitute any effective challenge either to the Government or to the two major working-class movements of Syndicalism and the reformist Social Democratic Party.

During these years several of the outstanding leaders of the pre-war working-class movement were removed by death. Anselmo Lorenzo, a notable veteran who had been active in the days of the First International, died at Barcelona in November 1914. Francisco Mora, the Vice-President and historian of the Socialist Party, died in 1924, and Pablo Iglesias (b. 1850), its founder and leader, the following year. The Anarchist writer, Ricardo Mella (b. 1861), also died in 1925. Among the Socialist leaders who took the places of Iglesias and Mora were Professor Julian Besteiro (?–1940) of Madrid University, Francisco Largo Caballero, the principal figure in the U.G.T., the journalist Indalecio Prieto, who held the leading position in Bilbao, and another professor, Fernando de Los Rios, who became the Party's principal agricultural theorist. The Anarcho-Syndicalists, for all their activity, threw up no outstanding leader, except Ángel Pestaña, who played a leading part in the negotiations with the Comintern. Among those who rallied to Communism for the time being, Andreas Nin and Joaquín Maurin, to be connected later with P.O.U.M., were important figures, and David Anguiano, Antonio García Quejido, and E. Toralba Beci played the leading parts in the establishment of the Communist Party.

PORTUGAL

In Portugal, where the Revolution of 1910 had overthrown the monarchy and set up what purported to be a constitutional Republic, *coups d'état* and insurrections succeeded one another at a headlong pace during the following years ; but Socialism had little to do with them. The small Socialist Party claimed to have had a continuous existence from 1876, but had never wielded any significant influence. The Trade Union movement was of greater importance, especially after 1918 ; but it was dominated by Anarcho-Syndicalism, and there was no love lost between the Anarcho-Syndicalists and the Socialist Party. Such strength as the latter possessed was mainly in the northern part of the country, especially in Oporto, the second biggest town and, apart from Lisbon, the only considerable urban centre. In Lisbon the Socialists had very little strength, and the Syndicalist Union ruled the roost, though the Party, with Alfredo Franco as its secretary in the 1920s, had its headquarters there. The Party's principal organ, *Republica Social*, edited by Joaquin de Silva, was published at Oporto.

In the confused struggles for power between monarchists and republicans and between republican conservatives, democrats and radicals, the Syndicalists sometimes came on the scene as abetters of the bourgeois left ; but the Socialists more often attempted to stand aside. Parliamentary elections, which were frequent until General Carmona established himself as dictator after the defeat of the radical insurrection of 1926, were again and again shamelessly rigged by the Government in power for the moment ; and the franchise, nominally manhood suffrage, was reduced to a mere fraction by the imposition of a test of literacy which excluded most of the workers and nearly all the peasants who made up the great majority of the people. To such conditions, as in Spain, Anarcho-Syndicalism was the instinctive response of the main body of industrial workers, when they responded at all. For the most part, however, the struggle went on between the politicians and the rival factions in the armed forces ; and the latter repeatedly overturned Governments and ousted elected Presidents from office long before their terms were up. A Communist Party was set up during the post-war excitements of 1919, but gained little strength. With the coming of the dictatorship in 1927–8, both Communist and Socialist activities were severely repressed, and Trade Union activity was made subject to the legal prohibition of strikes. Under the Republic the finances were in perpetual disorder, and inflation caused great hardships among both peasants and industrial workers.

CHAPTER XVII

RUSSIA FROM THE NEW ECONOMIC POLICY TO THE FIVE-YEAR PLAN

THE period of the Civil War in Russia — 1919 and 1920 — is usually described as that of 'War Communism', during which everything had to be subordinated to the requirements of the Red Army and to the need to ensure a sufficient supply of food to the armed forces and to the town-dwellers to prevent the dissolution of the Soviet régime. When the Civil War ended with the final defeat of Wrangel during the closing months of 1920, it became necessary to consider without delay how the structure of government and control needed to be modified to adapt it to the tasks of internal consolidation and development. The immediate problems, which were immensely urgent, were to lessen the acute discontent among the peasants, which had been prevented from leading to really widespread revolt only because the Whites had made themselves even more hateful to the peasants than the Bolshevik requisitioners of food, and to set about the restoration of production both in the countryside and in the industries which had suffered heavily under the impact of the Civil War. It was imperative both to find ways of inducing the peasants to grow more food and to make more of it available for consumption in the towns without continuing the drastic requisitions practised under War Communism and to begin building up an economic structure that would make it possible to proceed rapidly with industrialisation while doing what could be done to provide more consumers' goods for exchange with the peasants against supplies of food and agricultural materials.

There was also the closely related question of what was to be done with the Red Army, or rather with that part of it which was no longer needed for immediate military service. During the Civil War it had become necessary to draft into the Red Army large numbers of militants from the industrial proletariat, even at the cost of serious weakening of the industrial front ; and these elements of the Red Army had suffered very heavy losses in the fighting. The Red Army, however, had served also as a most important training-ground for new recruits to Communism drawn from the mass of the peasantry, and had become not only a highly efficient and disciplined fighting force but also a big potential instrument of Communist propaganda and administration. The question was whether to disband the part of it that could be spared from further military service and allow it to merge into the general mass of the population or to keep it somehow together and make use of it for some of the pressing tasks of civil reconstruction, and perhaps in addition to post Red Army men who had shown their capacity and reliability to key positions in the civil organisation — especially in the Trade Unions.

Trotsky, the chief maker and leader of the Red Army, appeared in this situation as the advocate of the latter of these policies. He wanted to keep the Red Army together and to use it for the execution of great civil enterprises under military discipline ; and he also proposed that Red Army men should be drafted in large numbers into the administration and especially into key Trade Union posts, in order to stiffen up the administrative system and to ensure that the Trade Unions should become reliable auxiliaries of the Soviet Government and the Party in carrying through the urgent tasks of economic reconstruction. Trotsky had no hesitation in proposing this 'militarisation' in the field of great enterprises of economic reconstruction or in wishing to impose Red Army militants on the Trade Unions even against the desire of their existing leaders or of the Trade Union rank and file. He saw the usefulness of large, disciplined 'industrial armies' for such immense tasks as the rebuilding of the devastated structure of transport — railway lines, bridges, roads, canals — and he was very mistrustful of the Trade Unions, in which Mensheviks and Social Revolutionaries still kept a considerable influence, and 'workers' control' and internal democracy were being strongly demanded now that the pressure of war conditions had been relaxed. Moreover, though the civil war had ended, it was in his view much too soon to say that the full strength of the Red Army would not be needed for further fighting, if not to meet fresh rebellions or interventions in Russia itself, to come to the aid of the Revolution when it broke out again in other countries — for example, Germany.

In the event, this policy of Trotsky was rejected. Lenin himself took the field against it, even before he announced the New Economic Policy in March 1921. Considerable use was indeed made for a time of Red Army units for urgent civil work ; but no attempt was made to post Red Army men to key positions, either in the Trade Unions or in the administrative machine — though, of course, a good number of them did find their way into such posts. In Lenin's view the supreme necessity, in the circumstances of the early months of 1921, was to execute a strategic retreat from the rigorous measures that the Civil War had forced on the Bolshevik Government, so as to alleviate peasant discontent and to restrict within narrower limits the direct responsibilities of the Government in the economic field. The Civil War, he pointed out, had made it inescapable that the Soviet State should take under full control much more of the economy than its leaders would have wished to do or could be in a position to handle efficiently. The inevitable result had been to undermine the incentives to production, above all in the countryside, and to subject industry to an improvised, highly authoritarian régime which had brought with it a prodigious growth of bureaucratic practices and of evasions of sheerly unworkable rules by distraught managers set on keeping their establishments working at any cost.

The answer to the problem presented by the general economic crisis that existed at the close of the Civil War was the New Economic Policy that began to be introduced on Lenin's initiative in the early spring of 1921. N.E.P. began almost exclusively as a step designed both to increase food supplies and to meet peasant grievances ; but it had immediate repercussions on other parts of the Soviet economy, and spread rapidly from agriculture into trade of all sorts, into industry and, before long, into the financial and budgetary fields. Its first essential but far-reaching application was the substitution for the war-inspired requisitioning of peasant surpluses of food of a fixed tax in kind on agricultural output, coupled with permission to the peasants to dispose of what remained to them, after providing for their own subsistence and paying the tax, by exchanging it for industrial or other goods they needed or even selling it for money payment in local markets. The new tax on peasant output was fixed at a rate a long way below the forced requisitions previously made, so as to give the peasants, on an average harvest, substantial surpluses to dispose of. But the main purpose was to give the peasants an economic induce-ment to increase output, by putting an end to a system which had allowed no such incentive. It was reckoned that the larger supplies of foodstuffs bartered or sold by the peasants would apply a stimulus to the output of industrial goods for supply to them in exchange and would thus contribute to industrial as well as to agricultural recovery. It was recognised that the new policy would inevitably be of most advantage to the better-off peasants, who would be in the best position to increase their output, and that it might tend on this account to increase rural inequality and to consolidate the position of just those peasants who were least in sympathy with Socialist or Communist policies ; but it was felt that, in view of the urgent need to get more food produced and made available for the towns, this prospect had to be faced — even if it did bear an unpleasing resemblance to Stolypin's efforts to establish a class of upper peasants as a bulwark against Socialism after 1905.

There were also unpleasing consequences to be faced in the industrial field. Large-scale factory industry, with its plant very badly dilapidated because of neglect during war and civil war, was plainly not in a position to increase its output at all rapidly to meet a rising peasant demand. Large measures of industrial reconstruction and capital investment were needed to make this possible ; and there were also serious shortages of necessary materials to be overcome. The only way in which, in the short run, the supplies of non-agricultural goods could be rapidly increased was by giving the fullest encourage-ment to those forms of small-scale production which could be developed without heavy capital costs — that is, mainly indi-vidual artisan production or production by small factories and by groups of Co-operative producers. The Bolsheviks, who were firm believers in the advantages of large-scale industry, were most reluctant to see this sector of the economy strengthened ; but here again necessity drove them on, for it was vain to expect the peasants to increase their output unless they could obtain what they needed in exchange for the surplus over their own consumption. Accordingly, in the early stages of N.E.P., the utmost effort was made to bring the artisans and the producers' Co-operatives into play as sources of non-agricultural supplies for the peasant households.

The new policy in dealing with the peasants came into operation too late to have its full effect on the spring sowings of 1921 ; and the hopes entertained of it were defeated at the outset by a calamitous failure of the harvest of that year. Largely as a consequence of this calamity, food prices rose sharply in relation to the prices of industrial goods, which were depressed by a competitive scramble to sell by the manufacturing concerns. This scramble was the more acute because, as a part of N.E.P., the entire system of financing industry and of supplying its workers with the means of living was being radically altered. Under War Communism, industrial enterprises, except the smallest, had been operated as state concerns, drawing their working capital from the state bank ; and their profits had accrued to, and their losses been borne upon, the state budget. Moreover, the workers had received their remuneration, for the most part, not in money wages, but in ration tickets which had allowed them to draw their means of life from state agencies, in relation to their basic needs rather than to any estimation of the value of their work. This system had highly equalitarian effects, but provided no incentive to high output. It was the product of a siege economy that left no surplus available for the rewarding of special skill or effort.

On the other hand, under N.E.P. the industrial workers ceased to draw rations in this way and came to be paid by the enterprises in which they were employed. They were still for some time paid largely in kind ; but such payments were valued at the ruling prices of the goods concerned, and the balance due was paid in money. This change opened the door to increasing wage-differentiation. But, immediately, its main effect was that the industrial concerns had to find the means of paying their workers, and could no longer simply draw what they needed for this purpose from the State Treasury. Similarly, they had to find the sums needed to pay for raw materials and fuel and to meet other necessary working expenses. They were ordered to pay their own way out of their takings, without looking to the State to finance them ; and though a new special Bank was established for the provision of industrial finance, what they could draw from it was strictly limited in accordance with the new principle of taking industry out of the state budget and compelling it to reorganise its finances on a commercial basis. The principle of 'separation' of industry from the State — though industries continued to operate under public ownership — was proclaimed ; and the immediate consequence was an acute shortage of working capital which forced industrial undertakings to sell off their supplies of finished goods as fast as they possibly could, and to run down their stocks of materials in order to meet their current liabilities.

In face of the consequent sharp fall in the relative [1] prices of industrial goods, the industrial concerns, thus left to provide their own working capital, speedily resorted to measures of collective self-defence. They grouped themselves into large 'trusts' and combines, which set out to prevent competitive underselling ; and they also, with every encouragement from the State, set to work to concentrate production in the more efficient plants in order to reduce their costs. Many of the less efficient units were shut down, and a number of the smaller factories were leased to Co-operative Societies or even to private persons, who resumed production in them as part of the new private sector established under N.E.P. As an outcome of these measures, the relative prices of industrial goods quite soon rose sharply : indeed, before long the boot was on the other leg, as agricultural output recovered from the disaster of 1921 and as the measures for procuring higher peasant production for the market yielded the desired results. In 1923 came the 'Scissors' crisis : industrial prices soared to relative heights which destroyed the power of the peasants to buy the goods offered for sale ; and a fresh crisis arose between town and country to threaten the entire Soviet economy.

By this time the leaders of the Soviet Union, who in the earlier phases of the Revolution had paid little attention to

---

[1] Relative only, because the rouble was still depreciating rapidly as the State continued to meet its heavy deficit by resort to the printing-press.

monetary or financial policy and had been unable to pay their way during the Civil War without constant recourse to the printing-press, had come to the conclusion that drastic steps were needed in order to stabilise the economy both internally and abroad, and to enable the State to meet its outgoings without resorting to inflationary finance. The attempt to take industry out of the state budget by forcing industrial enterprises to pay their own way had contributed towards this, but was not by itself enough. It was further necessary to levy in taxes enough to meet the current costs of government and defence and to provide resources for public investment either out of tax proceeds or by means of loans from persons or institutions that were in a position to save. Gregori Sokolnikov (1888–?), who replaced N. Krestinsky as Finance Minister in the middle of 1921, constituted himself the principal champion of a return to sound financist methods. New taxes, both direct and indirect, were instituted under his auspices, and loans were successfully raised from Soviet institutions that had resources to spare, as well as from individuals who were doing well out of N.E.P. Sokolnikov further set to work to provide a new currency unit, the chervonets, representing a value in gold, to serve first and foremost as a medium of foreign exchange, but also as an internal form of currency less liable to depreciation than the old rouble, which steadily and rapidly depreciated in relation to it as inflation continued. At the same time Sokolnikov set to work to reduce public expenditure by critical scrutiny of administrative costs, and was able greatly to reduce the gap between public outgoings and treasury receipts, as well as to force industry into further measures of cost-reduction by the drastic restriction of credit. In effect, Sokolnikov applied to the Soviet economy many of the traditional practices of orthodox capitalist finance, by restoring a gold standard and using financial deflation as a weapon for the control of the new forms of business enterprise sanctioned, and indeed enforced, under N.E.P.

Trade, as well as industry, was deeply affected by the new system. Under War Communism, the State had maintained its monopoly of foreign trade — which was continued under N.E.P. — but internal private trade had hardly existed save in the form of illicit 'black markets' which the state apparatus was unable to control. Under N.E.P. private trade speedily came back into its own. At the outset, the intention was that it should take largely the form of direct barter of peasant products for industrial goods, and that buying and selling for money should be limited strictly to transactions in purely local markets. But in practice it proved impossible to maintain these conditions, and freedom to buy and sell at prices settled by market conditions had to be allowed both for surplus peasant products and for the products of small-scale industry. From this, the market economy soon lapped over into large-scale enterprise. Factories bought their materials and even their fuel where and as they could, and disposed of a part of their output in the same way, though they were still supposed to give priority to the claims of state consuming agencies and to publicly owned consuming industries.

Under these conditions a new kind of private trader — the Nepman — speedily made his appearance, acting mainly as a middleman in bringing suppliers and purchasers together, and often acting as an agent in procuring supplies needed by industrial undertakings, especially where more than purely local transactions were involved. Many of these Nepmen were able to operate at very large profits, and to accumulate considerable fortunes, which could then be taxed by the State and drawn upon by the issue of public loans. To an increasing extent, the Soviet Union, under N.E.P., went back to the practices of capitalist industry and finance, with the difference that the major industrial enterprises were publicly owned, that all foreign trade was in the State's hands, and that credit remained a public monopoly, and with the further difference that it was always in the State's power to withdraw, or to modify, the conditions under which the market economy was allowed to work. The net result was a modified form of State Capitalism, explicitly designed as temporary and meant to give place to some sort of Socialism as soon as those in control of the State felt strong enough to resume the interrupted advance. It was never made clear how long N.E.P. was intended to continue, or by what steps it was to be wound up when the time arrived ; but Lenin, at any rate, clearly expected it to last for a number of years.

The introduction of N.E.P. had large consequences for the

Trade Union movement. Before War Communism set in there had been, as we saw, big differences of view concerning the place of the Trade Unions in the new society and especially concerning their relation to the dominant Communist Party. One view had been that the Trade Unions must maintain an independent position as bargaining agencies of the industrial workers, negotiating collectively with the managements of socialised industry in much the same ways as Trade Unions bargained with employers in capitalist countries, save that they could expect the Soviet employing agencies to show much more sympathy for working-class claims. Another view had been that, in effect, there would be nothing to bargain about now that class-exploitation had been removed ; that wages and conditions would henceforth be settled by the Soviet State as representing the working class ; and that the Trade Unions should become part of the state machinery and should devote themselves chiefly to the administration of welfare services on the State's behalf and to collaborating with the state managers in using every endeavour to raise productivity in the interest of the whole society. Cutting across these conflicting views were varying opinions about the part to be played by the Trade Unions and by the workers enrolled in them in the actual management of industrial concerns. There were in the early stages considerable Anarchist and Syndicalist elements in the Trade Unions ; and these for the most part claimed that in a workers' society the workers ought to be entrusted with the running of their own factories and workshops, either directly through elected factory committees or through Trade Unions organised on a decentralised, democratic basis, so as to afford to the rank-and-file workers a real opportunity to participate in management and control. To a considerable extent the advocates of this sort of 'workers' control' had their way during the early stages of the Revolution, when managers mostly taken over from the old order were forced to act largely under committee control. This improvised structure, however, was swept away during the period of War Communism, under which managers were given high authority to cope with the emergency as they thought best.

When the Civil War ended, the old controversies were quickly renewed. A 'Workers' Opposition' developed, including among its principal demands a reduction of bourgeois and intellectual influence both in the Communist Party and in the industrial apparatus of Soviet society, and also a large measure of Trade Union autonomy and internal democracy. Issues of 'industrial democracy' played a considerable part in the strikes in Petrograd factories which preceded the Kronstadt Rising of March 1921 ; and Anarchist elements hostile to centralised control and bureaucracy were prominent among the supporters of the Rising.[1] Its suppression was accompanied by sharp measures against Anarchists and suspected Anarcho-Syndicalists both in Petrograd and elsewhere. These measures, however, did not put an end to the dissensions within the Communist Party, in which Alexander G. Shlyapnikov (1883-?), who had been Labour Commissar in the Soviet Government of 1917, appeared as the leader of a 'Workers' Opposition', supported by the formerly very influential Alexandra M. Kollontai (1872-1952), who published a pamphlet stating the opposition's case. This Opposition had taken shape largely as a retort to the policy adopted by Trotsky as Commissar of Communications — a post which he had taken over in order to deal with the urgent task of bringing the railways back to a more efficient state. Towards the end of 1920 Trotsky had published a pamphlet expounding his policy of bringing the Trade Unions under state control and using them, under state-appointed leadership, as instruments for the promotion of state programmes of economic reconstruction. This proposal to 'nationalise' the Trade Unions had been rejected by the Communist Party leadership ; but a special Party Committee of Ten, on which Trotsky refused to serve, had produced a report which proposed, while leaving the Trade Unions as independent bodies, to take steps to ensure their co-operation with the State in measures for increasing productivity, combating slackness and absenteeism, and generally acting under party direction in furthering the economic projects of the Soviet State. In effect what was proposed was that the Trade Unions, like the Soviets and like other key institutions outside the state machine, should be so permeated by the Communist Party as to become the executants of its policy without being subjected formally either to it or to the State.

[1] For the Kronstadt Rising, see p. 212.

To this the 'Workers' Opposition' objected almost as strongly as it did to Trotsky's plan of complete incorporation of the Trade Unions into the state machine. But as the Committee of Ten included Zinoviev, Stalin, Kamenev, Mikhail P. Tomsky (1880–1936), who was the head of the central Trade Union organisation, and Lenin himself, the Workers' Opposition clearly stood no chance of getting its way. It was in fact brushed aside, and its leaders were demoted from positions of authority, though not liquidated as they would have been later, after the Party had put its ban on every form of 'fractional' activity. In 1921 the Communist Party was not yet set in the monolithic mould of 'democratic centralism' that was soon to be imposed on it. It was, of course, fully committed to the view that, when the Party had once reached a decision on a matter of policy, every member was under a firm obligation to carry out that decision, whether he agreed with it or not. But it was still permissible, until a matter of party policy had been finally decided, to form groups to carry on propaganda on behalf of divergent opinions and to canvass for support right up to the time when the authoritative decision was made.

Although Trotsky's proposal — to 'militarise' the Trade Unions and to turn them, in effect, into state agencies under leaders not chosen by their members but officially appointed to ensure their loyal service — was rejected, the policy actually adopted came a good deal closer to Trotsky's than to that of the Workers' Opposition. Shlyapnikov and his group stood for the independence of the Trade Unions both of the State and of domination by the party machine. They wanted the Unions to be both internally democratic, in the sense of being governed by their own members with a large amount of decentralisation to local and factory groups, and also direct instruments of proletarian democracy, responsible in a workers' society for the actual conduct of industry and exercising a large control over its management. They represented in effect the Syndicalist, or near-Syndicalist, element that existed inside the Communist Party, but was much more widespread among workers outside the Party — for example, among those who had been supporters of the Left Social Revolutionaries and among the small but active Anarcho-Syndicalist groups. The Menshevik elements that were still strong in a number of

Trade Unions were also keen upholders of Trade Union independence both of the State and of the Communist Party, but for the most part laid more stress on the function of the Unions in collective bargaining about wages and conditions than on the demand for 'workers' control'. The two questions were, however, closely intertwined; and, on both, the Workers' Opposition had to encounter the strong hostility of the Bolshevik leadership, including Trotsky's followers as well as Lenin's. Both these groups were absolutely against any form of dispersed 'workers' control', which they regarded as inconsistent both with efficient industrial management and with co-ordinated economic planning directed by the proletarian dictatorship. The dictatorship meant, in their view, centralised control by the entire working class, exercised through a firm centralised discipline; and they regarded any suggestion that each body of workers in a particular industry or establishment should exercise authority over its affairs, even as a trustee of the class as a whole, as a kind of 'fractionalism' or particularism that would open the door wide to corporate egoism and would destroy all possibility of co-ordinated action in the interests of the entire proletarian society. Though Syndicalist elements had been welcomed at the beginning as recruits to the Comintern in its struggle against the Socialist Right and Centre, there had never been any intention of allowing their views to prevail, or even to survive. They had been invited to rally to the Comintern for the purpose of being absorbed into it by conversion to the full Communist point of view; and it had been intended that they should pass, as speedily as possible, under reliable Communist leadership. The Red International of Labour Unions and its constituent groups in the various countries were regarded by the Communists, not as independent bodies entitled to shape their own policies for themselves, but as auxiliaries to be controlled and managed by the Comintern and, under it, by the national Communist Parties. The accomplishment of this subordination of the Trade Unions to the Parties gave rise to big difficulties, above all in France; but in Russia the Communist Party was in a strong enough position to be well able to enforce its will.

The principal leaders, however, except Trotsky, did not wish formally to make the Trade Unions part of the state machine. They wished them to remain as non-governmental bodies, and aimed at securing control over them for the Communist Party rather than for the Soviets or the Council of People's Commissars. The Trade Unions were to be permeated, rather than taken over, because they were more likely, if they kept their formal independence, to be of real help in the drive for higher production, and because they could be used, under such conditions, as powerful agencies for spreading Communist ideas and policies through the whole industrial proletariat. There was some ambiguity, and some real doubt, about the degree of independence that was to be left to the Trade Unions under this arrangement — particularly about the extent of their freedom to bargain collectively about wages with the bodies responsible for the conduct of industry, either nationally or in particular industrial plants. This matter was to give rise to trouble later and to occasion the displacement of Tomsky from his position at the head of the Trade Union movement. But in 1921 the Russian Soviet Republic was still without any general economic plan involving central determination of the amount of the 'wages fund' or of its distribution among different groups and grades of workers ; and it was still possible to proceed experimentally and to allow each industry and group some room for pressing its own case by collective bargaining, though there was already a strong presumption in favour of the centralisation of the major bargaining functions in the hands of the Central Trade Union Commission. At that stage industry had but recently emerged from the conditions of War Communism, under which the workers had received their incomes mainly, not in wages, but in rations distributed by the State. The entire structure of wage-payment was being worked out afresh, as industries were required to make themselves self-supporting financially and to meet their own wage-bills ; and the Communist leaders, provided they could ensure that the Unions were put under compliant Communist leadership, preferred to give them an important part in working out the forms of the new wage-structure in conjunction with the authorities responsible for the shaping of the general economic plan. Accordingly, rather than take over the Unions, they set to work to bring them more fully under the control of the Communist Party by driving the Menshevik and other opposition elements out of such key positions as they still occupied and by making the fullest use of party cells within them to secure compliance with party policy. In this they were before long so far successful that future opposition could come, in the main, only from dissident members of the Communist Party, and not from Menshevik or Syndicalist groups which rejected the Communist conceptions of the rôle of Trade Unionism in Soviet society.

One important count in the indictment put forward by the Workers' Opposition had been that 'bureaucracy' was undermining the foundations of proletarian democracy, in the economic as well as in the political field, and that the real proletarians, with whom the control ought to rest, were being more and more bossed and badgered by officials, some of them taken over from the old régime, who were not workers but bourgeois intellectuals, impatient of working-class attitudes and opinions. It would, indeed, have been astonishing if there had not been a good deal of truth in this charge. The Soviet Government had been forced, from 1917 onwards, to improvise an immense administrative machine for which it had no adequate personnel to draw upon ; and inevitably it had taken recruits where it could find them. The economic machine in particular had been staffed to a considerable extent by men who, under the need to earn a living under the new order, had been prepared to work in economic matters for the Bolsheviks, though they did not agree with them politically ; and among those who were Bolsheviks, and found themselves rapidly promoted to positions of authority, there were unavoidably many jacks-in-office who were all too prone to abuse their newly acquired powers. Moreover, the extreme scarcity of practically everything needed — of materials as well as of finished goods and components — had led to a formidably elaborate apparatus of 'controls' which easily degenerated into forms of 'red tape' exasperating both to managers in every field and to workers unable to get on with their jobs. It was natural to blame the 'bureaucracy' for these difficulties, and doubtless much of the blame was deserved. But at the bottom of the trouble was sheer shortage, which there was no easy way to remedy.

One big controversy arising out of this situation turned on the question whether, in order to lessen the shortages, both of consumers' goods and of machines and materials needed for industry, imports should be stepped up, despite the great difficulty of finding any means of paying for them. The financial authorities, striving to stabilise the currency externally as well as at home, were naturally hostile to such projects, and insisted that imports could be increased, in the absence of foreign loans, only if there could be a parallel increase in exports. Higher exports, however, could be made available only if the peasants could be induced to increase production for the market beyond the needs of the urban population ; and this was difficult both because part of any increase was bound to be absorbed in increased consumption by the peasants themselves and because the town-dwellers were still going terribly short. It was evident that, even if agricultural exports, particularly of grain, could be resumed on a bigger scale, what was exported would be, not a real surplus, but a denial to the home market of what was urgently needed by it. The only question was whether this need, despite its urgency, had to give way to the still greater needs for industrial goods to exchange against peasant products and for machines and materials for use in reviving industrial production.

This question of imports and exports was closely related to the even greater issue of the economic relations between the peasantry and the industrial population — or rather between the respective claims of peasant agriculture and large-scale industry. N.E.P., as we saw, had been designed initially mainly as a means of getting the peasants to produce more ; and the industrial and commercial aspects of N.E.P. were largely intended to procure more industrial goods for sale to the peasants in exchange for agricultural products. With this in view, the emphasis had been put on the revival of small-scale artisan production and on light rather than on heavy industries — for quick results could be got most easily in this way without heavy investment in new instruments of production, which the struggling economy was not yet in a position to afford. It had seemed necessary, in face of the immediate crisis, to postpone major projects of industrial development until the 'scissors' crisis had been overcome. Such a necessity was very unwelcome, both because it involved strengthening the position of the peasants — and especially of the more prosperous among them — and because the Bolsheviks were strongly convinced of the superior merits of large-scale industry, and felt a high contempt for the kinds of small-scale artisan manufacture that they were compelled to foster in its place. They no more wished to strengthen the artisan than the peasant element in Russian society. They wanted, as soon as they could, to replace small individual peasant holdings by large-scale industrialised farms ; and they were convinced that the prospect of Russia's survival under Communist rule depended on their ability to equip it with a thoroughly modern industrial structure of large-scale production, the foundations of which needed to be laid by an immense and rapid development of the heavy industries.

The Bolsheviks therefore greatly disliked N.E.P., and accepted it only because they had to, and on the understanding that it was to be no more than temporary. 'Temporary', however, might mean more than one thing ; and the question how long N.E.P. was to last soon became acute. There were not a few who feared that the very success of the new policy would before long render its removal impossible, in view both of the entrenchment of peasant agriculture and of the growing functions of the 'Nepmen' and the predominance of private enterprise in retail trade ; and those who felt these misgivings most strongly soon began to demand that a halt should be called and a renewed effort be made to resume the advance towards Socialism. There arose in particular a cry that the peasants, as the 'scissors' crisis was overcome and the relative prices of industrial goods were brought down, were being allowed to receive and to fritter away on consumption an undue proportion of the exiguous national income, and that steps should be taken to correct this without further delay. Trotsky was among the foremost exponents of a policy of rapid industrialisation, for which it was clear that the resources could be derived only from an intensified exploitation of the peasants — for the efforts under N.E.P. to attract foreign capitalist investors by offering concessions for industrial development had yielded no substantial results. It had become clear that Russia — or rather the Soviet Union, which came formally into being in December 1922 — would have to meet the costs of industrialisation out of its own scanty resources, at the cost of reduced domestic consumption while the change was being carried through ; and this meant in practice that the major part of the burden was bound to fall on the peasants, because there was no-one else to bear it.

In these circumstances the economist E. I. Preobrazhensky (b. 1886) advanced a theoretical formulation which gave rise to a hot controversy. The idea he put forward was that of a 'primitive Socialist accumulation' corresponding to the 'primitive accumulation' on which Marx had laid stress in his account of the early stages of capitalist development. The Soviet Union, Preobrazhensky maintained, needed to extract from the peasants the resources required for industrial investment in socialised industry, and only by these means could the advance towards Socialism be effectively resumed. Low agricultural prices, as well as heavy taxes on the peasants, were therefore indispensable as aids to Socialist progress. Those who opposed Preobrazhensky's views did so, for the most part, not out of any sympathy for the peasants — for whom the Bolsheviks, in general, had a high contempt — but because they were afraid that the peasants would be able to defeat the proposed measures by reducing their own production and thus bringing back the very crisis N.E.P. had been designed to put an end to. For the time being, these fears were strong enough to prevent the leadership from acting to any great extent on Preobrazhensky's or Trotsky's proposals. N.E.P. was allowed to continue ; but in the industrial field a shift nevertheless began from small-scale and light industries towards large-scale and heavy industries as soon as this was felt to be possible without provoking a fresh agricultural crisis. Any attempt to attack the peasant system of individual production, except by starting large state farms on uncultivated lands, was deferred ; and the major reliance for higher agricultural output continued to be placed on the encouragement given by N.E.P. to the middle peasants, who were much the most numerous group and were in a position to contribute in the aggregate much more than the big peasants, or *kulaks*, even if these latter drew the greatest advantage from the return to the 'free market'.

Preobrazhensky had begun to expound his views as early as 1921, in the infancy of N.E.P., and had been heavily criticised for them by Lenin. When he returned to the charge in 1923 with his theory of 'primitive Socialist accumulation', Lenin, though still living, was practically out of action ; and N. I. Bukharin (1889–1938) and A. I. Rykov (1881–1938) took up the renewed challenge, arguing that Preobrazhensky's policy would necessarily destroy the alliance between industrial workers and peasants on which the survival of the Revolution depended, and might easily lead not only to a sharp fall in agricultural output but even to widespread rural revolt. For the time being they had much the better of the argument ; but in effect Preobrazhensky's and Trotsky's ideas were rejected, not as wrong in themselves, but only as premature. The entire Communist Party had every intention of pressing on with the development of heavy industry as far and as fast as it possibly could ; and it was obvious that this would mean squeezing the peasants in order to get the required resources. The only real question was whether the squeeze should begin at once or should be delayed until the advance of peasant production had gone far enough to allow the peasants to meet it without such intense hardship as would inevitably forfeit all their good-will and probably drive them into active resistance. The attempt to pile up the 'primitive Socialist accumulation' was deferred, but not abandoned. It was destined to be renewed under the first Five-Year Plan and to have its sequel in the further attempt to replace individual peasant cultivation by the mass transition to the collective farm. This latter, however, had hardly been thought of, save in quite general terms, in 1923, though as early as 1921 Preobrazhensky had emphasised the importance of a rapid development of big state farms for grain growing, and had been urging that foreign capital should be invited for investment in large-scale experiments in capitalistic industrialised farming.

The period of sharp controversy over the effects of N.E.P. coincided in time with the struggle for leadership which followed Lenin's disablement and was intensified after his death in January 1924. Lenin, up to his enforced withdrawal, had been the unquestioned leader of the Revolution and the shaper of its essential policies. In 1921, after the end of the Civil War, N.E.P. had been his doing, almost forced by him on a reluctant Party, which could hardly have been induced to accept it save by his overmastering authority. But, after Lenin (if a long way after), Trotsky had been the second outstanding figure, first in the critical days of 1917 and then as the creator of the Red Army which had won the Civil War. Not only abroad had the names 'Lenin and Trotsky' been habitually coupled in designating the leadership of the Revolution; for no-one else could match or come near Trotsky's hold as orator and organiser on the mass of the revolutionary workers and soldiers. Outside Russia, it seemed almost a matter of course that, with Lenin's removal, Trotsky would succeed to the first place in the leadership; and this feeling was undoubtedly entertained widely inside Russia as well. It was not, however, shared by substantial elements in the Bolshevik *élite*, among whom there were many who regarded Trotsky as an upstart with a bad past of association with the Mensheviks, and of attempts to build bridges as a 'conciliator' between Bolsheviks and Mensheviks — and, perhaps, above all, as not being an 'old Bolshevik' and entitled as such to share in the fruits of Bolshevik victory. The fact that Trotsky was a Jew also, beyond doubt, counted against him, but considerably less among the Bolshevik leaders than among large sections of the common people; for anti-semitism, long endemic in Czarist society and much used as a deliberate means of diverting popular discontent, was not yet, in the 1920s, at all a marked attitude among the partisans of the Revolution, despite the prominence of the Jewish element in the Menshevik Party. It was mainly for the other reasons just stated that a good many 'old Bolsheviks' were not at all prepared to accept Trotsky as their leader in Lenin's place, and these were at no loss to find additional reasons for objecting to him. For Trotsky, in the course of his prodigious efforts to create the Red Army, to win the Civil War, and to re-establish the transport system, had often not minced his words in speaking of fellow-leaders whom he regarded as incapable or wrong-headed; and it was easy to accuse him of attempting to build a private empire through his control of the Red Army, and even of having Caesarist ambitions to make himself head of a régime resting on personal dictatorship. This was made the easier when Trotsky proposed, after the Civil War, to use the Red Army as a principal instrument of civil reconstruction, to plant out Red Army men in key positions throughout the administration, and to 'nationalise' the Trade Unions by subjecting them to state-appointed leaders drawn largely from his Red Army following.

It is, I think, most unlikely that Trotsky in fact cherished the ambitions of which he was chiefly accused. He was, I feel sure, most genuinely devoted to the revolutionary cause and devoid of merely *personal* ambition. But he did not brook fools or even disagreement easily, and was very impatient of anyone who, for good or bad reasons, threatened to get in his way. He was accustomed to giving orders and to having them obeyed ; and he liked making quick, fateful decisions without waiting to consult those whom they affected, or who felt they had a right to be consulted. He was imperious, and not tactful ; and these qualities, which had stood him in good stead during the fighting, now turned badly to his disadvantage. He had been able to work with, and under, Lenin because in the last resort he deeply respected Lenin's revolutionary instinct, and was prepared to give way to him even when they had disagreed. But there was certainly no-one else to whom he was ready to offer a similar deference : nor was he a man who could at all easily work as a colleague with others on equal terms. He was therefore highly vulnerable, despite his immense prestige ; and even while Lenin was still active there was no dearth of fellow-leaders eager to do all they could to undermine his influence both with Lenin and in the affairs of the Communist Party.

It must, I think, also be borne in mind that Trotsky was, by both instinct and conviction, more a Soviet than a Party man. We have seen how, in 1917, he stressed the rôle of the Petrograd Soviet, rather than that of the Bolshevik Party as such, in the preparations for the November *coup*, and how he differed from Lenin on this issue.[1] He had, as we saw, joined the Communist Party only in the summer of 1917, when the Mezhrayontsy merged their group in it in preparation for the second Revolution ; and his first experiences of the Party in action had shown up the hesitations of many of its leaders in responding to Lenin's demands for revolutionary action. He had by no means forgotten these experiences, as he showed when he wrote his celebrated essay on *The Lessons of October* in 1924,

[1] See p. 87.

and as he had indeed made abundantly clear in speech and action on many occasions. Grigory Zinoviev (1883–1936), the head of the Comintern and the leading figure among the Petrograd Communists, Trotsky plainly despised as a revolutionary babbler, whose brave words concealed an exceeding timidity at moments of crisis. L. B. Kamenev (1883–1936), too, he regarded as much too cautious and hidebound ; and between Trotsky and Stalin, the new secretary of the Communist Party, there had been a deep temperamental gulf from the first moment of their contact. This last antagonism was, in the event, to prove by far the most important ; for it was Stalin who was to emerge as Trotsky's rival for leadership and control after Lenin's death, and Stalin was able first to use Zinoviev and Kamenev as his allies in compassing Trotsky's overthrow, and then to discard them when they had served his turn. The veritable Caesar of the Russian Revolution was to be Joseph Stalin (1879–1953), not Trotsky ; but it would have required remarkable prescience to realise this, even as a potential danger, when Lenin died.

Immediately after the Bolshevik Revolution, Stalin's office had been that of Commissar of Nationalities — a post which had enabled him to get to know well the key persons in the areas under Soviet rule that were remote from the daily events of Petrograd and Moscow, the principal centres of party discussion and determination of general policy. In 1919 he had been called by Lenin to a second post which brought him into even closer touch with every aspect of the new machine of government and administration. This was the position of Commissar of Workers' and Peasants' Inspection, known as 'Rabkrin' — the special organ created by Lenin for the purpose of combating bureaucratic tendencies by subjecting every part of the administration to the continual scrutiny of reliable party members, themselves workers or peasants, who were authorised to intervene in any field for the correction of abuses such as bureaucratic inefficiency or corruption. In practice, the remedy often proved worse than the disease ; and Rabkrin got itself a bad name and presently earned Lenin's own denunciation for its ham-handed and even brutal methods, which stirred up a vast amount of discontent among hard-worked functionaries who found themselves the victims of its attentions,

Nevertheless, the man who was at the head of Rabkrin was necessarily very well placed for getting his hand on every part of the administrative machine, for knowing about everyone who played a part in it, and for favouring the advancement of some and the dethronement of others. Stalin largely escaped blame for Rabkrin's errors and offences, while he profited by its pervasive activity. Then, in 1922, after the displacement of the triumvirate which had served the Party as a secretariat, he was appointed to the new post of General Secretary of the Communist Party, with V. M. Molotov (b. 1890) as his chief assistant. In theory the Secretariat, even under the new arrangement, was no more than the servant of the Party's Central Committee, which operated in practice mainly through its two bureaux — the Political and the Organisation Bureaux. But Stalin was already a member of both these key bodies and the essential link between them ; and this combination of offices enabled him, aided by his experience at Rabkrin, to develop the post of General Secretary into one of immense power. The Organisation Bureau included among its functions that of assigning any party member to the particular duty in which he was considered best able to serve the Party and, in doing this, to move any member from one place to another, so as to prevent him from entrenching himself securely behind a local or institutional following. This power was used very extensively, and, no doubt, often for very good reasons. But it evidently gave the man who exercised it a very strong hold on the party machine, and indeed on the entire party membership, and Stalin was not the person to fail to make full use of such a chance. From the end of the Civil War, if not even sooner, Stalin set assiduously to work to make himself master of the Bolshevik party machine and of the administrative apparatus of the Soviet Government, in which party members held the key positions. This was the process which Trotsky, in his booklet on the *New Course* (written 1923-4), was presently to denounce as the 'bureaucratisation' of the party apparatus and to demand a reversal of it through a return to more democratic forms of party action.

For Trotsky, though his own methods were apt to be autocratic when he felt swift action to be imperative, held strongly to the view that the Communist Party could keep its vitality and advance the cause of the Revolution only if it were effectively governed by its rank and file and if this rank and file were continually renewed by new-comers among whom industrial workers drawn directly from the factories held the predominant place. Trotsky, himself regarded as an outsider and new-comer by the Bolshevik 'Old Guard', was up in arms against the continued supremacy of this 'Old Guard' in the determination of party and state policy and against the 'Old Guard's' habit of arriving at firm decisions without consulting the membership and then calling on the membership for complete obedience in the name of party loyalty. Something of this, he said, might have been inevitable during the Civil War ; but it was a dangerous error to keep to it in time of peace, when a 'new course' of Socialist construction needed to be planned and carried into effect. The new members who had rallied to the Party since the Revolution had no less right than the 'Old Bolsheviks' to take part in shaping policy for the future ; but, he asserted, they were being deliberately kept out and kept down by the bureaucracy that had been set up under the authority of the 'Old Guard'. With this charge against the 'Old Guard he coupled the charge that party membership had become inflated by the admission of a great number of persons who were neither workers nor peasants, but intellectuals, politicians, and former officials who had accepted service under the new régime and had provided a high proportion of the recruits to the state and party bureaucracy. He added the charge that many party functionaries who had come from the ranks of the workers had, under the influence of bureaucratic tendencies in the party machine, lost contact with the mass of the proletariat and become bureaucrats subservient to the centralising authority of the 'Old Guard'.

Trotsky was thus appealing not only for more democracy within the Communist Party, in order that policies might emerge from below rather than be imposed from the centre, but also for a change in the composition of the Party, in order to give it a more decisively proletarian make-up. After Lenin's removal, the second of these demands was to a great extent met, first by a grand purge, in the course of which a high proportion of the non-proletarian members were excluded from the Party, and then by an opening of the ranks which brought in a huge contingent of mainly proletarian members. This great change, however, was not matched by any concession to Trotsky's first demand, for a restoration of internal party democracy. On the contrary, Stalin was able steadily to increase his hold over the Party, and to make use of the purge as a weapon against dissentients. Trotsky's argument on this matter had turned largely on the growing tendency in the directing group of the Party to denounce as 'fractionalism' every sort of intra-party discussion that led to the formation of groups acting together for the advocacy of particular opinions about the policies that ought to be followed. He agreed, he said, that the existence of 'fractions' was to be deplored as a clear sign of *malaise* within the Party ; but he denied emphatically both that a 'group' holding a particular view different from that of the central caucus necessarily constituted a 'fraction' and that the existence of either 'groups' or 'fractions' could be prevented merely by denouncing them, save at the cost of killing the life of the Party and reducing it to a mere excrescence on the bureaucratic machine. He insisted that real and legitimate differences about the policies to be followed were bound to arise in any living Party that had to cope with changing situations both at home and abroad, and that such differences ought to be resolved by full and frank party discussion, and not stamped out by force. Force, he said, merely drove the dissensions underground, without resolving them : the only way of resolving them was by allowing the various points of view to be put forward, by groups as well as by individuals — for the individual was usually helpless if he had to act alone — and then reaching a collective decision democratically in the light of all the arguments that had been advanced. Trotsky was in no way questioning the need, at the existing stage of the Revolution, for keeping power firmly in the hands of a single Party : indeed, he strongly affirmed this need. What he demanded was that the controlling Party should make its own policy by constant and close consultation among its entire membership, and not take it ready-made from the authority of a central cabal.

It is easy to see that Trotsky might have taken a different view of the virtues of party democracy had he not felt confident that the rank and file of the Party — or at any rate of its proletarian elements — would be on his side against the widely unpopular bureaucracy which he denounced. He was hardly the man to be a stickler for democratic procedures unless he believed they would further the course he held that the Revolution ought to follow. He did, however, quite honestly believe that the success, and even the survival, of the Revolution depended on the sustained support of the industrial workers, and that this support was in danger of being lost. He thought that the New Economic Policy was being so applied as both to strengthen the hold of the *kulaks* in the villages and to enable the Nepmen and petty capitalists to establish themselves in a key position between the main body of peasants and the industrial workers, so as to cut the industrial proletariat off from direct contacts with the poorer peasants. As against the N.E.P. policy which was designed to come to terms with the village as a whole, ignoring the distinction between *kulaks* and poor peasants, Trotsky wanted a return to the class-war in the village, with the industrial proletariat co-operating with and egging on the poor peasants against the better-to-do ; and for this it seemed to him indispensable to evoke the active participation of the main body of industrial workers. This policy, far from being conceived in the immediate interests even of the poor peasants, was designed to render practicable a much more rapid development of industrialisation, which was bound in the short run to be mainly at the peasants', including the poorer peasants', expense. Trotsky was no friend to the peasant economy, which he most heartily despised. He considered that the peasants needed to be forced to make their contribution to the Revolution, even against their will, by supplying the funds for intensive industrial development; and he held that they could be compelled to do this most effectively by ceasing to pamper the *kulaks* and by turning the poorer peasants against them.

Yet Trotsky was evidently sincere when, in his *New Course* and in his articles in *Pravda* at the end of 1923, he rejected the charge made against him of 'underestimating the place of the peasantry' in the Revolution. He was able to show that he had been entirely in favour, in 1921, of that part of the N.E.P which was designed to appeal, above all, to the middle peasants for increased output by relieving them of the burden of requisitions imposed during the period of War Communism.

He showed, too, that in building the Red Army mainly out of peasant recruits he had given a practical demonstration of the importance he attached to the peasants as a force indispensable to the success of the Revolution. But at the same time he was always careful to speak, not of the 'dictatorship of the workers and peasants' but of the 'dictatorship of the workers with peasant support'; and his retort to those who accused him of underestimating the peasants was that his critics were guilty of the much more serious offence of underestimating the revolutionary potency of the industrial proletariat. In effect, Trotsky did underestimate the peasantry if it was under-estimation of them to deny their capacity for a real partnership with the proletariat in the revolutionary dictatorship. He saw the need — none more clearly — for the industrial workers to have the main body of the peasants on their side against the counter-revolution; but he did not regard the peasant, as such, as capable of playing a constructive revolutionary rôle. The peasant could, in Trotsky's view, play such a rôle only when he had been transformed into a Red Army soldier, and in his new function indoctrinated in Bolshevik conceptions. While he remained a peasant he could be placated and induced to keep the towns supplied and even to provide a surplus for export; and it was necessary to deal with him in such a way a to achieve this result. But it was also necessary to take steps to prevent him from entering into alliance with the private capitalists who were also being encouraged by N.E.P.; and this involved action to keep the class-struggle alive in the villages by stirring up the poorer peasants against the *kulaks*. Immediately, the greatest need of all was to keep down the prices of industrial goods to what the peasants could afford to pay, and to increase the supply of such goods by rapid in-dustrial development. But the advance towards a Socialist society must depend primarily not on the peasants but on strengthening the industrial proletariat by a rapid development of investment in large-scale industry. The industrial workers and the Red Army were the only reliable revolutionary forces : the peasantry was at best no more than an instrument they were compelled to use.

Holding this view, Trotsky was naturally a strong advocate of rapid advance towards a planned economy. He strongly supported Lenin in the importance he attached to the grandiose electrification plan which began with the establishment of the Electrification Commission (Goelro) in 1920 ; and he regarded his own task as President of the Transport Commission set up the same year to bring the railways back to an efficient condition as an essential step towards the institution of a general economic plan. Lenin at this stage still regarded as premature the setting up of any general planning body, though he accepted the need for constituting the Council of Labour and Defence (S.T.O.), made up of most of the principal members of the Council of Commissars, as a general co-ordinating authority in the economic field. Lenin was rather reluctantly persuaded to agree to the setting up of a General Planning Commission (Gosplan), attached to S.T.O. as an advisory body, which began work in April 1921, just as N.E.P. was being adopted ; but at the outset Gosplan was started only in a modest way, and little advance towards general economic planning could be made while the main emphasis was being put on getting N.E.P. into working order. Trotsky wanted a more powerful executive planning agency, because he wanted speedier industrialisation ; but Lenin had his eyes mainly on the electrification project, by means of which he hoped above all to revolutionise methods of production in the rural areas, and was afraid this project might be submerged in a wider scheme of general economic development. There was, of course, no difference of opinion about the desirability of a comprehensive general economic plan as soon as the conditions for it were ripe. What Lenin feared was that to attempt such a plan immediately might get in the way both of rapid electrification and of the essential measures to be taken under N.E.P.

While these great debates on Russia's economic policy were in progress, large changes were taking place in Russia's relations with the rest of the world. The ending of Allied military intervention and of civil war set the Russians free to attend to their enormous problems of economic reconstruction, but also confronted them with the need to establish terms of co-existence with the capitalist countries. In January 1921 the Allied Supreme Council recognised Estonia and Latvia as independent States, and in March an Anglo-Soviet trade agreement was signed. The same month a Peace Treaty was signed between

Russia, the Ukraine, and Poland and prepared the way for the establishment of the Soviet Union the following year. In April 1922 came the dramatic signing of the Rapallo Treaty between Russia and Germany — the two great outcasts of the post-war settlement in Europe. In June of that year came Lenin's serious illness and the murder of Walther Rathenau, and also, running on into July, The Hague Conference on relations with Russia to which Maxim Litvinov (1876–1951) presented his abortive scheme for the granting of large credits to the Soviets for economic and financial reconstruction. The U.S.S.R. came into being at the end of the year, and its new federal Constitution came into force in July 1923. In January 1923 the French occupied the Ruhr, and the long struggle against the occupation began. In July the Bulgarian counter-revolution overthrew and murdered Stamboliski, after the Bulgarian Communists had failed to come to his help. In Germany, through the spring and summer the Communists hovered on the brink of an armed rising, but ended by deciding that they had missed their chance. In September the Bulgarian Communists staged a belated revolt, which was speedily quenched in blood. As a sequel to these events, the policy of the Comintern underwent a further drastic overhaul,[1] involving the elimination of the German leadership that had been installed after the defeat of 1921 and a whole series of 'palace revolutions' in the European Communist movements. In January 1924 Lenin died, and on the following day Ramsay MacDonald's first Labour Government took office in Great Britain. In February Great Britain recognised the U.S.S.R., and soon afterwards negotiations began for a formal Anglo-Soviet Agreement. On May 31st a Treaty was signed between China and the Soviet Union ; and in June Poincaré was succeeded as Prime Minister of France by Edouard Herriot at the head of a progressive bourgeois Government. In August the French began the evacuation of the Ruhr ; and the Dawes Agreement on German reparations was signed. Early the same month the British Labour Government arrested J. R. Campbell (b. 1894), of the *Daily Worker* ; and with the dropping of the case it began to find itself in serious difficulties with the Liberals, on whom it depended for a majority. On October 8th it was

[1] See p. 638.

defeated in Parliament, and appealed to the country. In the course of the ensuing General Election occurred the episode of the Zinoviev 'Red Letter', disastrously mishandled by MacDonald ; and the Labour Government suffered a serious defeat.[1] Baldwin replaced MacDonald as Prime Minister, and the attempt to improve relations with the Soviet Union came to an abrupt end. However, in the midst of these developments, the French Government at length recognised the Soviet Union. Moreover, in 1925, as the outcome of a Trade Union delegation which had visited Russia and brought back a mainly favourable report, the British Trades Union Congress agreed to set up an Anglo-Russian Trade Union Advisory Committee with the principal purpose of improving relations between the British and the Soviet peoples.[2]

Thus, by 1924, the Soviet Union, though it had still very great difficulties to face, had gone a long way towards establishing itself as a power to be reckoned with in world affairs. There were many who hoped, in 1921, that the introduction of N.E.P. would mean the gradual abandonment of the attempt to build up the Soviet Union as a Socialist society, and that Nepmen and peasants between them would thoroughly undermine the socialistic character of the régime and lead to a restoration of capitalism and in due course to the overthrow of Bolshevik rule. There were, indeed, not a few among the Bolsheviks themselves who shared these fears and watched with deep misgivings the rise of the *kulaks* in wealth and influence, the domination of internal trade by private entrepreneurs, and the offers of concessions to foreign capitalists. Though such Bolsheviks acquiesced in N.E.P. under Lenin's powerful insistence, they were never happy about it, and were very soon urging that the time had arrived to call a halt, if not to bring the whole system to an end. Lenin, however, as long as he lived, remained insistent on the need to maintain N.E.P. and, confident that the dangers involved in it could be successfully dealt with, provided the State held firmly to its monopoly of foreign trade and went on rapidly with its plans of electrification as a foundation for a thoroughly mechanised economic structure. His policy was continued after his death by the triumvirate which took over power when he became too ill to maintain his hand at the helm.

[1] See p. 435.　　　　　　　　　[2] See p. 437.

To the last period of Lenin's life belongs his famous 'Testament', in which he wrote down his views about the future leadership of the Soviet State and of the Communist Party as its guiding and inspiring genius. This oft-quoted — and misquoted — document was not published in full until some years after Lenin's death, and even then not officially — it was indeed never published in an authorised text until 1956. It was, however, read to a meeting of party members in the spring of 1924, after the Central Committee had rejected Krupskaia's demand that it should be placed before the Party Congress ; and there is no real doubt about its meaning. The 'Testament' was dictated by Lenin in December 1922, a few days after his second stroke, and a postscript was added in January 1923. It was in this latter that Lenin definitely proposed Stalin's removal from his position as General Secretary of the Communist Party, characterising him as 'rude', and suggesting his replacement by someone 'more patient, more loyal, more polite and more attentive to comrades, less capricious, etc.' — but without saying who this successor should be. In the original 'Testament' Lenin had already attacked Stalin, saying that he had, as secretary, 'concentrated an enormous power in his hands', and adding, 'I am not sure that he always knows how to use that power with sufficient caution'. Trotsky he had described as 'personally, the most able man in the present central committee', but also as distinguished 'by his too far-reaching self-confidence and a disposition to be too much attracted by the purely administrative side of affairs'. Lenin had also expressed his fears of a possible clash between these two formidable personalities, and of the danger of such a clash leading to an actual split. He had insisted that the Party was liable to be unstable because it 'rests upon two classes' and 'if there cannot exist an agreement between these classes its fall is inevitable'.

In addition to these animadversions on Stalin and Trotsky, the 'Testament' referred to four other members of the Central Committee — Zinoviev, Kamenev, Bukharin, and Pyatakov. Of the first two, Lenin used the highly significant words that 'the October episode of Zinoviev and Kamenev' — *i.e.* their opposition to the Bolshevik *coup* — 'was of course not accidental', but added that 'it ought as little to be used against them as the non-Bolshevism of Trotsky' — *i.e.* before 1917. Of Bukharin, he wrote with some ambiguity, describing him as 'the most valuable and biggest theorist of the Party', but going on to accuse him of scholasticism and to express 'the greatest doubt' whether he could be regarded as 'fully Marxist'; for 'he has never learned, and I think has never fully understood, the dialectic'. Finally, Lenin spoke of Y. Pyatakov (1890-1937) as 'a man undoubtedly distinguished in will and ability, but too much given over to administration and the administrative side of things to be relied on in a serious political situation'. The last two were picked out for comment as the ablest of the Central Committee's younger members : there was no explicit recommendation as to the succession, except the negative recommendation that Stalin should be removed from the secretaryship. But, of course, Lenin's words, which could not be altogether withheld from knowledge, were very damaging to Zinoviev and Kamenev as well as to Stalin ; and that makes it all the more remarkable that these three should have stepped jointly into the succession.

The explanation is, of course, in part that the battle for the succession had been in progress for a long time before Lenin's death and had been going very badly for Trotsky, who was quite exceptionally bad at intrigue. Indeed, the break between Trotsky and the triumvirs had actually reached a decisive point the month before Lenin's death, with the publication in *Pravda* of the first of his letters on the *New Course* — subsequently embodied in the booklet he issued under that title a few months later. In attacking both the 'Old Bolsheviks' and the growth of bureaucracy in the Communist Party, Trotsky was tilting both at Zinoviev and Kamenev and at Stalin, well knowing that these three, who had already in effect taken over the direction of affairs, were already united for the purpose of destroying his influence. He remained, indeed, at this period a member of the Party's Politburo, as well as President of the War Council ; but his connection with the Politburo had already become hardly more than nominal, and he was already shut out from the inner councils of the Party, which had come more and more under Stalin's control. Stalin, however, did not feel strong enough at the time of Lenin's death to bid for the succession alone. He needed Zinoviev, who was both at the head of the Comintern and strongly entrenched in the Petrograd section of the Party ; and he also needed Kamenev, who occupied a central position of prestige in the 'Old Bolshevik' group. With the help of these allies, he saw his way to the elimination of Trotsky, despite his wide popularity and prestige ; and he proceeded to reinforce his position by means of a mass recruitment of picked new members — largely handpicked by his bureaucracy — to the ranks of the Party. In the course of this campaign nearly a quarter of a million new members — all drawn from the industrial proletariat — were admitted to the Party : a measure which Trotsky least of all could oppose, for he had been strongly urging the reinforcement of its proletarian basis.

It took a year from the date of Lenin's death to render Trotsky's position as a high officer-holder intolerable. During this year an intensive campaign against him was carried on by means of the party machine ; and in January 1925 he was forced into resigning his last public office, that of President of the Council of War. For almost another year the alliance between Stalin, Zinoviev, and Kamenev remained formally unbroken. But in December 1925, at the Fourteenth Party Congress, the allies fell out ; and within the few months the followers of Trotsky, Zinoviev, and Kamenev were acting together against Stalin in a new opposition. The development of this opposition followed on certain decisions taken, with the support of Zinoviev and Kamenev, earlier in the year. These included substantial concessions to the peasants, including new elections to a large proportion of the Peasant Soviets, which were held to have been chosen at unreal elections dominated by the local bureaucrats of the Communist Party. Orders had gone out to the party activists not to bully the peasants or persecute the *kulaks* ; and the freedom of *kulaks* and middle peasants to lease additional land and hire wage-labour had been substantially enlarged. Zinoviev and Kamenev took fright as this policy of conciliation began to take effect and as a fresh crisis began to develop because of the shortage of the industrial goods the peasants wanted to buy. They began to fear that the critics of N.E.P. had been right after all, and that the policy of giving way to the peasants and encouraging the private traders was becoming stabilised so as to present an insuperable barrier to Socialism. Accordingly, they began to echo Trotsky's demands for greater investment in large-scale industry and to call for a campaign against the *kulaks* and Nepmen. Stalin, characteristically, hit back hard at his critics, denying that their picture of the situation was correct and claiming that actually state and Co-operative trading were gaining ground at the expense of private trade and middle peasants profiting more than *kulaks* from the concessions and increasing in relative numbers. But at the same time Stalin adopted a part of his opponents' policy by accepting a stepping-up of industrial investment and agreeing that the increase should be directed especially to heavy industry, as a step towards making the Soviet Union independent of imports of machinery and other capital goods. With this policy he heavily defeated the rest of the opposition's proposals and criticisms and was able further to consolidate his hold on the Party and the Government. When M. V. Frunze (b. 1885), the Commissar for War, died in 1926, K. E. Voroshilov (b. 1881), Stalin's closest ally, replaced him, and M. Lashevich (1884–1928), who had been Frunze's deputy and a follower of Zinoviev, was removed from office. In October 1926 Trotsky was at length formally removed from the Politburo, thus losing his last recognition as a leader. But it took another two years to finish off the opposition. Though Zinoviev's control over the Petrograd Party had been broken early in 1926, soon after the Fourteenth Congress, another year was needed to evict him from the presidency of the Comintern ; and it was not until October 1927 that the remaining oppositionists were removed from the Party's Central Committee. A month later Trotsky and Zinoviev were both expelled from the Party. Zinoviev characteristically soon recanted his errors and was readmitted to the Party, though not to his former influence. Trotsky was first exiled to Siberia in 1928 and then, the following year, expelled from the Soviet Union to Turkey. It was not yet the fashion to execute dissenters who had been high up in the Party's counsels before their fall from grace. That came only later, when Stalin had become complete master and the 'personality cult' was reaching its height. But disagreement, denounced as 'fractionalism', had already become a heinous political crime.

Five years thus intervened between Lenin's death and

Trotsky's final expulsion from the Soviet Union. A very much shorter time was to elapse before Stalin was not merely carrying out the greater part of Trotsky's economic policy, but going a long way beyond it by the resort to agricultural collectivisation on an enormous scale. The part of Trotsky's programme that was not carried out was his demand for a reversal of the bureaucratic tendencies within the Communist Party. On the contrary, these tendencies continued to increase, as they were bound to do as personal more and more replaced collective leadership. Stalin's ascendancy also meant an increasing shift of the seat of power from the Soviets and the nominal Government responsible to them to the Party, which was under much more highly centralised control. Constitutionally, the Soviet Union was a federal State, made up of a number of independent Republics, of which the Russian was by far the largest; and though many key functions were in the hands of the Union, the Republics and the lesser Governments within them possessed considerable autonomous powers. The Soviets, at the higher levels, were mainly dominated by party members, and could be fairly well relied upon not to act against the Party's will; but at the village level it was often difficult, under N.E.P., to secure willing compliance except by rigging the elections — a process which, as appeared in the middle years of N.E.P., was liable to provoke peasant anger and even resistance. The Communist Party, on the other hand, was a unitary body covering the whole Soviet Union, with no autonomous fractions in the separate Republics or Regions — though it had, of course, its branches in all the important centres. It was organised as a single Party on the principle of 'democratic centralism', which was coming more and more to mean that policies were determined at the centre by the national, or supra-national, leadership and then passed down as orders which the entire Party was called on to obey without question. There were indeed still Party Congresses, and also Party Conferences of less authority, from which the leadership needed to get endorsement of its decisions; and debates on policy could still take place at these gatherings and also in the branches on issues on which no authoritative decision had yet been taken. But it became, from the middle 'twenties onwards, practically impossible to put forward policies that ran counter to those of the official leadership without being accused of 'fractionalism' and threatened with expulsion, which was freely resorted to against those deemed guilty of 'deviation'. The 'one Party', which had monopolised power after the Left Social Revolutionaries' departure from the Government over the issue of the Brest-Litovsk Treaty, had in its early days allowed a good deal of scope for the expression of conflicting opinions and even for the formation of groups to advocate them up to the time when a decision was officially pronounced. But under Stalin's leadership, and above all in the course of his bitter struggle against Trotsky, this relative freedom of discussion was rapidly destroyed, and the Communist Party was turned into a monolithic instrument for the enforcement of rigid obedience to whatever orders came down from the central leadership. It was not difficult for Stalin, with his heavy hand on every part of the party machine, to make sure that Conferences and Congresses should endorse what they were told to endorse ; and the compliance of the party bureaucrats in bringing this about was ensured by the knowledge in each man's mind that his continued tenure of office depended on faithful execution of directions and hints that came to him from the central machine.

'Democratic centralism' thus ceased to bear any resemblance to democracy, save on the assumption that democracy meant simply the unified action of the Party under the guidance of its central *élite* — which was precisely what Stalin did mean by it. For, according to Bolshevik theory, just as there could be only one Party expressing the collective will of the working class, so there could be only one policy that Party could correctly pursue, and this one policy must find expression through the party's leadership. To attempt to base policy on the untutored notions of the rank and file would mean a babel of conflicting voices, which would inhibit united action and lead the Party back to the discredited practices of 'bourgeois liberalism'. Only monolithic thinking could give the assurance of monolithic action ; and monolithic thinking could be secured only if conflicting opinions were kept from being heard. No doubt, many party members were unaware of what was happening to the Party and honestly regarded Trotsky's onslaughts on party bureaucracy as treasonable plottings against the Revolution he had done so much to make. Stalin could not have managed the Party so efficiently, or established his own ascendancy so firmly, had he not been able to persuade great numbers of Communists that he was doing no more than carry out faithfully and to the letter the precepts of Lenin and the true spirit of Marxism. He was able to persuade them of this because this view of his conduct was partly correct. Lenin had preached up intolerance as a revolutionary virtue, had been ready enough to fling charges of treason at old Socialist comrades who rejected Bolshevism, and had often not minced his words in speaking even of fellow-Bolsheviks whom he believed to be following a wrong line. But he had believed, none the less, in the virtue of open discussion as a means of arriving at an agreed policy among comrades, and had held bureaucracy in plainly genuine abhorrence. His bark, except at moments of acute crisis, had always been a good deal worse than his bite. Stalin, on the other hand, bit worse than he barked : the 'rudeness' or 'roughness' of which Lenin accused him was a matter even more of action than of words.

Having a centralised Party at his disposal, with an immense bureaucratic machine, Stalin found it easier to govern the Soviet Union by means of the Party than by indirect rule through the Soviet structure. Lenin had been at the head of the Party and of the Soviet Government. Stalin preferred to exert his power as Secretary of the Party, without holding any government office. This involved the development of a curious dual system of authority, in which laws and decrees, equally binding, could emerge from either the Soviet Congress or its Central Executive or its Presidium or alternatively from the Communist Party through its Congress or its Central Committee with its two immensely powerful Political and Organisation Bureaux. It became a mere matter of convenience to the leadership which channel was used. The dictatorship, vested nominally in the workers and peasants as co-operating classes, came in practice to be vested in the Communist Party, which was deemed to represent these classes, with the industrial workers predominant as the 'vanguard' of the class movement as a whole. The Soviet structure, which itself gave a preferred representation to the industrial workers as compared with the peasants, could still be used when such use seemed expedient ; but to an ever-growing extent the major policies were not merely worked out under the auspices of the Party, but also put into effect by its direct authority. In this again Stalin was following a lead which had been given by Lenin himself at the moment of the Revolution, for, as we saw, Lenin had insisted that the November *coup* should be carried through as far as possible under party auspices and control. After the *coup*, however, Lenin had constructed what was in form a Soviet and not a Communist Party structure of government and had himself acted officially as the President of a Council of People's Commissars deriving its authority from the Soviets and not from the Party. Stalin's decision to rule the Soviet Union from his party office rather than from the Council of Commissars was thus a most important constitutional decision which converted the entire Soviet structure into an appendage of the dominant Party.

That Stalin chose to act in this way may have been partly due to the fact that he was in a much better position for defeating Trotsky on the battleground of the Party than if the struggle had needed to be fought out mainly in the Soviets. In the Party he could make much more effective use of the fact that Trotsky was not an 'Old Bolshevik', but a new-comer with a Menshevik past. He could appeal to his fellow-veterans in the Party against the upstart, and could accuse Trotsky of wishing to undermine the Party's influence. He could, moreover, reckon on Trotsky's playing into his hands by allowing himself to seem to be attacking the Party when he attacked its 'Old Guard' and, however popular he might be among the masses, to antagonise a high proportion of those who held office in the party machine. Trotsky, on his side, appears to have been singularly unaware how many enemies he was making, and to have most remarkably underestimated both Stalin's ability in intrigue and the consequences of his own imperious and often contemptuous manner of handling his adversaries. Max Eastman, in his estimate of Trotsky's behaviour during the struggle, credits him, I think, with much too much nobility of character for his failure to answer back his calumniators during the period when Stalin and his allies were mobilising all their resources for a sustained onslaught. The explanation of Trotsky's conduct at this time is partly, as Eastman says, that he was seriously ill at a critical stage ; but it is also that he was unduly contemptuous and was quite unable to believe that his prestige could be so effectively destroyed. Whatever the explanation, he undoubtedly did play right into his enemies' hands.

What, in retrospect, were the real issues between Stalin and Trotsky ? It is none too easy to say ; for, as Lenin foresaw in his 'Testament', there was a very large element of sheerly personal antagonism, which made it impossible for the two to share power, or even to co-exist in the same country. It is sometimes suggested that the real issue was that of 'Socialism in one country' as against Trotsky's belief that the Russian Revolution could survive only if it could be turned into a World Revolution. Doubtless Trotsky, like Lenin, did hold this latter view in the early years after 1917 ; and he continued to hold it in the sense that he continued to maintain his doctrine of the 'permanent Revolution',[1] which involved a belief that the Russian Revolution was bound in due course to spread throughout the capitalist world. But Stalin, too, believed in the World Revolution : by 'Socialism in One Country' he meant only that it was possible to consolidate Socialism in the Soviet Union even if the spread of the Revolution to other countries was considerably delayed, and without waiting for it. Did Trotsky, after the defeat of the attempted German Communist *coup* of 1921, hold any very different view ? In one sense, yes ; but only because he believed that the Russian Revolution could not maintain itself without its reinforcement by Revolutions elsewhere, unless the Soviet Union both embarked on large schemes of industrialisation, centred on the heavy industries, and maintained its own revolutionary spirit by sustaining the revolutionary feeling of the Communist Party membership and urging them on to a renewed internal struggle against *kulaks* and Nepmen and against bureaucracy and traditionalism within the Party itself. Certainly, Trotsky's main quarrel with Stalin had at this time very little to do with international policy or with the affairs of the Comintern. The conception of 'permanent Revolution' entered into it in relation to internal policy — to the notion that the Revolution in Russia itself must be pressed ceaselessly forward — rather than in relation to the Soviet Union's dealings with the outside world.

The immediate issues were thus related mainly to the

[1] Trotsky's book bearing this title was written in 1928 and published in 1930.

question of industrialisation and to the place of the peasantry in the Revolution ; but on neither of these matters was there in reality a conflict of principle. Stalin, no less than Trotsky, believed in the need for the Soviet Union to become highly industrialised and to build up its heavy industries so as to make itself independent of imported supplies of capital goods. This was indeed an indispensable element in the establishment of 'Socialism in One Country' — much more so than if the Soviet Union had been able to draw supplies of capital goods from Communist Governments in the West. Nor had Stalin any love for peasants, or any wish to pander to them more than he was compelled to do — or to Nepmen either. No sooner was Trotsky out of the way than Stalin began to adopt the very policy in relation to industry that his rival had favoured ; and his methods in carrying through the collectivisation of agriculture were certainly far more ruthless in their effects on the peasants than anything Trotsky had proposed. In both these matters there was a difference about the appropriate timing ; but not much more than that, except that Stalin went much the further of the two. The really fundamental difference concerned the nature of the Party ; and even that developed largely because Stalin was in control of the party machine and Trotsky was not.

Yet Trotsky was too popular and prestigeful to be got rid of, unless he could be firmly labelled as 'Public Enemy Number One'. A vast anti-Trotsky myth had to be built up and implanted deeply in the consciousness of all good Communists. Trotsky had to be made into a symbolic figure of Caesarism, in order to conceal the growth of Stalin's personal domination. He had to be pursued, even in exile, with fantastic charges, because such charges could be used as a basis for the liquidation of Stalin's subsequent enemies, and also because there always remained groups of 'Trotskyists' strong enough to present a danger to orthodox Communist Parties outside Russia, and perhaps even inside as well. The story of Trotsky and of Trotskyism after Trotsky had been driven out of the Soviet Union belongs to a period that falls outside the limits of this volume. So does the history of the Soviet Union from the beginning of the Five-Year Plan and the drive for agricultural collectivisation. The present instalment ends with

Stalin's decisive victory and with the break-up of the triumvirate that held power for a year or two after Lenin's death.

It remains, in bringing this chapter to a close, to consider
briefly wherein consisted Lenin's contribution to the development of Socialist thought. I had a good deal to say about this
in an earlier volume of this study, in relation to Lenin's development up to 1914 ; [1] and I have no intention of going over that
ground again. I have also tried to make clear Lenin's part in
the destruction of what was left of the Second International
after 1914, and in the establishment of the Comintern. [2] But
at this point some attempt at a general appreciation seems to
be needed. To what extent was Lenin a faithful interpreter
and developer of Marx's doctrine, as he claimed to be, or a
perverter of Marxism, who led a large fraction of the world's
Socialists into a disastrous aberration from Social Democracy
and, under pretence of setting up the dictatorship of the
working class, in fact established the dictatorship of a monolithic Party over the common people ? I cannot hope to find
an answer that will satisfy more than a few readers ; for
Lenin's personality and achievements raise very strong emotions
and it is not easy to be objective in passing judgment.

First and foremost, it is evident that Lenin was a devoted
professional revolutionary. He gave his whole life to the cause
of revolution, and it never entered into his head either to
question the rightness of revolutionary action, or to set up any
other objective in competition with it as a motive. There can
hardly have been a moment in his waking life when he was not
thinking of and for the Revolution, so completely did the
revolutionary idea permeate all his studies and doings. Such
an attitude is, of course, abnormal, and was so even for a
Russian under the Czarist régime, though in Czarist Russia
not a few lesser men came near to it in the days of their youth,
and some maintained it all their lives out of an overmastering
hatred for the repressive system and for the bitter oppression
of the common people. How far Lenin was led to this state
of mind by the execution of his elder brother it is impossible
to say ; but undoubtedly he was deeply affected by that tragic
event. At all events, the destruction of Czarism and therewith

[1] See Vol. III, Part I, Chapters IX and X.
[2] See Chapter II of present vol.

presently of all oppressive Governments throughout the world became his passion and became linked inseparably in his mind with the victory of the oppressed classes over their class-enemies. He became a Marxist, and came to conceive of this victory as the triumph of the working class — the proletariat — over the bourgeoisie, with whom he grouped in his mind all the oppressors — monarchs, militarists, feudal landowners, bureaucrats, and police — indeed the entire apparatus of militarism, feudalism, and the police State in all its forms. It did not worry him at all that the Marxian diagnosis did not truly fit at all well the Russian situation, with which he was primarily concerned. He was well aware that in Czarist Russia capitalism was still a feeble, though a rapidly rising, force, and that the main body of the oppressed was made up, not of industrial workers — proletarians in the strict sense — but of peasants, some with a little land and some with none, whose outlook differed widely from that of industrial wage-earners. He gave much thought to the problem of the bourgeois Revolution in Russia, involving a struggle between the rising capitalists and the feudal elements, and also to that of the relation between proletarians and peasants in the struggle against both capitalism and feudalism. But whereas the general framework of his action was the largely pre-capitalist Russian society of the late nineteenth century, the framework of his general theory was that of a Marxism conceived mainly in terms of the advanced capitalist societies of the West, and he was continually adapting Marxism to the conditions prevailing in Russia and in other less advanced countries, rather than working out a theory of his own in terms of Russian conditions. The result was a Marxism that, while retaining the basic concepts of Marx's theory, differed considerably from Marx's own conception and still more from the Social Democracy of most of the Marxist epigoni of the West. Though he was deeply versed in the Marxian scriptures and in the literature of Western as well as of Russian Socialism, and though he had lived long in the West, he always saw situations primarily in Russian terms when he was planning active policies, and tended to transplant to other countries the precepts he had derived from his consideration of Russian needs. Of Western capitalism he tended to have two different visions, one taken straight from Marx and reflecting mainly the conditions of the 1840s and 1850s, on which Marx's diagnosis was largely based, and the other derived from a study of modern capitalism chiefly in its colonialist and imperialist aspects, rather than in its later developments at home. He was thus prone to a somewhat exaggerated view of the nature of capitalist exploitations of the proletariat in the advanced capitalist countries and to a judgment of contemporary capitalism based on its worst aspects — intensive exploitation of colonial peoples and internecine rivalries pointing the way to war ; and these attitudes put him out of all sympathy with reformism, both by hiding from him the real improvements that it had brought about in a number of countries and by giving him the assurance that reformist policies were impotent either to end colonial exploitation or to prevent war. He was none the less, up to 1914, a great admirer of the German Social Democratic Party, both because he thought highly of its closely knit, efficient organisation and because he took its revolutionary phraseology at its face value. The Germans, as he saw the matter, would have to make a Revolution in order to get rid of the Kaiser and the militarists, just as the Russians would have to, in order to get rid of Czarism ; and he believed, until 1914, that Kautsky and the anti-Revisionist German Socialists saw this as clearly as he did himself. He never understood, before 1914, how completely most of them had pushed this vital issue out of their thoughts and had come to think in terms of a coming parliamentary victory that would somehow clear the road for a sudden change-over to a Socialist society. He believed that the Germans, when they spoke of revolution, meant a Revolution in the same sense as he had in view : he took Kautsky for a great revolutionary theorist, when he was only repeating Marxian phrases that had lost their significance in face of German Social Democracy's parliamentary advance. Of other Western Socialist movements he knew much less, and he was not much impressed by what he knew. He greatly exaggerated the strength of potential revolutionary feeling in the West, and was apt to believe that this feeling *must* exist and needed only a disciplined revolutionary leadership to bring it into action. Hence his zeal for the creation of Communist Parties led exclusively by revolutionary devotees and for unrelenting war upon Centrists, even more than upon the right wing, at the cost of splitting the Socialist movements of the West at a point which was liable to isolate the new Communist Parties from the masses, rather than to make them effective instruments for drawing the masses behind them. In Russia, it was possible for the Bolsheviks, starting as a small, disciplined group, to make short work of the Mensheviks, and of the vast but formless Social Revolutionary Party. Lenin could not see why this triumph could not be repeated elsewhere : he did not realise that what had made it possible in Russia was the sheer fluidity of the situation after the collapse of Czarism, the weakness of the liberal elements in the population, and the entire absence of any practical middle policy, whereas in the West moderate reformist policies, whether sound or not, were thoroughly practicable and were bound to have a strong attraction for a considerable part of the industrial working class, as well as for substantial petty bourgeois groups.

So far as Russia was concerned, no-one saw more clearly than Lenin that the Revolution could be neither made nor maintained without mass peasant support. From 1917 onwards he was continually insistent that the union, or alliance, between industrial workers and peasants had to be taken seriously, as a real union and not merely as a euphemism for the action of the industrial workers in dragging the peasants along behind them. He was, indeed, strongly anti-*kulak*, because he well understood the danger of the mass of the peasants falling under *kulak* leadership and being thus drawn into the orbit of the bourgeoisie. This led him to emphasise the difference between *kulaks* and poor peasants and the need to stir up class-war in the villages. But it also led him later to take the middle peasants under his wing, because he saw that they represented the main element of productive support for the Revolution, to which so many of them owed their land. Lenin had no love for peasant agriculture, which he regarded as primitive and as destined to disappear. But he had no hesitation in 1917 in adopting the land policy of the Left Social Revolutionaries, though he was well aware that the immediate effect was bound to be an entrenchment of the peasant system. The needs of the Revolution meant that the main body of peasants must be on its side ; and the Revolution's needs were paramount. Lenin was impatient of those who argued that the industrial workers, as the spearhead of the Revolution, ought to dictate to the peasants and force them into Socialist causes against their will. Doubtless the time would come when it would be possible to reorganise agriculture as a large-scale industry, and therewith to render it immensely more productive. But one prerequisite for this was universal electrification and another the building of an industrial structure capable of supplying the countryside with an abundance of the products needed for a better standard of life. Pending these achievements, the peasants had to be given freedom to cultivate the land in their own way, which could not be a Socialist way. They should be given this freedom as the partners of the industrial workers in the workers' and peasants' dictatorship, not treated as mere drudges and conveniences for a ruling oligarchy of industrial workers.

Of course, in insisting on this real partnership, Lenin held to the view that the industrial proletariat was the spearhead of the Revolution and was destined to be the leader in the tasks of Socialist construction. The peasants, despite their indispensability, could be no more than junior partners ; but this was very different from being slaves. It was the Left Opposition that carried contempt for the peasants to the length of wishing to treat them as mere subjects, whose historic mission was simply to feed the towns as cheaply as possible in terms of industrial goods — and to fight, as Red Army soldiers, the battles of the industrial proletariat. Trotsky sometimes came near to this view, but was kept from falling right into it by his high respect for the Army he had made and by his belief that army service could be a powerful means of teaching peasants to think and feel differently, so as to become valuable recruits to the Socialist cause. That was why Trotsky found supporters in the villages, despite his emphasis on rapid industrialisation and his hostility to the rising class of middle peasants, as well as to the *kulaks*. But it was Lenin who, in the last years of his life, kept on insisting that the main body of the peasants must be treated as allies, and not as mere beasts of burden without rights of their own.

In relation to the industrial workers, Lenin's insistence on the supreme rôle of the Party in the building of the new society made him strongly hostile to whatever savoured to him of sectionalism — that is, of the pursuit of corporate egoistic aims as distinct from the aims of the working class as a whole. From an early stage he had realised the importance of Trade Unionism as a means of organising the workers and arousing in them a spirit of revolt ; but he had been bitterly opposed to 'Economism'[1] and to all who wished the Trade Unions to devote their main attention to the mere improvement of working conditions. He had insisted that the Party must set out to dominate the Trade Unions and to turn them into reliable revolutionary instruments ; and, when the Revolution had been made, he was hostile to those who wished the Unions to assume the control of socialised industry, holding that such a system would simply serve to entrench the corporate egoisms of the various trades. He was even more hostile to the idea that the factory committee of each establishment should be allowed to become the controlling power, preferring to see power in the hands of big centralised Trade Unions, which could be more easily controlled by the Party, to seeing it diffused among a host of autonomous corporations subject to little or no central direction. But he was against both these solutions, and strongly in favour of responsible one-man management as against any form of 'workers' control'. Seeing the proletariat as a class, which must be closely integrated for the fulfilment of its constructive tasks, he carried over into industry the conception of 'democratic centralism' which he had played the leading part in building up in the Party itself. He nevertheless opposed Trotsky's notions of militarising industry and turning the Trade Unions into subordinate government agencies, because he understood the importance of keeping Trade Unionism revolutionary and neither crushing it into the mould of bureaucracy nor, in attempting to do so, provoking widespread working-class revolt.

In handling Russian affairs, Lenin, given his revolutionary assumptions, showed himself again and again an eminently sensible person. If he was a fanatic, he never let his fanaticism run away with him in his handling of internal Russian problems, and, in the matter of means, he had an astonishing faculty of choosing the right course at the right moment. This very

[1] See Vol. III, Part I, p. 423.

flair naturally led him to advocate widely different ways of action at different times, and brought down on him the charge of inconsistency, and even of opportunism. If, however, it was assumed that the one valid objective was to make and consolidate the Revolution — and this was Lenin's postulate throughout — neither of these charges could be sustained ; for Lenin, even if he made some mistakes, always acted in complete consistency with this object. But what *was* the Revolution, to which everything else had to give way ? Was it just *any* Revolution that would avail to overthrow the Czar and the autocracy and to tumble the capitalists from their seats of power, regardless of what might replace them ? Certainly not, in Lenin's mind. It was the proletarian Revolution, that was to establish for a time the dictatorship of the proletariat, under which class-distinctions were to be swept away and the road was to be made clear for the advent of a classless society, the 'government of men' to be replaced by the 'administration of things', and the State, that instrument of class-coercion, to wither away. Lenin had, in these respects, a clear vision of the Revolution he was striving to bring about, and regarded this kind of Revolution as *the* Revolution that was growing in the womb of history, and was necessary and inevitable, however many set-backs might be met with on the road to it. He did not think of himself as making the Revolution, but rather as acting as midwife to it. For him, the Revolution already existed as a future fact : it needed, not to be made, but only to be speeded up and sensibly guided. This, of course, was all part of the Marxist gospel, and Lenin made no new contribution to defining the aims. Like Marx, he had no use for utopian visions of the coming society, in which mankind would begin to 'make its own history'. His exclusive concern was with the means towards an end already, in his view, well enough defined. The means, however, could not but affect the end, at any rate for a long time to come. If, in order to make and consolidate the Revolution, it was necessary to create a highly disciplined, centralised Party wielding an enormous apparatus of power ; if it was necessary to bring under the control of the Party not only the whole fabric of government but also every social institution capable of playing a formative part in its development ; if it was necessary to thrust into outer darkness everyone who ventured to dispute the Party's pre-eminence, or even to express dissent from its adopted policies, was it likely that out of such a situation would come the abnegation of power over men and the flourishing of the free spirit that was expected to characterise the classless society of the future ? Was there not an immense danger that the Party, practising dictatorship in order to destroy the very possibility of a return to the old order, would fall in love with its own authority and be most unwilling to renounce it when the danger of counter-revolution was no longer there ? Would not bureaucracy act as a canker at the heart of the dictatorship, and offer to any man who could establish a firm hold on it the chance of turning the dictatorship — no longer that of the workers, or even of the Party — into an engine of personal power ?

Lenin was by no means unconscious of some of these dangers — especially that of bureaucratic perversion of the dictatorship. He saw the importance, as soon as the Civil War was over, of a return to a sort of democracy within the Party, and did his best, while his health lasted, to bring it about. Under Lenin, the Party did really discuss policies before they were made. But he insisted that, when they had been settled, there should be implicit obedience to them — 'democratic centralism' in the proper sense of the term. He was, I think, too little alive to the ease with which such a policy could be perverted by a power-loving leader who could make himself master of the party machine. The fears he expressed about both Stalin and Trotsky rested rather on his fear that Stalin's 'roughness' or Trotsky's impetuosity might split the Party than on any apprehension that either might make himself into a personal dictator. About Trotsky, I think he was right in not fearing this. Indeed, the fervour of Trotsky's attack on the bureaucratic tendencies within the Party was not what would have been looked for in anyone whose supreme objective was the winning of dictatorial power. Trotsky was often dictatorial in manner, but I feel sure he was not a would-be dictator. But that was just what Stalin was, as the sequel plainly showed. And the practice of 'democratic centralism' opened the road to him.

It would have done so much less had it not been possible for Stalin, when the danger of counter-revolution inside the Soviet

Union had practically disappeared, to give dictatorship a new lease of life by perpetual insistence on the continuing danger from without. The attempt to build 'Socialism in One Country' involved building it in hostility to the capitalist States that were able, in the absence of Revolution elsewhere, to encircle the Soviet Union and hamper its development, even if they hesitated to take up arms against it. This external threat was, of course, greatly intensified by the rise of Fascism, at any rate from the moment when Hitler came to power ; and it must not be overlooked that the worst excesses of Stalinism took place after that event. But, in one way or another, it was always possible to justify the continuance of the dictatorship, and the failure of the State to show any signs of even beginning to 'wither away', on the plea that the Soviet Union was in a state of perpetual siege and could not afford to relax any of its authoritative severity. Lenin died long before Fascism had become formidable, except in Italy ; but he had plenty of opportunities after 1917 of observing the facts of encirclement and boycott, and of drawing the conclusion that it would be most perilous to loosen the controls. Indeed, the very need to retreat from War Communism to N.E.P. appeared to make more than ever necessary a strengthening of the Party's hold and of the discipline required to prevent the infection of re-established private trade from spreading throughout the economy.

Lenin, however, did clearly regard the dictatorship as no more than a transitional necessity, and as destined to be relaxed, and presently given up, in the course of the advance to a society without classes. He was never, I think, a lover of power for its own sake, or corrupted by it. His ruthlessness was always subordinate to his social purpose, which was to establish, in time, a free, classless society. It is generally admitted that in his personal relations he was unassuming to a degree, friendly, and equalitarian. If he had few social graces, that was because he had so little private life, living as he did for the Revolution and for little else. If N. K. Krupskaia (1869–1939) had been less devoted to the cause, she would have had a hard time of it. Indeed, she did have a hard time, but put up with it gladly.

In a sense, it is possible to find fault with Lenin only by

falling foul of his fundamental attitude — that is, by denying that it can be legitimate for any man to make himself so entirely the servant of the Revolution that nothing else counts. If *salus Revolutionis* is *suprema lex*, there is no more to be said. But is it ? Can it be, without the very concept of the Revolution being perverted, without the ends for which the Revolution is wanted dropping half out of sight, or without *power*, though not necessarily personal power, becoming the supreme object of worship ? Surely the Revolution, however important it may be, is not an end in itself, but only a means to something else — I should say, to the greater well-being and happiness of the individuals whose lives it affects. For Lenin, I feel sure, the Revolution, even if he regarded it in some sense as a means to human well-being, had come in effect to be something passionately desired in its own right, so that its effects on individual well-being, or happiness, dropped out of sight when its claims were being considered. For Lenin took from Marx the dangerous mental habit of regarding classes as somehow more real than the individuals of which they were composed and of identifying the emancipation of the proletarian class with the well-being of its individual members. He had, I think, only a feeble sense of human individuality, and almost none of personal happiness as a valuable state of mind. He looked on men, not as individuals with private desires that needed to be satisfied to the fullest extent compatible with the equal claims of other individuals, but rather as instruments to be made use of for furthering the revolutionary cause. This attitude not only made him callous about sufferings which he deemed necessary in the interests of the Revolution, but even indifferent to them, and therefore exempt from remorse or misgiving over their infliction. It can even be argued that Lenin had no effective sense of positive justice — only, in its stead, a passionate hatred of class-injustice, which blinded him to other kinds of injustice that could not be traced to class-oppression as their cause. Having accepted the Revolution as an unquestionable aim, he was prepared without compunction to take *any* action that he believed would help towards its success, and to denounce any person who did not share this attitude. Thus, though he was not a monster of natural cruelty — as Stalin undoubtedly was, or became — there was no cruelty which he would not have been prepared to justify if he really felt it to be necessary for the Revolution's sake.

Such an attitude is, in my view, fundamentally immoral and inhuman. I hold this because I believe that nothing counts finally as valuable except the well-being and happiness of individual men and women. I believe in Revolution only when and where I am convinced that it can be used to promote such well-being and happiness, and that these goods cannot be procured by less unpleasant means. Not only do I believe this : I also hold that not to believe it is sinful, and that whoever elevates the Revolution to the rank of an end in itself or regards a class as superior to, or more real than, the individuals who make it up, is guilty of sin against the spirit of humanity. On this count, I can exonerate Lenin no more than Stalin — though Stalin added to it other and perhaps worse sins, such as personal cruelty and the desire for unlimited personal power. I recognise that the Russian Revolution was, and remains, one of the very few great and admirable events in world history, and that without Lenin's utter devotion that Revolution would almost certainly have failed. For I do not at all share the view that the victory of Socialism is predetermined and can be scientifically predicted on a Marxist basis. I hold the world's future to be uncertain and unpredictable ; and for that reason I am all the more inclined, despite what I have found to criticise, to pay tribute to the man who, having achieved the Revolution almost by the sole power of his personal will, showed such mastery, till illness removed him from the helm, in steering it through the prodigious difficulties that beset it after its initial success.

Yet this praise of Lenin as the inspirer and leader of the great Russian Revolution cannot be left unqualified. His zeal for the Revolution and his interpretation of Marxism, which arose out of it, rendered him unable to see men as they really were, or to appreciate any quality in them apart from their capacity to contribute to, or to obstruct, the revolutionary cause. He believed most firmly that the only factor that counted in the making of history was class-interest, and that men in the mass would always act in accordance with this interest. When he was told, by Radek or by such Western Socialists as he had dealings with, that the proletariats of the advanced Western countries had for the most part no desire or will to resort to violence and civil war for the overthrow of their capitalist ruling classes, he simply refused to believe that this could be true, and persisted in holding that the Western Communist Parties, if they behaved with proper energy and resource, would be easily able to detach them from their obedience to their 'traitorous' leaders. The industrial workers, in his view, were absolutely destined to accomplish the proletarian Revolution ; and because this was so, he was prepared to split every working-class movement, in the complete confidence that the main body of the proletariat would speedily rally everywhere behind the Communists and would desert the 'social traitors' to follow the revolutionary lead. He was entirely unable to credit that any other consideration than class-interest, as he conceived it, could count in face of the appeal to class-solidarity. When Radek and others attempted to dissuade him from ordering the Red Army to advance on Warsaw by telling him that the Polish workers would not rally to its side, he was quite incredulous, and is said to have dismissed their fears with the remark, 'Let us test them with bayonets'. This blindness to the real force of the complex motives which move men to action may have served him well in relation to the Revolution in Russia itself ; but it led him, in relation to Germany and to the West, into the disastrous miscalculation which determined the policy of the Comintern in splitting the working-class movements of the Western countries in such a way as to make certain that the Communist Parties, instead of isolating the 'social traitors', would isolate themselves. The 'myth' of the coming World Revolution, resting on this theory of the universal preponderance of the class-war notion over everything else, so dominated Lenin's thought as to blind him to the very existence of the forces that furnished his enemies with their main basis of support. His greatness as the leader of revolutionary Russia had, as its antithesis, his disastrous misreading of the international situation through his failure to understand that most men are not simply units in a class, but also individuals moved by a diversity of motives of which, having no experience in himself, he did not accept the reality in others.

CHAPTER XVIII

THE UKRAINE

To the south of Russia proper lies the Ukraine, now a constituent Republic of the Soviet Union and, with White Russia farther north, recognised by the United Nations as a sovereign State. The Ukraine has its own language, or at least dialect, and had developed in the course of the nineteenth century a not inconsiderable literature of its own, including the work of at any rate one poet of high rank, Taras Shevchenko. It had also developed its own nationalist movement, mainly on a cultural basis, but with an increasing political element, which received a strong stimulus during the Russian Revolution of 1905. There was, however, much uncertainty about the extent of territory that could properly be called Ukrainian. The major area, the Eastern Ukraine, was part of the Russian empire ; but the Western Ukraine, comprising the eastern part of Galicia, was under Austrian rule, and in Galicia the Poles formed the dominant group, with Polish landlords exercising authority over Ukrainian peasants, but with Lvov, or Lemberg, as a centre of Ukrainian cultural nationalism. Michael Hrushevsky (1866–1934), the future leader of the Ukrainian Government of 1917, was a professor at Lvov University. Outside the Ukraine proper, East and West, there were large areas in the Russian border provinces inhabited by peoples, often called Ruthenians, who spoke languages or dialects closely akin to Ukrainian, but had for the most part no consciousness of nationality and no share in the Ukrainian nationalist movement ; and there were similar peoples under Hungarian rule in the Carpathian territory which became part of Czechoslovakia after 1918. In the Russian Ukraine there were considerable Russian populations in the larger towns, such as Kharkov and Kiev, and there had been much russification of the landowning classes ; but the countryside remained essentially Ukrainian.

Prior to 1917, both nationalist and Socialist movements had developed in both East and West Ukraine. In the West, the Ukrainian Social Democrats constituted one of the autonomous sections of the federal Austrian Social Democratic Party ; and in the East, Bohdan Iaroshevsky (1869–1914) had founded at the beginning of the century a Ukrainian Socialist Party, which in 1903 amalgamated with the left-wing nationalist Revolutionary Ukrainian Party, the combined body taking the name of Ukrainian Social Democratic Labour Party in 1905. The year before, in 1904, the Ukrainian Social Democratic Union had been founded as a section of the All-Russian S.D.P. There was also a non-Socialist Ukrainian Democratic Party, with a nationalist outlook. Panas Matiushenko, the leader of the *Potemkin* mutineers in 1905, was a Ukrainian : he was captured and hanged when, after escaping abroad, he returned to Russia in 1907. Of course, great numbers of Ukrainians served in the Czarist armed forces, and many learned to speak Russian as well as Ukrainian. There was a conflict between, on the one hand, the Russians and russianised Ukrainians of the towns, who tended to think in terms of an all-Russian Revolution against Czarism, and, on the other, those Ukrainians who gave their primary loyalty to Ukrainian nationalism. Most of the Ukrainian leaders, however, were not laying plans for an independent Ukrainian State. The Galician Ukrainians greatly preferred Austrian to Russian rule, and aimed only at autonomy within a federal Austrian empire ; while the Russian Ukrainians mostly had in mind a federalised Russian Republic, within which there would be room for national autonomy of the numerous peoples then under Czarist rule.

So matters stood at the time of the first Russian Revolution of 1917. The Ukrainians took their share in this Revolution, and the fall of Czarism compelled them to define their attitude to the new Provisional Government in Petrograd. In March 1917 a Ukrainian Provisional Government with a popular assembly — the Rada (Council) — was proclaimed under Hrushevsky as President ; and the following month an All-Ukrainian National Congress met at Kiev and called for the establishment, not of a separate Ukrainian sovereign State, but of a federal Republic within which the Ukraine would constitute an autonomous unit. From March to November intermittent discussions proceeded between the Rada and the successive Provisional Governments in Petrograd ; but nothing was settled pending the meeting of the proposed All-Russian Constituent Assembly. During the summer, in the Ukraine as elsewhere, the peasants began to seize the land ; and many Ukrainian soldiers deserted from the army and made for home. Then, in November, came the Bolshevik Revolution ; and the Ukrainian leaders had again to consider what line to take. On November 20th, the Rada proclaimed the Ukrainian People's Republic, but still stopped short of demanding separation from Russia. Most of the Ukrainian leaders at first expected the speedy fall of the Bolsheviks, and still hoped for an autonomous Ukraine within a federal Republic. The Bolsheviks had little strength in the Ukraine — almost none outside the big towns — the Ukrainian Social Democratic Party, led by Volodomir Vinnichenko, being quite distinct from the Russian S.D.P. On December 26th, however, the Ukrainian Bolsheviks, with help from Russia, proclaimed a Ukrainian Soviet Republic at Kharkov, in opposition to the Rada Government ; and desultory fighting began, with most of the Ukraine in the Rada's hands. Then came the Germans, in search of food supplies for their half-starving population and very ready to take the Ukraine under their control and use it against the Bolsheviks and, perhaps, when they had won the war, treat it as an area for German colonisation and as a stage in the drive to the East. The Germans recognised the Rada Government as the representative of an independent Ukraine, and summoned its delegates to the negotiations at Brest-Litovsk ; and the Bolsheviks, when they were forced to sign the Brest-Litovsk Treaty, had therein to recognise the Ukraine's independence and to renounce authority over the area assigned to it. Vinnichenko, who had been Prime Minister, was displaced in favour of the more right-wing Social Revolutionary, Vsevolod Holubovich, and the Rada found itself called upon to govern under conditions laid down by the occupying German authorities. This arrangement did not last long. In April 1918, with German support, the reactionary Hetman, Paul Petrovich Skoropadsky, a largely russianised nobleman, seized power and ousted the Rada Government ; he stayed in dictatorial power, subject to the Germans, until the great war ended with the collapse of the Central Powers in November 1918. Then Skoropadsky was at once overthrown, and a Republican Directory, with Vinnichenko as Prime Minister, took control, and found itself involved in war with the Bolshevik Government, with the complication that, for a while, the occupying German forces remained in the country, until they were gradually withdrawn under the orders of the Allies. The Bolsheviks, meanwhile, advanced into the area controlled by the Directory and captured Kiev in February 1919. Before this, in November 1918, a West Ukrainian Government had been constituted in East Galicia, and had given in its adhesion to the Ukrainian Directory ; and, in the South, the French navy had seized Odessa and other Black Sea ports, and, under their protection, counter-revolutionary Russian 'Whites' had begun to gather their forces for an attack on the Bolsheviks. The Allied intervention in support of the 'Whites' was beginning ; but the French, having no forces adequate for an advance beyond the seaports, were uncertain what to do.

The Ukrainian Directory was also uncertain. Its conflict with the Bolsheviks inclined it rightwards, and in February 1919 Vinnichenko was ousted from the Government because of his Socialist attitude. The 'Whites', however, made no secret of their desire to restore the old régime and to hand back to the landowners the land of which the peasants had taken possession ; and this the Directory, fresh from its defeat of Skoropadsky, was by no means prepared to endorse. When Denikin, after gathering his forces and securing plenty of military and other supplies from the Allies, advanced into the Ukraine and the neighbouring regions on his anti-Bolshevik mission, the behaviour of his forces in the areas they were able to occupy immediately antagonised the entire peasant population. Irregular bands, among them those of the Anarchist Nestor Makhno (1889–1934), ravaged his lines of communication and waged guerrilla warfare against him. Early in 1918 Makhno had joined forces with the Bolsheviks against the German-controlled Rada. Then, in July, he had returned to the Southern Ukraine and had organised his guerrilla army, which, moving from place to place, proclaimed the abolition of all state government and attempted to institute an Anarchist system (or unsystem) of purely localised control. For some time Makhno maintained a loose association with the Red Army ; but in the spring of 1919 he broke with the Bolsheviks, who insisted on the incorporation of his forces into it, and became little more than a free-lance marauder. He played an important part in harrying Denikin's forces and in occupying districts in the rear of their advance ; and, when Denikin was forced to retreat, Makhno again made a temporary alliance with the Bolsheviks against him, and presently against Wrangel, the last of the counter-revolutionary commanders. The end of the war of intervention was fatal to his chances. He was forced to escape across the frontier with a few followers, and disappeared from history.[1]

Meanwhile, the official general of the Ukrainian armed forces was Simon Petliura (1879–1926), a member of the Directory with some sort of Socialist background, but primarily a nationalist with no great concern for social policy. Petliura had been active in the Rada from the beginning, and had led the military side of the revolt against Skoropadsky in November 1918. He had then become Vinnichenko's principal rival in the Directory, and had opposed any attempt to come to terms with the Bolsheviks. In February 1919 he left the Social Democratic Party, ousted Vinnichenko from the Government, and attempted to secure French support for an independent Ukraine. The French, however, were set on strengthening Poland as the centre-piece of their projected 'cordon sanitaire' against Bolshevism ; and the Poles claimed not only the formerly Austrian Western Ukraine but also a large area of mixed population, formerly under Russian rule, which was also claimed by the Ukrainians. Petliura's attempts to secure Allied recognition therefore broke down.

A period of the utmost confusion followed. The Socialists, headed by Hrushevsky and Vinnichenko, wanted to make an attempt to come to terms with the Bolsheviks and were prepared to accept a Ukrainian Soviet Republic within a federal All-Russian State, on condition that the Ukraine should be autonomous and that freedom should be preserved for rival Parties, at any rate of the left and centre. The right-wing nationalists, on the other hand, remained set on securing Allied recognition for an independent Ukraine and, in hope of this,

[1] For Makhno and his ideas, see p. 211.

sent an almost incredible number of missions to the various European capitals, as well as to the Peace Conference in Paris, to plead the national cause and to represent the Ukraine as the inflexible enemy of the Bolsheviks. In March 1919 the Hrushevsky group, objecting strongly to the Directory's proceedings, set up a Committee for the Defence of the Republic in opposition to it. Petliura, who had been supporting the Directory, thereupon modified his line, persuaded the newly formed Committee to dissolve, and replaced the Directory's Government by a mainly Social Democratic Cabinet led by Boris Martos. The right wing thereupon attempted a counter-*coup*, but were defeated, leaving Petliura in control, but of what? Of little, indeed; for most of the Ukraine was in the hands of the Red Army, or of the Poles, or of the Russian Whites and the French, who had occupied the Black Sea ports. The new Ukrainian Government was driven from one place to another, travelling in an armoured train and exercising no authority except in the narrowing area occupied by its dwindling military forces.

Meanwhile at Paris the Peace Conference, at which the Ukraine had no official representation, repeatedly debated the Ukrainian problem, but mainly with reference to the West Ukraine, where the French and Italians were strong supporters of the Polish claims, whereas Lloyd George and President Wilson were critical and wished to put pressure on Poland to halt the offensive Pilsudski had launched against the West Ukrainian Government. The Poles, however, confident of French support, persisted in their attack, and the military position in East Galicia became so serious for the West Ukrainians that dictatorial powers were conferred on Eugene Petrushevich. The dictator was unable to check the Polish advance, and before long his forces had to withdraw into the East Ukraine, leaving all Galicia in Polish hands. The Paris Peace Conference then authorised the accomplished fact, while reserving judgment about the final disposition of the disputed territory.

While the Polish invasion of East Galicia was in progress Vinnichenko had been attempting to negotiate indirectly with the Russian Soviet Government. At this time Béla Kun's Soviet Government was in power in Budapest, but was well aware that its prospects of survival were almost nil unless it could get help from Russia. Vinnichenko proposed to Béla Kun that the Russians should recognise a Soviet Government of the Ukraine based on a coalition of Socialists and Communists, and that the Ukrainians should open the road for Russian forces to advance into Hungary across the Carpathians. The Bolshevik Government rejected this proposal, denouncing Vinnichenko as a *petit bourgeois* reactionary, with whom it would have nothing to do. It had, indeed, enough on its hands in its struggle with Denikin to make it wary of so dangerous an adventure, which would have embroiled it with Rumania as well as with Poland and might well have provoked further French intervention.

By mid-June 1919, Denikin's forces had captured Kharkov, and in August they were advancing on Kiev. Petliura, reinforced by the East Galician army, was also advancing on Kiev; and the two forces reached the city at the same time and occupied it from different sides. This soon led to a dispute, and the Ukrainians were compelled to withdraw. Then the East Galician army, without Petrushevich's agreement, opened negotiations with Denikin and concluded a treaty under which it laid down its arms. Petrushevich fled to Vienna, where he continued to carry on propaganda for Galician independence. Petliura, left in a hopeless military position, carried on the struggle until November, and then took refuge in Poland. There were violent mutual recriminations between the East and West Ukrainian leaders, the former accusing the Galicians of betraying the national cause, and the latter the former of being crypto-Bolsheviks because they refused to throw in their lot with Denikin, whom the Allies were by then supporting in his claim to be the saviour of All-Russia from Bolshevik rule. There were also important religious differences among the Ukrainians, the East being Orthodox, whereas the West was Uniate and recognised the Papacy; and in addition the East was predominantly Socialist, though not Bolshevik, whereas the West was by this time under anti-Socialist leadership. Moreover, the West was primarily anti-Polish, rather than anti-Russian, whereas the East was struggling for freedom from Russian control.

The Ukrainian war thus ended for the time being in the

destruction of both Ukrainian Governments ; but Makhno and other guerrilla leaders remained in the field harrying Denikin's rear. Denikin's success in his invasion of Russia was short-lived : during the winter of 1919–20 his forces were steadily driven back, until in March 1920 he was compelled to take refuge in the Crimea, where he handed over the command to General Wrangel. Admiral Kolchak, too, was liquidated by the Red Army ; and the Allies, realising the hopelessness of the policy of armed intervention, withdrew their forces from Russian soil. The Ukrainian Soviet Republic became firmly established with help from Bolshevik Russia ; and its nationalist opponents were reduced to entire impotence, though they continued to agitate actively abroad. It was in these circumstances that Petliura, a refugee in Poland, came to terms with Pilsudski, renounced Ukrainian claims to East Galicia, and secured in return Poland's recognition of the East Ukraine's claim to independence, subject to a fixing of frontiers which conceded large predominantly Ukrainian, or Ruthenian, border areas to the Poles. Petliura had no authority from the Ukrainian Directory, which had in fact ceased to function, for entering into this agreement, and his action was roundly denounced by many of his former supporters. Hrushevsky and Vinnichenko, who presently went back to Soviet Ukraine and accepted the new order there, hotly disputed Petliura's right to make any such arrangement. The so-called 'Treaty of Warsaw', did, however, make it possible for Petliura to set to work, with Polish aid, to create a new army to co-operate with Pilsudski in invading Soviet territory. His troops, few in number, took part in the Polish invasion of the Ukraine and in the capture of Kiev in May 1920 ; and on May 25th a new Ukrainian Government was set up in that city, only to be driven out a week or two later by the advancing Red Army, which retook Kiev on June 11th, and thereafter advanced into East Galicia and before long was threatening Warsaw. Then came the halting of the Russian attack, the defeat of the Russians before Warsaw, and, in October 1920, the armistice between Russia and Poland, leading on to the Treaty of Riga in March 1921. Even after the armistice, which involved his abandonment by the Poles, Petliura did not give up hope. He managed to occupy a small area in Volhynia, and there attempted to come to an agreement with Wrangel, against whom the Red Army was now directing its main forces. But nothing came of this attempt ; and after the signing of the Riga Treaty Petliura was forced to retreat into Western Galicia, where he remained, maintaining the semblance of a Government in exile, until 1923. He then went to live in Paris, where he was assassinated three years later by a Jewish workman, Samuel Schwarzbart, in vengeance for the pogroms which had taken place in the Ukraine during his tenure of power. Petliura was a strange figure. It is misleading to call him a 'brigand', for it seems clear that he was moved by a genuine desire for Ukrainian independence, though he was quite prepared to abandon East Galicia to the Poles in hope of securing Pilsudski's support for his claims in the Eastern Ukraine. A Socialist editor in his early days and an active member of the Ukrainian Social Democratic Party, he soon shed his Socialism in the course of the national struggle and allied himself with the right-wing nationalists against Hrushevsky and Vinnichenko, and later even with Pilsudski, who had a similar Socialist-nationalist past. What talent he had was as a military leader : as a maker of political policy he was of no account. The incredibly confused condition of affairs in the Russian-Polish borderlands enabled him to become a figure of European notoriety for some years after 1917 ; but his real significance was small. There was never any prospect of the Ukraine being able to establish itself as a really independent sovereign State, apart from Russia. If the Germans had won the war, a nominally independent Ukraine might have been maintained as a German puppet ; but from the moment of Germany's defeat there was no possibility of anything other than a Soviet Ukraine closely united with Russia in what was to become the Soviet Union. If the Bolsheviks had been overthrown, and the Russian Whites had been victorious, there would have been no chance for the Ukraine even of such autonomy as was achieved under the Bolshevik régime.

As for the Ukrainian Socialists, there is not a great deal to say. On the Bolshevik side the best-known leaders were Dimitri Z. Manuilsky (1883–?), later an active figure in the Comintern, who was a Ukrainian, and Christian Rakovsky (1873–?), who was neither Ukrainian nor Russian, but a

Bulgarian from the Dobrudja who had long played a leading part in the Balkan Socialist movement and was assigned to the leadership of the Ukrainian Soviet Republic.[1] Among the non-Bolshevik leaders of the Ukrainian Socialists the principal figures were Professor Hrushevsky and Vinnichenko, the former outstanding in the cultural nationalist movement, and the latter also a literary figure as well as a politician. Iaroshevsky, the founder of the Ukrainian Socialist Party, had died in 1914 ; and apart from Petliura there was no other figure of more than local importance, unless one counts the Anarchist guerrilla, Nestor Makhno, whose peculiar outlook has already been briefly described.[2] Boris Martos and Isaac Macepa, each for a time Prime Minister, were Social Democrats. The Ukrainian Social Revolutionaries, some of whom were badly tainted with peasant anti-semitism, threw up no leader of importance.

[1] For Rakovsky, see Vol. III, Part II, p. 588.   [2] See p. 211.

CHAPTER XIX

POLAND, 1914–1931

POLAND regained its existence as an independent State at the end of the first world war, after much of its area had suffered severely in the course of the fighting. Moreover, it came into being as a State whose frontiers were undetermined, and were to remain so for several years. Its claim to independence, in the conditions of 1918, rested principally on President Wilson's Fourteen Points, in which the basis for it was the right of national self-determination. But among the Poles themselves the claim usually went well beyond this. Most Polish nationalists demanded at the least an independent Poland covering the entire area of eighteenth-century Poland before the partitions ; and this meant the inclusion within its frontiers of great numbers of Ukrainians or Ruthenians, White Russians, Lithuanians, and Germans, some of whom lived as national minórities in areas chiefly populated by Poles, but others in areas in which Poles made up only a small minority of the total. Polish nationalists, in fact, appealed not only to nationality but also to history ; and some of them even extended their claims far beyond the territories of the eighteenth-century Polish Kingdom and had hopes of a Greater Poland that would include the entire Ukraine, White Russia, all Silesia, all Lithuania, and perhaps even the entire area of the Baltic States and of East Prussia and Pomerania, if not within a unitary Polish State at least within a federal Poland allowing a limited autonomy to the major non-Polish districts.

When war broke out in 1914 there were three Polands — Russian, Austrian, and Prussian — and the inhabitants of these three territories found themselves arrayed against each other in the war — Russian Poles on one side, and Austrian and German Poles on the other. The inhabitants were called up for service in the armed forces of the three great powers and their productive resources were treated as part of each power's resources in the struggle. In the course of the war much fighting took place on Polish soil and much territory changed hands, some of it several times over. Losses were heavy, both in manpower and in production ; and hardships were very severe. For most of the war period most of Russian Poland was in German occupation, and was subject to German military government with some delegation of functions to a Polish Council set up under German military control. The Germans made great efforts during the latter part of the war to enrol Polish recruits in their armed forces and to use Russian Poland as a source of supplies, and attempted to gain favour by promising some sort of self-government, but not independence, to 'Congress' Poland after the war, but not the extension of this autonomy to Prussian or to Austrian Poland. Many Poles, as long as they thought it likely that the Central Powers would be victorious, saw their best hope in the prospect of such autonomy ; and naturally the collapse of Russia in 1917 reinforced this view until the imminence of the defeat of Germany and Austria-Hungary became manifest in the summer of 1918. Thereafter, attitudes had to be hurriedly readjusted — a process that was by no means completed when the final collapse came in October and November of that year.

Of the three Polands, Austrian Poland, or Galicia, had been by far the least discontented. The Austrian Poles, though they were not among the two dominant ruling nations of Austria-Hungary, did occupy a position of considerable recognised importance in the Austrian empire and formed an influential group in the Austrian Reichsrath. They enjoyed a substantial measure of provincial autonomy and were able to use this in ruling over the large Ukrainian, or Ruthenian, population of Galicia, consisting chiefly of poor peasants. The Austrians had, no doubt, sometimes appeared to give some backing to Ukrainian nationalist claims in order to check Polish pretensions ; but, in general, Austrian policy had been favourable to the Polish aspirations to cultural freedom, and the aristocrats of Galicia had been well content with their situation as compared with that of their fellow-nationals in Russian — or indeed in Prussian — Poland. The Galician Socialists, led by Ignacy Daszynski (1866–1936), had formed an important section of the federal Austrian Social Democratic Party ; and in 1914 they, no less than the Austrian Germans, gave their support to Austria-Hungary in the war. They continued, indeed, to favour a federal reconstruction of the Austrian empire as long as the chance of its survival remained.

The Prussian Poles had much more reason for being discontented with their position in Germany ; for they had been for a long time obstinately resisting Prussian attempts at 'germanisation' — including the planting of German settlers on the land, as well as Prussian control of education and Prussian hostility to the Catholic Church. The Poles under German rule had, however, no such means of collective self-expression as the Poles of Galicia ; and even apart from this many of them hated and feared Russia and preferred German to Russian rule. During the war Prussian Poland, remaining securely in German hands, suffered much less acute hardship than either Austrian or Russian Poland ; and in 1918, before the German forces were compelled to withdraw, it experienced in some degree the impact of the German Revolution of November 1918, when Soldiers' Councils were formed among the regiments stationed in the area. Except in the industrialised parts of Silesia, however, Socialism was not a powerful force in the German districts of Polish population ; and the fate of Silesia remained in the balance for a considerable time after 1918 until it was split up between Germany, Poland, and Czechoslovakia.

Finally Russian Poland, with Warsaw as its centre, formed the heart of Polish nationalism and was the chief home of the Polish Socialist Party (P.P.S.), led by Josef Pilsudski (1867–1935), who was to appear as the outstanding leader of the new Polish State. The P.P.S., which had the support of the main body of the Polish industrial workers, was strongly nationalist and vehemently anti-Russian, though it included a left wing opposed to any form of collaboration with the bourgeois nationalist groups. Pilsudski, as we saw,[1] had been in his earlier days an active Socialist, conducting active propaganda for Socialism in his clandestine journal, *Robotnik* (*The Worker*), in which he drew a sharp distinction between bourgeois and proletarian nationalism. But, at any rate, from 1914 onwards

[1] See Vol. III, Part I, p. 495.

his Socialism waned rapidly, giving place to a radical form of nationalism resting on strongly anti-Russian sentiment. Unlike the bourgeois nationalists, the P.P.S. was never anti-semitic or even anti-Ukrainian. Its hostility to Russia became, for a time, less marked after the February Revolution; but after the Bolshevik Revolution and the defeat of Germany it came back, for the Socialists of the P.P.S. were keenly suspicious of the Bolsheviks' intentions in relation to Polish independence and to the settlement of the frontiers between Poland and the Ukraine. The Socialism of Pilsudski and of the P.P.S. was intricately bound up with the struggle against Russian domination. In rivalry with the P.P.S. was the Social Democratic Party of the Kingdom of Poland and Lithuania, of which Rosa Luxemburg was the chief inspirer. This Party, as we have seen,[1] stood, not for Polish or any other sort of nationalism, but for common action against Czarism with the Russian workers and with all the workers of the Czarist empire. Strongly internationalist and hostile to all forms of nationalism, it had fallen foul, not only of the P.P.S. leadership, but also of Lenin, on the issue of national self-determination, and stood for the cause of universal proletarian Revolution. In 1917 it gave its full support to both Russian Revolutions; and when the war was over it joined forces with the left wing of the P.P.S. to establish a Polish Communist Party, which was among the earliest adherents to the Third International. It had, however, even in 1918, far fewer supporters among the Polish workers than the main body of the P.P.S., which continued to follow Pilsudski in his rôle as national liberator.

When the war broke out in 1914, Pilsudski was in Galicia, where he had been attempting to organise a movement designed to build up on Austrian soil a force for guerrilla action against Russian rule in Congress Poland, with the passive support of Daszynski and the Galician Social Democrats. Pilsudski had organised his followers into corps of Riflemen, for whom he attempted to procure arms from the Austrian authorities. Soon after the beginning of the war he advanced into Russian Poland at the head of a tiny armed force and seized the town of Kielce, but was unable to secure Austrian backing until he had reluctantly agreed to the incorporation of his Riflemen

[1] See Vol. III, Part I, p. 491.

618

into the Austrian army, but as a distinct force under their own officers. During the early stages of the war heavy fighting took place in both Austrian and Russian Poland, the Russians successfully occupying a large part of Galicia and throwing back a German advance directed towards Warsaw. But in the spring of 1915 the Germans and Austrians launched big offensives in both areas, and the greater part of both was occupied. As a result, Russian Poland was partitioned between Austria and Germany, with a German Governor-General at Warsaw and an Austrian at Lublin. Rather more than a year later, in January 1917, the Germans and Austrians together set up at Warsaw a State Council and Diet for Congress Poland, in an attempt to win support for the raising of Polish forces to reinforce their dwindling armies. Pilsudski was made a member of this Council, which was kept strictly subject to the occupying military authorities and was soon at loggerheads with them over the terms of a proposed appeal to Poles to volunteer for service. In July 1917 Pilsudski resigned from the Council, after trying to persuade it to resign *en bloc* in protest against the restrictions imposed upon it. He was thereupon arrested by the Germans and imprisoned in the fortress of Magdeburg, where he remained until he was set free by the German collapse the following year. Soon after his arrest the State Council did resign and was replaced by a Council of Regents, under which a sort of Cabinet was allowed to take office, but was subject to the veto of the military Governor. Then came the Bolshevik Revolution in Russia, followed by the armistice negotiations at Brest-Litovsk. The Polish Regency Cabinet wished to be represented at these negotiations, but the Germans refused this ; and when a district of Russian Poland — that of Cholm — was handed over to the Ukraine the Polish Cabinet resigned and the Polish members of the Austrian Reichsrath, who had already demanded Polish independence, withdrew their support from the Austrian Government. In Russian Poland a new Cabinet, made up of officials, took office under the Regents, who also decided to set up a sort of Parliament, partly elected and partly nominated, under the name of Council of State. This body duly met in June 1918, but dispersed in July, and was never reassembled. Finally, as the signs of the impending collapse of the Central Powers became plain, the Polish Council of Regents, early in October, dissolved the Council of State and attempted to set up a new Government representing the whole of Poland to conduct elections for a new Assembly (Sejm) to be chosen by general suffrage. The new Government proclaimed the independence of Poland on November 3rd, 1918, but was thereupon dismissed by the Regents, who installed a provisional Cabinet of officials. A few days later the Galician Socialist leader, Daszynski, proclaimed a Polish People's Republic at Lublin in what had been the Austrian occupation zone. Then on November 11th, Pilsudski, released from prison, arrived in Warsaw and was tumultuously acclaimed. The Regents, who had been trying to form a new Government, were forced to resign and to transfer full powers to Pilsudski, pending the formation of a national Government for the whole of the liberated area. Poland, in eclipse since the partitions, got ready to resume its position as an independent national State.

Throughout the years of war there had been sharp divisions among the Polish leaders. The Austrian Poles, as we saw, had sided with Austria against Russia and had been ready, almost up to the moment of the Austrian collapse, to accept a federal solution that would leave Galicia with as much of the rest of Poland as could be united with it under Hapsburg rule. The Prussian Poles had remained under German rule, not without protests, but without being in a position to take any action. The Russian Poles, on the other hand, had been sharply divided between the so-called Russophils, who at first demanded only autonomy within the Czarist empire, but later came out for the full independence of a united Poland, to be achieved with the aid of the Western Allies and of President Wilson, on the one hand, and, on the other, the so-called 'Independentists', who at first tried to collaborate with the Austrians, but hoped to secure Polish independence through the victory of the Central Powers — or, perhaps it would be fairer to say, through the defeat of Russia. The main body of the Polish Conservative right wing — the so-called National Democratic Party headed by Roman Dmowski — supported the Allies and was represented during the war by the Polish National Committee with headquarters in Paris. The main Parties of the Left — the Socialists and the peasant Populist or

Liberation Party (Wyzwolenie) — took the opposite line. The other peasant Party — the Piast, headed by Wincenty Witos and supported mainly by relatively well-to-do peasants — had its main centre in Galicia, and was predominantly Austrophil till Poland became an independent State. Between Pilsudski, who ranked as a Socialist, and the very conservative Dmowski there was a deep personal enmity which prevented them from acting together even when they were both deeply concerned to see the new Polish State successfully established over the largest possible area.

Poland was, of course, mainly a peasant country, with holdings of every sort and size from the exiguous to the vast landed estate, the great estates being most extensive in the eastern part of the country. One of the biggest problems facing the new Republic in 1918–19 was that of land reform ; and in face of the widespread unrest in the countryside large promises of land redistribution were made. Some land, though not a great deal in relation to the whole area, was actually distributed to poor or landless peasants during the Republic's first years ; and a maximum size, varying as between the eastern provinces and the rest of the country, was laid down — all land holdings above the maximum being scheduled for gradual redistribution over a period of years. But before long the permissible maxima were increased, and the process of redistribution was greatly slowed down, leaving large areas still in the hands of great landowners, as well as a considerable number of lesser, but still substantial, estates in being. In the first Sejm chosen by adult suffrage, peasants were present in large numbers and were able to secure the passing, by a single vote, of a drastic land reform resolution, which had some effect in keeping the peasants quiet for the time being, though no actual law was enacted until 1920 under the stimulus given by the outbreak of the Russo-Polish War. As soon as the war was over the landowners began a strong agitation for modifications of the agrarian law ; and after the first spurt of activity little was done to give effect to it. In 1923 Witos, then at the head of the Government, made an attempt both to modify the law and, in doing so, to get some action taken upon it ; but the only effect was that he fell from office. At length, at the end of 1925, an Act was passed providing for the redistribution of two million hectares of land annually for ten years, on a basis of compensation highly favourable to the owners. But even this modified plan was not carried out : after Pilsudski's *coup d'état* of the following year the whole process of redistribution was allowed to die gradually away.

Up to Pilsudski's *coup* the question of land reform haunted each successive Government, and in each Sejm the issues were continually debated. The main reasons why so little was done were, first, that the landowning interest, which was strong in itself, was able to take advantage of dissensions among the groups which favoured some sort of reform concerning the extent of it and the conditions of compensation and redistribution, and, secondly, that Witos's Piast Party wavered continually between a centrist position and support of the right wing, so that there was never, after the first months, a majority in favour of any definite action. Stanislas Thugutt (1873–1941), the leader of the more radical Peasant Party, was in the Government in 1918–19 and again in 1924–5, but was never in a position to get his way ; and the Socialists, abandoned by Pilsudski from the very beginning of the Republic, were always far too weak in the Sejm to have any major influence on the course of events.

As we saw, the P.P.S. had split in 1906, when a large minority broke away to form the Left P.P.S., with a social programme closely akin to that of the Social Democrats. This new Party remained in being throughout the war, and then, in 1919, amalgamated with the Social Democrats to form the Polish Communist Party. The P.P.S. suffered a further split in 1916, when a right-wing minority, headed by Pilsudski, left it and became a part of his personal following in his subsequent struggle for personal power. The Russians, in 1919 and 1920, entertained strong hopes of a Polish Revolution on the model of their own, and looked to such a Revolution to open the way for the spread of World Revolution to Germany and the West. At the time of the Russo-Polish War of 1920 they still cherished these hopes and believed that the Polish workers and peasants would rise to support the Red Army as it advanced upon Warsaw.[1] But nothing of the sort occurred: on the contrary, the great majority of Poles rallied to the national

---

[1] See p. 256.

cause against the invaders, and what came about was the suppression of the Polish Communist Party, which was driven underground and forfeited a large part of its support. The P.P.S. continued in action, for the most part siding with Pilsudski in his repeated quarrels with Dmowski and the Parties of the Right and continuing to regard him as a 'man of the Left' right up to the *coup d'état* of 1926, in which not only the P.P.S. but also the Communists backed Pilsudski against the right-wing Government. Pilsudski, in effect, remained the hero of the Polish Left long after his policies had ceased to be at all in harmony with its own, not only because of his services in the cause of national liberation but also because he was the inveterate enemy of Dmowski and the conservative nationalists. Only after the *coup d'état* did the Socialists discover their mistake ; and then they were unable to offer any effective resistance to the new régime which he set up with the support of the army and the developing capitalist interests.

Pilsudski, temporarily endowed with plenary powers on the establishment of the Polish Republic, at first seemed willing to accept a democratic system of parliamentary government, though he was strongly opposed to those parts of the Constitution, adopted in 1921, which narrowly restricted the President's authority and provided for the subjection of the executive to the legislative power. Never, he said, would he accept office as President under such a Constitution : instead, in 1923, he retired formally into private life, without ceasing for a moment to exert his influence, which remained all-powerful in the army and allowed him to play off the political Parties one against another with devastating effect. In 1922, on his refusal to stand, a close friend of his, the former Socialist, Gabriel Narutowicz (1865–1922) was elected as President of the Republic, only to be assassinated a few days later by a nationalist fanatic and replaced by the Socialist veteran Stanislaw Wojcie-chowski (1869–1953), who remained ineffectively in office till he was driven out by Pilsudski's *coup* of 1926 in favour of the latter's personal friend, the engineer and former Socialist, Ignacy Moscicki (1867–1946). Up to the assassination of Narutowicz, Pilsudski had counted in the main as an adherent of democratic parliamentary government, though he wanted a more powerful President and a decrease in the number of political Parties representing a variety of fractional groups. But the killing of Narutowicz brought about a decisive change in his attitude, convincing him of the unreliability of the parliamentary system. The election of Narutowicz had been accomplished, against the candidate of the nationalist Right, by the votes of the Socialists and of the national minorities, including the Jews, and was intensely resented by the extreme nationalists. Pilsudski bided his time for the next three years, and then, in 1926, seized power by a *coup d'état* — still primarily as the opponent of the ultra-nationalist right wing. Even after the *coup* of 1926 the Socialists did not entirely cease to support Pilsudski : for example, Jedrzej Moraczewski (1870–1944), who had been Socialist Prime Minister in the first Government of the Republic from 1918 to 1919, came back to office as Minister of Public Works in 1925 and remained in that office for the ensuing three years, and Daszynski, who had been Vice-Premier in 1920–21, came back to office as Speaker (Marshal) of the Sejm in 1928.

The attitude and policy of the P.P.S. were indeed consistently rather radical than Socialist in any constructive sense. The Party was fairly strongly represented in the first Sejm elected in 1919, but lost ground considerably in 1922, when it won only 41 seats — less than one-tenth of the total. It did rather better at the next election, held in 1928, when its representation rose to 64, though it had to fight against the new Party, the Government Bloc, created by Pilsudski after the *coup* of 1926. Thereafter it declined in face of the growingly dictatorial character of the Pilsudski régime. In 1928 the Communists, despite their outlawry as a Party, were able to win 7 seats ; but their representatives were soon expelled from the Sejm after they had attempted to shout down the 'dictator'.

In the first Sejm, at the start of the Republic, the Socialists and their Peasant allies, supported by other Radical groups, had been able to enact some useful industrial and social legislation, including the eight-hours' day. But economically the country was in a very bad state, and mass starvation was averted only by the timely arrival of help from the United States. Then, in 1920, the Russo-Polish War diverted attention from economic measures, and after it had ended the Left was so weakened that little further progress could be made. In the autumn of 1923 there were extensive strikes and disturbances, which the Government, then in the hands of the conservative right wing, repressed with military force. Military action against a railway strike was followed by a brief general strike ; and in Cracow there was an actual insurrection, in the course of which the workers held most of the town for two days before it was taken by the military. These industrial disturbances were complicated and aggravated by troubles between the Poles and the national minorities which made up a considerable part of the population. Poland was committed under the Peace Treaties to set up a régime granting substantial cultural autonomy to these minorities, among which the most important were the Ukrainians in the eastern provinces and the Jews, scattered over most of the country, but most numerous in what had been Russian Poland. These minorities, as long as elections were relatively free, were able to return substantial contingents of members to the Sejm, thus complicating the political struggles of right and left and making it difficult to get coherent government majorities. Anti-semitism was strong in Poland, especially among the Parties of the right, such as the National Democrats : and the Polish right was also strongly hostile to Ukrainian nationalism, and, despite the treaties, used great violence in suppressing it, and indeed in attempting to 'polonise' the Ukrainian districts. Pilsudski, as we saw, had had dreams of a Greater Poland, to be constituted on a federal basis, with autonomy for the constituent national groups within their several areas. But these plans of federation rested on the idea of a Poland extensive enough to incorporate all Lithuania, the entire Ukraine, White Russia, most of Silesia, and perhaps even Latvia and Estonia, as well as East Prussia ; and even on this basis they could not have solved the Jewish problem, because the Jews lived intermingled with other nationalities and needed cultural rather than territorial autonomy.

These federal schemes, always opposed by a large part of the nationalist right wing, in effect lapsed when the hopes of such a Greater Poland were eclipsed after the settlement which followed the Russo-Polish War. During the war Poland had for a time entered into an agreement with Simon Petliura, the Ukrainian guerrilla leader, under which Petliura renounced the Ukrainian claim to Eastern Galicia in return for Polish help in establishing an independent Ukraine covering most of Southern Russia. This agreement was fiercely attacked by other Ukrainian nationalists, who regarded it as a betrayal of the Ukrainian nationalist cause ; and it came to nothing when the Bolsheviks successfully incorporated the main part of the Ukraine into the Soviet Union. But in the settlement of 1921 Poland was able to appropriate a considerable area in the east inhabited by populations much nearer to Ukrainian or Ruthenian than to Polish nationality and adhering to the Orthodox rather than to the Catholic Church, so that there remained in the new Poland, both in East Galicia and in the border provinces further north, a large non-Polish population keenly resistant to 'polonisation' and with a frustrated sense of kinship, both national and religious, as well as political and economic, with their Ukrainian neighbours in the Soviet Union.

Still farther north, the Poles, though they did not succeed in appropriating Lithuania as a whole, did successfully lay hands on a large part of its territory, including the ancient capital, Vilna — a mainly Polish city set in a predominantly Lithuanian or White Russian hinterland : so that there, too, a vexing minority problem existed in an area of great strategic importance. For the northern extension of the Polish State to Vilna and beyond cut off the Soviet Union from Lithuania, and thus from access to Germany and the West except through Poland. This removed the possibility of Russian aid to the German Revolution for which the Soviet leaders long continued to hope. The Vilna area, which the Poles held by force, was an essential part of the 'cordon sanitaire' which France sought to create as a barrier in the path of Bolshevism towards Western Europe ; and its acquisition by Poland was the most serious setback to Russia arising out of the settlement of 1921. The Silesian settlement also involved the inclusion in the new Poland of a German minority ; while in the south the incorporation of Transcarpathian Ruthenia in Czechoslovakia cut off its population, closely akin to the Ukrainians, from direct contact with the Soviet Union.

Poland was thus a multi-national State dominated by an intensely nationalistic ruling people, who resented and, through their governing classes, did their best to evade the obligations towards the national minorities put on them by the Treaties of

Peace. The resulting national conflicts operated strongly against the building up of an effective united working-class movement and aggravated the differences between the predominantly Polish P.P.S. and the Communists, who recruited much of their following among the national minorities and were able to make an internationalist proletarian appeal. The fact that the Communist Party was illegal in Poland and had to operate continually underground makes estimation of its real strength very difficult. It appears to have had a big following at first, but to have lost much of its appeal when, during the Russo-Polish War, it greeted the invading Red Army as a deliverer. When the fighting was over it set to work to rebuild its forces and succeeded in winning a few seats in the Sejm under the auspices of locally improvised political organisations which received a temporary legality for election purposes but were always liable to be broken up and to have their literature confiscated and their candidates, if successful, expelled by the Sejm and then arrested and sent to gaol. Its old leadership, drawn mainly from the pre-war Social Democratic Party, fell foul of the Comintern when its members mostly sided with Brandler in the dispute over the conduct of the German Communists in 1923 ;[1] and thereafter the control passed to a new group acceptable to the Comintern. There was a good deal of trouble in Poland on the question of the United Front tactics adopted by the Comintern after 1921, as many Poles regarded them as inapplicable to Polish conditions. In 1926, as we saw, the Communists, as well as the P.P.S., gave support to Pilsudski in his seizure of power, but soon had cause to regret their error. In 1928 the Communists and their near allies polled over half a million votes as compared with more than one million for the P.P.S.

The P.P.S., for its part, retained its strongly anti-Russian attitude and continued right up to 1926 to regard Pilsudski as the leader of popular nationalism against the conservative nationalism of the National Democrats and their allies. When the *coup* took place in May 1926 the P.P.S. had only just withdrawn from the coalition Government which had been formed to deal with the severe economic crisis and to take measures for stabilising the currency. The Socialist and

[1] See p. 647.

working-class leaders hoped that Pilsudski's seizure of power would be followed by the setting up of a Workers' and Peasants' Government dominated by the P.P.S. and the Popular Peasant Party; and these Parties called on Pilsudski to dissolve the Sejm and order new elections, in which they felt confident that the left Parties would be able to win a majority. But Pilsudski was set, not on strengthening but on undermining the influence of the Sejm; and it suited him best to leave in being a Sejm controlled by the right wing, but conscious of its weaknesses against the army and the current of popular opinion. As soon as this became evident, the P.P.S., after an internal struggle with the admirers of Pilsudski in its ranks, declared itself to be in opposition to the new régime; and in due course it fought the election campaign of 1928 as an opposition Party. On this basis it was able both to conclude an alliance with the German Social Democratic Party in Poland and to bring back into its ranks the major part of the Independent Polish Socialist Party, which had seceded from it in 1922 under the leadership of Boleslaw Drobner in order to adopt a more militant line. After the election of 1928 the old P.P.S. leader Daszynski was elected as Marshal (Speaker) of the Sejm, and another old stalwart, Herman Diamand (1861–1931), succeeded him as Chairman of the Party. Yet another veteran, Felix Perl (b. 1871), had died in 1927. In 1928 the reinforced Party had considerable successes in the local elections, as well as for the Sejm, and won, either alone or in coalition with the German Social Democrats and the Jewish Bund, majority control in a number of towns, including Lodz, Lublin, and also Vilna — this last in conjunction with the Popular Peasant Party. It also held the presidency of the City Council of Warsaw.

These successes, however, did not save the P.P.S. from being badly hit, as Pilsudski, with the support of the main body of the capitalist and financial classes, as well as of the army, set to work to build up a political following of his own in the form of a Non-Party *bloc*. The elections of 1928 had left Pilsudski unable to carry through the constitutional revision he wished for — a large increase in the powers of the President at the expense of the Sejm — as constitutional change required a two-thirds majority. Only in the election of 1930, at which opposition candidates were subjected to considerable repression, did Pilsudski's *bloc* succeed in winning an absolute majority ; and even then it fell short of the required two-thirds of the seats. Not until 1935 did Pilsudski succeed in forcing his new Constitution through the Sejm by the requisite majority — and even then only by a parliamentary trick. He did, however, at last get his way, but only to die within a few weeks of his success, leaving the so-called 'Régime of the Colonels' to inherit his power.

The Pilsudski régime, as it developed after 1926, and still more after 1930, was essentially a dictatorship, though it allowed the Sejm to continue a shadowy existence and retained most of the parliamentary forms. It rested on two sources of power — the immense prestige of Pilsudski himself and the army, which was devoted to him. It was able in 1926 to destroy the influence of Dmowski and the National Democrats, except in what had been Prussian Poland, and thereafter to break up Witos's right-wing Piast Peasant Party and drive its leader into exile. It thus destroyed the power of its conservative opponents and induced the bulk of their followers to rally behind it ; and it also kept the backing of many nationalists who had previously supported the Parties of the left. It was thus well able to deal drastically with its opponents — the P.P.S., the Communists, the Popular Peasants, and some of the national minority groups, including the Jews. At the outset, Pilsudski took a strong line against the Nazi régime in Germany — even to the extent of approaching the French with proposals for a preventive war. Only at a later stage, from 1936 to 1938, did his successors show signs of taking sides with the Nazis. The Polish dictatorship, as long as Pilsudski presided over it, had little in common with the ideology of Nazism. It was sympathetic to the poorer classes rather than to the conservative aristocrats, but found itself impotent to carry through major social and economic reforms in face of their determined opposition. Only after Pilsudski's death did his successors show ideological affinities to Nazism ; and these developments of the 1930s fall beyond the period covered in the present volume.

CHAPTER XX

THE WEIMAR REPUBLIC, 1922–1931

A FTER the abortive Communist rising of 1921 and the ensuing troubles inside the German Communist Party and between its leaders and the Comintern, the membership of the Party fell precipitately by more than one-half ; and the new leadership, under instructions received from the Third Congress of the Comintern, had to devise an entirely new policy. This new policy, laid down for world-wide application, went by the highly misleading name of the 'United Front', and a sharp dispute at once arose about the meaning of the phrase. A distinction was drawn between the 'United Front from Above', taking the form of negotiations for unity of action between the leaderships of the Communist Parties and those of the Social Democratic Parties or of the Trade Unions, and the 'United Front from Below' — by which was meant Communist action to stir up the masses by agitation on issues which were of immediate interest to the main body of the workers, in such a way as either to force the Social Democratic and Trade Union leaders to support the Communists' proposals or to drive them into opposition to the desires of their own followers. Up to a point both tactics were regarded as legitimate, with the proviso that, in using either, the Communist Parties should make no compromise with their Social Democratic enemies, but should persist in negotiating with them for the purpose of isolating them from their supporters. In this spirit the Comintern itself entered into negotiations, as we shall see, with the Second and Two-and-a-Half' Internationals,[1] but adopted in the discussions a quite uncompromising line, so that the negotiations speedily broke down. Similarly, in Great Britain, the Communist Party applied for affiliation to the Labour Party, making clear that it claimed the right to continue to advocate its own policy if it were accepted — which,

[1] See p. 682.

naturally, it was not. In Germany the question arose whether the Communists should be prepared to participate in the Socialist Governments that were in office in some of the German Länder ; but the main emphasis was on the 'United Front from Below' — above all, on the attempt to win support in the Trade Unions and on the Factory Committees set up by law in 1919 by calls for action to secure improved wages and conditions, in the hope that more vigorous immediate struggles with the employers might help to bring the masses over to a more revolutionary frame of mind. There were differences of opinion among the German Communists about the tactics to be followed in connection with the 'United Front'. A left-wing group, headed by Ruth Fischer (b. 1895), was alarmed lest, in pursuing the 'United Front from Above' or even by being too ready to compromise in pursuing the 'United Front from Below', the Communist Party might find itself, instead of capturing the Social Democratic and the Trade Union rank and file, being captured by its opponents and allowing its own members to be seduced. But the majority of the Communist leaders denied the reality of this danger, and defended the new policy as correct in view of the relative weakness of the Party after the disasters of 1921.

The entire policy of the 'United Front', of course, rested on a recognition by the Comintern that the prospect of immediate proletarian Revolution in most of Europe no longer existed after the set-backs of 1921. Indeed, at the Fourth Congress of the Comintern, held in November and December 1922, a great deal was said about the 'capitalist counter-offensive' that was in progress in the greater part of the world, and about the need to avoid any sort of 'putschism' under the existing unfavourable conditions. The Comintern leaders were still convinced that the opportunity for revolutionary action would before long recur. They had by no means given up the belief that world capitalism was approaching its 'final crisis' and that quite soon the economic collapse of capitalism would re-create the conditions needed for a renewed revolutionary advance, in which they still expected Germany to occupy a key place. But for the time being Revolution was, they admitted, impracticable ; and accordingly the task of the Communists was to prepare the way for it by enlarging their hold on the working class through participation in its day-to-day struggles to improve, or defend, its position under capitalism. This was the meaning of the 'United Front' policy which the Communist Parties had been called upon to adopt at the Comintern Congress of 1922.

The first showings of the new policy in action were in connection with the German railway strike of 1923, exemplifying the policy of the 'United Front from Below', and with the manifestations which followed the murder of Walther Rathenau in June of that year. The Social Democrats had joined the coalition Government of Josef Wirth, of the Catholic Centre, in October 1921 ; and under this Government a number of Emergency Ordinances for the protection of law and order were enacted in June of the following year. After Rathenau's murder these ordinances were replaced by a Law for the Protection of the Republic. There were huge demonstrations 'for the Republic', directed against the monarchist reactionaries; and the Communists, as well as the bourgeois Republicans, joined in these, but were thereupon formally warned by the Comintern against identifying themselves with the defence of the bourgeois Weimar Republic, on the ground that such a compromise went well outside any legitimate interpretation of what was meant by the 'United Front'. They then drew back, and concentrated their main attention on participation in the day-to-day economic struggle and on strengthening their hold on the Factory Committees. The policy of splitting the Trade Union movement by founding rival Communist Unions was definitely thrown over, and separate Unions were tolerated only where the exclusion of Communists from the 'free' Unions left no alternative open. By the time the Fourth Comintern Congress met in November 1922 the German Communist Party was able to congratulate itself that considerable progress was being made along these lines.

At this point the Wirth Government fell and was replaced by a right-wing Government headed by Wilhelm Cuno, of the People's Party, without Socialist representation. In January 1923 the Leipzig Congress of the German Communist Party voted in favour of joint action with the Socialists in face of a left-wing opposition headed by Ruth Fischer, Forkadi Maslow (1891–1941), and Ernst Thaelmann (1886–1944). At this moment the French, without support from Great Britain, marched into the Ruhr, on the plea that Germany had defaulted on its obligations in respect of reparations under the Versailles Treaty ; and the great struggle brought on by the occupation began. The Ruhr miners came out on strike on January 23rd, and a week later the French took over control of the railways in the occupied area. A general movement of passive resistance began among the Ruhr population and presently received the support of the German Government, which undertook to meet the cost of the resistance.

This is not the place for any full account of the Ruhr struggle of 1923-4. Our present concern is not with the events of the struggle as such, but rather with its effects on the internal situation of Germany as a whole. The French and Belgians marched into the Ruhr because they accused the Germans of wilful default in respect of reparations deliveries, and claimed the right to seize the Ruhr area as a pledge for German fulfil-ment of Treaty obligations. The Germans retorted that it was impossible for them to meet the fantastically large claims that were being imposed upon them — which was unquestionably true — but there were undoubtedly powerful forces in Germany which were hostile to the entire policy of 'fulfilment' and were doing their best to sabotage such deliveries as could have been made. The invasion of the Ruhr was, of course, calculated to make fulfilment more difficult, at any rate unless the population, employers and workers together, were prepared to co-operate fully with the occupying forces ; and even if they had been and if the French had been able to seize and carry away as much of the output of the area as they wished, the loss of Ruhr coal and steel would have led to a sharp economic crisis in Germany as a whole. It was, however, most unlikely that the population would be prepared to co-operate fully with the occupying authorities, who were likely to meet with bitter opposition both from the workers in the Ruhr industries and from the nationalist elements hostile to the policy of fulfilment ; and in fact these factions, though bitterly antagonistic to each other, did join hands in a common movement of resistance, which was intensified by the efforts of the French to use the occupation as a means of promoting separatist movements designed to establish new States permanently detached from the rest of Germany. The activities of these movements, headed by undistinguished puppets put up with French support, generated strong feelings not only in the Ruhr but also in other parts of Germany, and helped to force the German Government to give full support to the resistance. This support, involving the expenditure of very large sums in maintaining workers who refused to work for the French, or whose establishments were shut down, and also in compensating employers who were adversely affected, as well as in procuring supplies from abroad to replace Ruhr products for use in the rest of Germany, could be given only by an immense emission of additional paper money. The German mark had been falling in value on account of inflation before the Ruhr occupation began ; and, when the strain of the occupation was added, the inflation speedily became catastrophic, until, well before the end of the struggle, the currency had virtually lost all purchasing power both internally and in foreign exchange. A prodigious speculation against the mark greatly accentuated and speeded up this decline, which had terrible consequences both for the workers and, even more, for those among the German middle classes who depended on relatively fixed incomes. The purchasing power of both wages and salaries fell catastrophically ; and incomes from savings, pensions, and all forms of capital fixed in money value were practically wiped out. As against this all debtors were benefited ; for debts could be paid off at practically no cost, so that capitalist concerns which had been financed by loans òr debentures emerged as the debt-free owners of the capital assets they had acquired with the borrowed money. A great redistribution of property and income took place at the expense of the wage-earners, pensioners, and fixed-interest small investors ; and the ruin of a large section of the middle classes led to a rise of revolutionary feeling not only among workers who were supporters of the Socialist Parties but also among their bitterest opponents.

In effect, the Ruhr struggle plunged Germany into a revolutionary situation on two fronts. On the one hand, sheer misery, as the standard of living was brought down, supplied many recruits to the Communist Party, which wanted to overthrow the Weimar Republic and institute a proletarian dictatorship on the Russian model ; and, on the other hand, the counter-revolutionary elements, which wanted to displace the

Republic and to restore the rule of the military and institute a dictatorship of the 'Right', were also strongly reinforced and encouraged to believe that the fall of the hated Weimar régime was at hand. The Reichswehr, the authorised army of the Republic, had already entrenched itself in a position of large independence of the civil authority, and could not be relied on, any more than in 1920, to defend the Republic against counter-revolutionary attempts. It had also thrown off, contrary to the terms of the Versailles Treaty, a number of unauthorised armed units known as the 'Black Reichswehr'; and least dependable of all for the defence of the Republic were the numerous 'Free Corps' which still remained in being and gathered in many new recruits as economic conditions in Germany grew worse. Finally there were the Bavarians, demanding wide autonomy within the Federal Reich and maintaining counter-revolutionary armed forces of their own as well as a close contact with the local Reichswehr forces and the Free Corps, and also with the Nazi followers of Hitler — still at that time almost confined to Bavaria — who were demanding a march on Berlin to overthrow the Weimar Republic and were hoping to secure the co-operation of the Bavarian Government and of the Reichswehr in Bavaria for this adventure.

Thus, in the Germany of 1923, there were revolutionary plotters on both the extreme right and the extreme left, and the two extremes, very ready to fly at each other's throats, were nevertheless both in opposition to the French and Belgians and to those who either supported the separatist movements which they inspired or, out of fear or self-interest, were prepared to co-operate with the occupying forces. The resulting situation was exceedingly confused. The Government of the Reich was in the hands of a right-wing coalition headed by Cuno, who represented the capitalist interest that was profiting by the inflation, which it made no attempt to hold in check. The Socialists, mostly reunited in the Social Democratic Party, to which the non-Communist Independents — except a small group headed by Georg Ledebour — had returned in September 1922, were outside the Cuno Government, and on most issues, opposed to it, but were committed to the defence of the Weimar Republic and to hostility to both the revolutionary camps, which alike gained ground at the S.P.D.'s expense.

Through the spring and summer of 1923 the economic condition of the workers — and indeed of the whole people save those who profited by the mounting inflation — grew steadily and rapidly worse, until by the beginning of August it had become evidently impracticable for the German Government to carry on any longer its policy of meeting the costs of passive resistance to the occupying authorities in the Ruhr. Further emissions of paper money were manifestly useless when all their purchasing power had been lost — so much so that, the more money there was, the less would the whole amount in circulation avail to buy. The support given to the resistance had to be discontinued and, unless the entire Reich were to dissolve in chaos, a settlement had to be sought and external help secured in order to put the German economy back on its feet. In this crisis, the Cuno Government was displaced ; and a new 'Grand Coalition', headed by Gustav Stresemann of the People's Party, another representative of capitalist interests, took office, with the Socialists participating on the ground that it was necessary to rally all available forces for the defence of the State. By this time the capitalist class had extracted all the gains that could be got from the cancellation of its debts and was prepared to co-operate in measures designed to end the inflation. Stresemann himself had become convinced of the need to come to terms with the French and to invoke the aid of the United States and of Great Britain, both in bringing the French to terms and in coming to Germany's help in the financial field ; and he realised that this could not be done unless Germany were prepared, while demanding a revision of the claims made on her under the Versailles Treaty, to adopt a policy of 'fulfilment' and to make a real effort to carry out such of its terms as were, or could be rendered, practicable. Accordingly, on September 27th, 1923, the Stresemann Government proclaimed the ending of passive resistance in the Ruhr, and set to work, with the aid of Hjalmar Schacht, as head of the Reichsbank, to devise ways and means for the issue of a new, stable currency to replace the now worthless mark, and to persuade the Allied and American Governments to institute an immediate enquiry into Germany's capacity to pay reparations and into the measures necessary for making such payments possible. Out of these developments came, first of all, the issue of a new temporary money unit called Rentenmark, and purporting to be based on a mortgage on the real capital assets of the German economic system, but having really no basis at all except in the discontinuance of further issues of the utterly depreciated paper mark and in the cutting off of bank credit in terms of the old currency. Secondly, Stresemann's negotiations in London and the United States led to the appointment, under American chairmanship, of the Dawes Commission, which set to work to study Germany's capacity to pay and to prepare proposals for enabling the German currency to be stabilised on terms that would wipe the old mark currency out of existence.

Through the months of conflict in the Ruhr, it had been constantly on the cards that Revolution might break out in Germany, from either the left or the right ; and this was only prevented by the fact that the rival revolutionary forces, having diametrically opposite purposes, largely neutralised each other. The German Communists, as we saw, had been following, after their defeat in 1921, a cautious policy by which, under the slogan of the 'United Front', they had been attempting to win over the followers of the Social Democrats and had entered into less unfriendly relations with the left-wing elements in both the S.P.D. and the U.S.P.D. and, after these Parties had reunited, with the left wing in the new S.P.D. This element was strongest in Saxony and in Thuringia, in both of which, in 1923, predominantly left Socialist Governments were in office and were in serious dispute with the Government of the Reich. The question arose whether, in order to strengthen these Governments for resistance to the Reich Government and the Reichswehr, the Communists should join them and accept government portfolios. Some Communists favoured this course as in harmony with the slogan of the 'United Front', whereas the Communist left wing denounced it as involving a betrayal of Communist principles by coalition with 'social traitors' pledged to uphold the Weimar Republic. Moreover, as the chaos and misery caused by the Ruhr occupation increased, the question arose whether Germany had not again arrived at a revolutionary situation in which it had become incumbent on the Communists to return to an immediate policy of Revolution by attempting to use the general unrest as an opportunity for establishing a Communist dictatorship, though most of the Communists realised that the success of such an attempt was very doubtful and many saw that the consequences might be to provoke a successful counter-revolution of the right.

In these circumstances, the German Communists naturally took counsel with Moscow by asking for the Comintern's advice. They found, however, that the Comintern, too, was very uncertain about the course that ought to be followed. Heinrich Brandler (1881–?), then the German Communist leader, went to Moscow for consultations, and was kept there for several months while the Comintern was trying to make up its mind. In his absence the remaining leaders, uncertain of their future course, could neither definitely prepare for a revolutionary uprising nor decide not to prepare for one ; and when Brandler at length got back to Germany in October 1923, his Party was still at sixes and sevens, but he had his orders that the attempt must be made. Meanwhile, the leaders in Germany had come down on the side of joining the Saxon and Thuringian Governments, which were threatened with displacement by armed force by Reichswehr contingents ; and Brandler, on his return, became a member of the reconstituted Government of Saxony. The Reich Government then decided to depose the Saxon Government and to put Saxony under a Civil Commissioner appointed by the Reich ; and in support of this policy Reichswehr units were sent to occupy the country. Faced with military invasion, the Saxon Government felt itself too weak to resist, and allowed itself to be displaced ; and the Government of Thuringia soon suffered a like fate. The Communists, who had at last been making active preparations for a rising in other parts of Germany, but had relied on Saxony and Thuringia for their main support, saw that all chances of success had disappeared, and at the last moment called off the rising. The instructions to abandon it failed, however, to reach Hamburg in time ; and there a few hundred Communists rose and seized the centre of the city, but, without mass support, were speedily crushed. Elsewhere, the projected rising simply did not happen ; but the calling of it off did not prevent many Communists from being arrested and gaoled, or the Communist Party from being proscribed and driven underground.

While these events were occurring in northern and central Germany, revolution of the opposite kind was being hatched in Bavaria, where the right-wing Government headed by von Kahr was already at loggerheads with the Reich Government before the Stresemann Cabinet took office. The entry of Socialists into the Stresemann Cabinet greatly angered the Bavarians ; and there was much talk of a march on Berlin, to destroy the Weimar Republic, by way of Thuringia and Saxony, whose Socialist Governments were to be destroyed on the way. The Bavarians were in touch with the extreme right in Berlin, led by Admiral von Tirpitz, and were in hopes that the Reichswehr units in Bavaria, headed by General von Lossow, would join them ; but the fateful decision to take up active warfare against the Republic was deferred. On September 26th, however, the Bavarian Government declared a state of emergency, and conferred dictatorial powers on its Prime Minister, von Kahr. Stresemann, under pressure from the Reichswehr generals, retaliated by placing full executive powers in the hands of the Reichswehr Minister, who delegated them to the Reichswehr commander, General von Seeckt. This had the effect of making the Bavarian dictator formally subject to von Seeckt, and the question was then raised whether the Bavarians would give way and whether the Reichswehr in Bavaria would act with von Seeckt or with von Kahr.

Meanwhile, the group round Hitler, who had established his 'National Socialist' (Nazi) Party in Munich in 1921, continued to agitate for open war upon Berlin and secured the adhesion of General Ludendorff ; but this group was not nearly strong enough to act alone. It needed the support of von Kahr and, at the very least, the assured neutrality of von Lossow's Reichswehr forces. At this point, von Lossow made up his mind to refuse submission to von Seeckt and to place himself at von Kahr's orders ; and on October 22nd the Bavarian dictator took over control of the Reichswehr in Bavaria 'as trustee for the German people', thus openly defying the Government of the Reich and threatening civil war. It was at this point that Stresemann, eager to placate the right while preventing the right-wing extremists from overthrowing the Republic, authorised von Seeckt to take action against the Saxon and Thuringian Governments, which had thereupon to decide at once whether to offer armed resistance or to give way. Brandler, a member of the Saxon Government, refused to take responsibility for advising resistance unless the Social Democrats pledged their full support ; and the Social Democrats, conscious that they could not count on the backing of the main body of the S.P.D. outside Saxony and Thuringia, decided against armed resistance, and thus provided the Communists with an opportunity to put the blame for the calling off of the projected insurrection upon them. But, though the Saxon and Thuringian Socialists thus allowed themselves to be driven from office by the Reichswehr, their deposition made the position of the Socialists in the Stresemann Government finally untenable. There was no constitutional authority for the expulsion of the Saxon and Thuringian Governments, which was carried out by the Reichswehr under the special powers recently conferred upon it. The conferring of these powers had indeed made the position of the Socialists in the Government already quite unreal. On their resignation Stresemann at once formed a new Reich Government resting entirely on the support of the right-wing bourgeois Parties.

These events naturally did something to lessen the tension between Bavaria and the Reich. But there were powerful elements in Bavaria that were not prepared to stop short of a decisive effort to overthrow the Weimar Republic once for all and therewith to put an end to the Stresemann policy of fulfilment of the Versailles Treaty and agreement on this basis with the Allied Governments and the Americans. Hitler and Ludendorff, still hopeful of carrying von Kahr and von Lossow along with them, went on with their preparations, in consultation with the North German extremists, and finally decided to stage a rising in Munich for November 8th, not against von Kahr, but in order to force him to throw in his lot with them. On that evening, a large body of Nazis under Hitler's leadership forced its way into the hall where von Kahr was making a speech and, getting possession of his person and of von Lossow, called on them to give in their adhesion to the proposed march on Berlin. Von Kahr and von Lossow, under duress, pretended to agree, and it was announced that a new Reich Government was to be formed, with Hitler as Chancellor and Ludendorff in supreme command of the attack on

Berlin. Von Lossow was to be Reichswehr Minister : von Kahr was to continue as dictator of Bavaria.

Von Kahr and von Lossow had, however, no intention of acting on this arrangement. They had already made up their minds to come to terms with the Reich ; and on the following morning they put the Bavarian Reichswehr units and the police into action against the Nazis and their ultra-nationalist supporters, whose resistance was easily overcome. The Nazis attempted to retort with a mass demonstration ; but the police fired on the demonstrators and dispersed them. Hitler and other Nazis were arrested and sentenced to short periods of detention in fortresses. Ludendorff went off scot-free ; and, of course, von Kahr and von Lossow suffered no penalty for their previous refusal to accept the authority of the Reich. Nazism thus made its first unsuccessful bid for power by violent action ; and the failure left Hitler determined, in re-organising his forces, to find a way to power that would allow him to have the forms of legality on his side.

In the meantime the French, in occupation of the Ruhr, had been doing their best to foment separatist movements in the parts of Germany under their control. Local Separatist Governments, protected by French and Belgian forces, were set up, but were unable to exercise any authority. In November, as we saw, the German Government authorised the issue of a new currency unit, the Rentenmark, as a step towards stabilisation ; and in December, under British and American pressure, the Dawes Commission was appointed to consider Germany's actual ability to pay reparations. The same month, Wilhelm Marx, of the right wing of the Centre Party, took Stresemann's place as Chancellor ; but Stresemann, now Foreign Secretary, and committed to a policy of 'fulfilment' of the terms of the Versailles Treaty, so far as fulfilment was practicable, remained the chief controller of German foreign policy, acting closely with Schacht in the direction of financial affairs. The Dawes Commission reported in April 1924 ; and after long negotiations the Dawes Agreement governing Germany's reparations payments was signed on August 9th. Then at length the French and Belgians began the evacuation of the occupied areas, which was completed in November ; and Germany, aided by the large loan made available under the Dawes Agreement, settled down to the tasks of economic reconstruction on a capitalist basis acceptable to the Allied Governments, which still entertained extravagant hopes about the reparations that could be extracted despite the damage inflicted on the German economy by the struggle in the Ruhr.

Both the Fourth and the Fifth Congresses of the Comintern, held in 1922 and 1924, were largely taken up by mutual recriminations arising out of the disasters of 1921 and of October 1923. At both, the main blame was put upon two men — Brandler and Karl Radek, respectively the leader and the principal Comintern adviser of the German Communist Party at the time of the Ruhr struggle. The accusations made by the Party's new leaders against those who had been displaced after the defeat were, first, that the entry of the Communists into the Left Social Democratic Government of Saxony, headed by Zeigner, and into that of Thuringia, had been a capital mistake, and, secondly, that a rising could have succeeded had it been better organised, and also that it would have been better to go on and fail than to withdraw ignominiously at the critical moment. Brandler, in defending his conduct, fully agreed that the preparations had been badly defective, but pertinently pointed out that he had been summoned to Moscow and kept there during the two most critical months while the Comintern debated about the line to be followed : so that he had got back to Germany only when the opportunity for preparation had been already missed, to face a situation in which a rising could not possibly have led to anything short of dismal defeat. In the matter of his entry into the Saxon Government, the charge against him was that he had done this without exacting any of the conditions that could alone have justified such action. There had been, in connection with the discussion of 'United Front' tactics, a great many references to the possibility of Communist participation in a 'Workers' Government' that fell short of being a complete proletarian dictatorship ; and various definitions of what was meant by a 'Workers' Government' had been advanced. Such a Government, Zinoviev and others argued after the event, needed to be distinguished sharply from a mere Communist-Social Democratic coalition within the framework of bourgeois democracy. It must, he said, be a Government based on a repudiation of the bourgeois State, a Government dominated by Communists, and one that would from the outset expel the bourgeois civil servants from office and stand ready to defend itself in arms against bourgeois attack — including attack by the leaders of the Social Democratic Party, whom he dismissed as mere tools of the bourgeoisie. It must indeed be, according to Zinoviev's argument, which the Comintern endorsed, a Communist Government in all but name. This, clearly, the Left Social Democratic Governments of Saxony and Thuringia had never been : nor were the characters of these Governments in any essential respect changed by the entry into them of a couple of Communist Ministers. Brandler's reply was that when he got back to Germany in October, what appeared essential was to stiffen Saxony's resistance to the overthrow of the Zeigner Government by the armed forces of the Reich Government, and that, as soon as he had had time to measure up the situation, he had seen that, because there had been no proper preparation, a general Communist rising in Germany would stand no chance of success. He had found, even in Saxony, a widespread belief that the movement of Reich forces into that country was directed not against the Socialist Government but against the counter-revolutionary Bavarians, who were preparing for their *coup* against the Republic and were threatening to march into Saxony and Thuringia on their way to Berlin. This belief, Brandler argued, had been largely responsible for the failure to make ready for armed resistance to the Reichswehr when it threatened to march in. By inference, though not openly, Brandler also strongly criticised the Comintern leadership for failing to make up its own mind whether it wanted a German insurrection or not until the time for action had gone by.

Tangled up with this dispute was another, concerning the policy of the German Communist Party in relation to the Trade Unions. It was, as we saw, part of the tactics of the 'United Front' that the Communists should set out, not to split the Trade Union movement, but to infiltrate into the existing Unions and bring them over to a militant revolutionary policy. Their attempts to do this, however, were continually leading to expulsions ; and there was also, under the very depressed economic conditions of 1923, an immense drift out of the Unions by workers who could not afford to keep up their contributions. The left wing of the Communist Party argued that it was impossible, under these circumstances, either not to allow those who were expelled to set up new Unions or to refrain from attempting to organise the large numbers who had lapsed from membership. There was also an extreme left which regarded the existing Unions as hopelessly reactionary and, rejecting the 'United Front' tactics, wished to set up new Unions everywhere on a class-war basis and to endeavour to detach the members of the established Unions as well as to enrol those who had lapsed from them or been expelled. This extreme group was opposed by the new, as well as by the old, leaders of the German Communist Party ; but it still made its voice heard at the Comintern Congress of June and July 1924.

One reason why this question of Trade Union policy took a particularly acute form in Germany was that up to 1918 the German Trade Unions, though well organised and strong in certain industries, not only covered a much smaller fraction of the workers than the British Unions but were also by tradition divided into rival ideological groups. By far the biggest section, the 'Free' Trade Unions, were closely, though not formally, linked to the Social Democratic Party : the Christian Trade Unions, mainly though not exclusively Catholic, had their principal strength in the Ruhr and Rhineland, where the 'Free' Unions were relatively weak ; and there was a third, much weaker section — the so-called Hirsch-Duncker Unions — which was ideologically attached to bourgeois liberalism. During the war there was a great development of Unionism in the metal industries, and a strong shop stewards' movement emerged and tended to follow a militant policy, many of its leaders being connected with the Independent Socialists (U.S.P.D.), and not a few with the Spartacus movement headed by Rosa Luxemburg and Karl Liebknecht. In the course of the Revolution there was a great inrush of new members, who had previously been outside the Trade Union movement ; and the Workers' Councils, consisting mainly of delegates chosen in the workshops, included many of these newcomers and presented something of a challenge to the established Trade Union leadership. The 'Free' Unions, led at the centre mainly by Majority Socialists who had supported the war, made haste to arrive at collective agreements with the employers and to secure the fullest possible recognition, while doing their utmost to remain aloof from politics and to prevent their members from advancing claims that would hinder the conversion of industry to peace-time production. This attitude put them at cross-purposes with the left-wingers who were demanding all power for the Workers' and Soldiers' Councils and were pressing for revolutionary changes in the conduct of industry. In the view of the Majority Socialists and of most of the established Trade Union leaders it was not practicable to press for immediate socialisation : the first task, they urged, was to get production restarted as speedily as possible in order to keep the population supplied. The question of socialisation, they felt, would have to stand over, and to be decided on in due course by the Constituent Assembly that the whole people was to elect.

It was therefore of the first importance to the old leaders, while the Councils were still, pending the Constituent Assembly, the ultimate source of authority — and it was from the Councils that the Provisional Government had received its powers — to win control over the Councils and prevent them from falling under the domination of the left wing. In this they were remarkably successful ; for their nation-wide, efficient organisation enabled them to get their supporters elected as delegates to the Councils in large numbers, so that, when the Congress of Workers' Councils met, the Majority Socialist and 'Free' Union delegates were in a large majority and were able both to secure control of the Executive Committee which the Congress set up and subsequently to use it as a means of abolishing its own authority by handing over its powers to the Constituent Assembly. This, of course, meant a decisive rejection of the ideas of 'Council Government' and proletarian dictatorship and the recognition of a Republic in which the Socialists of all tendencies were in a minority. This was in full accordance with the parliamentary democratic conceptions of the Majority Socialists and of the old Trade Union leaders, such as Karl Legien (1861–1920) ; but it was naturally most unpleasing not only to the 'Spartacus' Communists but also to the left-wing shop stewards and to most of the supporters of the Independent Socialists. For the latter, even if they were not Communists and were divided on the issue of complete 'Council Government', almost all wished to maintain the authority of the Councils for the time being, to use them as instruments for pressing on with socialisation, and to give them at least some recognised place in the structure of the future government of the Republic. In Berlin particularly, and also in Saxony and Thuringia, the left-wing elements had majorities in the Workers' Councils, and were strongly opposed to the cautious policy of the Trade Union leaders. Richard Müller, the Berlin metal-workers' leader and the outstanding figure in the Berlin Workers' Council, was a major figure among the left-wing Independents, and was quite ready to work with the Spartacists until, against the advice of Liebknecht and Rosa Luxemburg, they committed themselves to an insurrectionary policy which cut them off from the majority of the left.

The victory of the right wing in the Congress of Councils and in its Central Committee and the defeat of the premature and ill-prepared Spartacist uprisings of 1918 and early 1919 left the Independents and the main body of left-wing shop stewards in a difficult situation. They were not willing to hand over control of the organised industrial movement to Legien and the General Commission of the 'Free' Trade Unions, or to disband their own organisation, which rested on direct election in the factories. In practice, where the old 'Free' Trade Unions were strong and well established, the old leaders got their way and came to terms with the employers, most of whom were eager to do a deal with them in order to re-establish workshop discipline and avoid widespread strikes directed against private enterprise and the maintenance of traditional industrial relations. But, especially where the 'Free' Unions had been weak, and huge numbers were becoming organised for the first time, it was impossible for the old leaders to prevent the establishment of new Unions arising out of the Workers' Councils and by no means prepared to accept the disciplined moderation of the old leadership. Thus it happened that new Trade Unions, mainly under left-wing leadership, grew up in localities and establishments from which the old Unions had been shut out before the war, and also that, even where the old Unions were relatively strong, their leadership was often challenged by shop stewards' committees under left-wing influence. In the early months following the Revolution of November 1918 there were continual strike epidemics, as the workers tried to improve wages in order to keep pace with the rising cost of living. In many of these movements the 'Free' Trade Unions succeeded in keeping or gaining control ; but there were areas, especially in Berlin, Saxony, and the Ruhr, where the left-wing influence remained strong, and new Unions or local groups followed militant courses which the General Trade Union Commission was unable to hold in check.

Germany remained in a condition of increasing inflationary pressure through the whole period from 1918 to 1924, when stabilisation was at length achieved with the aid of the Dawes Loan. Of course, up to 1923, when the French marched into the Ruhr, the inflation was much less violent than it then became ; but it was throughout on a sufficient scale to call for continual action to adjust wages to the rising cost of living, and therefore to encourage Trade Union militancy. It was under these conditions that the great argument developed between those who urged the need to preserve Trade Union unity by struggling for a more active policy within the established Unions and those who regarded these Unions as so reactionary that the only correct course was to break away from them and set up rival Unions that would follow a revolutionary policy. The Comintern, in its attempt to discredit the Amsterdam Trade Union International, and to build up the Red International of Labour Unions as its Communist-controlled rival, at the outset sided with the second group. But when, after 1921, the hopes of speedy World Revolution faded and the Comintern went over to the slogan of the 'United Front', it became an essential part of the new policy that Communists should remain in the 'Amsterdam' Unions and endeavour to win them over ; and the policy of setting up rival Unions became a dangerous heresy. The effect was to create sharp differences of opinion among the German Communists, many of whom had been working actively in the new Unions and against the old ; and these differences came out very plainly at the Comintern Congresses of 1923 and 1924. When, after the fiasco of the projected Communist rising of 1923, Brandler and his group were pushed out of the leadership of the German

Communist Party, the new leaders included a number, such as Ruth Fischer, who had been strong critics of the 'United Front' policy. These leaders took over authority at a time when, because of the acute hardships caused by the Ruhr struggle, members were lapsing from the Trade Unions, both old and new, at a prodigious rate, and the entire movement was being reduced to impotence. Even the eight-hours' day, the greatest single victory of the 1918 Revolution, though it had been given legal force, had to be surrendered in face of the absolute predominance of capitalist interests in the Stresemann Government and its immediate successors ; and wages, which had fallen heavily in purchasing power during the crisis, remained for some time after the stabilisation at a terribly low level.

The introduction of the Rentenmark in November 1923 had by no means solved the stabilisation problem. Additional inflationary issues of paper money had been stopped, and the new provisional currency had provided a temporary basis for commercial operations. But the Rentenmark, having no real backing, was in truth no better than a 'confidence trick', which could not continue to work unless something could be done to put the currency on a really new basis — and this was quite beyond Germany's power, in the prevailing conditions, without help from outside. Such help only the United States, with its abundant supplies of gold and its vast capital resources available for overseas investment, was in a position to provide on a sufficient scale. One essential purpose of the Dawes Commission on Reparations, for which the Americans supplied the chairman, was to prepare the way for a loan to Germany large enough to make it possible to set up a new currency on an assured gold basis. Stresemann, anxious to come to terms with France and to stop the disintegration of the German economy, had realised that his best chance lay, not in attempting a dircet deal with France, but in bringing in the British and the Americans to aid him in putting German capitalism on its feet. He was successful, as we saw, in inducing the Americans to participate in the Dawes Commission, which produced a report by-passing the question of Germany's total liability to pay reparations, but linking a proposal concerning the payments to be made during the next few years with a proposal for an international loan that would allow a gold standard currency to be introduced and would supply the Germans with immediate means of making international payments. While the negotiations were at an early stage the Labour Party came to office in Great Britain ; and soon after the issue of the Dawes Report Poincaré fell from power in France and was replaced by a left bourgeois coalition under Édouard Herriot. These political changes were highly favourable to the acceptance of the Dawes proposals ; and early in August 1924 the Dawes Agreement was signed. This involved a large measure of control by the Allied Governments over Germany's finances and the handing over of the German railways to a special agency subject to Allied participation ; and on this account the terms were violently attacked by the more extreme nationalists in Germany. The Dawes Plan, however, did make it practicable to stabilise the German currency, and as soon as this was achieved foreign capital — mainly American — began flowing into Germany in order to take advantage of the exceptionally favourable conditions for profit-making created by low labour costs and the German hunger for capital, which led to the offer of high returns to lenders and investors. With the aid of this foreign investment, including both long-term and short-term funds, German industry made a very rapid recovery in world markets, the very low wages helping German manufacturers to undersell their rivals and the abundant supplies of capital enabling them to lend customers the means of payment. Much of the recovery was unsound, both because of extravagant spending by public bodies on grandiose public works and because money revocable at short notice was lent or tied-up in long-term undertakings : so that the German economy became deeply dependent on a continued flow of loans from the United States. For the time being, however, an appearance of high prosperity was created, and German capitalism, freed from debt by the inflation, seemed to have taken on a new lease of life.

Under these conditions, as employment boomed, it became possible for the German workers to begin to climb out of the abyss into which they had fallen and, step by step, to bring wages back to a more tolerable level. For achieving this the old 'Free' Trade Unions were more favourably placed than their left-wing antagonists, whose power had been more seriously undermined during the crisis ; and the 'Free' Unions gradually regained some of their power — as indeed did the Christian Trade Unions, which were in much better favour with the Government.

Ebert, who had remained in office as President after the Social Democrats were driven out of the Government in 1923, died in February 1925 ; and the problem arose of electing a successor under the Weimar Constitution. At the election in March each of the main political groups presented its own candidate. Dr. Jarres, the candidate of the right-wing Parties, got 10½ million votes ; Otto Braun (1872–1955), the Majority Socialist, got nearly 8 million ; Wilhelm Marx, the right-wing leader of the Centre Party, who had been Chancellor in 1923 and 1924, got nearly 4 million ; Ernst Thaelmann, the nominee of the Communists, 2 million. Candidates of the Democrats and the Bavarian People's Party got respectively 1½ and 1 million ; and, finally, General Ludendorff, put forward by the Nazis, got only a little over a quarter of a million. This meant that no-one had a clear majority, and under the Constitution a further ballot had to be held. The Centre Party tried to persuade the right-wing Parties to support Marx ; but they refused. The Social Democrats, however, decided to withdraw Braun and to support Marx as the lesser evil — a remarkable decision in view of his extremely reactionary record. The Catholic Trade Unions, too, of course, rallied behind Marx ; and so did the Democrats. Confronted by this combination of forces, the right-wing Parties withdrew Jarres, and put forward Field-Marshal Hindenburg, then aged 78, in his place ; and the Bavarian People's Party and the Nazis agreed to support him. The Communists, wholly hostile to both Hindenburg and Marx, put Thaelmann forward again, though the Comintern, still following its 'United Front' tactics, tried to persuade them to join the Social Democrats in supporting Marx. At the second election, in April, Hindenburg got 14½ million votes, Marx nearly 13¾ million, and Thaelmann again 2 million. The aged Field-Marshal thus became President of the Republic, in which he had never professed to believe ; and the effect was further to strengthen the control exercised by the Reichswehr over the civilian Government. Dr. Hans Luther, formerly

Stresemann's Finance Minister, an expert administrator who had been Burgomaster of Essen, had succeeded Marx as Chancellor in January 1925, and remained at the head of the Government until May 1926, when Marx came back to office. It was under Luther as Chancellor that the Locarno Pact of October 1925, the direct sequel to the Dawes Agreement, was concluded and the North Rhineland, including Cologne, evacuated by the Allied forces in December of that year, immediately after the Locarno Treaties had been formally signed.

A General Election had been held in Germany in May 1924, soon after the publication of the Dawes Report ; and the main issue had been whether the Report should be accepted or should be rejected because of the indignity involved in the foreign control over German finances which it proposed. The Socialists lost heavily on this occasion, falling from 169 seats in the Reichstag to 100 ; the Communists polled 3¾ million votes and won 62 seats, and the Nazis, with nearly 2 million votes, had 32 seats. There was a majority in the new Reichstag for accepting the Dawes Plan, but not a large enough majority to carry through the constitutional changes it required. Accordingly, a further General Election was held in December 1924. The results were that the Social Democrats gained nearly 1¾ million additional votes, whereas the Communist vote was reduced by nearly 1¼ million, and the Communist representation reduced from 62 to 45. At the other extreme the Nazis lost over a million votes, and won only 14 seats ; whereas the Nationalist Party, which had also opposed the Dawes Plan, gained half a million. As the Social Democrats were supporters of the Plan, and as the Nationalists were in process of abandoning their opposition and were preparing to join the Government, this second election considerably strengthened Stresemann's position, and made the way smooth for the ratification of the Dawes Plan and for the inflow of foreign capital into Germany, now securely under the joint rule of the capitalists and the Reichswehr. For the time being, the period of revolutionary activity was definitely at an end. The Social Democrats settled down to a policy of moderate constitutional opposition ; and both Nazis and Communists were for the time being far too weak to present any serious challenge.

The Reichstag elected in December 1924 remained in being

until May 1928. By then, German recovery had advanced a long way, and working-class conditions had substantially improved. The effect was to strengthen the Social Democrats and seriously to weaken the extreme right. In comparison with December 1924 the Nationalist Party lost nearly 2 million votes, whereas the Social Democrats gained a million, polling over 9 million. The Communists also rose by about half a million, to 3¼ million; whereas the Nazis polled well under a million. The bourgeois capitalist Parties lost ground slightly; but many of the seats lost by the Nationalists went to splinter right-wing Parties, most of whose supporters were to go over to Nazism during the ensuing crisis.

In this changed electoral situation the Social Democrats returned to office in coalition with the capitalist Parties which had supported Stresemann's policy of 'fulfilment'. Indeed, they held formally a dominating position in the new Cabinet with their leader, Hermann Müller (1876–1931), as Chancellor, Rudolf Hilferding (1877–1942), as Finance Minister, Karl Severing (1875–1952), as Minister of the Interior, and Rudolph Wissell (b. 1869), the advocate of economic planning, as Minister of Labour. Stresemann continued as Foreign Minister; and the Democrats, the Centre, and the Bavarian People's Party, as well as the People's Party — Stresemann's — and the Social Democrats were represented in the Cabinet. On the face of the matter, the Socialists seemed to be in control of the key positions, provided they could work with Stresemann in foreign affairs, including the reparations problem — and this appeared to present no serious difficulty, as the Socialists were thoroughly in favour of the policy of 'fulfilment' of which Stresemann was the outstanding advocate.

Nevertheless, the reality was very different from the appearance. The power of the Reichswehr remained unbroken, and financial policy under the Dawes Plan was controlled by the Allies in conjunction with Dr. Schacht, who knew well how to use this control as a means to the consolidation of the power of the great capitalist interests in Germany. These interests, though they had supported Stresemann so far, were strongly opposed to the return of the Social Democrats to office and to Stresemann's desire to build up a 'Grand Coalition' resting on the joint support of the right-wing Social Democrats and of the middle classes for a bourgeois Republic based on private enterprise ; and, without endorsing the anti-republican policies of the Nationalists, the President, and the Reichswehr leaders, they showed active hostility to the new Government and especially to Hilferding, who found himself practically helpless in the hands of the Reichsbank and the great financial interests. Moreover, though the Social Democrats could work well enough with Stresemann in foreign affairs, it was another thing to work with Stresemann's People's Party, which was keenly hostile to the Socialists' desire to restore the eight-hours' day and to enact progressive social legislation, particularly in the field of unemployment insurance. The Social Democrats found their attempts to introduce and carry such measures blocked by their partners in the Coalition, and were able to achieve practically nothing — though, as we saw, the Trade Unions were able to improve the workers' position, to a limited extent, by successful collective bargaining. Inside the S.P.D. the left wing, now headed by the former Communist, Paul Levi (1883–1930), who had returned to it after his expulsion by the Comintern in 1921, took strong objection to Social Democratic participation in the Government on these terms, but were voted down. The Socialist Ministers took office, and, even when they had come to realise how little they could do, kept it mainly for two reasons — their desire for a settlement with France and of the reparations problem, and their belief that the best they could hope for in the near future was a consolidation of the bourgeois Republic against the counter-revolutionary forces of the Nationalists, the Nazis, and the military leaders. It seemed a great victory to have compelled Hindenburg to accept a Socialist Chancellor and to have defeated the Nationalists and Nazis at the polls ; and, in effect, the Social Democrats were content to be Republicans and to forgo any action that might upset the precarious prosperity that had followed the acceptance of the Dawes Plan. Even when, in 1929, Stresemann's own Party, the People's Party, demanded Hilferding's resignation as Minister of Finance, the S.P.D. Ministers allowed him to be driven from office without more than a protest, and remained in the Government without him.

In the meantime, Stresemann had been actively pressing his

negotiations for a revision of the Dawes Plan and for the evacuation of the part of the Rhineland still occupied by Allied forces. His object was, above all, to get Germany's total obligations for reparations fixed and to bring to an end the foreign controls over the German railways and over German finance as a whole, and also to secure the complete evacuation of the country by foreign controlling authorities as well as by foreign soldiers. At The Hague Conference of August 1929 he was successful in getting most of his demands accepted by the Allies. The Young Plan, drawn up by a new Committee under American chairmanship and embodying a draft final settlement of the reparations problem, had been issued in June, and provided the basis for The Hague discussions. There were further hitches before a settlement based on the Plan was finally adopted in January 1930 ; but a preliminary agreement was reached at The Hague in August 1929.

Stresemann thus appeared to have consolidated his position ; but immediately after The Hague Conference of August a deep rift in the Cabinet over unemployment insurance led to a crisis which Stresemann with difficulty adjusted by a compromise on October 2nd. The same evening he had a fatal apoplectic stroke, and with his removal the basis for the 'Grand Coalition' immediately disappeared. The Hague Agreement went through ; but the Müller Cabinet, which had been held together only by his influence, could no longer command a majority in the Reichstag, and was driven from office. In March 1930 the 'Grand Coalition' was dissolved over the unemployment insurance issue, and Heinrich Brüning, the right-wing leader of the Centre Party, became Chancellor. Just before then, in February, the death of Paul Levi removed the outstanding leader of the Social Democratic left.

Even before Brüning took office, at the head of a Government from which the Socialists were shut out, the German situation had been profoundly altered by the outbreak of the American stock market crisis in the autumn of 1929. There were many indeed who refused to attach any deep significance to this crisis and prophesied a speedy return to boom conditions. But the immediate effect of it was to bring to an abrupt end the flow of American capital into Germany, and to start a reverse flow as short-term loans were called in. The German recovery, as we saw, had been a direct outcome of the large-scale inflow of American funds ; and its continuance depended on this flow being maintained. The German financiers and capitalists had to a large extent borrowed 'short' and lent or invested at long term ; so that the American money could not be repaid when it was called in ; and, even apart from that, German economic development could not be maintained without a continual flow of foreign funds. With the Chicago wheat-market crisis of February 1930 and the renewed and much more severe crisis and panic in the New York stock exchange in May, the repercussions on the German economy became much more serious ; and Brüning found himself faced with a sharp internal collapse, which he tried to meet by transferring the burden to the workers. In face of widespread bankruptcies and mounting unemployment the trend towards passive acceptance of the capitalist-controlled bourgeois Republic was reversed, and the extreme Parties, the Nationalists and Nazis on the one hand and Communists on the other, gained ground rapidly at the expense of the bourgeois Parties and of the Social Democrats, who were made to share the blame for the swelling difficulties of the Republic. The period of crisis, which ended with Hitler's assumption of power three years later, set in.

The history of this struggle falls beyond the period covered in the present volume. Here, it remains to retrace our steps in order to see what happened to the German Communist Party after, having failed to make its projected rising in October 1923, it shed Brandler from its leadership and accepted instead a new group of leaders — Maslow and Ruth Fischer in Berlin and Ernst Thaelmann in Hamburg. These new leaders belonged to the left wing, which had been keenly critical of Brandler's and Radek's interpretation of the 'United Front' policy and had been opposed to the Communist entry into the left Socialist Governments in Saxony and Thuringia and also, for the most part, to the attempt to work inside the established 'Free' Unions instead of promoting a rival movement. Thus, although after October 1923 it had to be recognised that there was no longer any chance of a Communist-led Revolution, the new leadership felt itself called upon to adopt the most extreme policy that was consistent with the situation. The big strikes of August 1923, in which the 'United Front' had found its most significant expression, had been a direct cause of the fall of the Cuno Government and of the entry of the Social Democrats into Stresemann's 'Grand Coalition', which the Communists most vehemently denounced as treason to the working class. In face of the situation and of the fall of the left Socialists in Saxony and Thuringia, there could be no further notion of a 'United Front' based on co-operation with the S.P.D. ; and the Communists plunged into a campaign of violent denunciation of the Social Democrats, rank and file as well as leaders. The fact that the Trade Unions, mainly under Social Democratic leadership, lost half their members in the economic adversities of 1923–4, also affected Communist policy in this field, by making it seem less important to capture the seriously weakened 'Free' Unions than to build up a new revolutionary movement in the factories in opposition to them ; and this resulted in a falling off of Communist influence in the 'Free' Unions and in an attempt to secure the direct election of Communists to the legally constituted factory committees, in opposition to the 'Free' Trade Union nominees.

This left turn in German Communist policy lasted from 1923 to 1925, and was then sharply reversed. By mid-1925 Ebert had died and Hindenberg had been elected as President ; and in the presidential election the Communists had done very badly. It had become necessary to recognise that the new Communist policy was not paying a dividend ; and the blame was put, both in Germany and in Moscow, on Maslow and Ruth Fischer, who were thrust abruptly out of their positions, leaving Thaelmann in control. At this point, in Russia, Stalin had won his battle against Trotsky, but had not yet broken with Zinoviev or Kamenev ; and it suited the Russian book to tone down the revolutionism of the Communist Parties in the West. Accordingly, under Thaelmann the German Party took a distinct move to the right, especially in Trade Union affairs, resuming its attempts to gain influence in the 'Free' Trade Unions, which were recovering rapidly from the disasters of 1923–4. Once more, instead of running their own tickets in the factory committee elections, the Communists sought to get their candidates adopted by the Trade Unions and elected under Trade Union auspices ; and, with the Socialists back in opposition to the right-wing bourgeois Cabinet, it became possible again to woo the left wing of the S.P.D. During the period of economic recovery from 1925 to 1928 the German Communists followed a definitely non-revolutionary line in harmony with the current policy of Russia and the Comintern.

Then, in 1928, there was a further abrupt change of policy. The Social Democrats, having done well in the General Election of that year,[1] came back to office in Stresemann's new 'Grand Coalition' and thus again became open 'social traitors'; and at the same time Stalin, having settled accounts with Zinoviev, launched the new movement to the left in Russia that took shape in the First Five-Year Plan and in the mass liquidation of the *kulaks* and the hasty resort to agricultural collectivisation. The German Communists, too, though much less than the Social Democrats, had substantially increased their vote in the General Election and were encouraged to believe that Nationalism and Nazism were well on the ebb. Paradoxically, at this point the right wing of the German Communist Party — the old Brandler group — won a majority on the Central Committee of the Party and ousted Thaelmann from power. But its victory was short-lived: under orders from Moscow the right-wingers were promptly displaced and Thaelmann was put back at the head of a Committee that was prepared to carry out the Comintern's orders for a sharp turn to the left. From this point onwards German Communism became involved in the struggles which led up to Hitler's triumph in 1933. Social Democracy was again the arch-enemy: the 'Free' Trade Unions were again to be fought as betrayers of the workers' cause. The Communists, throughout these years, persisted in refusing to take the Nazi danger seriously, and even, at certain points, made common cause with the Nazis against the Social Democrats — for example, in the plebiscite by which an attempt was made to displace the Prussian Social Democratic Government in 1931.

After the fall of the Müller Reich Government in March 1930 the Social Democrats had passed into opposition in the Reich, but had kept their control of the Governments in Prussia and certain other States, and had thus continued as an important factor in internal politics. Already in 1928 the Communists had come into sharp opposition to the Prussian Government, in which

[1] See p. 651.

Otto Braun and Karl Severing (1875–1952) were the out-standing figures. The occasion had been the annual May Day demonstration in Berlin, customarily a joint affair of all the working-class bodies. In 1928 the Communists decided to hold a separate demonstration of their own ; and the Prussian Government, fearful of a serious riot, prohibited all demonstra-tions. The Social Democrats and the 'Free' Trade Unions accepted the ban ; but the Communists determined to defy the order. The chief of police, a Social Democrat named Zorgiebel, ordered the police to fire on the demonstrators, and a number were killed. Barricades were erected in the working-class district of Neukoelln, which held out for two days. The Communists issued a call for a general strike, but found no response. They themselves redoubled their denunciations of the Prussian Social Democratic Government and, as we saw, subsequently joined forces with the Nazis in an attempt to put it out of office. But in Prussia the Social Democrats, with declining power, held on to office until von Papen finally dis-placed them, without resistance, in 1932.

Opinions are bound to differ on the question whether the Social Democrats were right in joining the Reich 'Grand Coalition' in 1928, after their electoral success. Discontents were then already rising sharply, especially in the countryside ; but American capital was still flowing in, and there was a case for believing that the best thing that could happen, in the existing circumstances, was a consolidation of the Republic, with all its faults, through continued inflows of foreign funds. Stresemann's death and the onset of the great American depression, which cut off these supplies, entirely altered the situation ; and it is clear in retrospect that the Müller Cabinet would have done better to resign at once, instead of waiting to be pushed out a few months later. It also appears, in retrospect, that the Social Democrats were wrong in holding on to office in Prussia after Brüning had become Chancellor ; for this involved them in participation in his measures and helped to make Social Democracy widely unpopular, and to drive many of its supporters away — some to Communism, but many more to Nazism — as conditions grew worse and worse. Perhaps it was already too late, in view of the American collapse, to rally the working classes for a final struggle against Nazism : at all events, neither Social Democrats nor Communists, from their widely different standpoints, made any such attempt. The German Revolution had never recovered from the defeats that followed sharply on its initial success. Even from the early months of 1919 it had been in almost continuous retreat ; for there had never been a united German working class to carry it on, or even to defend it. It is easy, according to taste, to blame either the Social Democrats as having betrayed the Revolution by invoking Noske and the 'Free Corps' to put the left wing down, and for having left the old bureaucracy in authority and the Reichswehr free to reassert its power, or, alternatively, the Communists as having split the working-class movement again and again in pursuit of an imaginary proletarian dictatorship for which there was never a solid basis of working-class support. For my part, I blame both, and see the roots of the trouble far back in the record of German Socialism in the days of the Second International, when the Party signally failed to face the implications of the conquest of power against the old junker-militarist order, and preferred to live on evasions of the real issue, combining revolutionary phrases with reformist practices and never attempting to answer the questions involved in a real attempt to establish a Socialist society. These evasions were largely common to the Parties of Social Democracy in the advanced countries of the capitalist world : they were most disastrous in Germany because German Social Democracy was the strongest movement — indeed the model on which the Social Democratic Parties of other countries were largely based. The German people suffered most of all in the event ; yet there are all too few signs that the lessons have been learnt even now.

Whatever else may be in doubt, the disastrousness of the policy followed by the German Communists during the final years of the Weimar Republic is beyond dispute. Even if there was much to criticise and to blame in the policies of the Social Democratic Party during these years, it was both criminal and foolish on the part of the Communists to join hands with the Nazis against them. It can be argued that the main part of the blame rests not on the German Communists, who acted under Comintern orders with hardly any regard for the situation in Germany, but on Stalin, who drove them to act in this way.

This, however, is but a lame excuse ; for the Germans had no business to be so entirely subservient to Stalin's will. The entire episode was in fact the outstanding instance of the disastrous errors that arose out of the complete domination of the Comintern over the Communist Parties of the Western countries — and of Stalin himself over the Comintern. These conditions made it impossible for any Western Communist Party to be capably led ; for every leader who displayed any qualities of independent judgment was promptly weeded out at Stalin's orders. Thaelmann was acceptable as a leader precisely because he showed no such qualities and acted as a mere dummy at Moscow's call. The only interesting question is what induced Stalin to insist on a policy that was disastrous not only for German Communism but for the Soviet Union as well. The explanation most often offered by Communists was that Nazism presented no real danger and that its success in undermining the Weimar Republic would merely prepare the way for a Communist victory. Nazism was dismissed as the last, desperate throw of German capitalism in its death-pangs and as incapable of creating any régime that would not speedily collapse on account of its inner contradictions. Such a view was grossly misleading, as the event showed. Nazism may indeed have been incapable of enduring as a social structure without war ; but there was no assurance that, if it led to war and emerged as victor, it would not be able to impose its discipline for a long period upon the vanquished, and to destroy for a long time all hope of Socialist or Communist success. Even if its ultimate defeat in war could have been predicted — which in my opinion it could not — it is too much to suppose that Stalin really meant to procure a Nazi victory in Germany in order to bring on a world war that would lead to its overthrow. Clearly his calculations cannot have been on these lines.

On what lines, then, did he calculate ? He appears to have believed in a general 'scheme' of historical development in accordance with which revolutionary and non-revolutionary situations come about alternatively and to have held as a dogma of Marxism that, whenever a revolutionary situation seemed to be approaching, the task of Communists was to accelerate it by every means in their power, regardless of the character of the threatening revolution, and accordingly to abet the revolutionary forces even if their aims were utterly opposed to those of Communism. In the Communist interpretation of Marxism it was taken as an axiom that the next revolution would be the proletarian revolution and no other possibility was taken into account, the proletariat being assumed to be the only revolutionary force worthy of being considered. Accordingly, any movement that enfeebled the existing order must, *ex hypothesi*, lead towards proletarian revolution, and was worthy of Communist support. It may have helped towards this illusion that Stalin, like Lenin before him, was above all else a professional revolutionary and instinctively disposed to sympathise with revolution for its own sake. At all events, Stalin's responsibility for the support given by the German Communists to the Nazis in 1930-31 is indisputable ; and it is even arguable that in ordering this support he brought about Hitler's conquest of power and thus induced the second world war — not because he foresaw or planned these things, but because his dogmatic historical schema led him fatally astray. No doubt, the Nazis might have attained to power even if the German workers had joined forces in opposing them : what is certain is that the rift in the German working class, and the support given to the Nazis at a critical stage by the German Communists, handed the victory to Hitler on a plate.

If, in conclusion, one asks what contributions German Socialism made to Socialist thought between 1918 and its eclipse in 1933, the answer must be that it made almost none. In 1918 its leaders, on right and left alike, were entirely unready with any real ideas about the process of constructing a Socialist society. There were, of course, on the extreme left some who saw salvation in following, in all possible respects, the Russian example, and demanded 'all power for the Soviets' in one breath and the dictatorship of the newly founded Communist Party in the next. There were also revolutionaries, above all Rosa Luxemburg, who saw the folly of mere 'putschism' and were already fearful, even in 1918, of a degeneration of the Russian Revolution into a party dictatorship that would destroy the creative power of the working class and lead on to personal or caucus dictatorship. There were, on the other hand, men such as Kautsky, who not only abhorred dictatorship in any form but also, in effect, argued that the Russian Revolution ought not to have happened at all, or ought at any rate, in so backward a country, to have stopped short at the bourgeois-democratic stage. Such views, however, can hardly be held to constitute any original contribution to thought. In relation to the problems which confronted the German Socialists in 1918 hardly any thinking had been done, and very little was done during the ensuing years.

Thus, the Socialists, in the hour of their initial victory, seem to have had very little idea even about the basic institutions of the new society they were called upon to set up on the ruins of the Hohenzollern empire. The six men who constituted the first Provisional Government — the Majority Socialists Ebert, Scheidemann, and Otto Landsberg, and the Independents Haase, Ledebour, and Emil Barth — were never any of them theorists, and their initial action in leaving non-Socialists at the head of the departmental Ministries and appointing two Socialists, one from each fraction, to each Ministry to keep an eye on the Minister, without defining their powers, has all the air of an improvisation for meeting an immediate emergency. It had, however, very large consequences ; for it resulted in the old civil servants keeping their posts under the new Ministers, and thus carried on the administrative tradition of the old society into the new. This, clearly, was what Ebert at any rate wanted to do ; but it does not appear that the Independent Socialist Ministers had any alternative plan to offer, though both Ledebour and Barth did wish to keep power for the time being at least in the hands of the Workers' and Soldiers' Councils, and saw the danger of leaving authority in the hands of supporters of the old order. Nor does the danger of leaving the old judges and courts of law in being and thus carrying on the legal tradition of the old Reich appear to have been given serious consideration. Attention was centred almost entirely on the matter of choosing and convening a Constituent Assembly, which was to provide a formal Constitution for the new order ; and only the out-and-out advocates of 'Council Government' questioned that this Assembly should be chosen by universal suffrage, on parliamentary lines, as the only way consistent with democratic principle. The dispute took place between the Majority

Socialists and the Independents, not on the question whether there should be such an Assembly or not, but on the timing of its election and on the question what action the Government, as the creature of the Councils, was entitled to take before it met. One great issue in this connection was that of land reform. Should the great landlords east of the Elbe be immediately dispossessed in the name of the Revolution and their lands be made public property or handed over to the peasants ; or should the whole matter be left for the Constituent Assembly to decide as it might think fit ? This was a crucial issue ; for by leaving the landlords in possession, even temporarily, the Government provided them with a basis from which they could take steps to build up opposition to the new order — for example, by offering an asylum on their estates to the 'Free Corps' which were soon to give the Revolution so much trouble.

The Majority Socialists, upholders of parliamentary democracy, were eager to get the Constituent Assembly into action as quickly as possible, and were determined to leave over for its decision everything it was possible to leave. This, incidentally, gave them their best chance of defeating the Independents and the left wing generally, because they had by far the superior organisation for electoral purposes, and no time would be left for their opponents to build up an effective counter-movement. But it also involved the danger that the Socialists — all groups together — would fail to gain a majority if the elections were held at once ; and this, as we saw, was what actually occurred, so that the tasks of making the new Constitution and of deciding the basic principles on which the new society was to rest were handed over to a predominantly bourgeois body that would clearly not proceed to the establishment of a *Socialist* Republic. Indeed, the task of drafting the new Constitution fell at the outset to a non-Socialist, Professor Preuss ; and the Congress of Workers' and Soldiers' Councils, in which the Majority Socialists had gained the predominant position, made haste to abdicate its authority in favour of the Constituent Assembly, which was thus able to assume full powers unquestioned except by the right-wing extremists who rejected the Republic on any terms, and by the Communists, who were easily pushed aside in the troubles of the early months. The Majority Socialists, to say the least, aimed not at

Socialism directly but only at parliamentary democracy, which they regarded as the only legitimate road to Socialism ; and the Independents were divided enough on this issue not to be able to offer an agreed alternative, though they did try to delay the Assembly and to anticipate its meeting by making certain vital decisions on the authority of the Revolution and of the Councils as its embodiment.

Side by side with land reform, the great issue was that of industrial socialisation. Was capitalist property, or even the key sections of it, to be transferred at once to public ownership and control ? On this issue, as we saw, both Majority Socialists and many Independents were against upsetting the basis of industrial enterprise, and favoured leaving the matter over and attempting meanwhile to restore production under the existing firms, usually adding that there would have to be some arrangement for workers' participation in control. It was widely feared that any attempt at socialisation would further dislocate production and make the existing chaos worse ; and there were also fears that the Allied Governments would either veto socialisation or make it an excuse for confiscating the socialised properties as a contribution to reparations. There was also, on the part of the Majority Socialists, an assertion that such matters should be left to be settled by the Constituent Assembly, and, among the Trade Union leaders, many favoured not socialisation but some form of *Mitbestimmung*, or Co-determination, such as Karl Legien had advocated before the war.[1] The effect was that German industry came back to life under capitalist ownership and control, and that it was left to the Assembly to consider how much, if anything, should be socialised and what, if anything, should be done to meet the demand for workers' participation in control.

Thus it came about that, while the Constitution was being drafted at Weimar, a Socialisation Commission was set up to explore the general issue of public versus capitalist enterprise, and Rudolph Wissell appeared as the principal Social Democratic advocate of a planned economy, presenting his main proposals to the Assembly in May 1919. But Wissell, then Minister of National Economy, could not get his proposals accepted by the Assembly, and was soon forced to resign ;

[1] See Vol. III, Part I, p. 312.

and nothing came of the Socialisation Commission but a series of declaratory proposals which had no practical effect till they were translated into positive laws — and that they never were. All that did happen was the setting up of a statutory system of Works Councils, which had been promised in March 1919 ; but the powers conferred on these bodies were carefully restricted in order to prevent them either from taking on a political character or from having any real managerial control. Their main functions related to such matters as works welfare, though they also gave workers some measure of protection against arbitrary dismissal. They did nothing to alter the fundamental relations between employers and employed, or to set up any form of co-management — much less, to introduce any sort of socialisation. The German Socialists were, indeed, wholly unready to tackle the socialisation issue, which they had always pushed out of discussion as something that would happen 'after the Revolution' and that needed no consideration until the Revolution had occurred. The only pre-war projects that had been worked out were Legien's ideas of *Mitbestimmung*, or joint control by employers and employed ; and these were pushed aside by the employers as soon as they began to recover from the fright into which they had been plunged by the events of 1918. The railways remained socialised, as they had been before the Revolution ; and the management remained in essentials as before, except that Trade Union bargaining was now recognised and some amount of joint consultation was introduced. No major industry — not even the coal-mines — underwent socialisation : nor did the Majority Socialists appear even to regret this. German capitalism was allowed to remain intact and to reassert its power as soon as the immediate danger of Socialist Revolution receded. The Weimar Republic became a capitalist Republic, and was bound to do so from the moment when power passed from the Workers' Councils to the Constituent Assembly.

During the ensuing years, though hot controversies continued between Social Democrats and Communists and also between Social Democrats of the right and of the left, nobody made any considerable contribution to Socialist thinking. The Communists were too busy adapting themselves to the changing requirements of the Comintern to do any original thinking of their own, though they argued endlessly among themselves about the tactics of revolution and about such matters as the correct interpretation of the 'United Front'. The Social Democrats, too, were almost exclusively occupied with arguments about tactics and about the requirements of democratic principles and the wickedness of the Communist would-be dictators. Continually on the defensive, they felt no need to elaborate their ideas about a Socialism they saw no prospect of establishing. Hilferding, their chief financial expert, did indeed give much thought to the problems of a democratic tax structure, and Wissell did attempt to work out some of the essentials of a planned economy resting on state control rather than on general socialisation ; but apart from these two the new contributions were remarkably jejune. There was nothing in German Socialism after 1918 at all on a par with the great Revisionist controversies of pre-war days, or with Hilferding's work on *Finanz-Kapital*, published in 1910, or with Rosa Luxemburg's *Accumulation of Capital* (1913), though the second volume of this last, replying to her critics, appeared only in 1919, and her important small book on *The Russian Revolution*, edited by Paul Levi, only in 1922. Post-war German Socialism threw up no important new theorists, and fought out its theoretical battles too much under the shadow of Russia to strike out with original thoughts of its own.

CHAPTER XXI

GREAT BRITAIN TO THE FALL OF THE SECOND LABOUR GOVERNMENT, 1926–1931

AFTER the defeat of the British general strike in 1926 the Trade Unions, as we saw, were reduced to a purely defensive rôle until there had been time for them to rebuild their depleted funds and win back the members who dropped out as a consequence of the collapse. The political Labour movement, however, underwent no similar decline, but was rather benefited by the growing demand among the workers for improved conditions of unemployment benefit — these having been worsened after the fall of the Labour Government in 1924 by regulations under which benefit was refused to those alleged to be 'not genuinely seeking work' and the periods for receipt of 'Uncovenanted' benefit were cut down. During the years from 1927 to 1929 world trade and employment were in general improving, and the capitalist system appeared to be becoming less unstable ; but in Great Britain, mainly as a consequence of the mistake made by the Conservatives in restoring the gold standard at the pre-war dollar parity, unemployment remained high and social discontent grew rapidly in the 'depressed areas' chiefly affected by it. Consequently, at the General Election of 1929 the Labour Party considerably improved its position, winning 289 seats as against 151 in 1924. This put it a good way ahead of the Conservatives, who won only 260 seats, but still in a minority against its rivals when account is taken of the 57 Liberals. The Labour Party was thus for a second time faced with the necessity of deciding whether to take office without a majority of its own, though it was now in a much stronger position than it had been in 1924. Without hesitation its leaders decided to form a Government ; and Ramsay MacDonald again became Prime Minister without any pact with the Liberals, but in the knowledge that enough of them to keep him in power would be likely to do so if his Government limited itself to a policy that involved no attack on the fundamental institutions of capitalism. The unspoken understanding with the Liberals ruled out any important measure of nationalisation, even of the coal-mines, but appeared to be fully compatible both with measures designed to increase employment through the extension of public works and with an international policy aiming at the further relaxation of international tensions, at progressive disarmament by agreement, and at the liberalisation of international trade, especially by means of a 'tariff truce'. The main tasks in these latter fields fell to Arthur Henderson as Foreign Secretary and to William Graham (1887–1932), at the Board of Trade ; for MacDonald did not double the parts of Prime Minister and Foreign Secretary, as he had done in 1924. On the home front, conditions seemed favourable because a section of the Liberals, headed by Lloyd George and mainly inspired by the economist, J. M. Keynes (1883–1946), had come forward in the Report of the Liberal Industrial Inquiry on *Britain's Industrial Future* (1928) and in pamphlets published during the election — for example, *We Can Conquer Unemployment* by Keynes and H. D. Henderson — with an extensive programme of state control and positive action to increase employment at least as advanced as anything the Labour Party itself had produced until it issued its own *How to Conquer Unemployment* (written by the present writer) as part of its election propaganda. The Liberals were by no means united in support of the Lloyd George-Keynes proposals ; but it seemed reasonable to suppose that the Lloyd George group at any rate would be prepared to keep the Labour Party in office for the time being, on the assumption that it would do something to implement its declared policy on the unemployment problem.

When the second Labour Government took office in June 1929 the world economic outlook seemed favourable for action in this field and also in respect of international affairs. But hardly had it begun to settle down when the stock market collapse in the United States gave warning that all was far from well on the economic front ; and by the middle of 1930 it was evident that a world economic crisis was well on the way. The settlement of German Reparations under the Dawes Plan of 1924 was already proving to be unworkable, and it had become clear that it would have to revised. Much more serious, however, was the sudden drying up of the flood of American capital that had been pouring into Europe, and especially into Germany, since the adoption of the Dawes Plan. This withdrawal revealed the fact that economic recovery in Europe had been in reality dependent on the inflow of American money and that without it not only would the Germans be unable to pay Reparations but also the entire credit structure in Europe would be in danger of speedy collapse. It was, however, impossible to prevent the Americans, in their search for 'liquidity', from keeping their capital at home and even from seeking to withdraw what they could of their loans and investments in Europe ; and many European lenders found that they had locked up at long term resources which they had borrowed at short term from the United States. The full consequences of the American economic collapse became manifest only by stages. At first there were many who hoped that the stock market collapse would be followed by a rapid recovery and that the Americans would resume their lending on a scale sufficient to keep the European economies from disaster. It soon became clear, however, that the forces of disequilibrium in the United States were very powerful — especially the decline in the relative purchasing power of the farm sector — and that the Americans were plunging helplessly towards the worst depression capitalism had ever experienced and were dragging down with them the entire capitalist economy of Western and Central Europe.

The bleakness of the economic outlook became apparent only some time after the Labour Government had assumed office. But already in 1930 the numbers out of work were rising rapidly ; and the improved conditions of benefit which the Government introduced were causing the cost of their maintenance to rise faster still. At the same time, the spread of the depression was having adverse effects on British exports ; for, apart from the decline of the American market, each country, as its difficulties increased, turned to reducing imports in the hope of improving its balance of payments. Moreover, as openings for imports fell in one country after another, each exporting area did its utmost to discover alternative markets ; and Great Britain, as the principal country still operating under

Free Trade, was the obvious choice for the dumping of surpluses that could not be disposed of elsewhere. This seriously affected the British balance of payments, upset already by the American crisis; and the correct remedy, according to the traditional precepts of orthodox finance, was deflation designed both to bring down British prices and to encourage an inflow of foreign funds. Unfortunately Philip Snowden, the Labour Chancellor of the Exchequer, was as entirely orthodox in his monetary opinions as the most reactionary banker, and used all his influence and obstinacy — which were both very great — to prevent the Government from spending any money it could avoid spending. This meant that proposals to expand public works in order to increase employment — and with it purchasing power — were dismissed as much too costly, and that it was deemed preferable — because cheaper in immediate outlay — to maintain the growing numbers out of work in enforced idleness than to set them to useful labour. The Government, unable to shape any coherent programme for dealing with unemployment, remitted the problem first to the right-wing railwaymen's leader, J. H. Thomas (1874–1949) — almost the worst possible choice — and then associated with him George Lansbury and Thomas Johnston (b. 1882), the Under-Secretary for Scotland, together with Sir Oswald Mosley (b. 1896), a convert from Toryism who had been made Chancellor of the Duchy of Lancaster. There was no likelihood that this team would agree among themselves or that, even if they did, they would be able to shake Snowden's determination to pursue the ways of financial orthodoxy.

By the middle of 1930, when the Government had been in office for a year, registered unemployment had risen from 9·6 per cent in June 1929 to 15·4 per cent: by the end of 1930 it was up to 2½ millions. Meanwhile Mosley had taken the lead in calling for a bolder policy designed to increase employment and, failing to persuade Thomas, had put his proposals into a memorandum — the 'Mosley Memorandum' — which went to the Cabinet with Lansbury's and Johnston's approval. It was rejected; and Mosley thereupon resigned from the Government. In October the matter was carried to the Labour Party Conference, at which Mosley attacked the Government and defended his policy and was only narrowly defeated by 1,251,000 votes against 1,046,000 — a clear sign of the mounting discontent among the Labour Party's supporters in the country. Mosley continued his campaign, and in February 1931 issued a pamphlet, *A National Policy*, expounding his proposals, with the backing, among others, of such well-known leftists as John Strachey (b. 1901) and Aneurin Bevan (b. 1897). A little later, having failed to get the main body of the M.P.s to support him, Mosley left the Labour Party and set up a 'New Party' which before long developed into the embryonic organisation of British Fascism. Only four Labour M.P.s — one his wife — followed him into the New Party ; and of them John Strachey resigned almost at once. The others who had supported the Mosley Memorandum — including Bevan — refused to have anything to do with the new move. Mosley had undoubtedly expected a much greater following : he had no understanding of the sentiment of loyalty that bound nearly all Socialists to the Labour Party, however critical they might be of its policy. Nor had he himself any loyalty to the cause of the workers. Meanwhile the Government plunged on from one difficulty to another. Its legislative programme for the new session, announced in October 1930, contained nothing about the unemployment problem ; for it had no idea what to do about it, except to hang on and hope for the best.

What followed, however, was not a turn for the better but a more and more rapid deterioration. Under Liberal pressure, the Government even resorted to an attempt to cut the cost of keeping the unemployed by an Anomalies Act, which eliminated a substantial number, especially of married women, from the workers entitled to receive benefits. It also appointed a special Committee dominated by political opponents — the May Economy Committee — to report on means of reducing public expenditure. This committee duly produced a 'scare' report which, by making the situation appear even worse than it was, helped to bring about a foreign run on the pound sterling, and confronted the Government with the sheer impossibility of maintaining the pound's value, without the aid of large loans from abroad. Substantial loans were in fact secured, from the Central Banks of the United States and of France ; but they melted away in face of the ever-growing mistrust of sterling, and yet further loans were called for, with no assurance that they too would not be speedily dissipated. At this point the reactionary Governor of the Bank of England, Montagu Norman, seems to have used his influence with the Americans to induce them to attach stringent conditions to any further loans. At all events, that was what Snowden gave his Cabinet colleagues to understand. The Labour Ministers were faced with an ultimatum requiring them to cut unemployment benefits and to make other drastic economies at the expense of the working class as the only alternative to going off the gold standard, to which Snowden was fanatically devoted.

It seems clear that most of the Labour Ministers were by this time in a state of utter bewilderment. They did not understand international finance ; and they erroneously supposed that Snowden did. MacDonald was as bewildered as the rest. For a long time past he had been presiding over an Economic Advisory Council — of which Keynes, as well as Thomas and other Ministers — but not Snowden — were members. One expedient after another for dealing with the situation had been debated, Keynes pressing especially for a revenue tariff to reduce imports and bring in resources to the Exchequer ; but MacDonald had refused to allow any conclusions to be reached, and in the background was Snowden's rejection of every possible course except further and further deflation.

At length the final crisis arrived. MacDonald called on his Cabinet to accept drastic retrenchments at the expense of the unemployed ; and when a majority of them shrank back, he announced the Government's resignation and reappeared as the Prime Minister of a new 'National' Government made up mainly of Conservatives and Liberals, together with the few leading Labourites who had agreed to follow him — among them Snowden and Thomas, who thus passed, with him, out of the Labour movement they had served through the better part of their lives. The new Government proclaimed itself as taking office in order to 'save the pound' ; but almost its first act was to go off the gold standard, which had till then been regarded as inviolable. In this matter it had in reality no choice ; for things had gone much too far for the value of sterling to be maintained at the existing parity. But it went on to introduce, not the 'revenue tariff' which Keynes had asked for, but a thoroughgoing protective system which reversed the entire fiscal policy of a century.

The fall of the Labour Government in 1931 was even more ignominious than that of its predecessor seven years before, for it was the outcome of sheer and manifest incompetence in handling the entire situation in which Great Britain had been placed by the world economic crisis. That situation was admittedly very difficult : Great Britain could not by any means have escaped unaffected by the repercussions of the world crisis. What was amiss in the Government's policy was that it allowed the position to drift from bad to worse, making no attempt to apply either Keynes's policy or that to which it was committed by its own earlier pronouncements. This happened, not because most of the individual Labour Ministers were incompetent at their departmental jobs, but because they had no understanding of financial questions and, above all, because MacDonald could never make up his mind and allowed Snowden to veto every measure that might have helped to improve the state of affairs. Henderson, the most important figure in the Cabinet with these two, was entirely preoccupied during the critical period with foreign affairs — above all, with the Preparatory Disarmament Conference and with other efforts to reduce international tensions, and took very little part in the discussion of home affairs till the final stages of the crisis, when he joined those who refused to accept the 'economy' measures proposed at the expense of the working class.

MacDonald, in fact, had been getting more and more out of touch with most of his colleagues long before the decisive break came. He had been hobnobbing with 'society' people and enjoying the high social position his office gave him, mixing with only a very few of his Cabinet colleagues and often pointedly ignoring or snubbing the rest — including Henderson and Lansbury. He had ceased to be in any sense a Socialist, even of the very right-wing sort he had formerly been ; and he was easily able to convince himself that in the hour of national crisis he was the indispensable leader — even though he had no idea whither he wished to lead. During the war, because of his ambiguous attitude and thanks to the venomous attacks on him in the capitalist press, he had acquired the wholly undeserved reputation of standing nearer to the left than to the right wing ; and on this account the Clydesiders had brought him back to the Party leadership in preference to the honest but pedestrian J. R. Clynes. Since then he had shown again and again that all his sympathies were with the extreme right of the Party ; but until 1929 he had at any rate appeared to be still some sort of a Socialist, and the very woolliness and ambiguity of his public utterances had helped to conceal the extent of his defection from even the most moderate Socialist ideas. His action in 1931 exposed him finally : he was allowed to carry on for some years as the mere figurehead of a preponderantly Conservative Government ; but he counted for the nothing he essentially was.

Only a few of MacDonald's colleagues followed him into support of the 'National' Government. Snowden, raised to the rank of Viscount, pursued his former associates with the utmost venom in the General Election which immediately followed the crisis, but speedily quarrelled with the new team and resigned from the 'National' Government in protest against its tariff policy. Snowden had been, in most respects, much more a Socialist than MacDonald had ever been ; but he was essentially a doctrinaire, and he combined with his collectivism an impassioned devotion to Free Trade and to financial orthodoxy. These beliefs had rendered him quite incapable of accepting any unorthodox methods of dealing with the emergency, and had, no less than MacDonald's shilly-shallying, caused him to be mainly obstructive as conditions grew steadily worse. He was, moreover, the most self-righteous of men, and was quite unable to believe that in whatever he had done or left undone he had not been utterly right. After his resignation he simply disappeared from politics, living on to produce an autobiography in which he threw the maximum of blame on everybody else, but vigorously asserted his own infallibility. As for J. H. Thomas, he had never pretended to be a Socialist. He was a skilled Trade Union leader, who understood well the act of bargaining on the railwaymen's behalf about wages and conditions, but was entirely unsympathetic to their wider aims — indifferent about nationalisation, and actively hostile to their claims for a share in the control of the railway service. He had worked more closely than most with MacDonald during the Labour Government, and had been among the first advocates of a tariff to restrict imports. What he lacked most, as the sequel showed, was common honesty of purpose.

In the General Election which followed the crisis in the autumn of 1931 the Labour Party, having lost its best-known leaders and discredited itself by its failure to take any effective action, went down to disastrous defeat. Its M.P.s were reduced from 289 to 46, exclusive of 6 who were elected without official party endorsement. These 6 included 3 I.L.P. representatives, who stood without official support — among them James Maxton (1885–1946) — and 3 others, of whom 2 were closely associated with the I.L.P. During the period of office of the Labour Government the I.L.P. had been steadily losing patience with it ; and the Labour Party Executive had refused to endorse its candidates unless they agreed to accept the full party discipline. At the time of the election the I.L.P. was already more than half way towards secession ; and it finally left the Labour Party the following year, condemning itself to an isolated position between the Labour Party and the Communists in which it was unable to exert any effective influence.

The General Election cost most of the remaining Labour Party leaders their seats in Parliament. Of the members of the dismissed Cabinet only George Lansbury was returned, and was chosen as parliamentary leader not because he wanted the position but because there was no-one else. Clement Attlee (b. 1883) became his second-in-command, and later took over the leadership when Lansbury's pacifism led to his resignation, in face of the developing war situation, in 1935. Henderson, defeated in 1931, came back to Parliament only in 1933, already a dying man. He did not resume the party leadership, continuing to devote himself, while his strength allowed, to his tasks as President of the ill-fated Disarmament Conference, though by then all hopes of success had been squashed by Hitler's victory in Germany. He died, worn out, in 1935. Always, in most matters, on the right wing of the Party, he had served it most faithfully according to his lights and had been the principal architect of its fortunes during the post-war years. He had used every effort, again and again, to hold the Party together despite its divisions. During the war he had been mainly responsible for preventing the exclusion of the anti-war I.L.P. ; and despite the strength of his moderate convictions he had repeatedly taken the side of tolerance in intra-party disputes. Like many of his fellow-Trade Unionists of the older generation, Henderson had begun his political career as a Liberal, and had kept many of his Liberal convictions when he rallied early to the Labour Representation Committee. He hardly regarded himself as a Socialist until he joined hands with Sidney Webb to reconstruct the Labour Party on a basis of gradualist Socialism in 1917 ; and thereafter he was always firmly on the gradualist side. Henderson lacked personal magnetism and was not of much account as an orator, though he could make an excellent reasoned speech when the occasion required it. Sometimes he lost his temper, and was rude ; but he bore no malice and was utterly devoted to the Labour cause. The charms of fine 'society' had no attraction for him ; and he had no expensive tastes to lead him astray. Wanting in imaginative insight, he was nevertheless a thoroughly reliable leader, who could be trusted always to give of his best without regard for self.

With the *débâcle* of 1931 the first generation of British Labour Party leaders passed ingloriously out of action. Keir Hardie had gone long before, deeply disheartened by the war, in 1915 ; but up to 1931 the rest of the pre-war leaders — MacDonald, Snowden, Henderson, Thomas — had continued to dominate the Party. After 1931, with Henderson almost out of action, only George Lansbury was left, with Jowett, Clynes, and a few others who were out of Parliament for the time being. A younger generation — Clement Attlee, Herbert Morrison (b. 1888), and Hugh Dalton (b. 1887) among its principal spokesmen — was due to come to the front. How they fared in the task of rebuilding the Party by slow stages after its defeat belongs to a part of the story that falls beyond this volume's range. We are leaving the record, for the time being, with the Labour Party at the deepest ebb of its electoral fortunes since before the war, and with its prestige badly tarnished by the defection of its most widely acclaimed leaders, under circumstances that were no credit either to them or to those who stayed faithful to the Party in its sore trouble. Admittedly the Labour Government of 1929–31 was unfortunate in having to face a very difficult situation which called for a novel and adventurous approach. Admittedly it was precluded by its lack of a parliamentary majority from putting forward constructive Socialist measures with any prospect of carrying them through. It had, however, no excuse for its extreme pusillanimity in dealing with the problem of unemployment ; for in that field, had it set out resolutely to create additional jobs, it had the assurance of enough Liberal support to be able to carry its proposals in the House of Commons and to feel confident that the House of Lords would not venture to reject them. The plain fact is that it lacked the resolution to attempt even what the more progressive Liberals had been urging, and allowed itself to drift helplessly to disaster. Yet the Labour Party had, from its earliest days, proclaimed the duty of the State to maintain employment at a satisfactory level : the 'Right to Work' was one of the oldest and most persistent of Socialist slogans. Despite this, the Labour Government allowed itself to be bamboozled into believing that it was more economical to maintain millions of people in idleness than to set them to work producing useful things that the people needed. There was at the back of many Socialists' minds a belief that, as capitalism of its very nature caused unemployment and was liable to recurrent crises and depressions, nothing effective could be done without a change of system which was clearly beyond their immediate power. They failed, no less than their political opponents, to understand what Keynes was telling them about the effect of additional employment in generating yet more openings for employment, through the maintenance of purchasing power. Nor had they any understanding of the wider implications of Keynes's theories or of their importance in pointing the way towards a stabilisation of the economy that would give capitalism a new lease of life, on condition that it accepted a measure of subjection to public planning and control. If they had understood Keynes, most of them would not have rejected his advice on the ground that it would make capitalism stronger ; for they themselves wished capitalism to survive and to prosper until they were ready to replace it. They simply failed to understand the 'new economics' — which were still but half-stated in 1931, and began to be widely understood only when Roosevelt put a part of them into highly experimental practice under the New Deal. Perhaps the Labour Party should not be judged too hardly on this account ; for the failure of understanding applied fully as much to non-Socialists as to Socialists. They must, however, be judged by a somewhat different standard ; for they had been arguing for a generation in favour of policies which were closely akin to what Keynes proposed. Had MacDonald and Snowden, or either of them, been ready to give a constructive lead, the rest would have followed ; but no lead at all was given, except by Mosley, whom few trusted, and by Lansbury, who was dismissed as a muddle-headed left-winger who had never understood politics, and never would.

While the Labour Party was getting ready for its electoral advance of 1929, and also while it was frittering away its chances in office, small groups of left-wing Socialists were doing what they could to keep the spirit of militancy alive in the Trade Unions after the defeat of the general strike and of the miners in 1926. As we saw, the main body of employers deliberately stopped short of pushing their victory of that year to extremes, preferring to use the opportunity for coming to terms with Trade Unions that could no longer afford an open fight. The Trades Union Congress entered gladly, if without enthusiasm, into the 'Mond-Turner' negotiations which were set on foot by a powerful group of employers headed by Sir Alfred Mond of Imperial Chemical Industries. The lead in opposition to these discussions, which had the aim of bringing about better relations between employers and Trade Unions, was promptly taken by Arthur Cook, the Miners' Secretary, and James Maxton, the I.L.P. leader, who issued a joint manifesto and started a national campaign of protest. This campaign made little impression on the main body of the Trade Union movement, which was too dispirited to accept a call to militancy. It did, however, fit in with the growing dissatisfaction of the I.L.P. with the official Labour Party policy, and helped to accentuate the I.L.P.'s anger at the policy of the Labour Government during the ensuing years. In the event, nothing much came of the 'Mond-Turner' negotiations, for the Federation of British Industries and the National Confederation of Employers, when it came to the point, were not prepared to endorse the concessions to Labour which the Mond group of employers had been ready to make, and no regular joint machinery, such as the 'Mond-Turner' Conference had proposed, was ever set up. The Conference, however, did in fact help the Trade Unions to weather an awkward moment in their existence, without doing any particular harm ; for undoubtedly Mond's initiative had some effect in preventing other employers from making a frontal attack on the Unions at the point of their greatest weakness and disorientation. The membership of the Trades Union Congress, which had risen to more than 6½ millions at the peak of 1920, had already fallen to less than 4½ millions in 1926. By 1931 it was down to 3,700,000, and it continued to fall until 1934, when it was under 3,300,000. This final fall, however, was due mainly to the later phases of the depression, rather than to the effects of the general strike. The loss resulting from the strike was in the neighbourhood of a million — fully enough, in conjunction with the mounting unemployment, to deter the Unions from embarking on any perilous adventures.

CHAPTER XXII

THE BATTLE OF THE INTERNATIONALS, 1922–1931

IN an earlier chapter,[1] the story of the conflict between the rival Internationals was taken up to the foundation of the Vienna Union in February 1921. From that point there were for a time three competing Internationals — or four if the Syndicalist International set up at Berlin in December 1922 is to be included. The Anarcho-Syndicalists, however, did not at any point achieve a mass following, though they had a large body of supporters in Spain, and not a few in Italy and in Holland. The Anarchist movement in the Soviet Union came to an end when Nestor Makhno left the country in 1921. Thereafter the remaining Russian Anarchists were scattered over the world in exile, engaging everywhere in violent denunciations of the tyrannical régime that had been established in Russia, but unable to make any great impression because they were equally at loggerheads with the main bodies of opinion in the countries they went to. They had forcible writers and speakers in their ranks, from Emma Goldman and Alexander Berkman to Voline among the Russians, and from Rudolph Rocker (b. 1870) in Germany to Malatesta's successors in Italy ; but they did not constitute anywhere outside Spain a movement of real significance.

Of the remaining three Internationals — apart from the two rival Trade Union bodies centred respectively at Amsterdam and Moscow — the Vienna Union, as we saw, did not claim to be an International in any full sense. It was only a 'Working Union', designed to prepare the way for an inclusive International that would somehow reunite the warring Socialist factions. It actually lasted for only two years before it joined forces, at the Hamburg Congress of May 1923, with the revived Second, or Berne, International to form the new Labour and

[1] See p. 287.

Socialist International, which thereafter continued in existence up to the second world war. This fusion finally made an end of the Centrist movement which had aimed at a reconciliation between Communists and Social Democrats on the basis of a recognition that the methods of achieving Socialism would necessarily differ from country to country and that neither parliamentary democracy nor Soviet dictatorship could properly be laid down as a method binding upon all. At the outset, the 'Two-and-a-Half' International had seemed in many respects to be nearer to the Communists than to the parliamentarians of the Berne International; but the decisive and violently expressed repudiation of the centre by the Comintern had driven its adherents, even against their will, towards the opposite camp, and a number of particular events between 1921 and 1923 had further weakened the position of the Centrist elements. Their attempt to reconcile the two main rivals had indeed succeeded, in April 1922, in bringing about a joint Conference at Berlin of delegates from all three Internationals; but this reunion, never meant seriously by either of the extreme parties, had begun and ended in violent mutual recriminations. The Communist delegates, headed by Radek, had fiercely denounced the 'social patriots', who had retorted with abuse of the Communists for their behaviour to the Georgian Mensheviks and to the Social Revolutionaries who were about to stand their trial in Russia. Despite these irreconcilable attitudes, however, neither extreme party had been prepared at that stage to allow the proceedings to end in absolute breakdown. The Communists agreed that the Social Revolutionaries should be given an open trial and that foreign lawyers from the Berne International should be allowed to enter Russia to defend them; and they also agreed to the appointment of a joint commission to study the Georgian question. The representatives of the Second International, for their part, agreed in principle to the summoning, as early as possible, of a full joint conference representing all sections of the Socialist movement, at which the question of constituting a single inclusive International would be considered further. The delegates of the three bodies then managed to draw up an agreed manifesto, in which they appealed to the workers of all countries to organise mass demonstrations for the eight-hours' day and for measures to prevent unemployment and secure recognition of the right to work, and further called for 'united action of the proletariat against the capitalist offensive, for the Russian Revolution and the resumption by all countries of political and economic relations with Russia, and for the re-establishment of the proletarian United Front in every country and in the International'. The Committee of Nine — three from each body — which had already been set up, was to continue the negotiations and to take steps for the convening of the proposed inclusive Unity Conference.

In all this apparent oncomingness there was a deep under-lying unreality. The Communists had not the smallest intention of merging the Comintern in an inclusive International that would involve real co-operation with either the right wing or the Centrists they had been denouncing so vehemently. Nor had the right wing any intention of working with the Communists on friendly terms. But neither extreme Party wanted to take on itself the responsibility for breaking off the discussions. The Communists, chastened by the general set-back to World Revolution and by the onset of economic depression, had revised their tactics and had begun to speak in terms of a 'United Front' — to which it was possible to attach widely different meanings. What the Comintern leaders meant by it was an opportunity to attack the right wing and the centre from within a common organisation, instead of from outside, in the hope of using this vantage to detach the followers of their opponents from their leaders, and thus to strengthen the Communist movement in the world outside Russia. The right wing, on its side, was well aware of the strength of pro-Russian sentiment among the workers in most countries and was afraid of losing support if it appeared to be taking an intransigent line in dealing with the Russian Communist leaders. Only the Centrists of the 'Two-and-a-Half' International really wanted an accommodation, in the hope of bringing both extreme factions over to their middle point of view.

The farce of unity could not be kept going for long. The Committee of Nine met in Berlin in May 1922, but reached no conclusions. In June the trial of the Social Revolutionaries came on and, as we saw, led to the withdrawal of Vandervelde and his fellow defending counsel in protest against the methods by which it was conducted.[1] Largely as a result of this, the Committee of Nine refused to meet again, and the entire negotiations between the three Internationals came to an abrupt end, though Zinoviev and Losovsky, on behalf of the Comintern and of the Red International of Labour Unions, made a fresh approach to the rival Socialist Internationals and to the I.F.T.U. for joint action on the occasion of the French invasion of the Ruhr in January 1923. This approach arose in part out of the International Peace Conference which met at the Hague in December 1922 at the summons of the Amsterdam I.F.T.U. and was attended by 700 delegates representing a wide variety of Trade Union, Co-operative, Socialist, and pacifist bodies, including some Communists delegated by Trade Unions or Co-operative Societies in Russia itself. Nothing, however, came of the Zinoviev-Losovsky appeal, which was brusquely rejected both by Amsterdam and by the Socialist bodies.

These latter, indeed, had drawn much closer together after the breakdown of the earlier negotiations on unity. The Vienna Union lost one of its principal supporters when, in September 1922, the U.S.P.D., already much reduced by the Halle split of 1920,[2] decided by a majority to reunite with the S.P.D. in order to make a common front against the reaction after the murder of Walther Rathenau. The following month, Mussolini's March on Rome had left the sharply divided Italian Socialists in a sorry plight. These two events had sadly reduced the forces of the Centrists, who had also been disillusioned by the attitude of the Communists in the course of the unity negotiations. Probably the most important single factor in inducing the 'Two-and-a-Half' International to join forces with the Second was the practical disappearance of the U.S.P.D.; for, though a small section of that body, headed by Georg Ledebour, attempted to carry it on as an independent Party, it had no importance after the majority had rejoined the S.P.D. The Austrians, who had been the mainstay of the Vienna Union, were bound to be strongly influenced by the events in Germany, which they still hoped to join as a State of the Weimar Republic; and, even apart from that, they had been getting weaker at home, as the anti-Socialist Parties and the Catholic Church recovered from the disarray into which

[1] See p. 187.　　　　　[2] See p. 168.

they had been plunged in 1918. Even to the Austrian leaders, Otto Bauer and Friedrich Adler, there no longer appeared to be real hope of an inclusive International ; and in face of the Communists' attitude towards them they were left with no choice. Rejected with contumely by the Comintern, they made up their minds to do their best to draw the right wing into a more active defence of Socialism, which was by then under almost general attack from the capitalist side. Accordingly, at the Hamburg Congress of May 1923, the Second and the 'Two-and-a-Half' came to terms, and Friedrich Adler agreed, under some pressure, to become joint secretary of the new Labour and Socialist International which was set up there, but had its headquarters in London, where Arthur Henderson and the British Labour Party could keep a vigilant eye on its doings. At the outset Adler had as his co-secretary Tom Shaw (1872–1938), the British textile Trade Union leader, who had the advantage of being a good linguist. But when Ramsay MacDonald formed his first Labour Cabinet early in 1924, Shaw became a member of it, and had to withdraw from his office in the L.S.I. He was not replaced : Adler became sole secretary until the Labour Government fell from office in November 1924, when Shaw for a while resumed his position. Apart from Adler, the members of the Administrative Committee that took charge of the International's day-to-day affairs was made up entirely of British members. Its composition was almost entirely changed when the British Labour Government came into office at the beginning of 1924.

The new International had barely come into existence when urgent problems began to crowd upon it. In Germany the national resistance to the French occupation of the Ruhr was creating a situation which threatened the entire collapse of the currency and the dissolution of the Weimar Republic into sheer chaos. Behind the occupation lay the dispute over reparations and the French allegations of bad faith on the part of the German Government. On top of these troubles, immediately after the Hamburg Congress came the *coup d'état* in Bulgaria. Stambolisky's Agrarian Government was overthrown, and Stambolisky himself murdered ; and the Bulgarian Broad Socialist Party sided with Tsankoff against the Agrarians. Tsankoff's accession to power was accompanied by severe

measures against Stambolisky's followers ; and in September
the Bulgarian Communists, who had stood aside at the time of
the *coup*, joined hands with the Agrarians in an armed revolt,
which was bloodily suppressed. During the same month
occurred the Primo de Rivera revolutionary *coup* in Spain.
The European reaction seemed, almost everywhere, to be
mounting to new heights, and the European working class to
have sunk to its lowest point of influence since the end of the
war. Then the tide began to turn : the Austrian Socialists did
well in the elections of October 1923, and two months later
the British Labour Party also made big electoral gains, which
led to the formation of the first MacDonald Government. A
few months afterwards Édouard Herriot came to power in
France at the head of a Radical coalition ; and in both Denmark and Sweden the Socialists so increased their parliamentary strength as to be able to form their own minority
Governments. All these parliamentary successes greatly encouraged the moderate Socialists, though things continued to
go from bad to worse in Italy, Spain, Hungary, and Bulgaria,
and though the parliamentary successes in the West were soon
found to be no more than transitory. The Swedish Socialists
had hardly taken office when the British Labour Government
fell with a resounding crash and went down to defeat in the
'Red Letter' election. Meanwhile the German Social Democrats, after suffering a defeat in the election of May 1924,
achieved a considerable come-back at a second election near the
end of the year ; the reparations problem was settled for the
time being by the adoption of the Dawes Plan ; and steps were
set on foot to inaugurate a new currency to replace the utterly
depreciated mark. These developments provided the new
International with plenty of matters to discuss, even if it was
not able to exert any really significant influence on the course
of events. One of its major preoccupations was the Bulgarian
crisis. The Bulgarian Social Democratic Party had not been
officially associated with the Tsankoff *coup d'état* ; but a
number of its leaders had been privy to it, and on its success
the Party accepted participation in the new Government and
was thus associated with it in the suppression of the Agrarian-
Communist rising of September 1924. It took part, as a member of the Government *bloc*, in the ensuing General Election,

and thus secured a substantial number of seats in the new Parliament, despite the fact that the election was held under a very undemocratic voting system. The Social Democrats justified their participation by urging that the Tsankoff Government offered, under the circumstances, the best hope for Bulgarian democracy and by the statement that they were using their influence in it to limit the repression that followed the autumn revolt. Their influence proved, however, to be in this respect almost non-existent ; and in March 1924 they formally withdrew from the Government and resumed their independence, only to become themselves victims of the intensified repression of the ensuing years. The two rival Socialist Parties in Bulgaria, one of which had become the Communist Party, had, as we have seen, a very long record of intense mutual animosity, which helps to explain the Social Democratic attitude at the time of the Tsankoff *coup*. The reasons underlying the Communist failure to come to Stambolisky's aid have been discussed in an earlier chapter.[1]

The L.S.I., from the point at which the Bulgarian Social Democrats withdrew from the Tsankoff Government, gave them its full support in their opposition both to the Government and to the Communist-Agrarian rebels, whom it accused of resort to mass murder and violence that had provoked the Government to drastic measures of repression. It convened two Balkan Socialist Conferences in March 1924 and June 1925, at which it attempted to bring about common action by the Socialist Parties of the Balkan countries for the prevention of war between them — especially in Macedonia — and for the promotion of friendly relations. Shortly before the second of these meetings the civil war in Bulgaria had broken out again, and there had occurred the celebrated bomb outrage in the cathedral at Sofia.[2] Immediately before this rising the Communist members had been expelled from Parliament : they remained without representation till 1927, when they were allowed to form a 'Workers' Party', which won four seats at the ensuing election. Meanwhile the Social Democrats, in 1926, had expelled certain of their leaders who had been closely connected with the Tsankoff *coup* — among them Assen Tsankoff, who must be distinguished from his more famous namesake. Through all these events the dictatorship remained in being ; and even the moderate Social Democrats led by Janko Sakasoff were able to carry on their activities only under very severe handicaps. Up to the rising of 1923 the Communists undoubtedly commanded the major body of working-class support. When they were defeated and driven underground, they still remained a powerful group ; but the Social Democrats, working in alliance with certain sections of the Agrarians and urban artisans, gained some increased support, with the strong backing of the L.S.I., which was as bitterly opposed to the Communists as to the reactionary groups that were bent on imposing a form of Fascist rule on the Balkan countries.

In reporting to the first Congress of the new International, held at Marseilles in August 1925, the Secretariat presented a general review of events since the Hamburg Congress and offered its comments on the stage that had been reached. In its view, despite the maintenance of reactionary dictatorships in Hungary, Italy, Spain, and Bulgaria, there had been a marked improvement in working-class prospects over the two years. Credit was claimed for the Socialist Parties of Great Britain, France, and Germany for their united efforts to solve the problem of reparations, and for at least partial success in this field. The Secretariat also congratulated the International that the gains made in social and industrial legislation on the morrow of the war had been on the whole successfully maintained, despite the onslaughts made on them under cover of the depression. No fresh gains had been secured ; but it was held that the conditions were now becoming favourable for a further gradual advance, to be brought about by the combined action of the L.S.I. and the Amsterdam I.F.T.U. and their affiliated movements. The need for working-class unity in pursuance of this object was emphasised ; but there was no suggestion that this could be brought about by any sort of collaboration with the Comintern or with the Russians. On the contrary, the Secretariat appeared to believe that the world Communist movement, at any rate outside the Soviet Union, was on the point of breaking up under stress of its internal dissensions and that before long the erring Socialists who had remained outside the L.S.I. — or at any rate those of Western Europe — would come back to the fold.

The tasks confronting the L.S.I. in 1925 were described as essentially three : the struggle against war and for the establishment of conditions that would ensure 'a stable peace' ; the struggle against reaction, 'which blocks the way to the liberation of the working class from the fetters of capitalism' ; and 'the struggle for the improvement of the position of working people, a symbol of which must be the final victory of the Eight-Hour Day'. In other words, except in the countries where stark reaction was in power, what the L.S.I. contemplated was broadly a return to the activities of the Second International before 1918 — the gradual improvement of international relations and of working-class conditions by parliamentary and Trade Union efforts. The semi-revolutionism of the Vienna Union had totally disappeared : Communism was no longer a potential ally, whose policies could be regarded as at any rate partly appropriate in countries in which the road to gradual reform was closed by force : it was an enemy to be combated, in the hope that it would lose its appeal now that no prospect of early World Revolution could any longer be deemed to exist.

This attitude did not prevent the L.S.I. from pressing for the *de jure* recognition of the Soviet Government by all countries to which pressure could be applied. Actually, by the middle of 1925 the Soviet Government had been recognised by the German Republic (in 1922), by Great Britain, Italy, Norway, Austria, Greece, Sweden, China, Denmark, Mexico, Hungary, and France (in 1924), and by Japan (in 1925) — so that, of the great powers, only the United States still refused recognition. The L.S.I., in supporting the Russian claim, made clear that it hoped an early result of recognition would be a liberalisation of the régime inside Russia and a general release of the political prisoners — especially of those belonging to the rival Socialist Parties. It also demanded the evacuation of Georgia by the Red Army and the restoration of the independence of the Menshevik Georgian Republic, and therewith a cessation of Soviet interferences in the affairs of the independent border States, especially Estonia. It gave strong support to the Georgian rising of August 1924 and protested against the attempted *coup* in Estonia in December of that year. Its attitude towards Russia was substantially affected by the presence at its meetings of representatives of the exiled Russian

Parties — Abramovitch of the Jewish Bund and the Menshevik Party, Sukhomlin of the Social Revolutionary Party, and the Georgian Menshevik, Tseretelli, whom it authorised to prepare for publication a pamphlet dealing with conditions in Russia. When the British Trade Union Delegation returned from Russia at the end of 1924, the L.S.I. promptly issued a strong attack on the favourable statements made about the improving conditions of the Soviet economy, about religious freedom in Russia, and about other matters on which the leaders of the L.S.I. Parties held very different opinions. The L.S.I. statement accused A. A. Purcell (1872–1935) and Fred Bramley (1874–1925), the Chairman and Secretary of the British Trades Union Congress, in particular of whitewashing the Soviet Union in pursuance of their plea for Anglo-Russian Trade Union friendship, of ignoring the Russian attempts to undermine the I.F.T.U., and of acting against the interests of the movement they were supposed to represent.

With regard to Italy the L.S.I., of course, took up a line of strong hostility to the developing Fascist régime, and did what it could to help the Italian Socialist Party in the final phases of its opposition. When the Italian Socialist leader, Giacomo Matteotti (1885–1924), was murdered by the Fascists in June 1924, the L.S.I., in expressing its horror, protested that by this bestial crime Fascism had 'dealt itself a blow from which it will never recover'. The Italian proletariat, it declared, was 'the moral victor over the régime of Terror'. It recorded with approval the boycott of the Parliament by the Italian Socialists, and appeared to take a rosy view of the prospects of an early fall of the Fascist régime. It could, however, do nothing beyond protesting and offering limited help to Socialist refugees who were able to escape from Italy — mostly to France.[1]

By the time of the Marseilles Congress of 1925 the L.S.I. had some sort of affiliated Party in every considerable European country except Switzerland, but outside Europe had only the small Socialist Parties of the United States (15,000) and the Argentine (just under 10,000), and the tiny British Guiana Labour Union (1000). Among the Parties counted as members were the exiled Parties of Russia (Mensheviks and S.R.s), the

[1] See p. 392.

Ukraine, Georgia, and Armenia, and also an exiled Hungarian group, including Kunfi and Boehm, in Vienna. For these exiled Parties no membership figures were given. Among the others, by far the most numerous was the British Labour Party, with a membership of more than 3 million, mostly affiliated collectively through the Trade Unions. The Independent Labour Party, though affiliated to the Labour Party, was separately affiliated to the L.S.I. on a membership of 50,000, as were the small remainder of the Social Democratic Federation (2000), and the central Fabian Society (under 2000). Next in size to the Labour Party was the reunited German Social Democratic Party (869,000), followed by the Belgian Labour Party (621,000, including affiliated Trade Unions), and the Austrian S.D.P. (570,000). Only three others exceeded 100,000 — Czechoslovakia (nearly 200,000), Sweden and Denmark, with France next (99,000). Poland had 65,000, divided between three Parties ; but the P.P.S. included most of them. Czechoslovakia had actually five affiliated Parties — Czech, German, Ruthenian, Hungarian, and Polish ; but only the Czech (116,000) and the German (72,000) Parties had large memberships. The rest of the affiliated Parties were small, the Italians claiming no more than 31,000, and the Norwegians, a Social Democratic breakaway from the much bigger Norwegian Labour Party, which did not join the L.S.I. until 1938, only 8000. In all, excluding the exiles, the L.S.I. announced its affiliated membership as 6,280,000, of whom 752,000 were women, and the total vote of their parliamentary candidates at the most recent elections as 25,600,000, of whom nearly 8 million were in Germany and about $5\frac{1}{2}$ in Great Britain. These Parties had in all just over 1000 Members of Parliament, about $15\frac{1}{2}$ per cent of the total. They had 311 daily newspapers, of which more than half were in Germany.

The L.S.I. was governed between Congresses by an Executive of 38 members, with a Bureau of 9. In 1925, among the best-known executive members were Arthur Henderson, Otto Bauer, Jean Longuet, Louis de Brouckère, H. G. Tseretelli (b. 1882) of Georgia, Arthur Crispien, Hermann Müller and Otto Wels of Germany, W. H. Vliegen of Holland, Julian Besteiro of Spain, Antonin Nemec of Czechoslovakia, Arthur Engberg of Sweden, Zivko Topalović of Yugoslavia, Carl F.

Madsen of Denmark, Alexandre Bracke of France, and Claudio Treves of Italy. Victor Berger and Morris Hillquit of the United States were also nominally members, but had not attended any meetings since the inaugural one at Hamburg in 1923. A few well-known original members of the Executive had dropped out — among them MacDonald, Vandervelde, Stauning, J. H. Thomas, Troelstra, and Branting (who had died in February 1925). Quite a number of these — for example, Branting, Troelstra, Vandervelde, de Brouckère, Vliegen, Longuet, Bracke, Nemec, Müller, Madsen — and to a limited extent MacDonald — had been active in the Second International before 1914. The L.S.I. Executive was, on the whole, an assembly of veterans, largely drawn from the pre-war right and centre ; and it was also in effect almost exclusively European — and largely West and Central European at that. In the Balkans it had only a very small following ; and of the States bordering on Russia only Poland and Czechoslovakia supplied large contingents.

As we saw, in many matters the L.S.I. and the Amsterdam International Federation of Trade Unions worked fairly closely together. The I.F.T.U. had been set up at a Congress held at Amsterdam in August 1919, with the participation of the American Federation of Labor and of Samuel Gompers as its leader. At the Paris Peace Conference, Gompers had played an important part in bringing the International Labour Organisation into being, as a tripartite body representing governments, employers, and workers, to be attached to the proposed League of Nations but to be entirely self-governing within its own field of international labour 'legislation'. At the time of the Amsterdam Congress it seemed almost certain that the A.F. of L. would join the I.F.T.U. and would play an active part in its work. There were, however, dissensions even from the first. The Americans feared that the Germans would hold too strong a position in the I.F.T.U. ; and they also wanted it to keep aloof from all connection with politics, and especially with Socialist Parties. They also urged that the proposed rates of contribution were too high ; but this was probably no more than a secondary objection. When Gompers and his fellow-delegates got back to the United States they found there a labour ferment not unlike that which existed in Western Europe.

The United Mine Workers were demanding nationalisation of the mines, the Railroad Brotherhoods that of the railroads under the Plumb Plan ; [1] and there was much talk of setting up a Labour Party on the British model, with the Trade Unions as its basic components. There was also, as we saw, a considerable Communist and left-wing agitation in progress, and repressive measures were already on the way to put it down. The A.F. of L. leaders had, for the moment, to make some concessions to the state of working-class feeling : for example, Gompers himself accepted the presidency of the Plumb Plan League. The A.F. of L. leadership was, however, entirely opposed to the establishment of any sort of Labour Party and to any alliance with the Socialists — even those of the extreme right. Consequently their enthusiasm for the I.F.T.U. cooled very rapidly, and Gompers was soon bombarding its officers with demands that it should desist from making pronouncements on political matters and from intervening in political affairs. The I.F.T.U. answered that it was quite out of the question in the existing state of Europe to draw any sharp distinction between political and industrial issues, and quite indispensable to call on the governments to take action in the workers' interests. It also called attention to the fact that the A.F. of L. itself had made many political pronouncements, especially about Russia, and reminded Gompers of his own position in the Plumb Plan League. The I.F.T.U. clearly had the better in the war of words ; but that did not affect the outcome. The A.F. of L., at its Montreal Convention in June 1920, decided to leave the question of affiliation to the I.F.T.U. in the hands of the Executive. Much further argument followed : the Americans refused to pay dues to the I.F.T.U., and denied that they were affiliated to it. Gompers even wrote, in December 1920, a letter in which he declared 'the I.F.T.U. has become an international political body with Sovietism as its logical result and a revolutionary program for "socialisation" and "communism"'.

This was, of course, sheer nonsense ; but Gompers's attitude carried the day at subsequent conventions of the A.F. of L., and the breach with the European Trade Union movement became complete. I think what most of all accounted

[1] See p. 732,

for the A.F. of L.'s attitude was not that the I.F.T.U. was concerning itself with political issues in general — for so was the A.F. of L. — but rather that Amsterdam, despite its sharp hostility to Communism and to the R.I.L.U., was in favour of the recognition of the Soviets by the Western Governments, whereas the A.F. of L., like the United States Government, was not. In the United States anti-Communism took the form of a refusal to accept the existence of the Russian Communist State, as well as of sharp hostility to the Comintern and the R.I.L.U. The Americans did not make the distinction which even the right wing in Europe was compelled to make. They were against Communism in all its forms ; and therefore they would fight it wherever it raised its head. They were also, of course, strongly anti-Socialist, and were on this account indisposed to distinguish clearly between Communism and other forms of Socialism, regarding the former as, in Gompers's words, 'the logical result' of the latter. Before long even Gompers, shortly before his death in December 1924, was to modify in some degree his hostility to the Amsterdam International, mainly because, when the Socialist wave in Europe had been beaten back in the depression, both it and the L.S.I. had come to be more concerned with tasks of immediate salvage in Germany and elsewhere than with attacking capitalism or demanding general socialisation. But the change did not go nearly far enough to bring the A.F. of L. back into the Amsterdam International.

Indeed, at this point the I.F.T.U. itself became a battleground, largely under the impulsion of the British Trade Unions. At the Hamburg constituent Congress of the L.S.I. Jan Oudegeest (1870-1950), the Dutch co-secretary of the I.F.T.U., had declared the readiness of the I.F.T.U. to co-operate with the new Socialist International ; and the Communists, faced with the reunion of the right and centre, had decided to launch a new campaign for the so-called 'United Front' and to use the Russian Trade Unions as the front line in that campaign. The All-Russian Council of Trade Unions accordingly approached Amsterdam with a proposal for concerted action against war and Fascism. The Amsterdam Management Committee replied that it would have dealings with the Russian Unions only if they ceased attacking the

I.F.T.U. and became genuinely independent of the Communist Party and the Soviet Government. When this drew an angry retort from the Russians, communications were broken off.

At this point Fred Bramley, the Secretary of the British Trades Union Congress, strongly criticised the I.F.T.U.'s attitude at its Vienna Congress of June 1924 ; and after a hot debate the Congress passed a resolution regretting the absence of the Russians and instructing the Bureau to continue consultations with them, with a view to securing their affiliation on terms of accepting the rules and conditions of I.F.T.U. membership. At this Congress J. H. Thomas resigned the presidency and was succeeded by A. A. Purcell, who was a long way further to the left. A third, British, Secretary was also elected, to share office with Oudegeest and his German colleague. Johann Sassenbach, who had hitherto divided the functions. The following month the I.F.T.U. Executive invited the Russian Unions to affiliate. The Russians replied, proposing a conference between the Amsterdam International and its direct antagonist, the R.I.L.U. The I.F.T.U. then asked the Russians to state exactly what they wanted the basis of discussion to be ; and Tomsky, the Russian Trade Union leader, answered that the Russian Unions were prepared to co-operate in an International resting on the guiding principle of 'class-war to the knife' and 'a complete break with every form of class-collaboration'. He proposed a preliminary meeting between Amsterdam and the Russian Unions. Against the votes of the British delegates, the I.F.T.U. General Council rejected the proposal in February 1925, but declared its readiness to accept the affiliation of the All-Russian Council of Trade Unions under the existing rules.

This was followed, in April 1925, by a meeting in London between the Russians and the British T.U.C. General Council. It was there agreed to set up an Anglo-Russian Advisory Committee, representing the two bodies, the Russians agreeing to join a new Trade Union International based on the Amsterdam body, and the British to support an unconditional meeting between representatives of the Russians and the I.F.T.U. But, after many further interchanges, the I.F.T.U., against the votes of its British members, refused to modify its proposal of February 1925, and rejected a British demand that they should reconsider their attitude. By this time the British Unions were on the threshold of the crisis that led to the General Strike of 1926. When the General Strike broke down, and the British miners were left to fight on alone, the R.I.L.U. and the Comintern both launched fierce denunciations of the 'betrayal' of the miners, bitterly attacking the British T.U.C. The Russian Unions, meanwhile, collected very big sums in aid of the miners and called on the T.U.C. and the Amsterdam International to organise international support, including an embargo on the movement of coal. At several meetings of the Anglo-Russian Committee there were angry exchanges between the two sides, though the British representatives continued to urge an unconditional conference between the I.F.T.U. and the Russians. These events led before long to the winding up of the Anglo-Russian Committee and to the complete abandonment of the British attempt to bring the Russians into the Amsterdam International. The whole episode, indeed, had arisen out of a temporary movement of British Trade Union opinion sharply to the left after the visit of the British Trade Union Delegation to Russia in 1924. With the defeat of the General Strike this leftward trend was sharply reversed ; and the Amsterdam International was able to go its way without further trouble from the advocates of Trade Union unity.

It must not be supposed that, during this interlude in 1924–1926, the British Trade Unions had undergone any conversion to Communism. Purcell, Bramley, and George Hicks (1879–1954), the outstanding figures in it, were neither Communists nor favourable in any sense to Communism as a doctrine or policy. They were, however, both favourably impressed by what they saw or heard of Russian economic progress under the New Economic Policy and keen on the idea that Trade Union unity might be practicable even if there could be no unity in the political field. Almost untroubled by rival Communist Unions and not greatly troubled — despite A. J. Cook — by Communist influence inside the main Unions, they could not understand the intensity of anti-Communist feeling among their Continental colleagues, most of whom had a very different experience. It seemed to them to go almost without saying that the Trade Unions of all countries ought to constitute a single, united movement ; and they expected the R.I.L.U. to fade almost painlessly away if the Russian Unions came into the I.F.T.U. The British leaders of these years did want a more militant Trade Union policy, especially after the ignominious defeat of the MacDonald Government on the issue of the 'Red Letter'. They were 'leftists', in comparison with the leaders who preceded and followed them ; but that was a very different thing from being Communists or wishing to bring the British Trade Union movement under Communist control or influence. Bramley had been an active I.L.P. propagandist, Purcell a Guild Socialist : George Hicks, the leader of the building workers, was a long-standing member of the old S.D.F., W. M. Citrine (b. 1887), who succeeded Bramley as Secretary of the Trades Union Congress and was in charge of it during the General Strike, had been something of a left-winger in his youth as an electrician shop steward, but had moved a long way rightwards well before he took office. Arthur Pugh (1870–1955), the steel workers' leader who was Chairman of the T.U.C. at the time of the General Strike, had always been well known as a moderate.

Thus from 1926 Trade Union international relations were back pretty much where they had been three years earlier. The dispute between the British and the Continentals continued indeed into 1927, when the majority at the Paris Congress of August refused to re-elect Purcell as President and accepted the resignations of two of the three Secretaries — Oudegeest and J. W. Brown — leaving Sassenbach alone in office. Immediately after this, the British T.U.C. finally wound up the Anglo-Russian Committee, which had ceased to operate some time before. The following year the rift in the I.F.T.U. was patched up. Citrine was elected President ; and the British ceased to trouble the International while they tried to heal the serious wounds they had suffered as a result of their defeat in 1926.

Meanwhile, the Labour and Socialist International went on its way with fewer alarms and excursions than the I.F.T.U. The Marseilles Congress of 1925 decided to transfer the head-quarters from London to Zürich, and the removal took place before the end of the year. Adler continued as Secretary ; but the purely British Administrative Committee was replaced until 1928 by the Bureau, which included members from the leading countries. The next L.S.I. Congress did not meet until 1928, this time at Brussels. Through these years the active personnel on the Executive remained for the most part unchanged, except for members who resigned and returned as they took and left office in the Governments of their countries. Nor was there much change in the affiliated Parties. The Swiss at length joined the L.S.I. in 1926, followed by Iceland later in the year. As against this, the Norwegian Social Democrats withdrew on reuniting with the unaffiliated Norwegian Labour Party. No new non-European Parties came in except that Poale Zion, the Jewish Socialist Party, had been admitted with a mandate to represent the workers of Palestine. The Argentine Party split into rival factions. The Russian Mensheviks and Social Revolutionaries and the Georgian Mensheviks continued to be counted as affiliated Parties, with the same representatives as before. In Austria the German and Czech Parties, though working fairly closely together, were affiliated separately. In Great Britain the I.L.P. had fallen to a mere 30,000.

The long report presented by the Secretariat to the Brussels Congress, taken as a whole, hardly reads like the report of a body devoted essentially to the cause of Socialism. A very large part of it deals with issues, such as the policy and structure of the League of Nations, Disarmament, and Fascism, which, however important for Socialists, have little to do with the direct line of advance towards a Socialist society. The report indeed admitted that it had been, and was still, impracticable for the time being to attempt any such advance. Much was said about the advances made towards stabilisation of the various economies, and especially of that of Germany under the Dawes Plan ; and though the continuance of serious unemployment in many countries was noted, it was attributed rather to labour-saving technological developments than to any basic unsoundness in the capitalist economy. The report seemed to look forward to a period of increasing economic prosperity under conditions of growing stability : there was not a hint of the great depression that was to be started on its way by the American stock-market collapse only a year later. Communist vaticinations about a coming crisis were dismissed as the product of wishful thinking — which no doubt they were ; but there was also wishful thinking in the L.S.I., whose leaders appeared to be fully reconciled to a very gradual advance, even in the field of social legislation, and to be putting their principal hopes on the strengthening of the League of Nations as an instrument for peace and disarmament. On the subject of Germany the L.S.I.'s complacency was remarkable. It was greatly pleased by the S.P.D.'s relative successes in Reichstag elections, and showed no foreknowledge of the growing danger of Nazism, though it was fully alive to the success of Italian Fascism in completing its conquest of the Italian working-class movement. Italy had by this time joined the list of the Socialist Parties in exile, for which no statistics of membership could be given.

By July 1931, when the L.S.I. held its next Congress in Vienna, the view taken of world affairs was very different, and the Secretariat's report gave pride of place to the world economic crisis, which it described as 'the most serious that capitalism has ever experienced', and as dominating 'the entire political and social life of the world'. There was, however, no suggestion in the report that world capitalism was entering upon the 'final crisis' to which the Communists had been looking forward. On the contrary, though the importance of political factors was recognised, the crisis was described as 'a phase of the capitalist trade cycle' and was put on much the same footing as earlier crises 'which have always passed through the same phases — upward movement, boom, crisis, depression, and gradual upward movement again'. The L.S.I. reporters clearly expected capitalism to recover from the new crisis, as it had done from the others : it proclaimed as the great tasks of the Socialist Parties 'Fight the economic crisis, fight Fascism', and added that 'one thing is essential for both tasks — the maintenance and organisation of peace'. Far from setting out to use the crisis as a means of rousing revolutionary sentiment among the people, the L.S.I. desired to induce the Governments to take effective measures to deal with it, and proposed to carry on with the crusades for peace and against Fascism in which it had been engaged before the crisis occurred.

It was, indeed, recognised that the Fascist danger had become very much greater and more widespread as a consequence of the economic disaster. The Secretariat had to record that since 1929 Yugoslavia had been added to the list of countries subject to dictatorial rule, that Poland had moved a long distance towards dictatorship, and that the struggle against Fascism had entered on a critical stage in Germany, in Austria, and in Finland. As against this the Labour Party had been in office in Great Britain for nearly two years, and the Danish Socialists had held power in coalition with the Radicals for a similar period. In Czechoslovakia, too, a coalition including the Socialist Parties had been in office since late in 1929. Moreover, in Spain a Republican Government, in which the Socialists had a share, had recently taken office after the left-wing victory in the municipal elections of April 1931. Nowhere else in Europe did the Socialists hold office at the time when the report was made.

In a number of countries in which Fascism was advancing rapidly, the struggle turned in 1931 on proposals to revise the Constitution in such ways as to destroy parliamentary government. This was the position in Poland, Austria, and Finland, as well as in Germany. In Germany the Nazis had made large gains at the election of September 1930 ; and two months later Pilsudski's followers had won the Polish General Election, but had fallen short of the two-thirds majority needed for constitutional revision.[1] In Austria, in the same month, the Socialists had done well in the elections, but had not been able to prevent the increase of terrorism and violence by the armed bands of the Heimwehr.[2] In all these countries the L.S.I. had again and again protested against the attacks on free speech and parliamentary government, the arrests of leading Socialists and the murder of not a few, and the increase of violence on the part of the Fascist elements. There was, however, nothing it could do beyond protesting and appealing to world public opinion in the hope of having some influence on the would-be dictators. It also continued to protest strongly against the continued and indeed intensified persecution of political offenders both in the Soviet Union and in the countries already subject to forms of Fascist rule, such as Hungary and Yugoslavia ; and, through its special Matteotti Fund, raised to commemorate the murdered Italian Socialist leader, it did what it could to relieve some of the victims of Fascist oppression.

[1] See p. 629. [2] See p. 230.

All this, however, necessarily amounted to but little in relation to the rapidly increasing need.

One effect of the economic crisis was to bring the L.S.I. and the I.F.T.U. into closer association. In October 1930 the two bodies held a joint meeting at Cologne and set up a special Commission to prepare a report on the measures that ought to be taken to cope with the crisis. The Commission's report, issued a few months later, put its main emphasis on the failure of capitalism to maintain a level of purchasing power high enough to absorb the rapidly growing productivity, and strongly opposed the deflationary measures to which Governments and Central Banks were resorting under pressure of balance of payments difficulties. It urged the importance of maintaining wages in order to sustain working-class purchasing power and also the need to reduce working hours in order to spread employment and the desirability of raising the school-leaving age as a special means of diminishing juvenile unemployment. The report was a long document, stating in the main what was already the familiar policy of the Socialist Parties for dealing with depressions. The right to work or maintenance through insurance or assistance was asserted, as it had been so many times before ; and stress was also laid on the duty of Governments to provide additional employment by means of public works. Despite the association with it of the I.F.T.U. as well as of the Socialist International it had little effect. The depression went from bad to worse ; and the attempts to cope with it by deflationary measures — which in fact made it worse — persisted until President Roosevelt, on assuming office in the United States, inaugurated the series of measures known as the 'New Deal'. These, however, fell outside the period covered by the present volume.

The L.S.I., in 1931, still represented almost the same sections of the Socialist movement as it had done at the Brussels Congress of 1928. From 1929, when Arthur Henderson, on becoming Foreign Secretary in the British Labour Government, resigned from the presidency he had held from the beginning, Emile Vandervelde came back as President, resuming the office he had held in the Second International before 1914. By 1931 death had removed a few of the old L.S.I. leaders, notably Herman Müller (d. 1931) of Germany, Jakob Pistiner

(d. 1930) of Rumania, Joseph Wauters (1875–1929) of Belgium, and Herman Diamand (1861–1931) of Poland ; but for the most part the same persons were still at the helm. Tseretelli of Georgia had resigned from the Executive in 1929 ; and by 1931 a bitter quarrel had developed among the exiled Russian Social Revolutionaries, who removed Sukhomlin from his position on the Executive but were unable to agree on a new nomination. Rafael Abramovitch continued to represent the exiled Mensheviks. For Italy, the unification of the rival groups of Socialists in exile in July 1930 had brought Pietro Nenni (b. 1891) as a new Italian representative on the L.S.I. Executive. In the Argentine the split between the rival Socialist Parties remained unhealed, despite the L.S.I.'s efforts ; and no success had been met with in attracting further non-European Parties into its ranks. In February 1931 the British I.L.P. had made a renewed attempt to persuade the L.S.I. leaders to summon a Socialist Unity Conference open to all comers ; but the L.S.I. had replied that such a gathering would only provide disruptive elements with a convenient plat-form, and nothing had been done. The L.S.I. had continued to devote a great deal of its attention to the affairs of the League of Nations, and especially to disarmament, in connection with the Preparatory Disarmament Conference, which had at last arranged for the full Conference to meet in February 1932. Henderson, on behalf of the British Labour Government, had been particularly active in this field, and had kept in close touch with the L.S.I. after his resignation as its President. The L.S.I. had also given strong support to the proposals for an international Tariff Truce, in which William Graham, the Labour President of the British Board of Trade, was one of the prime movers.

In short, in 1931 the L.S.I. was continuing much the same activities as it had been pursuing before the world economic crisis, with the difference that it had been compelled to pay much more attention both to the growing Fascist danger and to the need for special measures to deal with the mounting un-employment in the capitalist countries. There was no sign of any movement towards securing a wider measure of working-class unity in face of these dangers or of any relaxation of the sharp antagonism between the rival Internationals.

We must now turn from the L.S.I. to its principal antagonist, the Comintern. That body, during its earlier years, met annually in full Congress, and between Congresses very great powers were vested in the Executive Committee. The theory on which the Comintern rested, as we saw, was that of a single, centrally directed movement to which belonged the control of the strategy and tactics of the World Revolution : so that the Communist Party in each country was to regard itself, not as an independent body with a right to determine its own policy and leadership, but as a mere section of the whole — with the corollary that the Comintern could issue orders to it and that the Comintern Executive had a right to override the decisions not only of the separate national Executives, but even of the national Congress of any particular Party. It is within this general framework of centralised control directed to World Revolution that the Comintern's history has to be studied — though, of course, the theory did not always work out in practice.

The Comintern duly held its first four Congresses in 1919, 1920, 1921, and 1922. But the fifth Congress met only in the summer of 1924, and it was then decided to hold future Congresses only in alternate years. In fact, despite the Comintern's rules, no Congress was held in 1926 ; and the next Congress assembled only in 1928. This long gap was certainly due to the fact that in 1926 and 1927 the struggle for power inside Russia between Stalin and his rivals was in full swing and would undoubtedly have been reflected in an immense faction fight in the Comintern if the Congress had been allowed to meet. By 1928 the more acute phase of this struggle had ended with the elimination of Zinoviev as well as of Trotsky ; and, though the further contest between Stalin and Bukharin was already well on the way, Stalin was firmly enough in power to feel able to take the risk of allowing the Congress to meet. It was in fact the occasion of Bukharin's swan song, and was speedily followed by his demotion from leadership in the Comintern, in which thereafter Stalin took a much greater direct part.

During the first few years of its existence, the Comintern had believed itself to be riding the wave of World Revolution and had, as we saw, been doing its utmost to wage war on the Centrists, even more than on the right-wing Socialists, in its endeavours to establish everywhere Communist Parties of guaranteed revolutionary devotion. But by 1921 it had become clear that the revolutionary wave was receding and that there would have to be a pause before the Revolution could be successfully extended to further countries. It was also plain, especially after the events in Germany in 1921,[1] that a *putsch*-ist policy, instead of bringing the mass of the workers over to the Communists, was having exactly the opposite effect. In Russia itself, after the Petrograd strikes of January 1921 and the suppression of the Kronstadt Rising, there had been the deep change of internal strategy embodied in Lenin's New Economic Policy, and in the more accommodating treatment of the peasants which accompanied it. These internal changes were bound to react on Russian external policy, and on the Comintern as Russia's instrument in its relations with the working-class movements in the outside world. Lenin himself had reproved foreign Communists who were subject to leftish infantile disorders; and at the Third Comintern Congress in June-July 1921 he appeared with the slogan 'To the Masses!' to adjure the Comintern Parties not to allow themselves to fall into sectarian isolation from the main body of the workers, but to establish contacts with them by showing a readiness to co-operate with them, even if this involved some sort of common action with bodies under right-wing or Centrist leadership. It is true that Lenin, in offering this counsel, also declared, in a phrase that became famous in his booklet on *Left-wing Communism*, that the co-operation which the Communists were proposing to the Socialists would support them 'as the rope supports the man who is hanged'.

Thus was born, in June 1921, the notion of the 'United Front' — that highly ambiguous phrase that was to give rise to so many disputed interpretations in the following years. As first put forward, whatever the ultimate intention behind it, the United Front involved a recoil from the extreme splitting tactics of the preceding years. Because of this, it encountered lively opposition from many Western Communists who, having been told so recently to cut themselves entirely apart from the 'social traitors' of the right and centre, found great difficulty in understanding why they should now be told to join forces

---

[1] See p. 169.

with them. It was explained to them that there were two opposite errors which it was of equal importance for Communists to avoid. One was 'opportunism', involving sacrifice of principle for the sake of getting immediate working-class support, at the cost of losing sight of revolutionary objectives. The other was 'sectarianism', which involved letting themselves be cut off from contacts with the working masses, by refusal to take part in campaigns for those reforms in which the main body of the working class was most immediately interested. Between these two, they were told, it was indispensable for the Communist Parties to steer their straight and narrow course. In practice, this meant that they must seek means of co-operating with the Parties from which they had recently broken away, while avoiding capture by these Parties and maintaining their rights of independent action, and further that they must work inside the existing Trade Unions, despite their right-wing leadership, and attempt to push them towards greater militancy, and must refrain from setting up rival Unions which would be too weak to put themselves effectively at the head of the industrial struggle.

Behind this change of front lay, of course, the realisation by the Russian leaders, or at any rate by most of them, that the prospect of immediate World Revolution had gone, and that the task of the Communists for the next few years was to build up their strength in order to be in a stronger position when the opportunity recurred, as they felt it was certain to do. Just as Russia had to take a long step back from the policies appropriate to the period of external intervention and civil war, and to devote itself to building up its own strength under the N.E.P., so World Communism had to go over from the tactics of immediate Revolution to those of leadership of the main body of the workers in the day-to-day struggle for improved, or against worsened, conditions.

There were other slogans besides 'To the Masses !' and the 'United Front' that arose out of the debates at the Comintern Congress of 1921. Much use came to be made of the cry for a 'Workers' Government'; and this too lent itself to very different interpretations. It could be taken to mean that where Social Democrats and Communists had between them majority support in a Parliament the Communists should be prepared to enter into coalition Governments which would then govern in accordance with parliamentary democratic practice, enacting advanced reforms and using their political power to strengthen the position of the working class. This is what it was actually taken to mean in those parts of Germany in which, in the State Parliaments, the coalition of a Socialist-Communist majority was momentarily effected.[1] But a 'Workers' Government' could also be taken to mean a Soviet Government applying a system of proletarian dictatorship ; and it was only by leaving it uncertain which of these was meant that the policy could secure general endorsement. Radek, who was in 1921 the Russians' principal adviser in West European affairs, clearly inclined to the first interpretation : Zinoviev, the Comintern President, no less clearly to the latter ; but for the time being the main body of Russian opinion was with Radek. Moreover, in 1922 there was a good deal of talk about a 'Workers' *and Peasants'* Government' ; and in 1923 the Russians got together an International Peasant Congress which decided to set up a 'Red Peasant International' just before the fall of Stambolisky's peasant régime in Bulgaria. This venture came to nothing for lack of any solid body of peasant support ; but it was clearly meant as the international correlative of the changed attitude taken up towards the Russian peasants in connection with N.E.P. In effect, under the changed circumstances the Bolsheviks were looking for means of increasing their effective strength in the world, not only among the industrial workers by taking a greater part in their day-to-day struggles, but also among those peasants who had a consciousness of being oppressed by the ruling classes.

Thus, in 1921 and for the next two or three years, Comintern policy moved sharply rightwards, and attempts were made to get a foothold for influencing the membership of the Social Democratic Parties and the Trade Unions that were under Social Democratic leadership. In face of the sharp rejection of the Communists' overtures by the Parties of the Second International, the new policy made much more headway in the Trade Union than in the political field. In the main, attempts to set up rival Trade Unions were abandoned, and the Communists had some success in winning positions of local

[1] See p. 642.

influence in the established Trade Unions. Even politically, the change in policy had some effect in Germany, where it provoked very sharp conflicts inside the Communist Party, and was enforced only by strong Russian or Comintern pressure. The Leipzig Congress of the German Communist Party in January 1923 endorsed the new line under Heinrich Brandler's leadership, only to be overwhelmed later in the year by the consequences of the Ruhr struggle and by its own, and the Comintern's, vacillations concerning the course to be followed in connection with it.[1] This *débâcle* was followed by the disgrace of Brandler, who was made a scapegoat by Zinoviev, though, in fact, the Comintern had been largely respor ible for the fiasco.

The events in Germany in 1923, followed by the negotiations which issued in the Dawes Plan, led to a further reconsideration of Comintern policy. A distinction was now drawn between two kinds of 'United Front' — one, the 'United Front from Above', involving co-operation at top level between Communist and Social Democratic Parties, and the other, the 'United Front from Below', rejecting such co-operation, but intended to involve the coming together of Communists and rank-and-file Social Democrats and Trade Unionists in common movements which the Communists hoped to be able to guide and control to suit their ends. Zinoviev came out in favour of the second kind of 'United Front' and of an interpretation of the phrase 'Workers' Government' that fitted in with it and made it involve some sort of proletarian dictatorship. Thus Comintern policy swung again leftwards, but not to the extent of any return to the tactics of 1919 — for it continued to be recognised that no immediate prospect of World Revolution existed, and that the immediate task was that of arousing the workers to greater militancy in pursuit of their short-run economic interests.

There were, moreover, cross-currents. As we have seen, the British Trade Unions were swinging leftwards after 1924 as the mining crisis approached and as economic conditions grew worse after the fall of the Labour Government. The chance of winning British Trade Union support to bring pressure on the Amsterdam Trade Union International was too

[1] See p. 655.

good to be missed ; and in 1925-6 the Russian Trade Unions were made use of to push the 'United Front' policy in Trade Union affairs. At the Fifth Comintern Congress in 1924 there had appeared to be a definite turn to the left with Brandler's replacement in the German leadership ; but in effect for the next year or two the Comintern was following different policies in different connections, and no clear line can be made out. These ambiguities help to explain why the Congress that should have been held in 1926 was never convened. In 1925 the German left-wing leaders who had replaced Brandler were driven out in their turn on a charge of left deviation ; and Ernst Thaelmann (1886-1944), who hastily accepted the new line, became the recognised head of the German Communist Party.

Meanwhile, the developing disputes inside the Russian Communist Party had been coming to a head. Stalin had already ousted Trotsky in the contest for leadership after Lenin's death ; and then, towards the end of 1925, Stalin and Zinoviev, hitherto allies, had fallen out, chiefly over the treatment to be accorded to the better-off peasants. The following year saw Trotsky and Zinoviev allied against Stalin ; and the year ended with Zinoviev's displacement from the leadership of the Comintern, and with his replacement by Bukharin — a definite rightward move. In 1927 the Communist Parties outside Russia underwent far-reaching purges of left-wing elements in their leadership, while in Russia the struggle between Stalin and his opponents went on unabated. In the same year came, in swift succession, the collapse of the Communist policy in China, the ending of the Anglo-Russian Trade Agreement, the abortive July rising in Vienna, and a series of other events which provoked a serious war-scare in the Soviet Union. Before the year ended, Trotsky and Zinoviev had been expelled from the Communist Party, and the 'United Front' epoch in the history of Comintern policy had come to a definite end. By the time the Sixth Comintern Congress met in 1928, it was being put about that a 'Third Period' in post-war history was about to begin, to be distinguished from the earlier periods of immediate Revolution and United Front tactics ; but no-one was at all clear what this 'Third Period' would involve. There were some, including Bukharin, who expected a continuance of capitalist recovery, thus agreeing with the diagnosis put forward in the report of the L.S.I. Secretariat to its Congress of 1928; whereas others prophesied an impending crisis in the capitalist world that would open the way to a renewed revolutionary advance. Bukharin, already well aware that he would not be left for long as leader of the Comintern, devoted a part of his presidential address to expounding the first of these views, and also strongly attacked the increasing rigidity of doctrine and policy which Stalin was seeking to impose on the Communist movement. He quoted a letter he had formerly received from Lenin, saying that 'If you drive out all intelligent people who are not very pliable, and keep only obedient idiots, you will certainly ruin the party'. It is not surprising that he was speedily relieved of his high office, or that no-one was appointed in his place. Stalin had no wish to be confronted with a rival who, from his point of vantage as the nominal leader of World Communism, would be in a position to challenge his authority.

Actually, no further full Congress of the Comintern was held, after that of 1928, until 1935 — by which time Hitler had been in power for two years in Germany, and the world depression was a long way past its nadir in 1932–3. During the intervening period Communism as a world movement had been gradually adjusting its ideas to the changes in the world situation arising out of the eclipse of the once-powerful German Labour movement and the effects of the depression on the Labour movements of the other leading capitalist countries. The fact had to be faced that the depression, though more devastating in its effects than any earlier crisis of capitalism, had brought with it not a recurrence of revolutionary action by the workers, but counter-revolution in the country on which Communist hopes had formerly been concentrated as the most likely to follow the Russian lead, and in the other advanced capitalist countries a most unrevolutionary demand for measures designed to get the capitalist economy back into working order and thus to limit the sufferings imposed on the poorer classes by unemployment and financial deflation. The 'Third Period' of which the advent had been announced in 1928–9 had turned out to be a period, not of triumphant proletarian advance, but of Fascist development on a grand scale and of a general retreat of the forces of Trade Unionism and

Social Democracy, as well as of serious dislocation in the Communist ranks. Generally speaking, the initial response of the Communists to the depression in its earlier years had been a turn to the left, because the crisis of capitalism seemed at first to offer a clear opportunity for intensified revolutionary agitation and for turning the masses against the Social Democratic leaders who seemed able to do so little on their behalf. For a very short time in 1928 the right wing of the German Communist Party had secured a majority on its Executive Committee, but had been promptly evicted under Comintern orders. Thereafter the German Party had returned to its obedience to the Comintern, and had found itself faced with the growing power of the Nazis, first plainly manifested in their success in the election of September 1930. During the depression the Comintern had stood by, unable to make any major impact on the course of events and increasingly troubled by the repercussions throughout the world of the internal struggles that had been taking place in the Soviet Union. The Russians themselves had enough to occupy them during these years with the carrying through of the first Five-Year Plan and with the immense problems of agricultural collectivisation. Stalin was too busy liquidating the *kulaks* and destroying the remnants of opposition inside the Soviet Union to be able to spare more than secondary attention for the affairs of the outside world. There were 'Trotskyist' troubles in many of the Communist Parties outside Russia ; and, though the depression naturally brought them many new recruits, especially among the unemployed and the youth, these recruits were none too easy to hold under the rigid discipline which it was regarded as necessary to impose without much regard for the differing conditions in each particular country. From the moment when, in 1924, Stalin first propounded the theory of building 'Socialism in a single country' the Comintern had been becoming more and more an auxiliary of the Russian Communists, to be used for the defence of the Soviet Union against its enemies, rather than an organised expression of a world-wide movement standing for the general interests of the working class. In the absence of any widespread revolutionary feeling among the workers in the capitalist countries, it could not really have been anything else. For, with Germany plainly out of the running so far as the Socialist, or Communist, Revolution was concerned—and with China, it appeared, utterly lost—where was the next Socialist Revolution to take place ? Certainly not in France, or in Great Britain, or in the United States, or even in India, where Gandhi's influence had become paramount. Certainly not in Italy, prostrate under Fascism. Certainly not in Scandinavia, which was weathering the depression relatively well, or in Austria, where Social Democracy was steadily giving ground before the increasing violence of the reaction, or in Poland, where Pilsudski had been rapidly increasing his dictatorial power, or in Hungary, where Horthy remained quite unshaken and the working-class movement in almost complete eclipse. There were, no doubt, greater revolutionary potentialities in Mexico ; and Revolutions, of a sort, were endemic in many parts of Latin America. But such upsets, even if they took a Communist or Socialist turn — which seemed unlikely — were almost irrelevant to the situation that faced the Comintern in the key areas of the capitalist world. The world depression furnished opportunities for trouble-making, but no more ; and trouble-making, though it might be of some use to the Soviet Union in its dealings with the outside world, could do nothing to bring back the extravagant hopes with which the Comintern had been launched on the morrow of the first world war.

At the point at which I am breaking off this narrative in the present volume the Nazis had not yet come to power in Germany, and President Roosevelt had not yet launched his New Deal in the United States. Nor, in the realm of economic thought, had the ideas of J. M. Keynes yet accomplished the revolution they were to bring about during the next few years. Keynes, following in the footsteps of J. A. Hobson, had indeed already proclaimed the folly of trying to meet the impact of unemployment by purely deflationary measures which only made it worse ; but the theoretical basis of his ideas and their potentialities for the reconstruction of capitalism on a foundation of full employment were still but little understood. Social Democrats, as well as Communists, were still arguing that crisis and mass unemployment were unavoidable recurrent phenomena of the capitalist system and could be cured only by the adoption of a socialised economy, though the Social

Democrats, in their hostility to Revolution, were calling for palliatives that would lead to a restoration of capitalism coupled with improvements in the condition of the workers under it, whereas the Communists were hoping for and prophesying its impending collapse, even though they were not ready with any immediate means of replacing it, short of a World Revolution that was evidently not going to occur. The Communists still looked on Fascism as no more than a resort by capitalism to violent, dictatorial methods of resistance to the claims of the working class, and refused to admit that it represented a new force, working indeed with capitalist support, but resting on nationalistic and militaristic foundations of its own. There was, no doubt, *some* justification for this view in relation to the forms assumed by Fascism or semi-Fascism in the Balkan countries, in Poland and Hungary, and even in Italy, though even in these countries it was most misleading to ignore the nationalistic and militaristic elements and to attribute to their relatively undeveloped capitalist classes a power and influence they certainly did not possess. In Germany, though capitalism was, of course, much stronger and more highly developed, it was even more unrealistic to regard Hitler as simply a capitalist stooge, and even to regard the advance of Nazism as something that would work itself out before long, because of its inability to resolve the 'contradictions of the capitalist economy', and would thus actually help towards Socialist or Communist Revolution. In due course the Communists were to come to an understanding that Fascism was their most formidable and dangerous enemy, and were to alter their strategy and seek for allies who would join them in a world-wide anti-Fascist crusade. But this realisation came only after Hitler had destroyed the Weimar Republic and consolidated his power in Germany as the first stage of his campaign for European, and even for world, domination.

Thus, the rival Internationals stood throughout the period covered by this volume for policies altogether too far apart for any real possibility of combined action between them to exist. The Berne International and its successor, the L.S.I., were consistently hostile to the entire conception of World Revolution and to the idea of exclusive rule by the representatives of the working class — and, of course, even more to the rule of a single Party claiming to represent that class. They were parliamentary democrats, and claimed no right to establish Socialism except with the consent of a majority of the whole people in each country, ascertained wherever possible by means of free parliamentary elections on a basis of universal suffrage. For the countries in which no possibility existed of such elections they had in effect no message : they could only protest against the undemocratic practices which ruled them out. As for the countries which did have, in the main, democratic parliamentary systems — and these were the countries on which their hopes were set — they envisaged a gradual conversion of the majority of the peoples to Socialism, a gradual improvement in social and economic conditions, and, when the majority had been won over, a still gradual transformation involving, during the stage of transition, a mixed economy in which Socialist and capitalist institutions would peacefully co-exist. For this gradual advance towards Socialism it was clearly needful to keep capitalism working as prosperously as possible and also to avoid war between the nations. Hence the devotion of the L.S.I. and its affiliated Parties to the cause of peace, to international arbitration, and to disarmament, and the desire, when their countries were laid low by the world depression, to aid the process of economic recovery rather than to use the depression for making the difficulties of capitalism worse.

As against these views, the Communists envisaged the world situation in quite different terms. For them, the Russian Revolution was the opening phase in a World Revolution that was necessarily destined to occur because, sooner or later, the capitalist system was bound to break under the stress of its inner contradictions, with Socialism as its only possible successor in the march of world evolution. The Russians had shown the way ; and the proletariats of other countries were under an inescapable obligation to follow their example and to use the methods which had shown their efficiency in carrying the Russian Revolution to victory and in enabling it to maintain itself in face of so many powerful enemies. Even when the early hopes of speedy World Revolution had to be deferred, they were only deferred, and not given up. The timing might be open to doubt : not so either the outcome or the methods to be employed. The coming Revolution was world-wide — one and indivisible, though the timing of it might vary from country to country. The essential task, therefore, was to generate revolutionary feeling among the toiling masses in all countries and to use every difficulty that beset world capitalism and imperialism as an opportunity for increasing the revolutionary ferment, without regard for the effects on immediate working-class conditions. It was, of course, necessary to take the side of the workers in relation to their immediate claims — for this was a necessary condition of winning their support for the Revolution — but the outcome of these day-to-day struggles mattered only as it affected the prospects of revolutionary success.

The Communists did not want capitalism to be patched up, so as to be able to carry on while Socialism was gradually introduced ; they wanted to destroy it and, while that was not yet possible, to harry and distract it as much as they could. Especially, while they were waiting for its collapse in its main centres of power, they did their best to carry on the struggle against it by stirring up trouble in the subject countries — colonies or economic spheres of influence — on which a part of its power depended. Russia being an Asian as well as a European power, their readiest means of doing this were in Asia, and above all in China, which had been passing through its own Revolution under the leadership of Sun Yat Sen. There were also opportunities in India, engaged in its struggle for Swaraj against the British, in Indonesia, under Dutch rule, and in the countries of the Middle East, from Egypt, under British occupation, to Persia, long the scene of conflict between Great Britain and Russia. Outside Asia and the Eastern Mediterranean, there were opportunities in Mexico and in many parts of Latin America for stimulating resistance to American imperialism, and in South Africa among the mineworkers oppressed under white domination. All these chances were seized on ; and emissaries of Russia and of the Comintern were continually active almost everywhere, and in addition numerous foreign revolutionaries were brought to the Soviet Union for training in the arts of revolutionary propaganda and Soviet apologetics. The collapse of the alliance between the Chinese Communists and the Kuomintang was a tremendous blow to the

Soviet Union and to the Comintern, not only because of its effects in the Far East but also because of its wider repercussions on Communist prestige. But the policy of stirring up trouble for the imperialists was not given up : it received a fresh impetus from the world depression, which fell most hardly of all on the countries most dependent on the world market for primary products. Social Democrats, as well as Communists, were, of course, ready to protest against the abuses of imperialism and to demand rights of self-government for the subject peoples ; but they tended to think mainly in terms not of colonial revolt or of Revolution in the less developed countries but of gradual concessions by the imperialist powers and of the introduction of democratic parliamentary government into the countries still subject to aristocratic feudal rule. It was no more possible for Social Democrats and Communists to work together in Asia or Africa or Latin America than in Europe or the United States. Although both were advocates of 'Socialism' and demanded social ownership of the means of production and a removal of racial discrimination, they attached different meanings to both Socialism and the means of arriving at it.

In cutting short the story of the rival Internationals at 1931 I am leaving the conflict between them unresolved, as it remains unresolved between the conflicting outlooks even to-day. It was bound to remain so unless either the Soviet Union collapsed, leaving no alternative basis for the strength of Communism as a world force, or Social Democracy lost the allegiance of the main body of the workers in the advanced capitalist countries — which, save in Germany, it never did. This conflict, moreover, was bound to dominate the affairs of world Socialism, even though there were always many individual Socialists who were highly critical of both the extreme parties and were neither prepared to regard the Soviet Union as a gloriously impeccable example to be followed nor content with the complacent gradualism of the parliamentary Socialist leaders of the L.S.I. The Centrists, as we have seen again and again, were ground to powder between the rival Behemoths.

CHAPTER XXIII

THE UNITED STATES: CANADA

As we saw in an earlier part of this work, Socialism in the United States, after advancing fairly fast up to about 1912, had already begun to lose influence before the outbreak of the European War in 1914.[1] I made some attempt to explain this fact in the third volume of this work ; and I need not go over the ground again. I need only say that the factors which were holding Socialism back before 1914 operated with much greater effect after the war and have continued to operate, after a brief interruption during the years of depression in the 1930s, right up to the present time. Chief among them, I feel sure, is the remarkable success of American capitalism in 'delivering the goods' on an ever-increasing scale — except during the depression, when the trend was for a while most sharply reversed — and the receipt of a large share in this advancing productivity by the American workers. This latter has, of course, been much more marked since the New Deal of the 1930s than it was before. The bargaining strength of the American Trade Unions has grown dramatically, and has been used to secure not only higher wages but also much greater social security and improved status, not by attacking the capitalist system but by squeezing it by means of continued pressure for better contracts of employment. Meanwhile, United States capitalism, formerly notable for its extreme antagonism to Trade Union claims, has for the most part fundamentally changed its strategy, and has realised the advantage of buying Trade Union and working-class support by making large concessions — which out of its abundant surplus it can well afford. In a rapidly expanding economy marked by almost continuous full employment it has paid the workers handsomely, in a material sense, not to spend their energies in attempting to overthrow capitalism but to

[1] See Vol. III, Part II, p. 776.

co-operate with it while taking good care to keep their powder dry in view of the possibility that these conditions may not last indefinitely.

This policy has been the easier to follow because American society, on account of the sharp decline in immigration, has become much more homogeneous than it used to be, with the consequence that European influence on American ways of thought — including Socialist influence — has declined sharply. The Socialist movement in the United States had always been largely dominated by European conceptions brought by the successive waves of immigrants : Socialism had never captured the imagination of the main body of American-born workers, largely because the American class-structure was much more fluid, and they did not feel themselves individually condemned throughout life to an irremediably inferior social position. The absence of a powerful and entrenched hereditary aristocracy and the possibility of rising in the social scale by personal effort made class-consciousness a much less powerful sentiment than it was in Europe ; and, though the 'frontier' for mass escape from wage-servitude had been almost closed well before 1914, the prospects of improved material conditions within the wage-system were good enough to take the edge off the desire to achieve revolutionary changes in the basic structure of society. In the minds of most Americans — including most workers — Socialism was an alien doctrine, inappropriate to conditions in the United States and even disliked because it seemed to involve greatly increased state interference with men's ways of life and the imposition of bureaucratic controls which ran counter to American conceptions of freedom.

Socialism, as it existed in the United States in 1914, was the faith of only a small minority, made up partly of immigrants from Europe or of their children who had taken over their ideas from immigrant parents and partly of idealists who based their Socialism much more on moral imperatives than on any conception of class-war.

The collapse of the Second International and the rallying of most of the major European Socialist Parties behind their respective Governments came as a great blow to the American Socialists, who had taken seriously the anti-war and anti-imperialist declarations of the International and mostly found it difficult to understand how the collapse could have come about. As there was, in 1914, no immediate question of the United States being directly involved in the fighting, the American Socialists did not have to face any problem of voting or refusing to vote for war credits. They were at the outset mere spectators ; and the first thought for most of them was whether they could do anything to bring the unwelcome struggle to an end. A small minority, including William English Walling (b. 1877), A. M. Simons (b. 1870), and John Spargo (b. 1876), came down on the side of the Allies, denouncing German militarism as the villain of the piece and the German Majority Socialists as its traitorous abetters ; and some at any rate of the Wisconsin German-Americans showed signs of 'pro-Germanism'. But the main body, without drawing fine distinctions between the combatants, was content to denounce the struggle as an 'imperialist war' arising out of capitalist-imperialist rivalries between the great powers, and involving the common people against their will and interest. In September 1914 the National Executive of the American Socialist Party sent to the European Parties a proposal for an international conference, to be held at Washington, in order to consider ways and means of bringing the war to an end. The Parties of the belligerent countries paid no attention to this appeal ; but some of the European Parties from neutral countries responded favourably, while urging that the proposed Conference should be held, not in the United States, but on European neutral ground. The A.S.P. accepted this suggestion ; and preliminary arrangements were made for the Conference to meet in January 1915 at Copenhagen. The Americans at this stage were still hoping that the Socialist Parties of the belligerent countries would agree to send delegates. When they found this was not the case, they lost interest. Camille Huysmans, the secretary of the International Socialist Bureau, had written deprecating the proposed Conference as premature ; and it was abandoned.[1] The A.S.P. thereupon refused to pay any further contributions to the Bureau, and allowed their membership of the Second International to lapse.

Thereafter, abandoning the attempt to bring the war in Europe to an end, the American Socialists, up to 1917, devoted

[1] See p. 30.

their energies to keeping the United States out of it. This ranged them, for a time, with President Wilson, and also, for longer, with a number of American pacifist bodies. For a while the Socialists, except the small pro-Allied group, advocated an embargo on all supplies to the belligerent countries for as long as the fighting lasted ; but presently they abandoned this demand when they found that it was ranging them with the supporters of Germany — for as the Allies had the command of the seas and trade with the Central Powers was already cut off by them, it would have meant in effect only a refusal to supply the Allied countries. When, in 1916, President Wilson, near the end of his first term, began to call for a programme of military 'preparedness', the A.S.P. strongly opposed this programme. They also took up the demand of Allan Louis Benson, in the *Appeal to Reason*, that no declaration of war should be made by the United States, save for the repelling of an actual invasion, until the issue had been submitted to a referendum vote of the whole people. Largely on the strength of this proposal, Benson was put forward as Socialist candidate for the Presidency in 1916, Eugene Debs (1855–1926) having refused to stand again, mainly for reasons of health. Benson did badly, getting only 585,000 votes — one-third fewer than Debs had polled in 1912 — partly because Benson was very much less a national figure than Debs, but also because the Socialist Party had been definitely losing ground, and because President Wilson, in 1916, still had a strong appeal to many American progressives on the verge of the Socialist movement.

The following year, as a sequel to the unrestricted submarine campaign launched by Germany, the United States entered the war, and the Socialists had to make up their minds what line to take in face of the accomplished fact and of the rising tide of nationalist feeling that went with it. At the St. Louis Party Convention of April 1917 the A.S.P. took up a strong anti-war line, only a tiny handful of delegates supporting John Spargo's pro-war minority report. This decision was endorsed by a two-thirds majority on a referendum vote of the whole membership. Thereafter, the American Socialists including the followers of the small and declining Socialist Labour Party, had to face a rapidly mounting opposition and met with increasing difficulties as the circulation of the Socialist

Press was hampered by the denial of the use of the mails by the Post Office, and as more and more Socialist speakers and writers were gaoled for offences against the special legislation that was speedily enacted to deal with anyone accused of hampering the draft for military service or of obstructing in any way the measures needed for the prosecution of the war. The courts of law gave short shrift to critics or opponents of American war policy ; and President Wilson himself completely backed up the more intransigent persecutors of the Socialists among federal office-holders. In addition to federal law-making directed against sedition — especially the Sedition Act of 1918 — one State after another enacted its own repressive laws. These fell on the right as well as on the left wing of the Socialist movement and were to a great extent supported by the Labor Unions of the American Federation of Labor, which took up a strongly pro-war line under Samuel Gompers's masterful leadership. Up to 1917, though the left-wing Trade Unionists of the I.W.W. had often met with scant mercy from the law and though State and federal forces had been often invoked against strikers, the United States had been, on the whole, a country in which political freedom of speech and organisation had been allowed fairly wide scope ; but from the moment when the country entered the war all this was abruptly changed, and not only anti-war speakers and writers, but also anyone who could be accused of hampering the prosecution of the war in any respect, found themselves in constant peril both of legal punishment and even of physical violence.

Moreover, the A.S.P.'s anti-war stand in 1917 lost it the backing of a good number of its best-known intellectual supporters, among them Allan Benson, Upton Sinclair (b. 1878), and C. E. Russell (1860-1941) in addition to those mentioned already. The pro-war Socialists began by organising, in hostility to the A.S.P., a Social Democratic League of America, which included a substantial group of well-known figures, but very few followers. This body soon merged with other pro-war progressive groups into a 'National Party', in which Charles A. Beard (1874-1948) also was active ; but the movement struck no roots, and speedily died away. For a while the A.S.P. seemed to be holding the ground well, despite these defections. It polled well in the municipal elections of the autumn of 1917, especially in New York, where Morris Hillquit (1869–1933), standing for the office of mayor, got more votes than any Socialist candidate had ever, or has since, received. But this appearance of strength was soon seen to be illusory. Party membership had been dropping steadily during the war years ; and the Party's position became much more difficult towards the end of 1917 as a consequence both of the Bolshevik Revolution in Russia and of the publication by President Wilson of his 'Fourteen Points', with which most of the Socialists could not help agreeing to a very considerable extent. First, the issue of the 'Fourteen Points', and then, a little later, the behaviour of the Germans at the Brest-Litovsk negotiations, led to demands for a modification of the anti-war policy laid down at the St. Louis Socialist Convention. Anti-German feeling in the A.S.P. grew stronger ; and at the same time a conflict began to develop inside the Party between those who wholeheartedly supported the Bolsheviks and the right-wing opponents of proletarian dictatorship. It seemed, however, impracticable under the prevailing conditions of repression to call together a full Party Convention at which these differences could be thrashed out ; and, under the Party's Constitution, nothing short of this could give authority to change the St. Louis policy. At length, in August 1918, the A.S.P. did call a policy meeting of its National Executive with the secretaries of its State regional organisations to consider the situation ; but this meeting accomplished nothing except a revelation of the wide dissensions that existed within its ranks. The anti-war policy remained officially unaltered, though it was clearly driving members out of the Party ; and the quarrel between the right and left wings over the Soviet Revolution remained wholly unresolved. There matters stood, until the collapse of the Central Powers in October-November 1918 confronted the American Socialists with a new situation, in which the issue was no longer that of supporting or opposing the war but had become a matter of the policy — revolutionary or reformist — to be adopted as the basis for action in the post-war period.

In general, the situation which arose in the United States when the fighting ended was peculiar. The entry of the United States into the war had given rise to a violent bout of 'hundred per cent Americanism', directed not only against those who took up an anti-war or pacifist line but also against every form of leftism, and against those immigrants who failed to identify themselves entirely with the American 'way of life'. This attitude weakened the Trade Unions, despite the support given to the war effort by most of their leaders ; for every attempt to press economic demands in face of rising prices was denounced as unpatriotic. Trade Unionism had never achieved in the United States anything like the degree of recognition it had achieved in Western Europe. Though it was strongly entrenched in some industries, at any rate among the skilled workers, it had failed to touch more than a tiny fraction of the vast immigrant industrial population, and there were very many employers, including a high proportion of the big business corporations, which rejected collective bargaining as inconsistent with 'freedom of contract' — though only a few of these had, up to the end of 1918, set up company Unions of their own in order to keep out independent Unions. The injunction had already been widely used as a means of preventing Union organisers from entering non-Union areas or establishments for the purpose of enrolling the workers in Unions, even of the moderate A.F. of L. type. Generally speaking, American employers were bitterly hostile to Labor Unionism ; and, though they were to some extent restrained from taking active measures against Unionism, as such, while the war lasted, they missed no chance of hitting hard at any Union which showed signs of militancy and did their utmost to identify the entire movement with its very militant left wing, of which the symbol was the I.W.W. That intransigent body, which, after the defection of the Western Federation of Miners, had its main strength among the immigrant workers of the Eastern and Middle Western States, had already lost most of its force well before 1917 ; but it was none the less ferociously attacked and used as a means of discrediting all forms of militant Trade Union activity. Moreover, the anti-Union employers found widespread support for their campaigns against the Labour organisations from middle-class opinion and from federal and state politicians of both the main Parties. President Wilson, though he ranked as a progressive in both international and social policy, was as hot as anyone against all those who appeared to him to be hampering the war effort, and positively encouraged his Ministers, such as the Postmaster-General, Albert Burleson, and, later, the Attorney-General, A. Mitchell Palmer, in their high-handed proceedings against Socialists and alleged Syndicalists who were charged with 'unamerican' seditious practices.

The end of the fighting brought, not a relaxation of this persecution or of the anti-union drive, but an intensification of both. The Trade Unions seized the cessation of the war pressure as an opportunity for pressing their economic demands ; and the big employers, instead of meeting them half-way, retaliated with an immense drive against the Unions, insisting on the 'open shop', by which was meant a denial of all rights of unionisation and collective bargaining, and by the widespread formation of 'yellow' company Unions designed to keep their workers apart from the democratic Labor Unions. At the same time, as the war had not been legally ended by the armistice, prosecutions under the Sedition Act continued, and those already gaoled for war-time offences remained in prison despite appeals for an amnesty. Against the Labor Unions the injunction procedure was used on a greatly extended scale. In 1919 there was a wave of strikes, many of which were violently suppressed by police and by state and federal troops ; and the big corporations engaged a host of labour spies and informers, who penetrated into the Unions, as well as into the left-wing organisations, for the purpose of sabotaging their proceedings and of informing against 'agitators' — a term which was extended to cover almost every kind of Labour or Socialist activity. Naturally this wholesale persecution had some effect in driving even the more moderate Unions leftwards : the A.F. of L. joined in the demand for an amnesty, and some of its Unions adopted fairly militant policies in combating the employers' attacks. An attempt was also made, with A.F. of L. backing, to counter the employers' campaign by unionising certain branches of large-scale industry in which Trade Unions had been hitherto held successfully at bay — notably steel. William Z. Foster (b. 1881), once active in the I.W.W. but latterly an opponent of 'dual Unionism' and a leading advocate of the policy of 'boring from within' the existing Unions of the A.F. of L., was put at the head of a Steelworkers' Organisation Committee which made a determined attempt to enrol the mass of unorganised workers. The Amalgamated Steel Workers, once a powerful Union, had lost its hold after its great defeat in the Homestead strike of 1892, and the industry had become a stronghold of anti-Union activity. In the renewed struggle of 1919 twenty-four separate Unions, each claiming a right to organise some section of the steelworkers, joined forces in a central, but continually bickering, Organisation Committee which directly enrolled members with a view to sorting them out subsequently into the appropriate sectional Unions. The Committee demanded the recognition of collective bargaining rights, the reinstatement of the numerous workers who had been discharged for Union activities, the abolition of company Unions, and a number of concessions in respect of hours and wages. The big steel corporations rejected these demands, and in September 1919 more than 300,000 workers came out on strike. They remained out for six weeks, in face of most violent anti-strike action by state police, in the course of which eighteen persons were killed. Then the strike broke down, and the workers drifted back, to remain ununionised until the C.I.O. launched its Steelworkers' Organising Committee in 1937 and succeeded at long last in winning recognition of Trade Union rights. Foster, subsequently a leading figure in the American Communist movement and several times Communist candidate for the Presidency, was at the time of the 1919 strike a Syndicalist, deeply influenced by European Syndicalist ideas and intent of 'boring from within' the A.F. of L. in order to bring it over to a militant industrial policy. After the failure of the steel strike he went over to the Communists and became their leading figure in the Trade Union movement.

Nevertheless, despite the bitterness of the industrial conflicts of 1919, the main body of American Trade Unionism remained under strongly anti-Socialist leadership, and the Socialist Parties, tarred by their anti-war attitude, gained few Trade Union recruits, though some of their old Trade Union stalwarts, such as Max Hayes (1866–1945) and James H. Maurer (1864–1944), remained faithful to them and they did get considerable backing from a few Unions outside the A.F. of L. — especially from the Amalgamated Clothing Workers, led by Sidney Hillman (1887–1946), whose membership was largely drawn from immigrants not yet fully assimilated to American ways of thought.

The American Socialist Party, which had lost membership heavily during the war, did, however, experience after the armistice a very rapid influx of new members. This came, for the most part, not from the A.F. of L. Unions, but from the unassimilated immigrants, who, except in the needle trades, were largely outside the ranks of the Unions. The effect was that the composition and attitude of the Party underwent a sudden and startling transformation. The new recruits flowed in at a prodigious pace, so that within a few months its total membership had become larger than it had been before 1914. The new members, however, were drawn mainly from different sources and were recruited for the most part, not to the regular state and local organisations of the Party, but to the separate language Federations to which it had given a special position exempting them from control by the State and local bodies and making them subject only to the party centre. Instead of regaining the members it had lost, who were largely American-born and included a considerable following in the Western States and among the farming and share-cropping communities, the A.S.P. became to a considerable extent a Party of immigrants from Eastern and South-Eastern Europe, who were naturally affected in a much higher degree by contemporary events in Europe and, above all, by the Russian Revolution and by the revolutionary wave that passed over Europe as the Hohenzollern and Hapsburg empires followed the Czarist empire into dissolution. Up to November 1918 the impact of the Russian Revolution on American Socialism had been lessened by the preoccupation of the Socialists in the United States with their own anti-war struggle ; but as soon as this was ended they had to meet the full impact of the European Revolutions on the American people and especially on the more recent immigrants who had not yet been fully assimilated. They had, moreover, to do this in face of a persecution that was maintained with undiminished vigour though the war was over : so that their best-known leader, Eugene Debs, was actually sentenced after the armistice to a long term in gaol for a speech delivered against the war while it was still in progress, despite the fact that the Department of Justice had expressed strong doubts whether the speech contained anything contrary to the law.

As the year 1919 advanced it became evident that a big split in the A.S.P. was unavoidable. From the moment when the Comintern was founded in Moscow in March 1919 it was inevitable that some sort of Communist Party would be established in the United States, either by capture of the A.S.P. by the Bolshevik sections of its membership or by their secession to form a rival Party. The only immediately doubtful point was whether the extreme left would remain in the A.S.P. in the hope of capturing it or would secede at once to form a new Party ; and on this issue there were sharply divided opinions. The A.S.P.'s National Executive was firmly in the hands, for the moment, of the opponents of Communism — of men who had been against the war, but were also strongly against any attempt to make a Soviet Revolution in the United States. But the Executive was due for re-election, and there was evidently bound to be a hotly fought contest between the rival factions.

Trouble inside the A.S.P. had begun to grow serious in November 1918, when the various Slav Federations of the Party in Chicago, without seceding from it, set up a Communist Propaganda League, and the Lettish Federation in Boston founded a left-wing journal, *Revolutionary Age*, edited by Louis Fraina, an old S.L.P. associate of De Leon who had crossed over to the A.S.P. during the war and had recently published a book, *Revolutionary Socialism*, embodying a forcible statement of the Communist case. In February 1919 Fraina's journal published a manifesto and programme drawn up by left-wing elements in the A.S.P., and a week or so later the New York left-wingers, still without seceding from the A.S.P., set up a 'Left Wing Section' of the Party with the declared object of capturing control. The left wing demanded that the A.S.P. should rescind its entire programme of immediate demands for social reform and should embark on the establishment of Workers' Councils with a view to an immediate proletarian Revolution, including workers' control of industry through workers' Soviets, repudiation of national debts, and socialisation of banks, railways, and all foreign trade, and should link up internationally with the Russian Bolsheviks and the German Spartacists for the furtherance of World Revolution.

From these points of vantage in New York and Chicago the left wing set out to capture control of as many locals as possible of the A.S.P., working in conjunction with the language Federations, which were already mainly in left-wing hands. The 'Old Guard' leaders of the A.S.P., instead of waiting while their opponents used every chance to undermine their influence, promptly retaliated in the New York region by expelling the locals which supported the left wing, and attempting to form new ones under their own influence. The left-wingers who had not been expelled retaliated by agreeing with the language Federations on a common list of candidates for the imminent Executive elections and pledging both groups to vote solidly for the combined list. The New York left wing also decided to convene, for June 1919, a national Conference of all left-wing groups to prepare the way for the capture of the forthcoming Convention of the A.S.P.

After the voting for the new Executive had taken place, but before the votes had been officially counted or the results announced, the A.S.P. National Executive held, in May 1919, a plenary meeting at which it decided to take strong action against its opponents. At this meeting the Executive began with the extraordinarily drastic step of suspending, by 8 votes to 2, the seven language Federations which had endorsed the left-wing programme — thus in effect expelling at one blow roughly one-third of the total membership of the A.S.P. On top of this, the Executive next proceeded, by 7 votes to 3, to revoke the charter of the Michigan State Federation, which, without actually joining the left wing, had passed a resolution threatening with expulsion any member who continued to advocate the immediate reforms laid down in the A.S.P. Programme. As if this were not enough, the Executive, instead of announcing the results of the election for its successor, declared that it had received so many accounts of irregularities in the voting that it felt obliged to order the actual voting papers to be sent to headquarters for inspection before deciding whether or not to validate the results. This last decision led to a revolt of the Massachusetts Section of the Party, which met the following day and decided to send delegates to the proposed left-wing Conference. The minority in Massachusetts which supported the Executive thereupon seceded and called on the Executive to recognise it as the true Massachusetts Section — which the Executive promptly did. The Executive also proceeded, after examining such of the ballot papers as had been submitted to it, to declare the Executive elections invalid and to lay down that the new Executive should be chosen, not by a further ballot, but by a Special Party Convention, which it summoned to meet at the end of August.

The outgoing Executive thus expelled or suspended considerably more than one-third of the entire party membership without giving the general body of members any chance of deciding what they wanted done. Whatever irregularities there may have been in the elections for the new Executive, it seems clear that the left wing had in fact captured, by fair means or foul, the majority of the seats. The expulsions, however, drastically changed the balance of voting power in the Party, and made it likely, if not certain, that at the coming Convention the 'Old Guard' would be powerful enough to carry the day. In these circumstances, the left-wingers who remained in the Party had to consider seriously whether they could do any good by persisting in their attempt to capture it, or would do better to secede at once and set up the Communist Party on which the hearts of many of them were set. On this issue they found themselves sharply divided. The excluded language Federations quite naturally decided to take steps to set up a Communist Party, and invited the rest of the left wing to act with them. But the other section of the left, made up mainly of native or assimilated Americans, fell apart on this issue, largely because many of its members did not wish to join a Party that would be mainly dominated by Slav and other recent immigrants from Europe, and still hoped that they might be able to win over the majority of the A.S.P. to their point of view.

When the national left-wing Conference met in June 1919 both sections of the left attended ; but as soon as the proposal to secede at once from the A.S.P. and to form a Communist Party had been defeated, the minority, made up mainly of the language Federations and of the already excluded Michigan delegation, left the Conference and proceeded to take steps to establish a Communist Party. The majority continued in session, set up a Provisional Council to conduct its affairs for the time being, and agreed to summon a further Conference to meet in Chicago at the same time as the emergency Convention of the A.S.P. The newly founded Communist Party also decided to hold a constituent Convention at the same place and time : so that three distinct but overlapping gatherings were due to be held in Chicago at the end of August. At this point the left-wing organisation, which had managed to get possession of a large number of the original voting papers for the election of the new A.S.P. Executive, announced that these showed the left-wing candidates to have been duly elected. These candidates thereupon held a meeting at Cleveland and proclaimed themselves to be the properly constituted Executive of the A.S.P. They then reinstated all the groups expelled or suspended by the old Executive, which retorted by expelling the Ohio Section in addition to those already excluded. The new 'Executive' did not, however, take any further action, or attempt to prevent the Convention called by the old Executive from meeting.

The proceedings at Chicago began on August 29th with a meeting of the left-wingers who still remained in the Party, designed to make plans for capturing the official A.S.P. Convention on the following day. But the old Executive, aided by the police, was successful in preventing the delegates of the excluded groups from occupying the floor of the Convention hall ; and after long disputes over the right of delegates to take their seats the remaining left-wingers were voted down. They then seceded from the Convention and, at a meeting of their own, decided to establish a Communist Labor Party distinct from the Communist Party already set up by the language Federations and the Michigan delegation. Attempts were made to reach agreement for a merger of these rival Parties ; but the negotiations broke down, and a year passed before the Comintern was able to induce them to come together. The main obstacle to unity between the two was that the Communist Party, from which the Michigan delegation were soon excluded as Centrists, was based on the language Federations and was essentially a Party of fairly recent unassimilated immigrants, mostly Slavs, whereas the Communist Labor Party represented mainly the extreme left of native or assimilated American

Socialism and had closer connections with the left wing in the Trade Union movement, including old stalwarts of the I.W.W. Louis Fraina and Charles E. Ruthenberg were among the left-wing leaders who tried to induce the two Communist groups to amalgamate ; but the language Federations defeated the proposal, and the Communist Party, under their influence, drew up a programme calling for the dictatorship of the proletariat and for outright opposition to all projects of social reform within the capitalist system. Meanwhile, the Communist Labor Party, after a fierce internal struggle which led to considerable secessions of the less extreme section of the left, drew up a very similar programme ; and both Parties declared their adhesion to the Comintern.

It might have been supposed that the rump of the A.S.P., having got rid both of the language Federations and of its most left-wing sections, would have moved sharply to the right and would have accepted the leadership of its old, moderate protagonists, such as Victor Berger (1860–1929) of Wisconsin. This, however, did not happen. The other outstanding leader who remained in the A.S.P. was Morris Hillquit, of New York, who was away ill throughout this period, but was able, even in absence, to exert a considerable influence through the New York delegation. Hillquit had taken no part in the old Executive's drastic action against the left, and, though no Bolshevik, stood a long way to the left of the Wisconsin group. In his absence, John Louis Engdahl, at the head of the New York delegation, sharply criticised the old Executive's policy, and when it came to the voting, at the Convention itself, for a new Executive in place of that which had been disallowed by the old one as irregularly elected, only one member of the old Executive, James Oneal (b. 1875), secured re-election. One big issue at the Convention was the line to be taken by the A.S.P. in relation to the rival Internationals. This was submitted to a special Committee of the Convention, which produced rival majority and minority reports. Both reports rejected out of hand the newly formed Berne International, dominated by the British and German Parties :[1] the majority proposed that a new International should be formed at a Conference to which all Parties accepting the class-struggle, including the Russian and German

[1] See p. 290.

Communist Parties, should be summoned ; the minority, headed by Engdahl, proposed affiliation to the Comintern, 'not so much because it (the A.S.P.) supports the Moscow programme and methods' as in recognition of the stand that Moscow was making against imperialism and against the combined forces of world capitalism. The Convention, instead of accepting either of these proposals, submitted them both to a referendum vote of the party membership, which resulted, in January 1920, in an endorsement of the minority report. The A.S.P. thereupon applied for admittance to the Comintern ; but that body, with applications already on hand from the two rival Communist Parties, left the application of the A.S.P. unanswered, being then busy with formulating the 'Twenty-one Points', to which, as they included a denunciation of Hillquit as a dangerous Centrist, the A.S.P. could hardly be expected to agree. At the A.S.P.'s Convention in May 1920 the dispute over affiliation was renewed, and the International Relations Committee again produced rival reports. The majority now favoured joining the Comintern only on condition of its readiness to transform itself into an inclusive International embracing 'all the Socialist forces' and not insisting on the dictatorship of the proletariat as a generally applicable dogma. The minority, including Engdahl, favoured unconditional affiliation ; and Victor Berger, as the spokesman of the extreme right wing, put in a third report, rejecting all further connection with the Comintern. The two main reports were again sent to a referendum vote, which resulted in a very small majority for conditional affiliation. At the following Convention, in 1921, both unconditional and conditional affiliation were defeated, and so was a proposal that the A.S.P. should join the 'Two-and-a-Half' Vienna Union. The following year, however, this last decision was reversed. The A.S.P. joined the Vienna Union, which shortly afterwards amalgamated with the Berne International to form the Labour and Socialist International. The A.S.P. thus in the end became an affiliated member of the L.S.I., with Hillquit and Berger as its representatives on the L.S.I. Executive.

By this time what was left of the A.S.P. had moved a long way to the right. But the shift was gradual, with the surviving left-wing elements putting up a strong fight on the question of joining the Comintern. Meanwhile, in 1920, the Party once more came forward with its old stalwart, Eugene Debs, who had refused nomination in 1916, as its candidate for President. Debs, as we saw, had been gaoled early in 1919 under the Sedition Act, and was still in prison, President Wilson personally rejecting the repeated demands for his release. Debs had to conduct his campaign from gaol : he had no chance to use his oratorical powers and was restricted to a mere 500 words a week of written communication with the outside world — a severe handicap because he was as poor and diffuse a writer as he was remarkable for his oratory. Nevertheless he polled 915,000 votes — the highest vote ever given for a Socialist candidate. The campaign was indeed largely concentrated on an appeal for an amnesty for him and for the host of political prisoners sentenced under the Sedition Act during and since the war ; but President Wilson remained obdurate, and it was left for the very reactionary President Harding to release Debs and a number of others after he had taken office. The demand for Debs's release and for a general amnesty commanded wide support beyond the Socialist ranks : even Samuel Gompers and the American Federation of Labor endorsed it, and Gompers himself went to visit Debs in prison in 1921. Sympathy on account of his continued incarceration undoubtedly helped to swell Debs's presidential vote in 1920 ; for by that time the A.S.P. had lost most of its influence. In 1919, just before the Communist split, it had numbered well over 100,000 members. The following year, at the time of the presidential election, it had fallen to less than 27,000 ; and two years later it was down to little more than 11,000. The A.S.P., in these circumstances, felt that it must find new ways of action, both in order to fight the Communists and to save itself from sheer extinction. Its leaders were aware that there existed a considerable body of, at any rate, socialistic opinion which it was quite unable to win over to its own programme, but which might be induced to support a reformist policy including some socialistic elements, such as the public ownership and control of railroads and other public utility services, as well as measures of social reform and opposition to the so-called 'American Plan' favoured by the big employers.

Accordingly, at the A.S.P. Convention of 1921, Morris

Hillquit introduced and carried a resolution instructing the National Executive to make a survey of all radical and Labour organisations in the United States in order to discover their possible willingness to collaborate with the Socialists on a platform not inconsistent with that of the A.S.P. and on terms which would allow the A.S.P. to keep its 'integrity and autonomy' within a wider political framework. The Executive was to report on this question to the Convention of 1922. Hillquit's resolution, which was endorsed in face of strong opposition, pointed clearly to an attempt to link up with non-Socialist Labour and other progressive groups and had behind it the idea of attempting to establish some sort of progressive Third Party in federal and state politics, if possible with a solid foundation of Trade Union support. What Hillquit had in mind was evidently some sort of grouping analogous to the Labour Party in Great Britain, but also wide enough to bring in at least a section of the farmers and other progressives who could be detached from their allegiances to the two existing major Parties. In some respects the situation in 1921 appeared to be favourable to such a move. The American Federation of Labor was disappointed with the scant success of its efforts to promote the election to Congress and to the state legislatures of candidates friendly to Labor Unionism and social legislation and hostile to the 'American Plan', and still more to prevent the election of candidates actively hostile to working-class claims ; and outside the A.F. of L. there were a number of growing independent Unions, such as the Amalgamated Clothing Workers and the important Railroad Brotherhoods, which were largely sympathetic to Socialist ideas, at any rate in certain limited fields. The Railroad Brotherhoods, in particular, had come forward early in 1919 with a plan for the public ownership of the American railroads and for their operation under a system of joint control by nominees of the management, the workers, and the State. This 'Plumb Plan', drawn up by Glenn E. Plumb, the legal adviser of the Railroad Brotherhoods, was endorsed not only by these bodies but also by the United Mine Workers and by the American Federation of Labor, Samuel Gompers actually serving as President of a Plumb Plan League set up to undertake propaganda for it. There was also widespread support, both in the Trade Unions and among progressives generally, for public control and operation of the major utility services ; and the Socialists were encouraged to hope that these movements might be preparing the way for a new Party which, despite their weakness, they would be able before long to dominate with Trade Union support. When, in the autumn of 1921, the Railroad Brotherhoods sent out an invitation to a Conference, to be held at Chicago in February 1922, for the purpose of adopting 'a fundamental economic programme designed to restore to the people the sovereignty that is rightly theirs', the A.S.P. accepted the invitation to take part.

The proposed Conference was duly held, and was attended by groups representing a wide range of viewpoints. Besides the Railroad Brotherhoods and a number of other Trade Unions, the bodies represented included the new Farmer-Labor Party, set up in 1920, which was attempting to revive the old Populist movement, and also the Non-Partisan League, which had been seeking to secure the adoption of progressive candidates by both the great Parties, and also the remains of Theodore Roosevelt's Progressive Republican movement, a number of religious social welfare groups, and the A.S.P. — to say nothing of a considerable number of nondescript reformers, ranging from advocates of particular reforms to sheer cranks. The Chicago Conference agreed to set up a joint body, to be called the Conference for Progressive Political Action, which was to campaign actively in favour of the more progressive candidates, irrespective of Party, at the congressional and state elections of 1922. This did not satisfy the Socialists, who had hoped for the creation of a new Third Party ; but they decided to support the C.P.P.A., though they had been given only one representative on its Committee.

Of the groups represented at Chicago, the Farmer-Labor Party appeared at this stage the most hopeful. It had been set up towards the end of 1919 in Chicago as the American Labor Party under the leadership of John Fitzpatrick (1871–?), the local head of the A.F. of L., and of the veteran Socialist Max Hayes, who had left the A.S.P. in Ohio when Charles Ruthenberg (1882–1927) had captured the Ohio Section for the left wing. Fitzpatrick had been closely associated with W. Z. Foster in the attempt to unionise the steelworkers, and was an influential figure in the left wing of the A.F. of L. Thereafter, in July 1920, the American Labor Party had joined forces with the Committee of Forty-Eight, a group of survivors from the old Progressive Party, to form the Farmer-Labor Party, which ran Parley Christensen (1880–?) of Utah and Max Hayes for the Presidency and Vice-Presidency at the election of 1920, and polled 300,000 votes. It had tried in 1920 to induce the A.S.P. to withdraw Debs and agree on a joint campaign ; but the Socialists had refused. In 1921 the Socialists' change of tactics seemed to make the Farmer-Labor Party a possible ally ; but the following year it was captured by the Communists, who successfully infiltrated into it through a number of auxiliary 'front' organisations. Fitzpatrick and Hayes left it, and it disintegrated ; and an attempt in 1924 by its Minnesota section to bring a new Farmer-Labor Party into being met with a similar fate when the Communists again succeeded in gaining control.

The Non-Partisan League, which had been organised in 1915 in North Dakota by the former Socialist Arthur C. Townley, was a much less hopeful ally ; though most of its leading promoters were, or had been, Socialists — among them Walter T. Mills (1851–?) and Charles Edward Russell. For the League had arisen out of disillusionment with the prospects of forming a 'Third Party' ; and its policy was essentially that of getting the candidates it favoured put forward under the auspices of either of the old Parties. In North Dakota the Non-Partisan League had for a time a spectacular success, until in 1921 the old Parties combined against it and succeeded in destroying its influence. It revived later, and succeeded in sending a few of its adherents to Congress. But it was throughout essentially a Populist, farmers' movement, with no real affinity to Socialism except in favouring state aid to farmers and public operation of grain elevators in the farmers' interests. In 1921 it was already a rapidly waning force.

The prospect of establishing any Third Party of the kind the A.S.P. desired was bound to depend on securing the support of at any rate a substantial part of the Trade Union movement, and especially, in the first instance, that of the Railroad Brotherhoods, which had taken the lead in setting up the C.P.P.A. But neither the Brotherhoods nor the other Trade

Unions which sent delegates to the Chicago Conference were prepared to go to the length of establishing a new political Party, so as to cut their connections with their friends in the older Parties. In 1922 the C.P.P.A. did play some part in defeating some very reactionary candidates, but did not achieve a great deal. At its second Conference, in December 1922, the Socialists vainly urged the immediate establishment of a new Party and were defeated only by 64 votes to 52. Their main support came, on this issue, not from the Trade Unions, but from the bourgeois progressive bodies. Even the Railroad Brotherhoods still preferred the non-partisan tactics of seeking friends in the existing Parties. The A.S.P. nevertheless continued to participate in the work of the C.P.P.A. and became much more hopeful when that body decided at its 1923 Conference to run its own candidates at the Presidential elections the following year, while stopping short of endorsing combined lists on a national scale for the congressional and state elections. The choice for Presidential candidate fell on Robert La Follette (1855–1925), the Wisconsin progressive, and the C.P.P.A. launched a big campaign. Its prospects were greatly improved when the A.F. of L., temporarily modifying its non-partisan policy, decided to support La Follette and the C.P.P.A.'s candidate for the Vice-Presidency, though not to join the C.P.P.A. itself or to endorse any proposal to set up a new Party. La Follette fought on a progressive, but entirely non-Socialist programme, which was endorsed by the S.P.A. Convention with the rider that the S.P.A. still adhered to its own Socialist principles.

In the ensuing campaign many attempts were made to brand La Follette as a crypto-Communist and to represent the C.P.P.A. as a crypto-Communist agency, though in fact La Follette roundly denounced Communism and the C.P.P.A. had firmly excluded all Communist participation in its affairs. In the event, La Follette got nearly 5 million votes — about 17 per cent of the total — carrying the day in his own State only, but running ahead of the Democrat, J. W. Davis, in 11 other States, mainly in the West. The Republican, Calvin Coolidge, won by a big majority. In the congressional and state elections the A.S.P. put forward its own lists, distinct from those of the other progressive groups, and did not do well.

Victor Berger won a congressional seat in Milwaukee ; but on the whole the Socialists fared rather badly in the state and local elections. The question then arose whether the C.P.P.A., having shown its ability to poll a respectable Presidential vote, should convert itself into a Third Party ; but at its Convention of February 1925 the Trade Unions rejected this proposal and left the groups which favoured it — mainly the A.S.P. and some of the farmers — to argue the question among themselves. The project then broke down because, whereas the remaining progressive groups wanted a Party based entirely on individual membership, the A.S.P. insisted on a federal structure which would admit the Socialists as an autonomous body, on the lines of the federal constitution of the Labour Party in Great Britain. When this proposal was rejected, the A.S.P. seceded from the C.P.P.A., which thereafter faded quickly away, leaving the Socialist Party again independent, but weaker than ever, with a membership that by 1928 had fallen to less than 8000 from the peak of 108,000 only nine years before. From that point there was some revival under new leadership. In the presidential election of 1928 the Party appeared with a new candidate, Norman Thomas (b. 1884), a former minister of great ethical fervour who had been coming rapidly to the front. Of the older leaders, Hillquit and Berger were still active, but were both disqualified for the office of President by their foreign birth. Debs, the 'grand old man' of the Party, had died in 1926, worn out by his efforts and sufferings for the cause ; and Thomas was his best available successor as the leading pro-pagandist of democratic Socialism. Debs, as long as he lived and was prepared to stand, had been the inevitable choice as Presidential candidate ; for though he had been always well on the left of the Party he was the only member of it who was known everywhere and possessed a really wide popular appeal. He had, moreover, taken care, as far as he possibly could, to keep aloof from internal party disputes. The right wing had never liked him, and had tried again and again to find someone capable of taking his place ; but again and again, except in 1924, when he had refused nomination, they had been forced to rally behind him as the one candidate capable of mustering a respectable vote. Debs's honesty and self-devotion were un-questionable. He was no great theorist ; but there was in

736

him a warmth of humanity which made a strong appeal to a great many simple people, especially in the Western States, who were inaccessible to more sophisticated approaches. He had made his great name first of all as a Trade Union leader who stood for a Trade Union spirit widely different from that of Samuel Gompers and the American Federation of Labor — indeed, for a spirit much more akin to the class-militancy of the Industrial Workers of the World. But he was a political Socialist and not a Syndicalist, and was quite prepared to work for piecemeal reforms as well as for Socialism and, above all else, was ready to rally at all times to the cause of the oppressed. This last quality in particular made him able to appeal successfully to such persons as small farmers and share-croppers as well as to industrial workers, and enabled him to play a big part in winning support for the A.S.P. in the Western States of the Union. His powers, however, had been failing for some years before his death : indeed, he never recovered from the effects of his imprisonment from 1919 to 1921, and the decline of the A.S.P. in the West was largely due to his removal from the leadership during and after these years. Without him, the A.S.P. had no-one capable of exerting a similar appeal. W. D. Haywood (1869–1925), who had something of the same appeal to the miners, oilworkers, and longshoremen, but not to the farmers, had been driven out of the Party because of his hostility to political action ; and there was no other major figure possessing the same sort of appeal.

Of the other leading A.S.P. figures after the split of 1919, Morris Hillquit was a New York lawyer with a considerable competence as an exponent of Social Democratic Marxism and in the legal field, but essentially a townsman and an intellectual without any great capacity for mass leadership. He had played a fairly active part before the war in the Second International ; and his Socialism was of an orthodox pre-war Social Democratic type. During the period of revolutionary ferment that began in 1918 he moved for a time some distance leftwards, but not far enough to prevent him from being a principal target for Communist denunciations as a leading exponent of the Centrism which the Comintern was attacking most bitterly of all. In the course of the exceedingly acrimonious conflicts between the A.S.P. and the Communists after the split, he moved back rightwards and became the principal exponent of the movement which led the A.S.P. into its abortive coalition with the non-Socialist progressives in support of Robert La Follette's candidacy for the Presidency in 1924. When the attempt to create a federal Labour Party in connection with that contest failed, and the A.S.P. returned to independence, he remained at the head of its sadly reduced forces as an orthodox Social Democrat of the pre-1914 brand, though he embarrassed his colleagues by taking up professionally certain big law cases in which his task was to uphold somewhat unsavoury capitalist interests. Outside New York, where he had a large following, he was never more than a secondary figure.

Victor Berger, as we saw in an earlier section of this study,[1] was also a highly orthodox Social Democrat, but of a much more reformist type than Hillquit. In 1919 he remained entirely unmoved by the revolutionary fervour that swept over so much of the Party and, while retaining his position in it, stood mainly aloof from its internal battles, waiting for it to recover its sanity, and in the meantime concentrating most of his energy on the affairs of Wisconsin and in particular of Milwaukee, where he was able to maintain his control over the local Party almost unimpaired. Berger was a collectivist, with a keen belief in the virtues of public enterprise ; but he was, above all, in practice a social reformer, deeply interested in efficient and progressive municipal and state administration. Internationally, he was a great admirer of German Social Democracy and utterly opposed to Bolshevism and to every sort of revolutionary policy. In his home state he had a strong enough following to secure repeated election to a seat in Congress, for the most part as the one and only Socialist to achieve this ; but on a national scale he made no considerable impression and had no wide popular following. He remained active in Wisconsin up to his death in a street accident in 1929. Of the other post-war A.S.P. leaders only James Oneal made any substantial mark ; and his rôle was rather that of a doughty foe of Communism than that of a constructive Socialist leader. James H. Maurer, long President of the Pennsylvania Federation of Labor, was notable as the one outstanding Trade Union figure who remained throughout his career loyal to the

[1] See Vol. III, Part II, p. 805.

Socialist Party. He did manful work for it in the Trade Unions, especially in the educational field, but never became a great popular figure.

As for the De Leonite Socialist Labor Party, after De Leon's death in 1914 it was never of any real account, despite Lenin's praise of De Leon as an outstanding Marxist thinker. After 1914 its leading spokesman was Arnold Petersen (b. 1885), who waged bitter verbal war upon the American Communists as well as upon the A.S.P. But the S.L.P., which had never been much more than a sect, even in De Leon's day, had become more and more sectarian in its old age, and need not detain us further.

On the Communist side, undoubtedly the outstanding personality in 1919 was the journalist John Reed (1887–1920), whose account of the Bolshevik Revolution, *Ten Days that Shook the World*, takes rank as a revolutionary classic. Reed was a new convert of the revolutionary period and, above all else, a romantic revolutionary. He took a leading part in the attempt to win the A.S.P. for Communism in 1919 and in founding the Communist Labor Party when that attempt had failed. In these efforts he worked closely with Louis Fraina, who subsequently changed his name to Lewis Corey and became a professor and a well-known economic historian. In 1920 Fraina was accused of being a police spy, but was exonerated after an enquiry by the Communist Party. Two years later he quarrelled with the Party and was charged with the crime of organising an opposition group in Mexico. He remains a somewhat enigmatic figure ; but he undoubtedly played a leading part in bringing about the split in 1919 and was a journalist of high controversial ability.

Yet another outstanding figure in the affairs of American Communism in 1919 was the Irish leader, James Larkin (1876–1947), who was then resident in the United States.[1] Larkin had left Ireland in 1914 after the defeat of the great Dublin strike of 1913–14, intending to return home after a visit of no very long duration to the United States. In America he worked with the Socialist Party, in fairly close association with Eugene Debs, and also spoke on behalf of the I.W.W. and other left-wing groups. Strongly anti-war, he rallied in 1917

[1] For Larkin's career, see Vol. III, Part I, pp 240 ff.

to the cause of the Russian Revolution, and took part, with C. E. Ruthenberg and Bertram D. Wolfe (b. 1895), best known much later, for his book, *Three Who Made a Revolution* (1948), in the Left-Wing Committee which organised the campaign for the capture of the A.S.P. at the Convention of August 1919. A few months later, together with other left-wing propagandists, he was arrested and, after long delays in prison, was put on trial on a charge of 'criminal Anarchism' and sentenced to prison for a period of from five to ten years. He remained in gaol until the Governor of New York, Al. Smith, released him in 1923, when he was deported to Ireland. Throughout his nine years' absence he had remained, in form, secretary of the Irish Transport and General Workers' Union ; but on his return he found it impossible to work with the leaders who had taken charge while he was away. Quarrelling violently with these leaders, he led a group of supporters who forcibly seized the Union headquarters and kept possession until he was displaced by a legal action. He then founded a new Union — the Workers' Union of Ireland — which met with considerable success, especially in Dublin, and he also took an active part in the municipal affairs of that city. Larkin was a most powerful and rousing orator who, like his co-worker, James Connolly (1870–1917), firmly maintained the compatibility of his faith in Communism with his membership of the Roman Catholic Church ; but his connection with the American movement was no more than an episode.

Luckily, it does not seem necessary in this work to enter into any detailed account of the infinite varieties and endless disputes of American Communism after the two rival Communist Parties had been forced to amalgamate in 1920 under strong pressure from the Comintern. The American Communists, consisting largely of East European immigrants, but with a number of native Americans and West Europeans among their leaders, showed a bewildering propensity to factional disputes, so that every amalgamation supplied the occasion for a fresh split. Even in 1920 the establishment of the United Communist Party promptly led to the secession of a minority which accused the Moscow-inspired leadership of departing from the true revolutionary path and proceeded to set up a rival Communist Party composed largely of immigrants from Russia. By 1921 there were, or had been, no fewer than twelve Communist Parties, united only in their deep hostility to the Socialist Party and, of course, to the American 'way of life'. In face of the persecution to which the entire left was subject, the Communist Parties had been driven underground and were unable, even if they had wished, to fight elections or even to conduct open propaganda. When, in 1921, the Comintern altered its tactics in view of the evident decline of the World Revolution, the main Communist Party, which had Moscow's support, changed its line and took the lead in setting up an above-ground Workers' Party as a 'front' organisation behind which the underground Party maintained its existence and attempted to keep the control in its own hands. W. Z. Foster, the steelworkers' organiser of 1919, became a prominent figure in the Workers' Party and, in due course, its Presidential candidate in 1924. A quarrel speedily developed between those who wished to keep the Workers' Party as a mere tool of the underground Communist Party and the 'Liquidators', who wanted to abolish the latter and concentrate all their activities in the Workers' Party, or upon infiltration into other above-ground bodies, such as the Farmer-Labor Party ; and most of the best-known Communists, including Foster, Earl Browder (b. 1891), Charles Ruthenberg (who died in 1927), Jay Lovestone (b. 1898), who later became a prominent anti-Communist and official adviser on international policy to the A.F. of L., and James P. Cannon (b. 1885), took the latter view, which was reinforced when, on the occasion of a secret Convention of the underground Communist Party in August 1922, the police succeeded in seizing all the party records.

The Workers' Party, thus left to conduct its own affairs, soon divided itself into two factions, one led by Foster, Browder, and Cannon and the other by Ruthenberg, Jay Lovestone, and the Hungarian Josef Pogany, now known as John Pepper, who was in America as the representative of the Comintern. The main question at issue was the attitude to be adopted towards the attempts that were being made to establish a Labour Party. Foster at first opposed participation in these attempts, but then changed sides and advocated support for La Follette and the C.P.P.A., which strongly rejected it. in the Presidential contest of 1924. Moscow, however, decided against supporting La Follette, and Foster again changed sides to follow the Moscow line.

By this time, in Russia itself, the struggle between Trotsky and Stalin had taken precedence of all other issues. Max Eastman (b. 1883), one of the foremost literary champions of American Communism, published in 1925 his *Since Lenin Died*, an emphatic eulogy of Trotsky embodying an account of Lenin's unpublished 'Testament'[1] and a sharp attack on Stalin ; and a faction fight soon developed among the American Communists between Stalinists and Trotskyists, with the Stalinists still divided into rival factions, each attempting to get the Comintern on its side. Then Zinoviev quarrelled with Stalin and was displaced from the leadership of the Comintern ; and a little later Bukharin, who had replaced him, was accused of right-wing deviation and was thrust out in his turn. Through these successive phases Foster managed to maintain his leadership of the main Communist Party up to 1929. In 1925 the Party almost split in a dispute between the Foster and Ruthenberg factions, of which the former had the majority. But Moscow intervened to prevent Ruthenberg and his followers from being displaced from their leading offices ; and Foster had to give way. Then, in 1927, Ruthenberg died, leaving Foster in control. In June 1928 the Trotskyists, headed by James Cannon and Max Shachtman (b. 1903), were expelled for left-wing deviation and set up a rival Workers' Party, and a little later Lovestone and Benjamin Gitlow (b. 1891), after being summoned to Moscow, were thrust forth as supporters of Bukharin, and set up yet another splinter Party, the Communist Party Opposition. At this point Moscow also decided to discipline Foster, who was displaced as party secretary by his former follower, Earl Browder. Pepper, who had been closely associated with Ruthenberg, was recalled to Moscow and presently disappeared in the purges of the 1930s. Foster retained his membership of the Party and came back to the leadership when Earl Browder was finally displaced in 1945. A. J. Muste (b. 1875), who had been a protagonist in the Lawrence textile strike of 1919, formed in 1929 a new body, the Progressive Conference for Labor Action, and during the

[1] See p. 583.

depression of the early 'thirties took a leading part in setting up unemployed clubs. In 1933 he founded yet another abortive Party — the American Workers' Party, which for a time attracted some notable recruits, including Sidney Hook (b. 1902), a Marxian theorist of some importance, and James Burnham (b. 1905), later famous as the author of *The Managerial Revolution*. In 1934 it amalgamated with the Trotskyists in yet another Workers' Party.

These are only a few among the countless splinter organisations which arose out of the American Communist movement during its early years. But enough has been said to illustrate the extreme faction-proneness of the movement, largely a consequence of its failure to strike any firm roots among the main body of the working class, and of its dependence on the stream of East European immigrants, which had begun to dry up with the imposition of severe restrictions on immigration after 1913.

I am conscious that what I have written in this chapter is for the most part a chronicle of very small beer. For the plain truth is that at no point after 1914 did Socialism amount in the United States to a movement of any real significance. This applies as much to the Communists as to the A.S.P. or to the surviving rump of Daniel De Leon's rival Socialist Labor Party ; for though American Communism made more noise in the world than its Socialist rivals, much more of the noise was due to its opponents' than to its own efforts. Neither Communism nor democratic Socialism made, at any point between 1914 and the 1930s, even as much impact as the I.W.W. had made for a few years earlier in the century, or even as much as the Socialists had made on the A.F. of L. at an earlier stage. The rapid increase in the A.S.P.'s membership in 1918 and 1919 was due almost entirely to the inrush into it of Slav and other East European immigrants which followed the Revolutions in Russia and accompanied the post-war upheavals in Europe in 1918-19. This ferment doubtless spread to some extent to the existing membership and propelled almost the whole of the Socialist movement for a time a long distance to the left. But it did not bring in any large body of new recruits from among the native or assimilated membership of the Trade Unions or threaten even for a moment to wrest the control of the Trade Union movement from its old, mainly anti-Socialist leaders. Certain Unions, notably the Railroad Brotherhoods, did move towards demands for public ownership and workers' participation in industrial control ; but they did this without becoming in any way revolutionary or even converts to the idea of a Labour Party on the reformist British model, and even the moves they did make towards political action did not last long or in any way alter their fundamental attitude. This was no doubt partly because the United States, unlike the other belligerent countries, emerged from the war with its productive power, not impaired, but greatly increased, and because American capitalism, far from being faced with any prospect of dissolution, was more powerful than before. But this is not, I think, the whole explanation. Nor does it suffice to say that the drastic curtailment of immigration, especially from the poorer European countries, cut off the main supply of revolutionary material — though this was unquestionably a factor of real importance in the 1920s, because it enhanced the bargaining power of the A.F. of L. Unions and offered them better prospects of immediate advantage from 'pressure group' policies directed at the established major Parties. There was, over and above these factors, an absence of fundamental discontent with the existing social institutions and a strong tendency to conform to the American 'way of life' that largely barred the way to the acceptance of revolutionary ideas blowing over from Europe and served to brand these ideas as 'unamerican' and therefore unworthy to be taken seriously except as threats to American institutions.

It is true that, in the period before 1914, this 'American spirit' had not prevented the growth of a very militant minority Trade Union movement, which found its chief expression in the I.W.W. This movement, however, had never spread to the main body of members enrolled in the A.F. of L. Unions. It had grown up mainly, in the early stages, among the miners and oil and lumber workers of the still thinly populated but rapidly developing Western States and, in spreading from these areas to the Middle West and the East, had found its following mainly among the immigrants who supplied most of the less skilled labour in the great cities rather than among the born Americans or the fully assimilated immigrant groups. In

California, Oregon, Washington, and the other Western States, the I.W.W. and its predecessor, the Western Federation of Miners, had been largely movements of native Americans, Irishmen, and assimilated Europeans : in Lawrence and Paterson and Chicago the I.W.W. found its rank-and-file support mainly among workers relatively new to American conditions. It is true that some of the A.F. of L. Unions — notably the United Mineworkers — were forced into industrial militancy by the extreme anti-Unionism of the big employers ; but, even so, militancy in industrial relations failed to convert these Unions to either Socialism or Syndicalism, which seemed to most of their members to be alien creeds sponsored for the most part by foreigners on whom they looked down as inferiors destined for the less remunerative and less prestigeful kinds of labour. Even if the 'frontier' was already becoming closed, there was still large room for social mobility in a society advancing rapidly in economic wealth ; and there was also a widespread tendency to despise and distrust politicians, which rendered unappetising proposals for expanding the range of state action in the economic field. In effect, the ferment that affected the Socialist movement in 1919 quite failed, despite the extremely reactionary attitudes of the big employers and of Congress, to spread to the main body of the American working class.

How, then, did it come about that Socialists themselves, old-stagers as well as new-comers, got into the highly excited condition in which they clearly were for a time after the end of the war ? Of course, not all did : Victor Berger and his Wisconsin followers stayed precisely where they had been, continuing to advocate and to practise their reformist policies just as they had been doing for many years past. But they were the exception ; and for a time they lost almost all their influence on the main body of the A.S.P. In New York and Massachusetts and in Michigan and Ohio the main body of Socialist opinion, among native and assimilated Americans as well as among the swollen language Federations, moved sharply to the left, so that, even after the two Communist Parties had both broken away, the rump of the A.S.P. continued to pass resolutions in favour of adhesion to the Comintern until that body had made perfectly plain that it was not prepared to accept them at any price. I do not think this was mainly due to realisation that the prospect of any substantial advance towards Socialism by constitutional methods was manifestly non-existent, at any rate for a long time to come. It was probably due much more to the ferocity with which every kind of Socialism, even the mildest, was denounced as Bolshevism, and to the severe persecution to which every sort of supposed leftism was subjected from the moment of America's entry into the war. With only a few exceptions, the right as well as the left wing of the A.S.P. had opposed the war, and had thus exposed itself to the accusation of treason ; and, when the persecution was continued after the war was over, the effect was to push the Socialist movement, in self-defence, further left than many of its members really wished to go. But it is undeniable that, over and above this, the European revolutionary ferment, though it failed to arouse a response among the main body of the organised workers, did for the moment strongly affect the Socialists and push them temporarily a long way leftwards, leaving them to recoil only when, after the split, they found themselves subject to violent attack from the Communists, who, under orders from the Comintern, were making war even more ferociously on the Centrists than on the adherents of the constitutional right wing. Under the impact of this un-measured violence of language, the depleted A.S.P., as we have seen, before long moved abruptly rightwards and for a while almost sank its Socialism in an attempt to bring the Trade Unions, the farmers, and the liberal bourgeois groups into a progressive alliance in which they, as Socialists, could hope to play only a minor part. When this attempt broke down, mainly for lack of Trade Union support, the A.S.P. resumed its isolation, and found itself reduced to sheer impotence not only while the wave of economic prosperity continued to flow, but even when the American economy plunged into the colossal depression of the 1930s.

The great American depression of the 1930s, which was ushered in by the Wall Street collapse of 1929, falls outside the scope of the present chapter. Throughout the 1920s the American economy, despite serious troubles on the farming front, appeared to most people to be in process of a rapidly expanding prosperity under capitalist auspices, so that leading economists, such as T. N. Carver, could write almost without challenge books in which they claimed that the United States had had its economic revolution without any political upheaval and was well on the way to establishing universal prosperity under the benevolent reign of private enterprise. Throughout this period, despite the advancing industrial economy, free Trade Union membership, which had risen rapidly in 1919 and 1920, was falling almost continually in face of the growth of company Unions and the 'open shop'. The A.F. of L., which had over 4 million members in 1920, had fallen below 3 million in 1923 and below 2¾ million by 1930. Over the same period, total Trade union membership fell from 5 million to less than 3½ million, or from nearly 20 per cent of eligible workers to about 10 per cent. These figures include Canada ; but this does not materially affect their import. In effect, the employers were able to keep Trade Unionism almost wholly outside the big mass-production industries, except coal-mining, and to destroy the powerful position which the rail-road Unions had built up during and immediately after the war. The so-called 'American Plan', based on the 'open shop', did, to a great extent, succeed not only in wrecking the Socialist movement but also in keeping Trade Unionism from becoming a really powerful force in the most rapidly expanding sections of the economy. Socialism and Communism were reduced as movements to impotent factions, fighting one another with the utmost bitterness, but making no impact on the main body of American opinion ; and even Trade Unionism could not hold its own, save here and there, until the depression and the 'New Deal' of the 1930s had prepared the way for the new broom of John L. Lewis's United Mineworkers and Philip Murray's C.I.O.

CANADA

Of Socialism in Canada during the period covered in this volume there is not much to say. As we saw, a Socialist Party of Canada had been set up in 1905, to unify the scattered organisations already in being ; and a second body, called the Social Democratic Party, had been founded in 1911, and had joined the Second International, to which the S.P.C. refused to adhere because it objected to the presence there of the

British and Australian Labour Parties, regarding those bodies as inadequately Socialist. Neither the S.P.C. nor its rival had any large following, though the former succeeded in electing a few scattered members to the Provincial Legislatures in Alberta and Manitoba. During the war the S.P.C. grew somewhat stronger, and there was a considerable growth of militancy, especially in connection with the struggle over conscription. When the war was over, the militancy for a time increased, especially in the Western provinces ; and a considerable movement grew up in support of the idea of 'One Big Union' to carry on a more intense and more closely co-ordinated struggle in the industrial field. This movement reached its culmination in the general strike at Winnipeg in the early months of 1920 — a struggle marked by considerable violence which ended in the defeat of the strikers and in a serious set-back for the Canadian left wing. At the same time Labour Parties, largely in alliance with the rising organisations of farmers, were being founded in a number of Provinces ; and in 1920 Angus McDonald (b. 1890) was elected from Ontario to the Federal Parliament as the candidate of the Labour Party and the United Farmers of Ontario. The following year James Shaver Woodsworth (1874–1942), who had come into prominence as editor of the strikers' newspaper — the *Western Labor News* — during the Winnipeg strike, was elected for Winnipeg as a Labour Party nominee. Woodsworth, who had been trained for the ministry, had taken up a strongly anti-war attitude during the conscription struggle and had been discharged from his position as director of the Social Research Bureau set up jointly by the Provincial Governments of Saskatchewan, Manitoba, and Alberta. He had then become a travelling propagandist for Socialism, and had built up a popular influence which made him the natural leader of the rising Socialist and Labour political movements. His outstanding follower in these movements was the English-born teacher, M. J. Coldwell (b. 1888), who was active with him in establishing the Co-operative Commonwealth Federation in 1932, with a moderate Socialistic programme, on the basis of which it tried to enlist the support of the more progressive farmers as well as of the workers. Only at this point, which falls beyond the range of the present narrative and coincides with the most severe impact of world depression on the Canadian economy, did Canadian Socialism begin to act politically on a national scale. A Canadian Communist Party had indeed been set up in 1920 ; but it was weak, and was speedily outlawed ; and, acting underground, it was unable to exert any significant influence.

CHAPTER XXIV

LABOUR MOVEMENTS IN LATIN AMERICA FROM 1914 TO THE EARLY 'THIRTIES

IN the preceding volume of this work an attempt was made to present a general picture of the growth of Socialism in Latin America up to 1914, and some parts of the story were carried a long way beyond that date because of the great difficulty of finding a convenient stopping point.[1] I now find myself in a similar difficulty ; for it is nearly impossible to give any clear account of the developments which took place in the 1920s without continuing the record to cover a part of the 1930s as well. The first world war and the Russian Revolution of 1917 both had a profound influence on the Labour movements of the Latin-American countries ; but this influence was felt very unevenly from country to country, and the major consequences had only begun to show themselves by the date — approximately 1931 — at which the present volume is designed to stop short. I shall therefore be very brief, and shall leave fuller treatment over for the ensuing volume, if I survive to write it.

The first major impact of the war of 1914–18 was felt in the decline of imports and of capital investment — and also of immigration — from Europe. The scarcity of European consumers' goods forced the Latin-American countries to develop light industries of their own — especially textiles — and these helped to foster industrialisation, mainly in light rather than in heavy industry. There was also an increasing replacement of European by United States investment, which had, up to 1914, been relatively small except in Mexico and other parts of Central America ; and the inflow of American capital was a powerful factor in stimulating feelings of economic nationalism, while at the same time the decline in British investment weakened British influence even in the Argentine, which had

[1] See Vol. III, Part II, Chapter XXII.

very close links with the British market and had drawn from Great Britain most of the capital invested in railways and public utilities.

After the entry of the United States into the war in 1917, many of the Latin-American countries were induced to abandon their neutrality and to join the Allies. Up to that time there had been sharp divisions, and many Latin Americans had tended to sympathise with the Axis powers, whose agents had been very active. Throughout the left-wing movements, the Russian Revolution exerted a very powerful influence. Until then, as we saw, the predominant influence on the working-class movement in most parts of Latin America had been Anarcho-Syndicalist, rather than Social Democratic, though even before 1914 the Anarcho-Syndicalists had begun to lose ground wherever small-scale artisan production was replaced by large-scale employment. After the Russian Revolution, and still more after the Third International had begun from 1920 to interest itself actively in the cause of World Revolution, not only the left-wing elements in the Socialist Parties but also many former Anarchists and Syndicalists became converts to Communism. Communist Parties were speedily set up in many parts of Latin America ; and Communist influences became powerful in many of the Trade Union movements, most of which were still at an embryonic stage. It is not at all easy to measure the real strength of these Communist or Communist-dominated movements at any moment ; for, particularly in the Trade Union field, the Communists became past-masters in the art of carrying on organisations with high-sounding titles, but in many cases with no large or assured actual following. Moreover, the Communist Parties themselves were often outlawed, and had either to carry on a clandestine existence or to operate under other names, in what came to be known as 'front' organisations. They were, moreover, in some degree affected by the endless splits that occurred among the followers of Communism in the United States, and also later by the appearance of a variety of Trotskyist groups, as well as by the breaking away of disillusioned elements and by the growth of rival doctrines based on specifically Latin-American conditions rather than on comprehensive theories of anti-capitalist revolution.

The emissaries of the Third International who were

specially charged, in the early 1920s, with carrying the message of Communism to Latin America were first the Indian, M. N. Roy (1893–1954) — from 1920 to 1922 — and then the Japanese, Sen Katayama (1858–1933) — the latter an old stalwart of Japanese Socialism already well known in the United States. In some countries, notably Uruguay and Chile, the pre-1914 Socialist Parties went over to Communism and accepted the Twenty-one Points insisted on by the Comintern. In others, notably Argentina, a section of the Socialist Party split away and before long converted itself into a Communist Party. In quite a number of countries no Socialist Party, or at all events none that counted, had existed in 1914. The Brazilian Socialist Party, for example, was founded only in 1916. The Argentinian Socialist Party, started in 1894, alone had a long continuous existence. That of Uruguay dated only from 1910, and that of Chile, led by Luis Recabarren (1876–1924), only from 1912. Thus the Communists were able to enter a still mainly untilled field, though there had, of course, been Socialist groups and Trade Unions, in many cases ephemeral, in the majority of countries. From 1920 onwards Communist progress was rapid. In that year, Communist Parties began operations in Uruguay and in Bolivia ; in 1921, in Argentina and in Brazil ; in 1922, in Mexico and Chile ; and in 1925 in Ecuador and in Cuba. Peru followed in 1929, the year of the first continental Communist Congress at Montevideo, and then came Colombia and Costa Rica in 1930, and Venezuela in 1931.

During the years of war, anti-imperialist feeling in Latin America had been much stirred up by United States intervention in the affairs of a number of American States. The Dominican Republic had been occupied in 1916, and Haiti the previous year ; and in 1916–17 United States forces had advanced into Mexico and a naval force had occupied Vera Cruz. Further aggressive acts followed in the 1920s — for example, in Honduras in 1924 and in Nicaragua in 1925. The effect was to stir up a strong current of anti-imperialist feeling, directed especially against the United States, but also against all forms of penetration by foreign capital which resulted in the creation of business enterprises under foreign ownership and management.

This anti-imperialist sentiment extended over a very wide range. It affected not only the working classes but also many of the middle classes — not only students and intellectuals, but also employers and traders, who feared exposure to the competition of foreigner-owned businesses in command of more up-to-date and efficient business techniques, and resented the high living standards of foreign specialists who settled among them, just as the workers resented the much higher wages paid to foreign workers. It is true that the need to import capital for purposes of economic development was widely recognised; but this did not prevent fears of domination by foreign capitalist interests from being widely felt. Nationalist and xenophobic sentiments tended to cut across the traditional divisions between right and left, giving rise to conflicts within the Socialist and Trade Union movements as well as within the older groups and parties. In general, the foreign-owned enterprises, at all events in the urban areas, paid better wages and offered better working conditions than most indigenously owned concerns; but this did not prevent the rise of anti-foreigner sentiment even among many who benefited by it in a material sense. The dominance of reactionary influences in the United States during the years after the 1914–18 war tended to make both the United States Government and the great business corporations interested in the Latin-American field the allies of the most reactionary political elements in Latin America — the old landed aristocracies and the small groups of financiers interested in large-scale economic development; and such alliances tended to turn both nationalists and a large section of the middle classes — including many small employers — as well as the organised workers into forces hostile to imperialist, and especially to North American, economic penetration. But there were also cross-currents; for the Socialists were naturally, for the most part, eager for rapid industrial development as a means of strengthening the industrial working class, which had in most parts of Latin America little contact with the unorganised masses of rural labourers and impoverished small cultivators still largely subject to feudal control.

This was a situation of which the Communists, working in close connection with the Comintern and its agents in America, were able to take advantage. The policy of the Comintern in the years after 1920 was aimed at using the working classes of the Latin-American countries as instruments in an intensive struggle against imperialism, and especially against the economic imperialism of the United States. It was, however, also based on a class-war theory which excluded all forms of alliance either with the bourgeois left or with the Socialist or Social Democratic Parties or groups that rejected the idea of proletarian dictatorship. This prevented the Communists, until much later, from attempting to put themselves at the head of all the forces hostile to imperialism, and compelled them to concentrate their efforts largely on winning over the Trade Unions and trying to bring them together in Central Confederations in each country under Communist leadership and influence. In this they had considerable success, especially among the heavily exploited miners and oilworkers and among the transport workers — that is, among the working-class groups that were directly experiencing the consequences of large-scale economic development, mainly under the auspices of foreign concerns. Among these groups they were able, to a considerable extent, to oust the formerly predominant influence of the Anarcho-Syndicalists and even to win over many former Anarcho-Syndicalists to their point of view. They had much less success among the skilled artisans and other workers in small-scale employment; and usually the result of their activities was not the establishment of working-class unity under Communist control, but the division of the Trade Union movement into rival factions, each with its own central organisation, and with many Trade Unions refusing, in the hope of maintaining a limited solidarity, to connect themselves with any of the rival centres.

Up to this time the Trade Unions of Latin America had been, for the most part, entirely without formal connections with those either of the United States or of Europe. But from 1920 onwards they came under growing pressure to establish such contacts. The Communists, of course, were doing their best to induce the movements which they controlled or influenced to join the Red International of Labour Unions set up at Moscow [1] and also to bring about closer relations between

[1] See p. 335.

the various national Centres in Latin America that were following their lead. Much less actively, the predominantly Social
Democratic Unions attached to the Amsterdam I.F.T.U. were
conducting counter-propaganda in the hope of attracting the
non-Communist Unions into its orbit ; and, with much greater
initial success, the American Federation of Labor joined hands
with the Mexican Trade Unions in establishing a Pan-American
Labor Federation as early as 1918. This body continued in
nominal existence up to 1930, but was never effective over
most of the continent. The Trade Union Centres of Argentina,
Uruguay, Chile, and Brazil were among those which refused
to join it ; and what support it received outside Mexico and
the United States came largely from groups of Unions under
strong government influence and control in countries subject
to dictatorial rule by *caudillos* acceptable to the United States
and its corporations active in Central America. Even the
Mexicans of C.R.O.M. — the Mexican Regional Workers' Confederation — were by 1919 strongly criticising the A.F. of L.'s
failure to make an effective stand against the high-handed
actions of the United States Government both in Latin America
and against the I.W.W. and other left-wing groups inside the
U.S.A. The disputes grew hotter at each successive Pan-
American Labor Congress ; and after the angry withdrawal
of the Cubans in 1930, which had been preceded by the virtual
secession of the Mexicans at an earlier stage, the Pan-American
Federation practically ceased to exist.

Meanwhile, the Anarcho-Syndicalists had not given up the
battle. In 1928, under the leadership of F.O.R.A. — the
Anarchist-controlled Regional Workers' Federation of Argentina
— a Congress held at Buenos Aires set up a Continental Labor
Federation, which affiliated to the European Syndicalist International — the International Workers' Union — but failed to
establish itself and speedily disappeared. F.O.R.A., at this
time, was already losing influence to the rival Trade Union
Centre — the General Union of Workers — which was favoured
by the Socialists and concentrated on immediate economic issues
rather than on revolutionary objectives. The following year,
1929, the U.G.T. and F.O.R.A. amalgamated ; and the combined body — the General Confederation of Workers (C.G.T.)
— decided to affiliate to the Amsterdam International, and soon

755

passed mainly under Socialist control. The same year, the Communists brought together at Asunción a Conference which set up a Latin-American Trade Union Confederation (C.S.A.L.) with headquarters at Montevideo, as a regional section of the R.I.L.U. Purporting to represent the Trade Unions of most of the Latin-American countries, it had in most only a limited, and in some no more than a nominal, following. It lasted until 1936, after which what remained of it was absorbed into the then much more important Confederation of the Workers of Latin America (C.T.A.L.), organised and led by the Mexican Vicente Lombardo Toledano (b. 1893).

Toledano's period of greatest influence came well after the period covered in the present volume. He made his name first as a lawyer and teacher, holding the Professorship of Law and Philosophy in the University of Mexico from 1918 to 1933. He became active in left-wing politics, and entered the Trade Union movement as a lieutenant of Luis Morones (b. 1890) in C.R.O.M. — the Regional Confederation of Mexican Workers set up in 1917. Thereafter, he became a convert to Marxism, and, during the 1930s, entered into friendly relations with the Communists after they had shifted their line to advocacy of the Popular Front. In 1936, after the collapse of C.R.O.M., he established a new Mexican Trade Union Centre — the Confederation of Mexican Workers (C.T.M.), with himself as secretary ; and on this basis he went on in 1938, with help from Léon Jouhaux of the I.F.T.U. and from John L. Lewis (b. 1880), then the leader of the C.I.O., to found in 1938 the C.T.A.L. — Confederation of Workers of Latin America — which became for a time by far the most important and extensive labour organisation that had ever existed in that part of the world. Lombardo Toledano was a powerful writer and speaker as well as a remarkable organiser. He was widely accused of being a Communist, but always denied the charge and seems indeed never to have actually joined the Communist Party. He did, however, act closely with the Communists, both in the 1930s and after the outbreak of the second world war, in the course of which his ascendancy in the Mexican movement declined, until he was finally expelled from the C.M.T. in 1948, still keeping his position at the head of what was left of the once dominant C.T.A.L. and maintaining a strong intellectual influence in many parts of Latin America. The Mexican movement, which under his leadership had collaborated actively with President Cardenas in the extensive measures of social and economic reform which he launched during his period of office (1934–40), fell to pieces during the second world war, and has never regained its unity. The case of Lombardo Toledano well illustrates the extreme difficulty of breaking off the account of Latin-American Socialist and Labour development at any point short of 1939 ; but I shall try, wherever it is possible, to leave out of account developments that occurred after 1930, save where they appear to be inseparably linked with earlier events.

Enough has been said to show that throughout the 1920s the growing Trade Union movements of Latin America were in a great deal of a mess, with rival groups, mainly Anarcho-Syndicalist, Communist, and Social Democratic, continually contending for influence and, as a consequence, making united action impossible over any wide field. The Socialist Parties, rent asunder by Communist secessions, and even in some cases captured by the Communists so that new ones were set up as minority groups, laboured under similar difficulties, and were, moreover, no less liable than the Trade Unions to be broken up, or driven underground, by successive dictators who were put into power, as a rule, by military *coups d'état* and received the support both of the reactionary creole aristocracies and of the United States and the American business corporations. The Latin-American dictators of these years were mostly of this sheerly reactionary type : the new type of dictatorship based on nationalistic demagogy and seeking to enlist working-class support with a mixed bag of xenophobic and material appeals hardly appeared until later, and reached its zenith only after the second world war.

In stirring up anti-imperialist feeling and, still more, in turning it to constructive use, both Communists and Anarcho-Syndicalists were, to a considerable extent, hampered by their acceptance of a doctrine of revolution in which the working class alone was accorded a revolutionary rôle. Even in the more advanced Latin-American countries, the industrial workers were far outnumbered by the peasants and the landless labourers, among whom, save in a few areas, hardly any organisation existed. Moreover, except in Argentina and Uruguay, where most of the inhabitants were of European stock, the main mass of the people was made up of indigenous Indians or of *mestizos* — *i.e.* persons of mixed racial ancestry — with varying elements of African Negro origin. Exact statistics are impossible to come by ; but according to the best-known general estimate, in Brazil about 30 per cent of the total population were Negroes and nearly 3 per cent Indians of unmixed blood ; while in Mexico the Negroes were over 5 per cent and the pure Indians nearly 28 per cent. In Guatemala the pure Indians constituted a clear majority, and in Bolivia, Peru, and Ecuador they were between 40 and 50 per cent of the total — Negroes being relatively few in these countries. In Argentina, on the other hand, and in Uruguay, the pure Indians and Africans were negligible in number ; and they were also few in Chile and in Paraguay. In the Caribbean islands the Negroes were more than two-thirds of the total population. Over the entire continent from 1850 to 1950 the number of overseas immigrants into Latin America seems to have been about 17 millions, of whom 7 millions went to Argentina, 4 to Brazil, 2 to Chile, 1½ to Cuba, and 1 to Uruguay, but only half a million to Mexico, the remaining million being widely scattered over the other countries. Of these immigrants the largest number (6 millions) came from Italy, predominantly to Argentina. There were 4 million Spaniards, 2 million Germans, 1 million Portuguese, half a million Russians, a quarter of a million French, and a quarter of a million Jews, besides one million or so from the Far East (mainly Japan and China) and half a million from the Near and Middle East — leaving a residue of 1½ millions from all other sources.

Thus, except in Argentina and Uruguay, the great majority of the Latin-American peoples were Indians or *mestizos*, with, in a few areas, a large admixture of Negroes. In most countries, urban populations were greatly exceeded by dwellers in rural areas. Even in 1950, only in Chile and Argentina was the urban population as high as 60 per cent of the total. In Cuba and Venezuela it was over 50 per cent, and in Uruguay just under 50 per cent. In Peru, Bolivia, Guatemala, Panama, and Brazil it was between 30 and 40 per cent, and in most of the other countries it ranged from 30 to 25 per cent, or even less. In most parts of Latin America, even in 1950, the proportion of illiterates remained exceedingly high. Of the leading countries, Argentina, with 15 per cent, had easily the lowest rate. Costa Rica, Cuba, and Uruguay had rates of 20 to 25 per cent, Chile 28 per cent, Panama 37 per cent, Paraguay 40 per cent, Colombia 44 per cent. Brazil, Mexico, and Ecuador had rates of 50 per cent, Peru 52 per cent, Venezuela 58 per cent, Guatemala, Honduras, and the Dominican Republic 65 per cent, Nicaragua and Salvador 70 per cent, Bolivia 75 per cent, and Haiti actually 80 per cent. Many of these percentages, high though they are, represent substantial progress since the period dealt with in this volume. Illiteracy rates were, of course, much higher, as a rule, in the rural areas than in the towns, and put immense obstacles in the way of both political and economic organisation. The literacy barrier and the sharp differences in living standards between regular urban workers and country-dwellers also put powerful difficulties in the way of co-operative action between organised workers and peasants, and sometimes, as we saw earlier in the case of Mexico,[1] led to deep antagonisms between them.

The rural populations of Latin America were not only to a great extent illiterate and desperately poor ; they were also mostly landless, the land being still, for the most part, in the hands of the landed aristocracy, and much of it left uncultivated even where there was intense population pressure. The landlords cultivated, or used for ranching, or let out on onerous terms of feudal service, such land as they pleased ; and such cultivation as there was was in many cases badly hampered for lack of access to water, as well as by the use of exceedingly primitive methods. It was evident that the basic economic and social problems of Latin America were quite insoluble without a fundamental reorganisation of the system of land tenure, followed up by great campaigns of land development, irrigation, and agricultural education. But the old-established land-owning aristocracies were utterly hostile to land reforms that might undermine their power ; and the investors of capital from abroad were entirely uninterested in agricultural development, except for large-scale fruit-growing for export in parts of Central America, or in other forms of land development except

[1] See Vol. III, Part II, p. 839.

for the extraction of minerals or oil. It usually suited the foreign investing concerns best to come to terms with the land-owning interests, rather than to encourage any developments that might stir up rural revolt. Native capitalism, where it existed, tended to take the same line, and to oppose any movement that might interfere with the ample supplies of very cheap labour made available by the inflow of starving surplus workers from the countryside into the towns. Even the Mexican Revolution failed for a long time to make any real impression on the condition of the main body of the rural population — and has made only a very limited impression on it even to-day.

Up to 1914 Latin-American Socialism rested almost entirely on European foundations, and had produced no really distinctive thinker of its own. Anarchist, Syndicalist, Social Democratic, and other doctrines imported from Europe had contended for support ; and many of the contestants had been themselves emigrants from Spain, or Italy, or Germany, or France. The Argentinian Socialists, headed by Dr. J. B. Justo (1865–1925), had been in closest touch with the Second International ; and Justo had produced his own version of the Marxist gospel in an attempt to apply it to Argentinian conditions. His argument, as we saw earlier,[1] had been that it was unnecessary for a country to go through a process of advanced industrialisation in order to render it ripe for the growth of a Socialist movement. Justo contended that in Argentina the place of a developed industrial proletariat could be taken by the mass of surplus rural labourers who migrated to the towns in search of employment, even if there were no jobs available for them in large-scale industries. In fact, Socialism in Argentina had been built up largely on the basis of the support given to it by the large body of such migrants, much more than on any success in enlisting the support of the rural workers. This notion, however, though it fitted fairly well the conditions of the overcrowded capital, Buenos Aires, at a stage when industrial development was still not far advanced, was of little help as an answer to the problem of social revolution, or of social development, for the continent as a whole, in view of the preponderance in most areas of rural over urban population. The crucial question for Latin America was bound to be the

[1] See Vol. III, Part II, p. 827.

land question — and this was a question which most of the Socialists were singularly ill-equipped to tackle in any constructive way — even in Mexico, where the Revolution that had begun just before the first world war had forcibly drawn attention to the claims of the impoverished rural population.

The Communists, when they set to work in the early 1920s to gain control of the forces of revolution in Latin America, did, to some extent, realise the key importance of the land problem, and did their best to put themselves at the head of peasant revolt and to stimulate it wherever they saw a chance. They worked, however, on the basis of a theory which assigned to the industrial proletariat the necessary leadership of the revolutionary forces, and were prepared to give the peasants only a subordinate place under this leadership. Mostly townsmen, they were all too apt not only to despise the peasant, but also to regard him as a potential reactionary wherever his lot improved. Though they had some success in stirring up scattered peasant risings, they were no better equipped than the Socialist Parties with any constructive land policy and, in default of one, tended to put their main emphasis on demands for the removal of racial discrimination, as a part of the anti-imperialist crusade, rather than on economic issues connected with land distribution and development. The Communists' attitude changed substantially in the 1930s, after they had been ordered over by the Comintern to support Popular Front movements. But during the period covered by the present chapter, their class-theory, with its strong emphasis on the primacy of the industrial proletariat, stood in the way of their working out any conception of Socialism or of Socialist policy really appropriate to the situation of the Latin-American continent as a whole.

The one outstanding attempt to devise a specifically Latin-American conception of Socialism — if it was Socialism — applicable to the prevailing conditions was that of the Aprista movement founded in Mexico in 1924 by Victor Raoul Haya de la Torre (b. 1895), then an exile from his native Peru, from which he had been driven on account of his activities in the student movement and in the foundation of Popular Universities in opposition to the dictator Augusto Leguia. On leaving Peru, Haya de la Torre visited first North America and then Europe, including the U.S.S.R., and thereafter settled for a time in Mexico, where he founded the Alianza Popular Revolucionaire Americana (A.P.R.A.) as an international movement designed to cover every part of Latin America, or, as he often significantly preferred to call it, Indo-America. For a time it looked as if A.P.R.A. might succeed in building up a mass following in many countries, and not only in Peru, where it rapidly became by far the most widely supported Party. It was, however, involved from the outset in bitter conflict with the Communists, whose conception of the class-struggle Haya entirely rejected. Instead of a movement under exclusively proletarian leadership, Haya preached the need for a common front of the workers, the intellectuals, and the middle classes against the landed aristocracy and its allies, the foreign capitalists and their native supporters. He rejected the separate nationalisms of the various Latin-American peoples, and called for common action on a continental scale, including the international public ownership of land and other key resources and the development of a continent-wide system of social security. In methods of organisation A.P.R.A. had much in common with the Communists : Haya was insistent on the need for a strongly disciplined Party under centralised direction and control, and was himself a leader of markedly autocratic and uncompromising temperament. Until 1931, when Leguia was at length overthrown, Haya directed A.P.R.A. from headquarters-in Europe, first in London and then in Berlin. Returning to Peru on Leguia's fall, he became A.P.R.A.'s candidate for the Presidency, and was regularly elected only to be overthrown by Sanchez Cerro, who clapped him into gaol. In 1933 he was liberated by Cerro's assassination ;. but a new dictator, Oscar Benavideo, proscribed the Apristas, and Haya had to seek refuge in the Colombian Embassy — an incident which had its sequel in a dispute between Peru and Colombia that in the end found its way to the International Court of Justice at The Hague. This part of Haya de la Torre's life, however, belongs to a later period than is dealt with in this chapter.

Haya's Aprista movement called, as we saw, for an alliance of workers, peasants, and middle classes — including indigenous owners of capital — against foreign capitalism and imperialism and against the indigenous landed aristocracy. It therefore set out to improve labour relations, except with the foreign-owned corporations, and thus came into conflict with the more militant Trade Union groups as well as with the Communists. The crippled Peruvian printer, journalist, and poet, José Carlos Mariategui (1891–1930), who became the outstanding theorist of Communism in Latin America, began his political career as a supporter of A.P.R.A., from which he broke away only in 1928 to found the Peruvian Communist Party. Mariategui was a chronic invalid, tied to a wheeled chair ; but in spite of this he was active as an organiser as well as in conducting journals and writing books. As a student he received a bursary for study in Europe, and came back a Marxist, though not of an orthodox type. His best-known book bears the title, *A Defence of Marxism* ; but in his interpretation Marxism, as applied to Latin-American conditions, involves, above all else, a solution of the land question by making the Indians masters of the right to land. He rejected the view that this could be done by reviving the decaying traditions of primitive land communism, and insisted on the profound difference between it and modern Communism, which he regarded as the product of industrial development. This, however, did not mean that he shared the contempt for peasants that was so frequent among urban Marxists. On the contrary, his devotion to the pursuit of full equality in all matters for the Indians with the whites over-rode his bias in favour of the industrial proletariat, and brought him into conflict with his fellow-Communists at the Monte-video Communist Congress of 1929, which rejected his thesis on the agrarian question. In addition to the *Defence of Marxism* (1927) Mariategui published *The Contemporary Scene* (1927) and *Essays in Interpretation of Peruvian Reality* (1928), as well as many studies in his review, *Amauta*, which was repeatedly suppressed. His influence extended far beyond Peru, and his death at 39 was a very serious loss to the Latin-American Communist movement.

A third theorist who deserves mention in connection with the attempt to reshape Socialist thought, in order to bring it into closer conformity with Latin-American conditions, is the Salvadorian Albert Masferrer (1891–1933), who was for a time Consul for Salvador in Brussels, where he began to elaborate his doctrine of the 'vital minimum', embracing not only the living wage but also a complete system of social security to be embodied in the legislation of each country. Masferrer began by interesting himself primarily in educational reform, and on his return to Salvador founded a 'rational' school rather on the lines of Ferrer's venture in Spain.[1] But he speedily launched out into the advocacy of his wider social ideas ; and when he found that politicians were making use of them for what he considered claptrap slogans he left Salvador and was expelled successively from several countries of Central America, settling finally in Costa Rica, where he died in 1933. Masferrer held that starving men do not make revolutions, and that the necessary first step towards the regeneration of Latin America lay in the adoption of far-reaching measures to establish a tolerable minimum standard of living for all. He was, in effect, the first prophet in Latin America of the 'Welfare State', and was by no means without influence on the subsequent course of social legislation in a number of its countries — though much of the legislation that was passed was put so little into effect as to yield almost no positive results.

In terms both of theory and of policy, the Aprista movement made the outstanding contribution to the formulation of a distinctively Latin-American left-wing social movement. The policy of A.P.R.A., as set out by Haya de la Torre, turned on five main points — struggle against North American (Yankee) imperialism, political unity of Indo-America, socialisation of land and of major industries, internationalisation of the Panama Canal, and world solidarity of all oppressed peoples and classes. The first and fourth of these points ranged the Apristas on the side of anti-imperialism, whereas the second and the fifth set them in opposition to the xenophobic nationalism that was so often linked with anti-imperialism in people's minds. The third point — socialisation — took a radically new shape when it was linked with the demand for political unity of all the Indo-American peoples ; for it then came to be a demand for internationalisation, rather than for a separate structure of public ownership and development of resources within the frontiers of each distinct State. Finally, the conception of Indo-America, rather than of Latin America, as the essential unit for transforming the conditions of living, challenged not only

[1] See Vol. III, Part II, p. 770.

the narrower forms of nationalism but also the whole conception of white superiority over the indigenous peoples, and in effect implied also full equality of Negro rights in those areas in which Negroes rather than Indians made up a large part of the most deeply impoverished and ignorant social strata.

'National sovereignty', Haya proclaimed, 'disappears in proportion as the volume of capital investment by Yankee capitalism in our countries grows greater.' He saw Yankee imperialism as a challenge, not to the reassertion of independence by each individual State into which it penetrated, but to oppose to it a wider conception of Indo-American solidarity and to build up Indo-America into a single, unified confederation of peoples on a foundation of complete racial equality. This was the element of Aprista doctrine and policy that gained for the movement the enthusiastic allegiance of many idealists and intellectuals who were repelled by the cruder forms of nationalism and at the same time felt the Communist conception of dictatorship by the industrial proletariat to be out of relation to the needs and realities of the Latin-American peoples. This idealism lay at the root of A.P.R.A.'s appeal ; but it has also to be recognised that by setting itself in opposition to the cruder forms of nationalism, A.P.R.A. made it much more difficult to build up a solid basis of mass support. For it was obviously a most formidable task to find means of uniting so many States, with so widely differing economic and demographic conditions, into a coherent political unit capable of giving practical effect to the Aprista programme. In each country, it was a great deal easier for demagogues to play on nationalistic feelings and to promise reforms that could be arrived at within an existing political unit. It was easy to represent the Apristas as visionaries, as well as to denounce them, among the industrial workers, as betrayers of the class-struggle who would have the Trade Unions make peace with the employers instead of struggling manfully for proletarian demands.

In face of these difficulties, A.P.R.A. never succeeded in building up a mass following on a continental scale. In Peru, indeed, it did become a mass movement, with cells and groups not only in the towns and industrial areas, but throughout the countryside as well, and with a big following among the Indians, whom it managed to reach on a scale previously quite unknown.

It also won a substantial popular following in several other States, including Paraguay, Venezuela, and Cuba. But over most of Latin America, though it had enthusiastic supporters, these were largely intellectuals rather than workers, and failed to establish themselves as powerful political forces or effectively to challenge the demagogic nationalism of which Peron later became the most notable embodiment. Even in Peru, where the Apristas were strong enough in popular support to elect Haya to the Presidency, they were not able to prevent him from being ejected by a military *coup*, or their own Party from being outlawed and driven underground. The Aprista movement had, indeed, too much vitality to be snuffed out by repression : it kept on coming back long after the period covered by the present chapter. But it did fail to establish itself as a continental force such as Haya dreamed of, or to win over the main body of Latin-American Socialist and working-class opinion to a practical acceptance of the need for united action over the entire continent. Moreover, an essential part of the Aprista programme — its strong hostility to Yankee imperialism — lost some of its force when, in the 1930s, Franklin D. Roosevelt proclaimed his 'good neighbour' policy, and for a time the force of popular 'anti-American' feeling grew considerably less.

After Mariategui's secession from A.P.R.A. in 1928 to form the Peruvian Communist Party, bitter hostility developed between the Communists and the Apristas over the issue of class-war. But when the Communists, in the 1930s, went over, in face of the rising threat of Fascism, to the policy of the 'Popular Front' the Apristas were in a position to tell them that they had been advocating this very policy from the beginning, and to urge that A.P.R.A. was itself already the Popular Front which the Communists now professed to desire. Naturally, the Communists repudiated this view ; for what they were aiming at was a Popular Front under proletarian leadership and control, and not a Party in which workers, peasants, intellectuals, and even capitalists could take part on equal terms. The Apristas were indeed socialisers, especially in relation to the ownership of land ; but they were political advocates of parliamentary democracy and not of any sort of dictatorship, proletarian or other. They were idealists, with an ethical passion to put an end to racial discrimination and to bring into self-consciousness and power a new Indo-American supra-nationalism that would supersede colour bars and all forms of racial antagonism. In the long run, their policy on this issue is the only one that offers real hope of solving the fundamental economic problems of the Latin-American continent. Yet it is hardly surprising that, during the thirty years since A.P.R.A. was born, it has failed to carry any important part of its programme into effect. The way of the internationalist is hardest of all where he is faced, on the one hand, by imperialism armed with vastly superior economic resources, and on the other by a rising wave of popular nationalism which can adapt its slogans to the state of popular feeling in each particular State or region. Haya's programme was, in the circumstances, unrealisable and utopian ; but, for all that, it may well prove to have been of far greater lasting value than any of its rivals.

It remains to refer briefly to a few of the more important developments between 1914 and 1930 in certain particular countries in which the working-class movements had achieved some real strength. In Chile, as we saw earlier,[1] the working-class movement had developed considerable militancy before 1914, especially among the miners in the northern region. A Central Trade Union Federation, known as F.O.C.H., had been set up in 1909, and, after moderate beginnings, this body moved sharply leftwards during the first world war. In 1912 the Socialists, who had previously acted within the old-established Democratic Party, broke away and set up an independent Socialist Workers' Party. The Democratic Party, strongly sympathetic to Socialism in its earlier days, had by this time lost most of its reforming impetus ; and the secession from it was led by the outstanding Trade Union leader Luis Recabarren (1876–1924), who was also the general secretary of F.O.C.H. After the war, under Recabarren's influence, the Chilean Socialist Party joined the Comintern, and F.O.C.H. became affiliated to the Red International of Labour Unions, the Moscow-centred rival of the Amsterdam I.F.T.U. But serious troubles soon developed inside F.O.C.H. The railwaymen seceded from it in 1923, and were followed by a number

[1] See Vol. III, Part II, pp. 826 and 834.

of other Unions. F.O.C.H.'s power steadily waned ; but no new Trade Union Centre took its place until 1936. Till then, the Unions in the various industries acted separately, sometimes under the influence of one or other of the rival working-class parties.

During the war the activity of foreign capital in Chile was much reduced ; and the landed aristocracy took advantage of the country's economic difficulties to re-establish its political power. This led to an alliance of Liberals, Radicals, and Socialists, who combined in 1920 to secure the election as President of the Liberal leader Arturo Alessandri. Alessandri came forward with a substantial programme of social and industrial reforms, and, in face of violent opposition, succeeded in enacting laws providing for insurance against accidents, compensation for dismissal, and the establishment of arbitration for the settlement of labour disputes. In 1924, however, Alessandri was overthrown by a military *coup* ; but the army groups behind it were sharply divided among themselves, between a conservative faction that wished to restore the aristocracy to power and a left-wing faction animated by socialistic ideas, but lacking any clear theoretical standpoint. The leaders of this second group were the colonels Marmaduke Grove (b. 1878) and Carlos Ibanez (b. 1877). The Trade Unions, which had been antagonised by the slow progress of Alessandri's reforms, mostly supported Grove and Ibanez : the Socialist Workers' Party, then affiliated to the Comintern, stayed neutral, while the non-Communist Socialists mostly backed the revolutionary colonels. In the hope of consolidating working-class support the military directorate produced a Labour Code recognising the Trade Unions as legal persons, restricting night-work for women and children, prescribing a minimum wage, and introducing sickness insurance. The disputes inside the military Government, however, continued ; and the more conservative elements began to gain the upper hand. This led to a revolt of the military left under Grove and Ibanez, who in 1925 ousted the Directory and called on Alessandri to resume power. The Communists at the outset supported Alessandri, but rapidly changed their minds, though he came forward with an advanced reform programme, including a new democratic Constitution which, among other changes, guaranteed the separation of Church and State and the right of free association, and also gave legal sanction to the 48-hour working week. When, however, strikes broke out on a large scale, Alessandri took fright and embarked on a policy of repression which cost him much of his popular support. The following year, the revolutionary Colonel Carlos Ibanez was elected President as the candidate of the left. He governed, however, as a dictator ; and in 1931, when the world depression was already beginning to hit the Chileans hard, a general strike forced him to resign, leaving authority in the hands of a conservative Vice-President. The following year there was a left-wing *coup d'état*, led by Colonel Marmaduke Grove, who with the support of the air force and the navy proclaimed Chile a Socialist Republic. Grove at once introduced an emergency programme of relief measures, including the release of objects pledged at the pawnshops by those in distress, the opening of land colonies for the unemployed, and the provision of credit for small businesses. These measures were enough to cause the reactionaries, with the support of most of the army, to organise a counter-revolutionary *coup*, led by Carlos Davila. But the new military junta was unable to establish itself in power : within a few months, Davila was in flight and soon afterwards Alessandri was re-elected as President.

Though the Chilean Socialist Revolution of 1932 failed, it had important long-run consequences ; for it had evoked widespread popular enthusiasm, and led to a rapid reconsolidation of Trade Union strength as well as to the growth of the best organised and most powerful Communist Party in Latin America. These developments, however, belong to a period well outside the scope of the present chapter.

In Brazil, though Socialist groups existed at an earlier stage,[1] no Socialist Party was established until 1916. A dispute at once arose in its ranks between the advocates of war neutrality, chiefly Germans and Italians, and those who favoured intervention on the side of the Allies, mainly native Brazilians and Portuguese. In 1921 the Party decided by a majority to join the Comintern, and the minority then split off, and in 1925 set up a rival party, which made little headway. In 1928, with considerable Trade Union support, a Labour Party was founded,

[1] See Vol. III, Part II, p. 833.

modelled largely on the British, and rapidly increased its membership to 800,000 in 1930, only to fade away in the later 'thirties when Getulio Vargas established a kind of corporative State. Until 1929 there was no central Trade Union organisation ; but during that year two rival bodies appeared, one under Communist and the other under Syndicalist influence. The Communists, however, lost control of the Brazilian C.G.T. in 1933, and proceeded to set up a third body — the United Trade Union Confederation. In 1937 Vargas dissolved all these bodies and forced the workers into his new corporative framework. The outstanding personality of the Brazilian movement during this period was Luis Carlos Prestes (b. 1898), a romantic figure who had, at the outset, no connection with Communism, though he was later accepted as its leader and became an executive member of the Comintern. By training a military engineer, Prestes was involved in insurrectionary attempts as early as 1922 and 1924. At the head of a mixed band of soldiers and peasants, he managed to maintain himself for well over two years by moving from area to area, until in 1927 he at length took refuge in Bolivia. Up to this point he had been simply a rebel, without any clear programme, but with a remarkable power of arousing popular enthusiasm. Invited to Moscow, he was there made much of, and in 1934 at length joined the Communist Party, returning to Brazil the following year to participate in its struggle against Vargas. He was soon arrested, and spent the next nine years in prison, being released only on the fall of Vargas, to resume his leadership of the Communist Party.

In Argentina, as we saw,[1] the powerful Socialist Party of Dr. J. B. Justo and Alfredo L. Palacios (b. 1880), which was actively associated with the Second International, had suffered a split in 1913, when the poet Manuel Ugarte (1878–1932) broke away at the head of a small nationalist group. During the war of 1914–18 the Socialist Party favoured neutrality, though its best-known leaders were partisans of intervention on the side of the Allies. In 1917 the Party split again, the left wing breaking away to form an International Socialist Party, which presently joined the Comintern and duly reorganised itself as a Communist Party. Despite the split, the old Party

[1] See Vol. III, Part II, p. 832.

continued to grow, and was able to return 18 deputies at the General Election of 1925. It had joined the re-formed Second International, and followed a strictly parliamentary line. In 1927, however, it suffered a third, and far more disastrous, split, when a faction led by Antonio de Tomaso seceded on the ground that the official party policy was not sufficiently nationalist. The seceders carried the majority of the Socialists' popular following with them ; and in 1930 the Independent Socialists polled 109,000 votes and won 10 seats, whereas the old Party, with 83,000 votes, could win only a single seat. This same year the Liberal President, Hipolite Irigoyen (1852–1933) was driven from office by a military *coup*, headed by the generals Augustin Justo and Uriburu. This Justo had no connection with the Socialist leader, J. B. Justo, who had died in 1925. The remnant of the old Socialist Party joined hands with the Liberals in protesting against the military *coup*, but attempted no active resistance. The Independent Socialists, on the other hand, ranged themselves on the side of the generals, and helped to bring about the election of Justo as President. This attitude soon cost them a large part of their following, and they fell to disputing among themselves, and presently broke up. The old Party, however, though it regained its strength for a time, soon began to lose ground seriously to the Communists.

In Uruguay, as we saw,[1] Emilio Frugoni (b. 1880) had organised a Socialist Party in 1910. Ten years later the Party decided by a majority to join the Comintern, and the minority broke away under Frugoni's leadership. Throughout the 1920s this latter Party remained very weak, though Frugoni regained a seat in Parliament in 1927. When the world economic depression hit the Uruguayan economy, the President, Gabriel Torra, succeeded in maintaining himself in power by a *coup d'état*, and Frugoni fled to Argentina, but subsequently returned and resumed his leadership of the Socialist Party. During the ensuing years, despite the electoral weakness of the Socialists, Uruguay made very considerable advances in social legislation, building on the foundations laid earlier under the great Radical President, Battle y Ordonez. These developments, however, belong to a period outside the range of this chapter.

[1] See Vol. III, Part II, p. 833.

The two remaining countries about which it seems needful to add a few sentences are Colombia and Nicaragua. In Colombia the outstanding event of the 1920s was the struggle put up by the Trade Unions against the United States-owned United Fruit Company. This struggle was begun by the Trade Unions before they had come under Communist control, and opened with several victorious local strikes for improved conditions. But in the course of the big strike of the banana-plantation workers of Santa-Marta, the Communists gained côntrol of the movement and tried to turn the strike into a political battle. In the ensuing repression more than 1,000 persons were killed, more than 3000 wounded, and about 500 sent to prison. The strength of the Trade Unions was broken, and fierce repression continued for a long time after the workers' defeat. A new Colombian Labour Party was started in 1930, but only in 1937 were the Trade Unions able to organise a new central Federation. These events took place in a country which had previously preserved for a remarkably long time a stable, fairly liberal régime.

In Nicaragua the main interest is attached to the activities of the rebel leader Agusto C. Sandino (1893–1934), who was neither a Communist nor even a Marxist, but a romantic anti-imperialist Radical who espoused, above all, the cause of the unfortunate rural workers. Nicaragua was occupied four times by United States forces under successive American Presidents ; and this situation continued until Franklin Roosevelt at length withdrew the United States occupying contingents in 1933. The matters at issue were the right of the U.S.A., under the terms of the Bryan-Chamarro Treaty, to build a canal across Nicaragua and to establish naval bases in that country. During the fourth occupation, in 1927, Sandino, then only an army lieutenant, disobeyed an order to surrender arms to the Americans, and formed a small revolutionary army which managed to maintain itself in the mountains for the ensuing six years, equipping itself mainly with captured arms and fighting both the United States forces and those of the pro-United States puppet Government. Sandino was often described as a 'bandit' ; and no doubt he was often compelled to supply his forces by raids upon the country. He was, however, essentially a revolutionary fighter against imperialism, and his exploits won him great renown throughout Latin America. None the less, he aroused the fierce hostility of the Latin-American Communist Parties, both because he refused to establish a Soviet Republic in the areas his soldiers controlled and because he agreed with the Apristas in desiring to base the struggle against imperialism not solely on the proletariat, but rather on an alliance of peasants, workers, and indigenous middle classes against foreign penetration. In 1933, on the withdrawal of the United States forces, he led his soldiers down from the mountains and demanded that land should be provided for them. Invited to dine with President Somoza, he was arrested by national guards as he was leaving the palace, and was shot out of hand. His movement died with him, and Somoza continued to govern Nicaragua as a dictator for many years.

What has been written in this chapter sufficiently illustrates the chaotic condition of Latin-American Socialism during the period under review. The only movements which tried to give themselves a continental rather than a narrower, state basis were those of the Apristas and the Communists ; and these two, despite their common hostility to Yankee imperialism, were bitterly antagonistic to each other. Nor did either succeed at any point in building up a really solid body of support in all parts of the continent. The Apristas had indeed followers in many countries besides Peru ; but they never spread effectively to either Argentina or Uruguay. The Communists succeeded in establishing 'front' organisations and Trade Union Centres over a wider area ; but in many places these hardly existed except on paper, and, where they had some real strength, they tended to follow divergent policies from state to state and to show considerable recalcitrance when they received orders they disliked from the Comintern. The Comintern itself suffered from ambiguities of policy because of its attempt both to insist on a strictly proletarian basis for the various Communist Parties and at the same time to show its solidarity with national 'liberation' movements even when these were not under Communist control. The position became for a time easier for the Communists in the 1930s, when, in order to rally all possible support against Fascism, they went over to the advocacy of the 'Popular Front' ; but it did not remain easy when Fascism and nationalism came to be more and more closely allied in those movements which came later to be called 'Peronism', and made effective appeals to a considerable section of the industrial workers on a basis of aggressive nationalism combined with an attack on the traditional landed aristocracies. But these developments came for the most part well after the period covered in the present volume ; and I am forced to cut short the story of Socialism in Latin America at a most inconvenient point in order to avoid advancing too far into the period that I have reserved for my final volume.

CHAPTER XXV

THE RISE, FALL, AND RENAISSANCE
OF COMMUNISM IN CHINA

IN China, as we saw in an earlier chapter of this study,[1] there was, up to 1914, practically no Socialist *movement*, though there were Socialist ideas, of which the outstanding exponent was Sun Yat Sen (1866-1925). The socialistic element in Sun Yat Sen's thought found expression mainly in his conception of 'People's Livelihood' as one of the 'Three Principles' on which he held that political action should be based. This principle ranged him against the powerful forces that were holding the Chinese people in poverty and subjection and were wasting the nation's substance and preventing its economic development. It put him against the imperialists who were exploiting China from without and were seeking either to establish spheres of influence for themselves or to act together in a 'consortium' for the domination of the whole country. It set him against the 'war lords' who established their control over particular areas and wasted the people's substance in their internecine conflicts, in which they were often ready to abet the imperialists in order to enlist their support against rival war lords. It set him against the landlords and usurers — against the former as a class whose exactions impoverished the peasant cultivators and left most of them without means of improving their methods of cultivation or of getting access to markets on fair terms, and against the latter as a group which profited by the peasants' difficulties to exact grossly excessive interest on their loans. It also, to some extent, set him against capitalists who employed labour under unfair conditions ; but he was much less hostile to the capitalists as a class than to the landlords because the capitalists were, on the whole, on the side of economic development : so that in their case what he felt to be needed was rather an enforced improvement

[1] See Vol. III, Part II, Chapter XXVI.

in industrial conditions than their immediate displacement. In industry, Sun Yat Sen wanted a planned economy in which a new kind of government would take the lead in a process of rapid economic development, in part operating the new industries under its own auspices, but also in part using the capitalists as its agents under controls that would ensure rising standards of living for the workers they employed.

Sun Yat Sen's essential ideas were discussed in the preceding volume of this study,[1] and there is no need to discuss them a second time. He was fundamentally a democratic nationalist who regarded democracy as carrying with it the requirement that a satisfactory standard of living should be assured to the entire people and therefore ranged himself on the side of a democratically controlled plan of economic development, involving the use of advanced techniques adopted from the West, but adapted to suit Chinese conditions and to develop rather than destroy the traditional Chinese way of life, for which he had a high respect. As we saw, after being called to the Presidency of the Chinese Republic in the Revolution of 1911 he renounced his office in the hope that the whole country could be unified as a Republic under Yuan Shih-kai, and accepted instead a post which was designed to make him the responsible executant of a great plan of economic reorganisation. But Yuan had quite other ideas and attempted to make himself emperor; and Sun Yat Sen found himself wholly without power to put his projects into effect. Instead of the national democratic unity of which he dreamed, China broke up, especially after Yuan's death in 1916, into a number of territories dominated by contending war lords, with Sun and the Republicans maintaining only a precarious foothold in the South and with the Japanese profiting by the preoccupation of the Great Powers with their own war in the West to establish under the 'Twenty-one Points' of 1915 an effective hegemony over a large part of the country.

Then came the Revolution in Russia, followed by the Soviet Government's renunciation of the unequal treaties which had been forced on China before 1914. For some time after the Bolshevik Revolution the Russians were in no position to take any effective action in the Far East. Only when the Civil War

[1] See Vol. III, Part II, p. 922.

ended in 1920 did Asiatic Russia come effectively under Bolshevik control ; and even then it took time to liquidate Japanese intervention and the remaining White Russian forces. But, as soon as the Civil War ended in Asiatic Russia, the question of the relations between the Russian and the Chinese Revolutions became of immediate and considerable importance. The Russians, regarding themselves as the inaugurators of a World Revolution destined speedily to extend to all countries, had to make up their minds what policy to adopt in relation to the unfinished Chinese Revolution, and also what course of action to recommend to their own supporters in China, who were still no more than a handful, mainly of intellectuals, but were already meditating the establishment of a Chinese Communist Party as an adherent of the Comintern.

The Chinese Communist movement had originated in a small way as a direct outcome of the Bolshevik Revolution. It began in the spring of 1918 with the formation of Marxist study-groups in Pekin under the influence of two intellectuals, Li Ta-chao and Ch'en Tu-hsiu, both professors in the University. About a year later came the so-called 'Fourth of May' movement, the first wave of the succession of anti-imperialist demonstrations and manifestations of the years after the war. This movement was not by any means exclusively, or even largely, Communist : it began at a time when Communism still barely existed as an organised force. But, though it originated mainly among intellectuals and especially students, it is notable because it drew to itself a substantial working-class following and gave rise to the first wave of strike action with a political purpose. Spreading from town to town, it included a widespread boycott of Japanese goods, and was accompanied by a growing literary and artistic movement of cultural nationalism. This same year — 1919 — Sun Yat Sen, in conjunction with Tang Shao-yi and Wu T'sing-fang, set up a new Republican Nationalist Government in Canton in opposition to the war lords who were in control of Northern and Central China.

In the spring of the following year — 1920 — the Chinese students in Paris formed a Communist Youth Group — the first definitely Communist Chinese organisation ; and Yang Ming-chai returned to China accompanied by V. S.

Voitinsky (b. 1887) as a representative of the Comintern. Voitinsky got into touch with Li Ta-chao at Pekin and with Ch'en Tu-hsiu, then at Shanghai, and with them made the initial moves towards setting up a Chinese Communist Party. They began in August by founding in Shanghai a Communist Youth Group, which became the nucleus for the larger Chinese Communist Youth Organisation set up in 1925. The following month a Conference met in Shanghai to consider the creation of a Communist Party, the delegates including Chang T'ai-lei Shao Li-tzu, and Chang Tun-sun, as well as Ch'en Tu-hsiu ; but no decisive result immediately followed, the decisions of the Second Comintern Congress in favour of Communist collaboration with national liberation movements in colonial countries not having become known in China at the time of the meeting. Almost at the same time Wu Pei-fu, the Chihli war lord, joined forces with Chang Tso-lin, of Manchuria, to destroy the Anfu clique which controlled the Pekin Government, headed by Tuan Chi-jui — which there-upon collapsed. Its successor at once opened negotiations with the Russian Soviet Government and with that of the recently established Far Eastern Republic ; and a provisional agreement was reached, only to be abandoned when the Pekin Government, in the hope of currying favour with the Western powers, broke off the negotiations. The Russian Government then changed its line, and in October 1920 Chicherin dispatched a letter to Sun Yat Sen, as President of the Republic in South China, proposing trade negotiations. This letter, however, failed to reach Sun Yat Sen till the following July — by which time further steps had been taken towards the formation of a Communist Party in China. In July 1921, at a Congress opened in Shanghai and continued at Kashing, a body of twelve delegates established a Chinese Communist Party, with Ch'en Tu-hsiu, who was away at Canton, as Chairman. Mao Tse-tung (b. 1893) was among the delegates, and C. Maring (whose real name was H. Sneevliet [1]) of Indonesia was present on behalf of the Comintern. At the same time a Chinese Labour Union — a forerunner of the All-China Labour Federation set up at Canton the following year — was estab-lished in Shanghai, with Chang Kuo-t'ao as its leader, and

---

[1] For Sneevliet, see p. 823.

the attempt to organise the Chinese urban workers on a national basis was begun. Two or three months later a branch of the Communist Party was founded in Hunan, with Mao as secretary — the first step towards the creation of a revolutionary peasant movement to act in alliance with the urban workers — and P'eng Pai began to organise a similar peasant movement in Kwangtung.

All these activities were still on a very small scale. The same year — 1921 — the Southerners got together as many members of the 1913 Parliament as they were able to secure ; and this rump Parliament formally elected Sun as President of the Chinese Republic. In 1922, however, the Southern war lords fell foul of Sun's Government and drove him temporarily out of Canton, which he regained only the following year. Early in 1922 there had been an extensive strike of Chinese seamen in Hong Kong which had spread to Canton and the neighbouring areas, and had met with remarkable success. The Communists were active in these movements and succeeded in gaining many positions of influence in the Trade Unions that were set up to conduct them. Chang Kuo-t'ao represented the Chinese workers at the Conference of Eastern Toilers held in Russia in January 1922 ; and on his return an All-China Labour Federation was set up, and held its first Conference at Canton in May 1922, with 170 delegates representing about 100 Trade Unions in all. At the same time the Communist Youth of China held their first Conference ; and the same month came the Second Congress of the Chinese Communist Party, which chose Ch'en Tu-hsiu as General Secretary and Chairman of the Political Bureau. This Congress also issued the first Manifesto of the Party, defining its policy of support for the 'democratic revolution'. The Manifesto declared that such support did not involve 'surrender to the capitalists', but that the destruction of the feudal system was absolutely necessary to increase the power of the proletariat, and was in the proletariat's class interest. It declared that the opposition of capitalists and proletariat would develop only when Chinese capitalism, still in its infancy, had made further advances, and that when that stage was reached the proletariat would need to launch the struggle 'for the dictatorship of the proletariat' allied with the poorer peasants against the bourgeoisie, but that, for the time being, the primary need was for a programme in the common interests of workers, peasants, and petty bourgeoisie, as a prerequisite for their liberation from their present oppression and for 'a democratic united front of workers, poor peasants, and petty bourgeoisie'. The workers, however, 'must not become the appendage of the petty bourgeoisie within this democratic united front, but must fight for their own class interests'. 'It is therefore imperative that the workers be organised in the Party [*i.e.* the Communist Party], as well as in Trade Unions.' Proclaiming itself to be 'the party of the proletariat', the C.C.P. announced that its aims were 'to organise the proletariat and to struggle for the dictatorship of the workers and peasants, the abolition of private property, and the gradual attainment of a Communist society '. Its immediate programme included 'the quelling of internal disorders, the overthrow of military cliques, and the establishment of internal peace ; the removal of oppression by international imperialism, and the complete independence of the Chinese nation ; the unification of China proper (including Manchuria) into a genuine democratic Republic ; the liberation of Mongolia, Tibet and Sinkiang, and the establishment of a Federated Chinese Republic unifying them with China in a free federation ; the unlimited right to vote for all workers and peasants, regardless of sex, in all assemblies and municipal assemblies, and absolute freedom of speech, assembly, publication, association, and strike action ; and also protective legislation for workers, peasants, and women — including, among other measures, the eight-hours' day, factory legislation and insurance, abolition of the contract system, protection for the unemployed, limitation of land rents, a national land tax, a progressive tax on incomes, abolition of all extraordinary taxes, such as *likin*, abolition of all legislation restricting women's rights, and the institution of an improved educational system'.

This was at one and the same time a revolutionary and a reformist programme. Its specifically labour demands were reformist : its revolutionism was kept carefully within the limits of the 'democratic', as distinct from the Socialist or Communist Revolution. Its immediate intention was to work for a democratic united front made up of workers, peasants, and petty bourgeoisie, while retaining its identity as a Party within this front and seeking to organise within it an independent Trade Union movement under Communist influence. The ulterior purpose was declared to be that of developing the strength of the workers' fighting organisations, in order 'to prepare the way for the establishment of Soviets in conjunction with the poor peasantry and to achieve complete liberation'. The Chinese Communist Party further proclaimed itself 'a section of the Communist International' and declared that 'only an alliance of the world proletariat and the oppressed peoples can lead to the liberation of the world'.

In all this there was some confusion. The C.C.P. called on 'the oppressed masses of all China' to fight in common with the workers and poor peasants *under the party banner*, and thus appeared to be contemplating a united front led by, or even included within, the Communist Party. It made no mention of any other Party as destined to form part of the proposed united front — none, for example, of the Kuomintang, the Party of Sun Yat Sen, and of the democratic Revolution. The delegates, however, can hardly have supposed that the, as yet tiny, Communist Party could become the mass Party of the people in the struggle for the democratic Revolution, even if they hoped it might become a mass Party for the proletarian Revolution that was to follow. Nor was it clear from the wording whether the word 'proletariat' was meant to include the peasants as well as the industrial workers, or whether the rôle of the peasants was regarded as parallel or subordinate to that of the industrial workers. All that was clear at this stage was that there were to be two successive Revolutions, national-democratic and proletarian, and that the C.C.P. meant to work for the present in the interests of the former, but also to organise and prepare its forces for the latter. The ambiguities of the policy laid down in the summer of 1922 were before long to give rise to many difficulties and disputes; but for the time being they provided a foundation for considering on what terms it was practicable for the Communists to play their part in the national Revolution on the basis of some sort of united front of workers, peasants, and petty bourgeoisie. It will be observed that no mention was made of the greater bourgeoisie as forming any part of such a front, and that there was no suggestion that Communists should join the KMT, or even become its allies.

The Kuomintang was at this time the loosely organised Party of Sun Yat Sen and of the national Revolution. It was a broadly based nationalist party, including large bourgeois elements and by no means united behind Sun's radical and in many respects Socialist policy. Its membership and following were indeed highly indeterminate, especially in Central and Northern China, where the contending war lords held political power. It was, in fact, less a Party than a loose league of groups and interests united against the war lords and the imperialist powers and broadly committed to the struggle for national independence under some sort of democratic Republic. However, with all its limitations it was the only existing mass organisation of the Chinese Revolution ; and the Communists could not avoid defining their attitude towards it.

They did this at a Plenum of their elected Central Committee, attended by Maring (Sneevliet) of the Comintern, in August 1922. It was then decided that the Communists, without dissolving their own Party, should join the KMT as individuals and endeavour to secure key positions within it by 'boring from within' — to use the American phrase. The policy of collaboration with the KMT received the approval of the Fourth Comintern Congress, held in Moscow in November 1922, at which Radek argued in favour of an alliance between the Communists and the KMT, though nothing was said officially at Moscow either for or against the policy of Communist infiltration into the KMT's ranks. This particular decision seems to have been made on Maring's own responsibility, and accepted with some hesitation by the Chinese Communist leaders, after Maring had secured Sun Yat Sen's agreement to it. Sun subsequently made plain, in a manuscript note that has survived, that he did this only on condition that the Communists concerned would accept the discipline of the KMT leadership

At all events, the infiltration was effected. At this point A. I. Yoffe (?–1923) arrived in China as the representative, not of the Comintern, but of the Russian Soviet Government. He went first to Pekin, where he attempted to negotiate with the new Chinese Government that had been set up there under the control of the war lord, Wu Pei-fu, after Wu had quarrelled with his former ally, Chang Tso-lin, and had driven him back to

Manchuria. Wu, however, was not at all inclined to come to terms with Russia at the cost of antagonising the Western powers ; and after some months of fruitless waiting Yoffe proceeded southwards and in Shanghai met Sun Yat Sen, who, as we saw, had been driven out of Canton that June. Yoffe, having given up hope of arriving at terms with Pekin, was now prepared to do a deal with Sun ; and after considerable discussion the two issued their celebrated communiqué of January 1923, already cited in part in the preceding volume of this study.[1] In this document, Sun and Yoffe agreed that the conditions necessary for the introduction of either Socialism or Communism did not yet exist in China ; and Yoffe further declared that 'China's permanent and most pressing problem is to achieve national unification and full national independence', and pledged the warmest sympathy and support of Russia and the Russian people for these objectives. This declaration obviously fitted in very well with the policy of Communist infiltration into the KMT ; and it also prepared the way for Russian help in reorganising the KMT itself as a centralised and disciplined mass Party. Soon afterwards Sun was able to return to Canton, which again became the headquarters of the Southern Republican Government.

Meanwhile, in February 1923, a general strike had broken out on the Pekin-Hankow Railway, mainly under Communist leadership. Wu Pei-fu ruthlessly suppressed the strike, shooting a considerable number of the workers, including the leading Communists involved, among whom were Lin Hsiang-ch'ien and Chao Shih-yen. The extremely severe measures adopted to crush the strike showed the Trade Unions their weakness in face of the readiness of the war lords to employ armed force against them and strengthened the desire of the Communist leadership to get control of the KMT. The Third Communist Party Congress, meeting in June at Canton, issued a Manifesto calling for co-operation with the KMT in the national struggle, and on this occasion included 'the peaceful and moderate merchants' among the groups conscious of oppression. It asserted that the KMT 'should be the central force of the national Revolution and should assume its leadership', while criticising it for looking to foreign help in the

[1] See Vol. III, Part II, p. 926.

national Revolution and for concentrating on military action and 'neglecting propaganda work among the people'. It urged the KMT to correct these errors and to take the lead in mass propaganda, but at the same time stated its own special task to be propaganda among the workers and peasants, and re-affirmed its devotion to working-class interests. Ch'en Tu-hsiu was re-elected as General Secretary and head of the Politburo. The Central Committee, meeting in August, decided to maintain the Trade Unions' independence of the KMT, while continuing the policy of Communist infiltration into that body. The following month Michael Borodin (1890–1954) arrived in Canton as an emissary from Russia to Sun Yat Sen and proceeded, in conjunction with Sun, to reorganise the Kuomintang as a centralised Party on the Russian model. A national Congress of the KMT was held in Canton in January 1924 to carry through the reorganisation, and pronounced in favour of alliance with the Russian Soviet Government and with the Chinese Communist Party and of giving support to the workers' and peasants' movements. On the new KMT Executive Committee were three Communists — Li Ta-chao, T'an P'ing-shan, and Yü Shu-te — and also six alternate members, one of whom was Mao Tse-tung. Shortly afterwards, the KMT established the Whampoa Military Academy for the purpose of training military leaders for a new revolutionary army, with Chiang Kai-shek at its head and Chou En-lai (b. 1898) as chief of its Political Department. Thus the reorganised Kuomintang set on foot its preparations for taking the offensive against the war lords who dominated most of the country.

Throughout 1923 a shadowy Republican Government con-tinued to exist at Pekin under Wu Pei-fu's protection. The nominal President was Ts'ao Kun, under whose auspices a new Republican Constitution was proclaimed in October of that year. But in 1924 the so-called Christian general, Feng Yu-hsiang, ousted Wu from Pekin, and under his auspices the former Prime Minister of 1916, Tuan Chi-jui, took office as Chief Executive. Tuan, conscious of his weakness, proceeded to open negotiations with the Southern Government, and towards the end of the year Sun Yat Sen proceeded north-wards to confer with him and Feng about the possibilities of unification. In January 1925 the Chinese Communist Party, holding its Fourth Congress first at Canton and then at Shanghai, decided to develop its organisation by establishing special Bureaux for Northern and Central China, under the leadership respectively of Ts'ai Ho-shen and Chang Kuo-t'ao. In February Tuan held a series of Conferences with Sun and other leaders on the question of national reorganisation ; but in the midst of these Sun Yat Sen fell seriously ill and died at Pekin in March 1925, thus depriving the Kuomintang and the Chinese Revolution of their outstanding and most respected leader. In these circumstances nothing came of the projected settlement, and the rival war lords continued their internecine conflicts. In May the All-China Labour Federation held its Second Congress at Canton, this time with 281 delegates representing 166 Trade Unions. Liu Wei-min was elected Chairman, and Teng Chung-hsia Secretary-General. The same month serious troubles broke out in Shanghai, where anti-foreign demonstrators were fired on by the police of the International Settlement, 13 being killed. A general strike in Shanghai followed and spread to other areas, including Hong Kong, whose workers seceded to Canton and blockaded the British port. In an affray at Shameen, near Canton, British marines fired on the strikers, and a number were killed and wounded. A wave of anti-British and anti-Japanese demonstrations spread over most of the Chinese cities. The Communists put themselves at the head of this movement, known as the 'May 30th Movement' ; and the membership of the C.C.P., which had been less than 1000, rose suddenly to more than 20,000. At the same time, in Hunan, Mao Tse-tung began organising the peasants as a revolutionary force ; but for some time little attention was paid to him by the Communist leadership, which was busy working inside the KMT and had its eye mainly on the Trade Unions and the urban working class.

The death of Sun Yat Sen was mourned by great demonstrations throughout China. As we saw,[1] he left behind a 'Testament' which served, at any rate nominally, as the basis for the Kuomintang's policy of national reconstruction. To commemorate his work and to prepare leaders for the coming Chinese Revolution, the Sun Yat Sen University was set up in Moscow in 1925, with Radek as its first President.

[1] See Vol. III, Part II, p. 922.

In January 1926 the Kuomintang held its Second National Congress at Canton ; and on this occasion the Communists largely dominated the proceedings, securing 7 representatives and 24 alternates on the Central Executive Committee. This, however, was more than the right wing of the KMT could stomach ; and in March Chiang Kai-shek organised a *coup* against the Communists and induced the KMT Executive to pass a resolution banning them from leading positions in the Party. Even this, however, did not lead to a rupture between the KMT and the Communists, who continued to hope that the main body would follow them rather than Chiang, who was busy putting the finishing touches to his preparations for the projected Northern Expedition against the war lords of Central and Northern China. In May the All-China Labour Federation, now representing more than half a million Trade Unionists, held its Third Congress in Canton, and elected Su Chao-cheng as Chairman. In July the Northern Expedition began, and made a rapid advance into Central China, occupying Hankow in September 1926. In November the National Government, which included 3 Communists, moved from Canton to Wuhan, in Hupeh ; it represented those elements in the KMT which were still prepared to co-operate with the Communists. Chiang, on the other hand, and the KMT right wing, were by this time ranged openly against the left. Borodin, who had been mainly responsible for reorganising the KMT, had been dismissed before the Northern Expedition set out ; and when the Indian, M. N. Roy, arrived in China in December 1926 to represent the Comintern, he found the entire arrangement for which Borodin had been responsible already broken up.

The Wuhan Government continued for a time as the representative of the alliance between the KMT and the Communists ; but it had no control over Chiang or the armed forces under his command. Chiang continued his military advance, aided by strikes and peasant disturbances and by large-scale desertions from the armies of the war lords who attempted to oppose him. By March 1927 he had taken Nanking and was advancing on Shanghai. A rising under Communist leadership took place in Shanghai as he approached the city, and helped him to capture it ; but the following month Chiang, having broken with the Wuhan Government, organised an anti-Communist *coup* in Shanghai and Nanking, disbanded the left-wing organisations, and executed thousands of Communist and Trade Union and other left-wing activists. While this reign of terror was in progress the Chinese Communist Party held its Fifth Congress at Hankow, still in the hands of the Wuhan Government whose authority Chiang had thrown off. The C.C.P. at this Congress reported a membership of 50,000. The delegates roundly denounced Chiang and the right wing of the KMT, but were still reluctant to admit that the alliance with the KMT had utterly broken down, and hoped to maintain good relations with the Wuhan faction. The C.C.P. was still led by Ch'en Tu-hsiu, who continued to advocate united action with the left KMT. The members of the Political Bureau chosen at the Congress included, among others, Ts'ai Ho-shen, chief of the North China Bureau of the Party, Li Li-san, the leader of the Party's left wing, Ch'ü Ch'iu-pai, soon to succeed Ch'en as General Secretary, Chang Kuo-t'ao, a leading Trade Unionist, who had been secretary of the All-China Labour Federation, T'an P'ing-shan, Minister of Agriculture in the Wuhan Government, Su Chao-cheng, the Wuhan Minister of Labour, and Chou En-lai, subsequently among Mao's chief lieutenants in the long struggle of the 1930s and 1940s. It thus represented all the main Communist groups ; but this apparent unity was short-lived. In June 1927 the Chinese Communists were still appealing to the KMT left wing to put itself at the head of the Revolution and to lead the struggle against Chiang and his right-wing supporters ; and at the beginning of July they were still trying to come to an agreement with the Wuhan Government. But then, under instructions from Moscow, they abruptly changed their policy, ordered their representatives to leave the Wuhan Government, and reorganised the Political Bureau so as to exclude Ch'en Tu-hsiu and his supporters. Thus ended the co-operation of the Communist Party with any part of the KMT, and with it Ch'en's leadership of the Party. At the same time Borodin left Wuhan and made his escape to Russia with such of his coadjutors as did not fall victims to Chiang's reprisals. The Russian influence was driven out of China ; and Ch'en was made the chief scapegoat for the collapse of the C.C.P.'s attempt to collaborate with the nationalist revolutionary movement.

In order to carry into full effect the changes in Communist leadership and policy involved in the new turn of events, the C.C.P. held an Emergency Conference in August 1927. Ch'ü Ch'iu-pai was chosen in place of Ch'en as General Secretary of the Party ; a new Central Committee, excluding Ch'en's supporters, was elected; and it was decided to adopt a more radical programme and no longer to pander to the susceptibilities of the KMT. The numerous executions of Communist and Labour leaders under the orders of Chiang and the forcible breaking up of many of the left-wing organisations had struck a hard blow at the C.C.P., which also found difficulty in extracting itself completely from its entanglement with the KMT. The repression of the left grew steadily more severe and forced the Communists and the Labour Unions more and more underground. But it also provoked local insurrections in a number of areas — especially in Hunan under the leadership of Mao Tse-tung. This Hunan insurrection was essentially a peasant movement, though it proclaimed itself as a workers' and peasants' uprising. As we saw, Mao had been busily organising the Hunan peasants for the past two years ; and in 1927 his movement had already a following of more than 2 millions. The Hunan insurgents now demanded complete separation from the KMT, the establishment of a workers' and peasants' revolutionary army, the confiscation of the landlords' property, the setting up of a local Communist régime, and the organisation of Soviets. The rising was speedily crushed, and Mao was even reprimanded by the Communist Central Committee for conducting it ; but the peasant movement remained unsubdued, and Mao continued to lead it.

There were other local risings. In September Communist bands occupied Swatow and held it for a few days before they were driven out ; in October P'eng Pai set up Soviets in Kwantung and maintained them for several months ; and in November Mao again organised a local Soviet régime in part of Hunan. Then, in December, the workers rose in Canton under Chang T'ai-lei — who was killed in the fighting — and set up the short-lived Canton Commune. This rising, unlike Mao's, had the full support of the Communist leadership and of the Comintern. It was followed, in January 1928, by a further peasant rising, this time in South Hunan, led by Chu

Teh, who a few months later joined forces with Mao to form the Fourth Red Army — still without the support of the C.C.P. leadership, which continued to assign little importance to peasant movements and to insist that only the urban proletariat could play the leading rôle in the Revolution. In view of the control of the cities by the Kuomintang's forces and of the severe repression to which the urban workers were subject, such a policy held no hope of immediate success, and indeed threatened to provoke reprisals disastrous to the workers' movement. But the Communist leadership was by this time in a state of extreme disorientation. Up to the moment of Chiang Kai-shek's revolt, the Communists had reckoned on being able to capture control of the Kuomintang and use it as their instrument, first for carrying through the bourgeois Revolution and thereafter for laying the foundations for a proletarian seizure of power. Led mainly by city intellectuals and under the spell of the Russian Revolution, they had been directing their main organising effort to the Trade Unions, which had risen by 1927 to a membership of nearly 3 millions, attached to the All-China Labour Federation. They did realise that a successful Revolution must have peasant support ; but they thought of the peasants as no more than auxiliaries to a movement led and controlled by the much less numerous, but more articulate, workers of the towns, whereas Mao had already understood that the Chinese Revolution, in order to advance beyond the purely bourgeois stage, would need to be primarily a peasant movement, based on a programme with a directly rural appeal. Unable at this stage to influence the national leadership, Mao persisted in going his own way, standing somewhat aloof from the central councils of the Party and resistant to Russian and Comintern influences. By acting in this way Mao saved Chinese Communism from the complete disaster that faced it when Chiang turned savagely upon it in 1927 ; but for the time being his influence extended only to a small area, and over most of China the Communists and their Labour allies were confronted with utter defeat.

Meanwhile, at Moscow, the Russians and the Comintern had been engaging in acrimonious debates about Chinese affairs. Trotsky had been vigorously attacking the Chinese policy of Stalin and the Comintern. He had attacked them for continuing to support Chiang Kai-shek right up to his *coup* of April 1927, and had taken the view that the C.C.P., instead of capturing the KMT, as Stalin hoped, was well on the way to being captured or liquidated by it. Stalin and the Comintern, however, persisted even after Chiang's *coup* in attempting to maintain the alliance with the KMT left headed by Wang Ching-wei, the leader of the Wuhan Government ; but Wang, well aware that the C.C.P. was set on capturing his Government and in no mind to accept Communist control, struck back in July 1927 by expelling the Communists from it and, with the support of the generals on the spot, launching an anti-Communist repression only less ferocious than Chiang's. In face of this, both the C.C.P. and the Comintern were compelled to think out a new line. During the period of alliance with the KMT they had been trying to act in terms of a united front including not only the workers and peasants and the petty bourgeoisie but also the nationalistic elements in the greater bourgeoisie and even among the landowners. They had indeed contemplated that, on the victory of the bourgeois Revolution, these latter groups would desert the alliance ; but they had reckoned on the continued support of the main body of the petty bourgeoisie as well as of the workers and peasants. They tried to interpret Chiang's defection in class terms, as meaning that the greater bourgeoisie had gone over to the side of the landlords and capitalists, and even of the foreign imperialists, against the Revolution ; and they then set their hopes on reconstructing the united front, with the aid of the left KMT, so as still to include the petty bourgeois elements represented by the Wuhan Government. When Wang turned on them, this hope disappeared, and it became necessary to think out both a new policy and an explanation of what had happened that would hide up the disastrous errors of judgment of which they had been guilty. This they found partly in denunciations of Chiang and the bourgeoisie for betraying the Revolution and partly in similar denunciations of the tergiversations of the petty bourgeois Government at Wuhan. There was, however, no way of disguising the fact that Communism in China had suffered a quite appalling defeat.

Driven from pillar to post in China, the Communist Party was in no position to hold a regular Congress on Chinese soil.

Its Sixth Congress met in Moscow in the summer of 1928, at the same time as the Sixth Congress of the Comintern. Such a gathering, especially in view of the disorganised state of the Party, was bound to be much less than fully representative and also to be more than normally subject to pressure from the Comintern leaders. In the policy which it laid down, an attempt was made to steer a course somewhere between the alleged right-wing deviations of Ch'en Tu-hsiu, which had been condemned already, and what was termed '*putsch*-ism'—by which was meant the stirring up of immediate insurrections that held out no prospect of durable success. As we saw, there had been, in 1927 and the early months of 1928, a succession of uprisings, both among the peasants and in some of the cities ; and some of the blame for encouraging this form of action was now laid on Ch'ü Ch'iu-pai, the new General Secretary of the Party. Ch'ü was reprimanded and was ordered to remain in Moscow as the C.C.P. representative with the Comintern, his place as General Secretary being taken by Hsiang Chung-fa, who had been one of the Communist Ministers in the Wuhan Government. Chou En-lai was made head of the Organisation Bureau, from which post he moved subsequently to the leadership of the Military Bureau, at first assigned to Hu Wen-chiang. Li Li-san, the former Youth leader, was chosen to preside over the Propaganda Bureau, and Liu Shao-ch'i, later Chairman of the All-China Labour Federation, over the Labour Bureau of the Party. Finally P'eng Pai, who had led the peasant Soviet movement in Kwangtung the previous year, was made head of the Peasant Bureau.

The Sixth Congress also rewrote the C.C.P. Constitution and adopted a series of resolutions completely recasting the Party's policy in view of the changed situation. It set out from an admission of defeat : the revolutionary wave, it said, had definitely receded, and some time was bound to pass before its flow was resumed. But it was also strongly asserted that a renewed revolutionary onflow could be confidently expected, and that the C.C.P. must set to work immediately to prepare for its coming. The World Revolution was still treated as a certain future event, and armed insurrection as its necessary procedure. Accordingly, though it was needful to guard carefully against all forms of '*putsch*-ism' that would only exhaust the strength of the workers' movement to no good effect, it remained an indispensable task to prepare for the armed uprising that would be called for as soon as the period of recession came to an end. No indication was given — indeed, none could have been given — of how long the recession would last ; but it was clearly thought of as lasting not so long as to make preparation for the coming insurrection immediately unimportant. Even when the 'trough' had been surpassed, the Revolution to be achieved would be not Socialist but only bourgeois-democratic, though it would now have to be carried through, not with the support of the bourgeoisie, who had gone over to the war-lord, imperialist camp, but against them. But it could not yet be a Socialist Revolution, because the conditions were not yet ripe. Nor must it on any account be spoken of as a 'permanent' Revolution — that was Trotskyism, and deadly sin : it implied a continuous rising of the revolutionary wave, which was contrary to the facts of the situation. The task of the Communist Party was to accomplish the first Revolution — to complete the destruction of feudalism, landlordism, and imperialist intervention — no longer as the temporary ally of the bourgeoisie, great or petty, but in spite of their betrayal of the united front.

This could be done only if the C.C.P. could succeed in putting itself at the head of a real mass movement of the workers and peasants, who together constituted the sole remaining revolutionary force. In order to do this, the Party needed to steer a careful course between opposite dangers. On the one hand, it must avoid taking up a dictatorial attitude towards the mass movement ; for this would only antagonise the masses and destroy the Party's influence. The C.C.P. must not *order* the workers to strike, or the peasants to revolt. It must permeate and inspire the mass movement, without seeking to substitute the Party for it. Communists must join the Trade Unions and work within them, even when they were under reactionary influence, as well as help to bring new, militant Unions into existence. Similarly they must work with and inspire the peasant movements, and keep clear of dictating to them. Here, however, the C.C.P. came up against a most formidable difficulty. Its real allies were the poorer and middle peasants, not the prosperous peasants who ranked rather with the bourgeoisie ; but it was dangerous to insist on this, because the immediate need was to stir up a mass peasant movement on the broadest possible basis, and this involved appealing to the peasantry as a whole, rather than stirring up antagonisms in the villages, except against the landlord class. Moreover, popular peasant movements were apt to take as their objective the confiscation of the landlords' property in order to divide it up equally among themselves ; and the C.C.P.'s Moscow Congress expressed itself strongly against such equal division, which it regarded as an expression of a petty bourgeois attitude and as going right against the Communist objective of making the land common property in the hands of village Soviets, which should control its distribution and use. The Congress in its resolutions repeatedly warned the Chinese Communists against having anything to do with peasant projects of equal distribution and insisted on the key importance of procuring Soviet control of the land. It did not, indeed, stress nationalisation of the land, which had been its declared policy in the past, for fear of antagonising the peasant movement. It sought a half-way house in urging Soviet control and in warning Communists, at one and the same time, to avoid antagonising the better-off peasants and to be mindful of their duty to fight on behalf of the poorer peasants against their oppressors — not easy tasks to combine.

This problem of Communist policy in relation to the land and the peasants was indeed the crux of the difficulty the Sixth Congress was attempting to face. Up to 1927, or even to 1928, the Communists in China had never admitted that the peasants could play more than an entirely subsidiary part in making the Revolution. They had, with few exceptions, been city-minded, and had looked to the city proletariat, under their direction, to take the lead, drawing the peasants after it, but allowing them virtually no share in the determination of revolutionary policy. They had frowned on Mao's preoccupation with the peasant aspect of the Revolution, and had even censured his efforts from time to time. Now, however, in face of the collapse of their power in the cities, the countryside, which the war lords and the KMT could not effectively police, had become the area most open to them for purposes of revolutionary preparation ; and they were compelled, willy nilly, to take a fresh look at the peasant movement and to give greater recognition to its importance. Even so, they remained entirely unwilling to concede to the peasants an independent rôle in revolutionary leadership : they clung to the idea that the urban workers must lead the peasantry and continue to play the dominant part. They did, however, see that for the immediate future much more could be done in the countryside than in the cities, and that the most urgent task was to find a workable solution of the agrarian problem. This solution, in its immediate aspect, they regarded as forming part of the bourgeois-democratic, and not of the Socialist, Revolution, because they saw collectivisation of agriculture to be quite impracticable for the time being, and were aware of the danger of a solution that would serve merely to entrench the system of small property and small-scale cultivation.

One great difficulty that faced the C.C.P. in re-defining its attitude to the peasants was that both the land system and the character of peasant movements differed from one part of China to another. Over most of Southern and Central China the main body of the peasantry was made up of poor peasants and landless labourers, and the peasant movements tended to be largely in the hands of these groups.· In the North, on the other hand, there were large numbers of relatively well-off peasants who owned their land, side by side with tenant-farmers and bigger landed estates. In areas of both types the middle peasants formed a large and important element ; and the C.C.P. declared emphatically that the Revolution could not succeed without their backing. But whereas, in many parts of the South and Centre, there was already in being a bitter class-struggle in which the richer peasants were arrayed against the poor and the landless, in other areas — and especially in the North — this was not the case, the peasantry of all types being in the main united against war lords, landlords, and onerous taxation, and therefore supporters of the Revolution as far as it was directed against these evils. It therefore appeared impracticable to recommend a uniform policy to be followed over the whole country. In the North, and in similar areas elsewhere, it seemed needful to avoid antagonising even the richer peasants, so as to throw them into the arms of the counter-revolution ; whereas, over most of the South and much of the

Centre, this had already occurred and the C.C.P. was accordingly free to take the side of the more heavily exploited groups. Even in such areas, however, it would be fatal to antagonise the middle peasants, who must be induced to support the Revolution and could be persuaded to do this if attention were concentrated on the demand for confiscation of the landlords' estates, in which they could hope to share, and if no threat were directed against their holdings. This meant that there could be no single, simple policy : each area would have to be considered separately, and action adapted to its particular conditions. Everywhere the Communists should endeavour to play a leading part in the peasant movements ; but what that part should be would vary from place to place.

Thus, in relation to movements for equal distribution of the land, which the Congress had roundly condemned in its general resolutions on policy, the special resolution dealing with the peasant problem was much more equivocal. The resolution recognised that in many areas the demand for equal distribution was bound to arise ; and it laid down that where, in areas containing a high proportion of poor peasants and landless labourers, this demand came clearly from the local peasant movement, the Communists should support it, 'but should also criticise it '. They should support it as a step leading to the liquidation of agrarian feudalism, but should criticise it as 'an illusion of petty-bourgeois Socialism'. Nor should they agree to equal distribution in areas where middle peasants constituted a majority ; for it would inevitably, in such areas, antagonise the middle peasantry and destroy all prospect of revolutionary success. This was certainly a dusty answer, open to widely different interpretations ; but it was not easy to find a way out of the dilemma.

A great deal was said in this resolution about the problems of peasant organisation. On the one hand, much stress was laid on the need to organise 'the village proletariat and semi-proletariat', including the craft workers as well as the landless rural labourers, and to secure for these groups both an independent organisation of their own and a place of high influence in the general peasant movement. Much emphasis was also put on the need for close association between the peasant movements and the workers' movements in the near-by small towns and cities, and also for an infiltration of urban workers into the village organisations in order to give them a more proletarian character. Great stress was also laid on the need to enrol women as active participants in the peasant movement and on the important part that could be played by organisations of Youth. The Communists were urged, while maintaining the character of the peasant organisations as broadly representative of the peasant masses, to miss no chance of winning leadership in them and to play a vigorous part in their day-to-day struggles. In the villages, it was laid down, 'guerrilla warfare' would be 'the chief instrument' of struggle. Under this head were included refusal to pay rents and taxes, confiscation and distribution of landlords' land, 'killing of oppressive gentry and landlords', and the setting up of peasant delegate committees and village Soviets. Guerrilla warfare, however, was not enough : it should lead on, in suitable cases, to local revolts in promising areas leading to the taking over of all power by the Soviets and to the creation of peasant armies. Communists were, however, at the same time warned that such revolt 'can be a starting-point in the nationally victorious masses' revolt only on condition that it is carried on in alliance with a new revolutionary tide among the proletariat in the cities'. In other words, the peasants could not hope to make the Revolution without the full participation of the workers in the cities, and under their guidance — a condition which appeared to rule out such revolts for the time being. The resolution, however, went on to say that 'the Party should lead the spontaneous revolts of the peasants'; and the party members were left to make what they could of this equivocal advice.

It was, nevertheless, made plain that the resolution contemplated the existence of Soviet-controlled enclaves of territory, on which local Soviet régimes would be able to maintain themselves against the armies of their antagonists. In such areas the Soviets were urged to build up reliable and disciplined armed forces of their own, and to establish the nuclei for a 'Red Army' of workers and peasants that would be gradually consolidated as the great instrument of revolutionary force. Training of cadres for this army was to be taken seriously in hand, and at the same time Communists were to work actively within the militia corps maintained by the landlords and within the bandit units established by landless and workless elements in order to bring as many as possible of them over to the revolutionary side.

Thus, the Moscow Congress did its best to formulate a new policy for the Chinese Revolution, in such a way as to throw the blame for past defeats on the errors of right 'opportunists' and left 'putsch-ists' rather than on the Communist International or the Russian Government, which had been in fact chiefly responsible for the policies that had led to the disaster. It had been under Comintern and Russian influence that the C.C.P. had attempted to co-operate with the KMT, first from outside and then by infiltrating into it. The united front of workers, peasants, petty bourgeoisie, and greater bourgeoisie had been wholeheartedly approved by the Comintern leaders, as had the reduced front, omitting the greater bourgeoisie, after Chiang's defection. Borodin had been an active party to the attempt to continue co-operation with the Wuhan Government after Chiang had set to work killing Communists and dissolving the Labour organisations. According to the resolutions of the 1928 Congress the Kuomintang, left as well as right, was made up entirely of reactionary elements ; but this had been discovered only when Wang, as well as Chiang, had sent the C.C.P. about its business. Nothing, however, must be said at the Congress to criticise either the Russians or the Comintern — above all, nothing that might give countenance to Trotsky's vehement opposition to Stalin's Chinese policy. The entire blame had to be shared between the Kuomintang 'traitors' and the C.C.P.'s own errors and inefficiencies.

The resolutions passed by the C.C.P. delegates at Moscow involved a fundamental revision of policy, above all because they recognised the primary importance of the land question and of the peasants' place in the revolutionary movement. Yet they still rested quite largely on illusions. They grossly exaggerated the part that industrial workers were capable of playing in the Revolution. In Russia in 1917 the industrial sector formed only a small part of a predominantly peasant economy ; but the big, up-to-date establishments were strategically placed in Petrograd and Moscow for exerting a decisive influence at the critical moment, and included a substantial element of heavy industry employing mainly male workers, who provided the nucleus for an armed revolutionary force. Chinese industry had no such highly developed sector of heavy indsutry ; nor could any one city occupy the key place taken by Petrograd in the Russian Revolution. In Shanghai textiles predominated, and foreign influences put powerful obstacles in the way of revolutionary action. Canton was the most revolutionary city, but was a centre rather of commercial than of industrial enter-prise. A high proportion of Chinese industrial workers were handicraftsmen, or artisans, widely scattered in small groups or working on their own account, and not easily organised into any comprehensive class movement. It was sheer fantasy to suppose that the industrial proletariat could be the principal makers, or even the guides and leaders, of the Chinese Revolu-tion, either bourgeois or Socialist ; but it was difficult for either the Comintern or the Chinese Communist leaders to admit this, because the leading rôle of the industrial proletariat ormed part of the dogma of revolutionary Marxism. As we have seen, even in raising the peasant movement to a status of primary importance in revolutionary strategy, the Communists remained unable to conceive of it as really leading the Revolu-tion and continued to insist that it must be induced to act under the inspiration and guidance of the industrial workers.

Nevertheless, the turn in policy was decisive because, for the most part, after 1928 it was only through the peasant move-ment that the Chinese revolutionaries were able to act at all, on any considerable scale. Thereafter Mao ceased to be a minor and much criticised figure among the C.C.P. leaders, and rose rapidly to primacy among them because, by continuing to act on the principles for which he had been so often criticised, he was able to maintain continuously a high level of revolutionary activity and to defy the immense efforts which Chiang Kai-shek made to eliminate his movement. From 1928 onwards there were always in China Soviet areas, sustained by the organised force of a Red Army, in which revolutionary action was taken against landlords and other exploiters, land dis-tributed and taxes made more fair, and full-scale war carried on against the regular armies of Chiang and his lieutenants with varying fortunes, but on the whole with quite remarkable success. The story of these exploits falls, for the most part, outside the period covered in this volume, which stops short of the Japanese invasion of Manchuria in 1931. But the beginnings were made between 1927 and 1929, with the setting up of the first Chinese Soviets and the formation of the first Red Armies in Hunan and Kiangsi and Hupei. By 1930 this new movement had developed far enough for a national Conference of delegates from the Soviet-controlled areas to meet at Shanghai and propose to establish a Central Soviet government of China, and to draw up its code of organic laws. There was, indeed, a· long road still to travel before such a Government could have any real existence ; but the indispensable foundations were being laid.

Meanwhile, the C.C.P. as a whole had been undergoing further vicissitudes. The Sixth Congress, meeting far away in Moscow, had been by no means fully representative ; and it took some time before its decisions became generally known to the members of the Party. In June 1929 a Plenum of the Central Committee, meeting in Shanghai, at length ratified the Moscow decisions and set the Party on its new course. In August Mao and Chu Teh established a Soviet system in parts of Kiangsi ; and the same month P'eng Pai, the creator of the Kwangtung Soviets of 1927, was captured and executed in Shanghai by the KMT. The following month, under the leadership of the former C.C.P. Secretary, Ch'en Tu-hsiu, a conference of opposition groups was held in Shanghai and attempted to concoct a rival policy to the one approved at the Moscow Congress. Associated with Ch'en were leading C.C.P. figures such as P'eng Shu-chih and Liu Jen-ching. Ch'en's expulsion from the C.C.P. speedily followed ; and thereafter he and others maintained fractional opposition Parties, usually denounced as followers of Trotsky, who was said to have advised Ch'en to form his opposition *bloc*.

By this time Li Li-san had become the leading figure in the C.C.P. hierarchy, having succeeded Ch'ü Ch'iu-pai when the latter was censured at the Moscow Congress. It thus fell to Li's lot to put the new Moscow policy into effect, by steering the required middle way between 'opportunism' and '*putsch*-ism' and by preparing for insurrection while actually stopping short of it until the new revolutionary wave arrived. The question was, who was to say when this had happened. Li found himself subject to constant demands from Moscow for a more active policy. In July 1930, under the impression that the revival was at hand, Li decided to act, and ordered a peasant force from the Soviet-controlled areas of Hunan to attack and occupy the city of Changsha. The result was a heavy defeat; and Li found himself accused of '*putsch-ism*' and threatened with removal from the leadership. He was able, despite this failure, to command a majority at a Plenum of the Central Committee held in September 1930 at the instance of Ch'ü Ch'iu-pai, who had recently been sent back from Moscow to report on the situation in China. But Pavel Mif, who had come to China in May to represent the Comintern, accompanied by a large group of students trained at the Sun Yat Sen University in Moscow, took up a strongly hostile attitude to Li, and received the Comintern's backing. The returned students took a strong line and, with Mif's support, set out to gain control of the Party. When, in November, the Comintern formally condemned Li's line, he was forced to resign his offices. After a stiff struggle the new-comers, with Mif's support, gained control of the party machine, ousting the old stagers led by Lo Chang-lung, Chairman of the All-China Labour Federation, and Ho Ming-hsiang, who was caught and executed by the KMT the following year. Li, deposed from power, soon left for Moscow, where he recanted his alleged errors and was presently taken back into favour. Meanwhile Ch'en Shao-yü, a leading figure in the group which had come from Moscow with Mif, took Li's place at the head of the Party as Secretary-General.

During this period Mao Tse-tung, who had been elected to the Party's Central Committee at the Moscow Congress, though not present, had been consolidating his position in the highlands of Hunan and Kiangsi. Until almost the end of 1930 he was left there undisturbed by any major military attack; but in December 1930 Chiang Kai-shek launched his first big offensive against the Soviet-controlled area, which lay in difficult country and lent itself well to irregular defensive action. The attack, successful at the outset, was before long beaten back; but it was followed by a second and a third offensive, each with bigger forces, in the spring and summer of 1931. These renewed attacks were also beaten off; and in November 1931 the first All-China Soviet Congress met at

Juachin, in Kiangsi, and set up the Chinese Soviet Republic with Mao as its Chairman and Chu Teh as Commander-in-Chief of its armed forces. Mao was also chosen as Chairman of the C.C.P.'s Central Committee, and thus at length received recognition as the outstanding figure in the Chinese Communist movement. By that time Japan had invaded Manchuria and was revealing its intention to convert China into a satellite country ; and the C.C.P. found itself faced with a fresh enemy. In February 1932 the Chinese Soviet Republic declared war on Japan, and began to call for a new united front directed against Japanese imperialism. Chiang Kai-shek, however, preferred coming to terms with the Japanese to giving up his attempt to overthrow the Chinese Soviets. He launched one attack after another, each bigger than the last, against the Soviet areas, until at last in October 1934 Mao decided to evacuate the area he had defended so manfully and to lead his Soviet forces to join those of another Soviet region that had been established in Northern Shensi. The famous 'Long March' across China began ; and about a year later Mao's army reached its goal. A year later still, in the autumn of 1936, Mao's forces were joined by those of Chu Teh, which had stayed in Szechwan ; and early the following year a new Shensi-Kansu-Ningshia Soviet Government was founded in North-West China, with its capital at Yenan, and Chang Kuo-'tao, a veteran of the movement who had been chairman of the C.C.P.'s Organising Bureau and General Secretary of the All-China Federation of Labour as early as 1921, as its Chairman. Then came the full-scale Sino-Japanese War of 1937, leading among other things to Chang Kuo-tao's secession to the KMT and expulsion from the Communist Party in 1938. These events, however, belong to a later period than this volume is meant to deal with : the record of the present chapter ends with the beginning of the 'Long March' in October 1934.

We have thus to leave the story of the development of Chinese Communism right in the middle, at a point at which the Comintern's confident hopes of impending world capitalist collapse and of a renewed revolutionary wave were still unfulfilled in China, though the great economic recession had come upon the world and prophecies of the early demise of capitalism were again very much in the air. In China the revolutionary movement had made little progress towards regaining its hold on the cities : its achievements had been in the country areas, and the peasants, rather than the industrial workers, had taken the lead and proved their fighting capacity against Chiang's attempts to destroy them. Chinese Communism, under Mao's inspiration, had taken its own line in growing independence of Comintern and Russian influence, and had worked out its own interpretation of the Marxian gospel. Ch'iu Pang-hsieu, chosen as General Secretary of the C.C.P. in 1932, had given place to Chang Wen-tian early in 1934 ; but Mao, with Chu Teh and Chou En-lai as his principal lieutenants, had become the outstanding personality and the outstanding national leader.

CHAPTER XXVI

JAPAN, 1914–1931

IN Japan, as we saw in the preceding volume of this history,[1] the Socialist movement had been all but wiped out by the arrests and executions of the so-called 'Anarchists' in 1910–1911 and by the suppression of the entire Socialist press and the prohibition of all Socialist meetings. These measures also reacted strongly on the Trade Unions, which had been largely under Socialist or other left-wing leadership. Many of them disappeared, and others were driven underground. Only a moderate group, headed by Bunji Suzuki (1885–1941) and organised in a central body, the Yuaikai, was allowed to exist openly, with the support of a number of employers who hoped to guide the workers into pacific courses. Suzuki and his followers were, of course, roundly denounced by the Socialists who were still at large ; but, until the first world war was at an end, Japanese Socialism was practically in abeyance.

The war, however, fostered rapid industrial development. Japan, though in alliance with the British against Germany under the Anglo-Japanese Treaty, took little part in the fighting beyond occupying the areas in China previously held by the Germans, policing the seas in the Far East, and providing convoys for vessels carrying Japanese goods to Europe. Instead the Japanese devoted their main attention on the one hand to pressing their demands upon China — the 'Twenty-one Points' [2] — and establishing their influence over the Chinese economy, and on the other to supplying the European Allies with large quantities of exports and taking the place of the belligerents in many parts of the world market. These conditions led to a rapid growth in the number of industrial workers and to a state of full employment highly favourable to working-class claims. With prices rising sharply, strikes grew numerous

---

[1] See Vol. III, Part II, Chapter XXVII.
[2] See p. 776.

despite continued repression ; and even the unmilitant Yuaikai was drawn into activity and turned into something much more in the nature of a real Trade Union movement than it had been at the outset. This caused the employers who had supported it to withdraw their help and to set up a rival body, the Roshi-Kyochokai or Society for Harmonising Labour and Capital. This move was ineffective : the Yuaikai changed its name to Nihon-Rodo Sodomzı (Japanese Federation of Labour) and rapidly expanded its membership, with a programme that embodied demands for the eight-hours' day, the six-day working week, and universal suffrage. During 1918 there were widespread riots on account of the scarcity and high price of food — especially of rice ; and Socialism reappeared as a social and economic force.

This was the position when the war ended ; and the Japanese Government had to make up its mind what attitude to take up towards the swiftly growing Trade Union movement and the increasing popular pressure for political reform. The victory of the Allies, in its impact on Japan, had the aspect of a victory for democracy over autocracy and militarism, and led to a greatly increased interest in Western liberal and democratic ideas. Many Western writings on politics and economics were translated and published, either for general sale or in limited editions issued by special societies of intellectuals, in many cases connected with the Universities ; and a number of progressive journals, such as the *Kaizo*, published articles by Western democratic writers and engaged in lively discussions of Western Socialist ideas and policies. As against this it seemed for a time as if Japan might become involved in a large-scale continental war against the Bolsheviks in the Far East ; but after the withdrawal of the European Allied forces and the defeat of Kolchak the Japanese were gradually induced, under strong American pressure, to withdraw from their Siberian adventure and also to modify their attitude towards China. Japan took part in the negotiations which led up to the Washington Treaties of February 1922, and was a party both to the Five-Power Naval Treaty regulating the relative sizes of the fleets of Great Britain, the United States, Japan, France, and Italy and to the Nine-Power Treaty guaranteeing the territorial integrity of China and providing for equal opportunity in all parts of China for the commerce and industry of all nations ; and these Treaties helped to prepare the way for the Soviet-Japanese Treaty of 1925.

In respect of the Trade Unions, the Japanese Government was not prepared for any measure of positive recognition ; but continuance of the former policy of repression had become impracticable, and in effect the Unions were allowed to exist and to develop, though they acquired no positive legal status. The question came to a head in connection with the setting up of the International Labour Organisation as an organ of the League of Nations under the Versailles Treaty. The I.L.O. was based on a tripartite structure, which required participating governments to appoint half the delegates after consultation with employers' and workers' organisations. The Yuaikai claimed the right, as the largest Trade Union body, to be consulted ; but the Government rejected its claim and insisted on appointing all the delegates itself, despite the requirements of the I.L.O. Constitution. This led to a great outcry ; and the Government, though it maintained its position at the constituent Washington Conference of the I.L.O. in 1919, was forced thereafter, under international as well as home democratic pressure, to give way and to consult both the Japanese Federation of Labour and the Railwaymen's Union, the largest Trade Union outside the Federation, and to include both Suzuki and the Railwaymen's leader, Narazaki (1865–1932), as delegates to subsequent I.L.O. meetings. Similar troubles arose in India, where in 1919 the Government passed over M. N. Joshi, the nominee of the Indian Trades Union Congress, in favour of B. P. Wadia ; but in this case the two agreed to share the delegation, with Joshi formally in the position of substitute.

On the suffrage issue the Japanese Government rejected the demand for universal or manhood suffrage, but did, early in 1918, greatly extend the franchise by reducing the qualification from payment of 10 yen in taxes to that of 3 yen. The agitation, however, continued ; and in 1925 a coalition Government, formed after the General Election of 1924, carried through an Act establishing manhood suffrage. There was still no question of enfranchising women, who up to the war period had been even forbidden to attend political meetings.

Save as a pressure group, acting chiefly through the Trade Unions or through small groups of intellectuals largely connected with the Universities, neither Labour nor Socialism had yet become, in the years after 1918, a substantial political force. The two main political parties were the Seiyukai, the traditional conservative party, and the Kenseikai, known later as the Minseito, which largely represented business interests. At the first Election after the electoral reform, in 1928, eight workers' representatives secured election, but not as members of a solid Labour or Socialist Party. They were, in fact, divided into three groups — the Rono, led by Oyama, the Nichiro, led by Aso, and the Shamin, led by Professor Abe. Organisation was, however, spreading from the industrial workers to the small farmers; and attempts were being made to effect an alliance between these two. In 1925 a conference representing both elements was held in Tokyo; but sharp divisions emerged. The Federation of Labour and other moderate groups seceded; and the Farmer-Labour Party (Nomin Rodo-To), set up by the remaining delegates, was immediately dissolved by the authorities on the ground that some of its demands were a danger to the State. By this time Communists were beginning to be active and to gain some influence over the main left-wing Trade Union groups; but they had little mass following, and the older Trade Union movement remained strongly hostile to their attempt to give economic unrest a political turn.

The first Japanese Factory Act — a very mild measure — had been passed in 1911, and had come into force in 1916. Mainly as a consequence of Japan's membership of the I.L.O. a new Act was passed in 1923 and came into force, after further amendment, in 1926. It limited the working hours of children under 16 and of women to eleven a day and prohibited night work for both, but contained no restriction on the working hours of adult male workers. It also provided very limited compensation in case of disablement through industrial illness or accident and introduced a system of allowances for funeral expenses in case of death at work. Health insurance also was introduced in 1926; and the Government also passed an amended ordinance for the settlement of labour disputes and repealed the police ordinances under which strike action had hitherto been a penal offence — this latter a provision which it had been found impracticable to enforce for a long time past. Japan thus took the first few steps towards the adoption of a code of labour legislation in line with the stage reached in its industrial development.

This period of relative liberalism, however, was not destined to endure. It came to an abrupt end at the onset of the world economic depression and with the development of the Manchurian crisis in 1931–2. The victory of the Kuomintang in China after Chiang Kai-shek's break with the Communists[1] had unified most of China under a Government that was committed to make a stand against foreign privileges and concessions ; and, with both Great Britain and the United States following, on the whole, a conciliatory policy towards Chiang after his break with the Soviet Union, Chinese anger was directed mainly at the Soviet Union and at Japan, especially in relation to the affairs of the Russian-controlled Chinese Eastern Railway and the Japanese-controlled South Manchurian Railway. The Manchurian dictator, Chang Hsieh-liang, opened in 1929 a renewed attack on the Russian administration of the C.E.R., expelling and arresting the Russian officials on the plea that they were using the railway administration for political ends. The Soviet Union promptly retorted by military force, making armed incursions into Manchuria and defeating Chang's forces in a series of engagements without any formal declaration of war. Chang was compelled to give way and to reinstate the Russians in control of the railway. The Western powers made a number of protests to the Soviet Union, but without effect.

Trouble next developed in connection with the South Manchurian Railway, the position of which Chang set out to undermine chiefly by refusing to pay the interest on the debts incurred on its construction. Japan protested, but was unable to secure any redress ; and, inside Japan, nationalist feeling developed rapidly, helping to undermine the position of the Minseito Government, which was also being seriously shaken by the onset of world depression. By the end of the 1920s Japan had barely recovered from the disaster of the great earthquakes of 1923 ; and the Minseito, whose economic backers in

[1] See p. 786.

big business aimed at being on good terms with the West, restored the gold standard just as the great depression was setting in. Japan was hit hard by the depression at a very early stage — above all, by the abrupt fall in silk exports to the United States ; and the attempt to maintain the balance of payments by sharply deflationary finance involved both heavy unemployment and deep agricultural distress. These conditions, instead of strengthening the left-wing forces, resulted in a wave of nationalist and militarist feeling and in demands, not merely for a change in economic policy, but for an attempt to retrieve the situation by active measures of military intervention directed against the Chinese nationalist boycott of imports from Japan and against Chang's intransigent behaviour in Manchuria. The Japanese militarists, riding on this current of national feeling, decided to resort to open war in Manchuria, and seized its capital, Mukden, in September 1930. Before the end of the year the Minseito Cabinet had fallen, and the Seiyukai party had come back to power. The short epoch of relatively peaceable and liberal rule came abruptly to an end ; and thereafter Japan stood committed to a policy of imperialist expansion which the Western powers, preoccupied with their own economic difficulties, showed themselves impotent to check. Hitler's advent to power in Germany early in 1933 seemed only to confirm the eclipse of Japanese liberalism and to encourage drastic action against the Labour and Socialist movements. From 1931 up to the end of the second world war in 1945 the predominant mood in Japan was one of militant imperialism, wearing the label of 'Co-prosperity' to cover the claim to Japanese predominance in China and throughout the Far East. In such a climate of national opinion there was no chance for Socialism, or even for Trade Unionism, to make its voice heard. Communism, indeed, survived as an underground and heavily persecuted movement ; but other forms of Socialism were virtually extinguished until, in 1945, the Japanese people found themselves confronted with the necessity of accommodating themselves, in defeat, to the conditions of a radically changed Asia in which India, Burma, Indonesia, Korea, and presently Indo-China were emerging as independent powers, and China itself was plunging into the renewed civil war from which Communism was soon to emerge as victor.

CHAPTER XXVII

INDIA: INDONESIA

IT would be an unrewarding and indeed, for the most part, an impossible task to set out to record the history of Socialist development between 1914 and 1930 in a number of countries in which significant developments did take place during these years without giving rise to movements distinctive enough in thought or action to provide means of marking off the Socialist elements from others with which they were inextricably entangled. This holds good above all for India, where many thinkers and leaders in the movement for national independence were strongly influenced by Socialist ideas, and some, such as Jawaharlal Nehru (b. 1889), were already proclaiming capitalism to be irreconcilable with democracy and looking forward to Socialism as the necessary outcome of the democratic struggle for national independence, but where, with the exception of the Communist Party, no significant formulation of Socialist policy and no important distinctively Socialist organisation developed till the 1930s at the earliest — and not a great deal of either until after the achievement of Indian independence at the end of the second world war. No account of Indian Socialism up to 1931 could be more than a gathering of scraps ; for, save in its Communist form, Socialism existed only within the framework of the movement for national independence that had begun under the auspices of the Indian National Congress and found during this period, in Mahatma Gandhi (1869-1948), a leader who can fairly be called neither Socialist nor anti-Socialist, not because the issues involved had not presented themselves to his mind, but because other issues seemed to him much more urgent and also more fundamental. I believe there were occasions when Gandhi, in private conversation, referred to himself as an Anarchist ; but this was only in order to emphasise his dislike of centralised state action and his belief in voluntary action directly inspired by strong ethical conceptions. If both parliamentary Socialism and, still more, Communism were antipathetic to him, so were capitalism and exploitation in all its forms. He believed, above all else, in the virtues of the local community animated by the spirit of mutual service, and deeply mistrusted 'politicians' who spun their webs of intrigue and pursued their quest for power in a spirit remote from that of the ordinary simple people. Even Communism, which took shape in an Indian Communist Party in 1924, but had found earlier expression in the writings of M. N. Roy, its outstanding theorist in its early days and the main spokesman of India at the Comintern, was in its practical manifestations an affair much more of anti-imperialism and of World Revolution than of distinctively Socialist thought or policy, though Roy did, of course, attempt to find, in the developing class-struggle, a foundation for the Revolution which, he felt sure, the bourgeois nationalists would seek to halt, and even to betray, as soon as they saw it threatening their interests as a class.

In India, as in some other underdeveloped countries, Communism began chiefly as a movement among a limited group of intellectuals. It could indeed hardly have begun in any other form in view of the very limited character of the working-class movement. It was, however, able to secure early successes in the Trade Union field. The All-Indian Trade Union Congress, at the outset closely connected with the Indian National Congress, was set up only in 1920 — largely as the outcome of a considerable expansion of industry during the war. Because of the scarcity of sufficiently literate workers to fill key offices, many Trade Unions had to rely on officials drawn from the educated classes ; and this was undoubtedly an important factor in facilitating the introduction of politics into Trade Union affairs, and helped the Communists to increase their influence during the period of widespread industrial unrest that followed the end of the war in 1918. By 1927 the Communists won control of the A.I.T.U.C. ; but that body had not at any point represented nearly the whole Indian Trade Union movement, and the Communist victory soon led both to the establishment of a rival Trade Union Federation and to the refusal of a number of important Unions to connect themselves with either fraction. Meanwhile, in 1926, under the directions of the Comintern, the Indian Communists had set up a new Workers' and Peasants' Party, designed to broaden their appeal ; but the Socialists, to the extent to which they existed as a recognisable force, still remained within the Indian National Congress and did not attempt to set up an independent Party of their own, or even, until 1934, to organise a Socialist fraction inside the Congress movement.

Manabindra Nath Roy (1893–1954), who, during the early years of the Comintern, was not only the outstanding leader of Indian Communism but also the chosen emissary of that body both in Latin America [1] and in China,[2] had taken a very active part in the early debates at Moscow on the question of Communist policy in relation to imperialism and to nationalist movements in colonial countries. He had emphasised the view that the native capitalists of these countries would speedily make common cause with the feudal classes and with the imperialists against the workers, and that the great need was to strengthen the proletarian elements on the side of revolution without making fruitless and debilitating concessions to the bourgeois nationalists. On this issue he had even crossed swords with Lenin and had succeeded in making his influence felt. Within a few years, however, he had become seriously dissatisfied with the line taken by the Comintern and by the Party in India ; and in 1928 he was excluded from the latter as a 'deviationist'. Thereafter Roy was for a time largely isolated, being subject to constant attack both by his former Communist colleagues and by their opponents. He continued, however, to take his own outspoken line until he was arrested and put on trial by the Government in 1931, and, despite the efforts of a Defence Committee in which Jawaharlal Nehru participated, spent the ensuing years in prison. His later career, as a supporter of the British against the Germans in the second world war and as leader of his own Radical Democratic Party during the post-war years, belongs to a later section of this history.

The post-war period in India opened with the introduction of the Montagu-Chelmsford constitutional reforms of 1919, which were designed to grant a measure of self-government on a provincial basis, subject to high property qualifications for

[1] See p. 752.   [2] See p. 786.

electors and to a division of the field of government into two —
'reserved' and 'transferred' subjects respectively — and to the
maintenance of a reserved power to override the mainly elected
Legislative Councils whenever they adopted measures which
the Governments of India and the United Kingdom felt unable
to accept. This was the system known as 'dyarchy', which
was quite unacceptable to the leaders of the Indian National
Congress. At the outset the Congress boycotted the elections,
with the result that the new Councils were made up of
'moderates' who were prepared to work the system, and were
widely denounced by those who followed the Congress lead.

These were the circumstances under which Gandhi rose to
a position of undisputed pre-eminence as the national leader of
Indian opinion. The new Constitution left the central government of India still in the hands of the Viceroy and his Executive
Council, with limited participation by two mainly elective
Chambers, chosen on the basis of an exceedingly high property
qualification for electors, but, even so, open to being over-ridden
by the Viceroy at any point. Moreover, before the Montagu-
Chelmsford reforms came into force the Central Government
had armed itself, under the notorious 'Rowlatt Acts', with
special powers of great extent to put down 'sedition' and deal
with any kind of revolutionary or conspiratorial action. These
measures were brought in at a time when, at the end of the
first world war, the country was seething with discontent ; and
it was in response to their introduction that Gandhi launched
the first nation-wide movement of Satyagraha, which means
something nearly equivalent to organised passive resistance.
When the Rowlatt Acts received the Viceroy's assent, Gandhi
retorted by ordering a day of national mourning and general
cessation of business. Contrary to his intentions, violent rioting
broke out in a number of areas, especially in the Punjab ; and
on April 13th, 1919, General Dyer, who had been called in
by the civil authorities to suppress the rioting at Amritsar,
ordered his soldiers to fire on the crowds, killing about 400
persons and wounding a much larger number.

The Amritsar Massacre, for which Dyer was later condemned both by the Hunter Committee of Inquiry and by a
resolution of the British House of Commons (July 8th, 1920),
but was upheld by the House of Lords, greatly worsened the

state of feeling in India. When it was followed immediately
by Gandhi's arrest, rioting spread beyond the Punjab, in face
of the proclamation of martial law. The introduction of the
Montagu-Chelmsford reforms thus took place under most unfavourable conditions : well before the first elections were held,
late in 1920, Gandhi had proclaimed a national policy of 'non-
violent non-co-operation' in opposition to a Government for
which he had 'neither respect nor affection'. At the meeting
of the National Congress at Christmas 1920 the demand was
made for complete Home Rule by the following September,
and Gandhi was given almost unlimited powers to organise
the campaign. Soon after this, in April 1921, Lord Reading
succeeded Lord Chelmsford as Viceroy and found himself faced
with a rapidly spreading movement of civil disobedience, which
was to be launched on a national scale early the following year.
In February 1922, however, at Chauri Chaura in the United
Provinces, an angry crowd of peasants and Congress volunteers
massacred 21 policemen and village watchmen ; and in face
of this Gandhi, faithful to his creed of non-violence, called off
the entire campaign. He was nevertheless arrested on charges
of disaffection and plotting to overthrow the Government, and
was sentenced to six years' imprisonment. Further movements
of repression followed ; and, in face of Gandhi's action, Congress found itself largely paralysed, and wide differences
opened up in its ranks between those who wished to carry on
the policy of electoral abstention and civil disobedience and
those who favoured contesting the elections in order to use the
Montagu-Chelmsford Councils as sounding boards for opposition to the Government. At the second election, held late in
1923, a large section of the National Congress broke away from
Gandhi and contested seats as a Swaraj (Home Rule) Party,
winning nearly half the seats in the Central Assembly and
clear majorities on at least two of the six Provincial Councils.
At the centre, when their demand for Swaraj was rejected by
the Government, they mustered enough support in 1924 to
throw out the Finance Bill, which had to be put into force
by the Viceroy under his special powers. The Swaraj Party did
not, however, go to the length of absolute resistance : in effect,
it acted thereafter as a more or less constitutional opposition,
continually demanding revision of the Montagu-Chelmsford

Constitution in advance of the ten-years' period, at the end of which it was due to come up for reconsideration in any case.

These developments had taken place, especially in 1920 and 1921, against a background of severe economic distress, due to the failure of the harvest in 1920 and to the industrial slump of 1921. But after 1921 a series of good harvests much reduced the distress; and in 1922 and the following year a beginning was made with protective industrial legislation, including the regulation of child labour and of working hours and conditions. 1921 had been a year of widespread strikes as well as of peasant troubles; but with the better harvests popular unrest became less, though political agitation continued in full force, and serious disturbances in Bengal were met by further repressive ordinances. Meanwhile, Gandhi had been released unconditionally in January 1924; but, faithful to his doctrine of non-violence, he found himself in opposition to the policy of many of the Congress leaders, and was unable to resume his position of uncontested leadership. For a year, in 1926–7, he went into retirement from political activity. But in 1928 he resumed his campaign in favour of civil disobedience unless full Dominion status were granted within a year; and this policy was endorsed by Congress, with the full support of the Moslem League, in December of that year.

Meanwhile, the British Government had decided to advance the date for reconsidering the constitutional question; and in 1929 the Simon Commission, which included no Indian representative, was set up to enquire and report to the British Parliament. The Congress, under Gandhi's influence, boycotted the Commission, which carried on its work in India to the accompaniment of continual outbreaks of strikes and popular disturbances, but, thanks to Gandhi's restraining hand, of remarkably little violence. In 1930 Gandhi launched a renewed campaign of civil disobedience and was again arrested and condemned to detention for an indefinite period.

But the campaign continued, despite the arrest and imprisonment of more than 27,000 of his followers. Before his arrest, he had refused to attend the first Round Table Conference, summoned by the British Labour Government to meet in London; but the following January he was released from detention and, after negotiation with the Viceroy, agreed to call off the civil disobedience campaign, and was induced to attend the Second Round Table Conference, from which he returned to India disillusioned. He then restarted civil disobedience, and was once more arrested in January 1932. In September of that year he announced his intention of starving himself to death unless the Government abandoned its proposal of separate electorates for the depressed classes — the Hindu 'untouchables', whose champion he had consistently been against the upholders of caste distinction. A compromise was reached on this issue, mainly through fear of his death. Further arrests, threatened and actual hunger-strikes, and hurried release of Gandhi followed ; but the record of these events would take me too far beyond the period covered in this volume. Politically, Gandhi's influence waxed and waned ; and for some time after the failure of the Round Table Conferences he devoted himself increasingly to his campaign against the abuses of the caste system, and less to directly political issues. Whether his influence as a political leader rose or fell, his position as a moral teacher rose continually higher, and its effect extended to an immense number of persons who were unable to accept in full his rejection of all forms of violence.

In economic matters Gandhi, as we saw, was not a Socialist in any sense familiar to the West. He looked for the accomplishment of the non-violent revolution on which his hopes were set, not to the industrial workers as a class — and not indeed to any *class* — but to the broad masses of the people, and above all to the great peasant masses and to the idealists in all classes on whom he called to help them. He believed, above all else, in simple ways of community living and in the renovation of the Indian villages as centres of communally organised production, both in agriculture and in rural industries based on hand labour and small-scale manufacture for domestic or local use. In this connection he laid great stress on the virtues of Khaddar — cloth produced by home spinning and weaving — both in order to reduce dependence on imports and on the products of power-driven factories and because he regarded the practice of such simple crafts as valuable for the human spirit. Gandhi's insistence on the *panchayat*, or village community, has something in common with the views of Western Anarchist-Communists, in that both stress the value of non-coercive small-scale co-operative community living ; but his emphasis was different because he was fundamentally much more a moralist than a political revolutionary and rejected the entire concept of class-conflict. Sharp antagonisms were to appear later within the ranks of Indian nationalism between the industrialisers, who looked to modern industrial techniques for the means of escape from primary poverty, and the Gandhists, who saw large-scale industrialism as the enemy of human freedom and of real democracy. But as long as India remained a subject country, the National Congress had to find room within it for partisans of both these views, as well as of many intermediate positions, just as it had to accommodate both Bombay millowners and Trade Unionists in revolt against them. These internal conflicts led to many strains ; but throughout the 1920s only the Communists were prepared to break away from a national liberation movement that set out to unite all classes against British rule rather than to regard itself as a mere section of a world movement of proletarian class-revolt.

Even after the dissensions of the war period and of the disturbed years after 1918, the Indian National Congress remained in essentials a moderate body, limiting its demands to Home Rule without calling for complete independence or a separate Sovereign State. Its claim was rather for an assured position as a self-governing Dominion : not until 1930 did it declare its aim to be complete national independence. Though, like India itself under British rule, predominantly Hindu, it made its appeal not on a religious basis, but to all the Indian peoples irrespective of their religious affiliations. It had indeed a large Moslem following : the Moslem League, founded as early as 1906 to press the claims of the Moslem minority on the basis of an acceptance of British sovereignty, was still relatively uninfluential except among the wealthier classes. The very notion of a separate Pakistan for the areas where Moslems formed the majority had not yet emerged. The best-known Moslem leaders were for the most part still either attached to the Congress or prepared to work in with it ; and, especially in the villages, communalist troubles and religious conflicts were very much less frequent than they became in the 1930s. In most areas of mixed population Hindu and Moslem peasants, and also those who belonged to other religious communities, usually lived side by side without much friction, sharing common economic grievances against landlords, money-lenders, and tax gatherers, but taking little part in national politics and seldom joining together on more than a local scale. The Congress indeed claimed, and Gandhi personally soon secured, a big peasant following ; but a high proportion of the peasants were too poor and too uninstructed to be reached by political appeals. Even Gandhi, with his reputation of saint-hood and his capacity to transform political into moral and human issues, could at most overcome only momentarily the immense obstacles in the way of uniting them in support of a common crusade ; and his doctrine of non-violence, deeply attractive though it was to great masses among the Hindu peoples, appealed much less to most Moslems or even to those Hindu peoples, such as the Marathas, who had a strong military tradition. Gandhi's influence repeatedly rose and fell, usually rising when he issued the summons to one of his great campaigns, and falling when, distressed at outbreaks of the violence he had done all he could to prevent, he called off his campaign rather than allow it to continue to be marred by violent action. Yet, even when his political influence was at its lowest, his moral influence remained very great ; and even among those who rejected his political prescriptions, there were many who continued to be deeply under his moral inspiration.

In this environment there was hardly any room for the growth of a Socialist movement. There was, of course, a continuous cry for land reform — for the ending of the *zemindari* system, under which, in the large areas over which it operated, the local landowners doubled the parts of landlords and tax gatherers for the Government, collected rents from the tenants, and paid over 45 per cent of their receipts as land-tax. There were also constant complaints of the exactions of the money-lenders (*banias*), who were able to exact prodigiously high rates of interest, and to whom, in many parts of the country, practically every villager was not merely in debt, but so deeply in debt as to have no hope of ever liquidating his obligation, which was passed on to his children when he died. Gross under-nourishment was almost universal in these areas ; and disease was everywhere, with hardly a hope even of a minimum of medical attention. In the towns there were, no doubt, many who were substantially better off ; but the industrial workers were for the most part both grossly underpaid and subject to serious unemployment, which often drew them back to the villages in search of the merest subsistence, without their being able to make there any contribution to higher production — for there were already too many crowded on too little cultivable land. The prevailing conditions of indebtedness and sheer poverty made it impossible for the villagers to improve their methods of production, even if they had known how ; for they had neither capital nor the means of getting credit save on fantastically uneconomic terms. I am not saying that these hopelessly debilitating conditions existed everywhere in India ; but they were very widespread, especially in the northern and central provinces. Only in a very few places, such as the Punjab, had Co-operative credit societies been introduced, under government surveillance, on any substantial scale. Most of rural India suffered under the double burden of a landlordism that made no contribution at all to the improvement of land or village and of a system of moneylending that was utterly extortionate ; and the Government, though most of its servants did their best according to their lights to administer the laws impartially, was in its relation to the peasants essentially a policeman and not a source of help.

In these circumstances there was, of course, always bitter discontent, and therewith the possibility of hunger riots when bad harvests reduced large masses to sheer starvation. But even at the worst times the isolation of the villages made it vastly difficult to organise the people on any large scale ; and the nationalist movement was further hampered by the fact that its leadership was drawn largely from the wealthier classes and that, in its quest for national unity, it was unwilling to risk antagonising its wealthier supporters, either among Bombay millowners or even among landlords. Gandhi was indeed always on the side of the common people ; but even he was concerned much more with his crusade on behalf of the Hindu untouchables against the abuses of the caste system than with the basic economic wrongs of the peasantry as a class. He was involved in a continuous struggle with the Mahasabha — the national organisation that stood for strict Hindu orthodoxy and for the maintenance of caste — but was at the same time anxious to carry the main body of Hindus with him and not to cause a split that might destroy the power of the National Congress. He stood for equality and co-operation of all groups and creeds in his crusade for self-government ; but he was not prepared to carry on his crusade on any basis that would subordinate national unity to the struggle of class against class.

It was Gandhi's strength, however, that no considerable section of the National Congress could afford to do without him, because of the immensity of his personal prestige. This personal ascendancy forced the wealthy to modify their policies in order to come to terms with him, and prevented the left, who were on the side of the workers or the peasants, from breaking away to set up parties devoted to the interests of these classes. Only in the 1930s did any distinctively Socialist or Peasant Parties, other than the Communist Party, begin to emerge ; and when they did they emerged as Parties within the orbit of the Congress and owing allegiance to it as long as national independence had still to be won. Accordingly, there is almost nothing to say in the present volume of an Indian Socialist movement : all that existed was an intellectual current favourable in some degree to Socialism but — save in the exceptional case of the Communist Party, which was, in fact, an advocate of Revolution rather than of any constructive Socialist idea — unorganised and unable to command any large popular following.

Something must be said, however, of the repression to which those who attempted to organise and lead movements of protest and collective self-assertion among the Indian working classes were subjected, wherever these movements took any kind of militant form. The outstanding example of this repression was the extraordinary Meerut conspiracy trial of 1929 and the following years, in which 31 prisoners, 3 of them British and the rest Indians, were arraigned on a charge of 'conspiracy to deprive the King of his sovereignty' over British India. The Meerut trial, held before a Civil Servant acting as a judge and without a jury, actually lasted for three and a half years, of which the case for the prosecution occupied much more than half. For all this time, the accused men remained in gaol ; and long before the trial ended the funds raised for the defence had been exhausted. A Conservative Government was in power in Great Britain when it began, but was replaced by a Labour Government before it had been more than barely started. But the change of Government was of no benefit to the prisoners : throughout the Labour Party's period of office the trial was allowed to continue, and the end came only when the so-called 'National Government' had been in power for more than a year. The men who were on trial were largely Communists, but included left-wing Socialists unconnected with the Communist Party. Heavy sentences, including one of transportation for life and eight others of transportation for ten years or more, were passed on those convicted, the lightest being of imprisonment for three years. These sentences were indeed greatly reduced on appeal ; but even those who got off most lightly had spent three and a half years in prison before they were convicted. Yet they had not even been accused of any act of rebellion, or even of violence. The principal charge against them was that they had organised a subversive Workers' and Peasants' Party, which had served as a 'front' organisation for the Indian Communist Party and had established Trade Unions on a basis of class-struggle and opposition to British imperialism as well as to the employing class in India.

It is a fact most discreditable to the second MacDonald Government that, even while it was attempting to negotiate a settlement with India at the Round Table Conference, it allowed this trial to proceed towards its wretched conclusion. Doubtless the excuse was the Government's reluctance to put pressure in such a matter on the Government of India, which was determined to pursue relentlessly not only Indian Communism but anything that could be regarded as allied to it as a subversive force. This, however, is no valid reason for the Labour Government's inaction, which did much to destroy Indian faith in the good intentions of the British Labour Party. In Great Britain, many Socialists protested strongly against the Meerut proceedings ; but the Labour Government disregarded their protests, and rank-and-file interest in Indian problems was too small for them to be made effective.

It was while the Meerut trial was in progress that the first steps were taken to establish non-Communist Socialist organisations in certain parts of India. Among the older Indian leaders who had become advocates of Socialist ideas one of the best known was Lala Lajpat Rai (1856–1928), the principal leader in the Punjab, who was a well-known figure in England and America as well as in India ; and it was in the Punjab that, in December 1930, a Conference met to establish a Socialist Party, with H. N. Brailsford as the principal speaker. It consisted mainly of intellectuals, but had the support of the Railwaymen's Trade Union, which was among the strongest and best organised sections of the working-class movement. Its sponsors included both Hindus and Moslems. A similar movement, led by M. R. Masani and Asoka Mehta, was being developed at about the same time in Bombay ; and there were parallel movements in other areas. Remaining within the orbit of the National Congress, these nascent Socialist groups directed themselves mainly to the founding and officering of Trade Unions, and were able to make a growing contribution to the development of the Indian Trade Union movement, in rivalry both with the Communists and with the followers of Gandhi — for Indian Trade Unionism had everywhere a strong political tendency and most Trade Unions were led largely by literate adherents of one or another political Party or group.

These premier Socialist organisations were formed largely out of young people who had been brought into mutual contact in the course of the civil disobedience movements, in many cases in prison, and had come to the opinion that it was necessary for Socialists, without leaving the Congress, to set up distinctive propagandist agencies of their own. Not until 1934 did the local Socialist organisations come together on a national basis to form the Congress Socialist Party, which remained in association with the Congress until after India had won its independence at the end of the second world war. Acharya Narenda Deva and Jai Prakash Narayan speedily rose to positions of leadership in this Congress Socialist Party. In the earlier stages the Indian Socialists made many attempts to co-operate with the Communists ; but in the course of the 1930s the two drifted further apart. The history of Indian Socialism, as an organised movement, thus falls beyond the scope of the present chapter.

British Socialists up to 1914 had a good record in respect of Indian problems. Keir Hardie's small book, *India* (1909), written after his visit in the course of his journey round the world in 1907, was a pungent attack on the system of British rule — especially on racial discrimination and on the economic conditions of the people and the destruction of native craft industries by the competition of factory-made goods imported from Great Britain. Hardie was much abused in the British press for his speeches in India, most of all for hobnobbing with native 'agitators' and for saying that India ought to be a fully self-governing Dominion, in the same way as Canada ; but, in fact, his utterances in India were very moderate — considerably more so than the book in which he gave an account of what he had seen. H. M. Hyndman, too, was in his earlier years a pungent critic of British imperialist policy ; but his *Awakening of Asia* (1919) appeared only after his support of the British cause in the war in 1914–18 had destroyed his influence among the Socialist left wing. Annie Besant, after her conversion to Theosophy in 1889, became an outstanding supporter of Indian claims to self-government and, during her long residence in India, wrote extensively on political as well as on religious matters and greatly influenced the development of the Congress movement. Other notable friends of India in Great Britain included George Lansbury, H. N. Brailsford, and Bertrand Russell, who was for some years the very active President of the India League organised by Krishna Menon. Ramsay MacDonald, too, was in his earlier days a strong advocate of Home Rule for India, though he shilly-shallied when he was called upon to take action as Prime Minister from 1929 to 1931. The Labour Party at its Conferences passed many resolutions in favour of Indian self-government ; and Indian Socialist or radical Nationalist speakers were welcomed by Labour audiences when they visited Great Britain. There was, however, it must be admitted, no really deep interest in Indian questions among the main body of British Labour supporters, or in the electorate as a whole ; and it was always possible for British Governments to disregard Socialist protests against misrule in India without provoking mass resentments. On account of this apathy, Indian Socialists and Nationalists often accused the British Labour movement of insincerity in its professions of support for Indian claims. The root of the trouble, however, was not that the Labour Party was insincere, so much as that most of its members were preoccupied with other issues that seemed to them more pressing, and, knowing nothing of India at first hand, were not prepared to do more than make occasional protests until the rising tide of Indian Congress Nationalism forced them to take notice. C. R. Attlee, who as Labour Prime Minister was to accept India's claim to independence after the second world war, signed the Simon Report which preceded the Round Table Conference of 1930, and, though rejected by the Indian Congress, provided the main basis for the Government of India Act of 1935. Attlee, at that time, saw insuperable obstacles to the concession of Dominion status to India in the conflict between Hindus and Moslems, in the position of the Indian States governed by native rulers under treaty arrangements with Great Britain, and in the impracticability of establishing at once an independent Indian army. By 1945 he had changed his mind in face of the further development of provincial Home Rule under the Act of 1935, of the growth of an army largely led by native officers, and, most of all, of the evident impossibility of continuing to enforce British rule. In the 1930s, however, the fact that Attlee had signed a Report which was rejected by the main body of Indian opinion helped to discredit the British Labour Party in the eyes of Indians who had previously looked for British Labour backing in their national struggle for self-rule.

INDONESIA

In Indonesia a small Socialist movement was in existence even before 1914. The leading personalities were H. Sneevliet — alias Maring — (1883–1942), the Dutchman whose activities have been mentioned in earlier chapters. It had supporters especially among the railway workers : its principal indigenous leader was Semaoen. Both Sneevliet and Semaoen were active later in the Communist Party. Until after the war the movement existed only in Java, which continued to be its main stronghold. In 1918 the main nationalist organisation, Sarekat Islam, adopted Socialist ideas and elected Semaoen as a member of its executive committee. The following year a Central Trade Union organisation was set up, but split soon afterwards into rival moderate and extremist factions. The old

Socialist Party (I.S.D.V.) went over to Communism and became in 1920 the Indonesian Communist Party. I.S.D.V. had been affiliated to the nationalist Sarekat; but in 1921, having become definitely Communist, it cancelled its affiliation, continuing nevertheless to co-operate fairly closely with Sarekat Islam for the next two years. It then set up a left-wing nationalist organisation, Sarekat Rakjab, as a rival to the older body. In 1926 and 1927 there were nationalist risings in both Java and Sumatra; and Achmad Soekarno (b. 1901) emerged as the outstanding nationalist leader.

CHAPTER XXVIII

AUSTRALIA AND NEW ZEALAND

Australia

WHEN the first world war broke out in August 1914, Labour Governments were in power in most of the individual States, and Andrew Fisher (1862–1928) resumed office as Prime Minister of the Australian Commonwealth in the course of the following month. When Fisher resigned in October 1915 and came to London to represent the Commonwealth, his successor at the head of the Labour Government was William Morris Hughes (1864–1952), of whose earlier career something has been said in the preceding volume of this history.[1] .The Labour Party at the outset supported the war, in face of lively opposition from the supporters of the Industrial Workers of the World and from a section of the Trade Unions which had come under its influence. From its establishment in Australia in 1907 the I.W.W., under the leadership of Tom Barker, had been vigorously advocating a programme of industrial unionism, with the 'One Big Union' as its final objective, and had been conducting a growingly intense campaign against the arbitration system favoured by the Labour Party and the Trade Union moderates. The heavy sentences on left-wing leaders in connection with the Broken Hill strikes and lock-outs of 1908–9 and the Brisbane dispute of 1912 had aroused very strong feeling ; and the influence of the I.W.W. had increased, though it never included any large membership or came near to making the One Big Union a practical project. What its propaganda did help to achieve was a certain amount of amalgamation of Trade Unions into wider industrial bodies, and therewith a strengthening of the sentiment in favour of greater class-solidarity. The feeling that greater unity was needed gained ground in the political field as well, and in

[1] See Vol. III, Part II, p. 853.

1915 the Australian Labour Party for the first time set up a Federal Executive, made up of representatives of the Parties in the various States. This, however, did nothing to narrow the gulf between the right and left wings : on the contrary, this gulf was widened by differences on the war issue. By the end of 1916 the Labour Party itself had split on the question of military conscription for service overseas, and the Hughes Government, reconstituted as an anti-Labour Coalition, had set out to destroy the I.W.W. by proscribing it under the Unlawful Associations Act and was busily engaged in prosecuting the left-wing leaders hostile to the war effort. From this point onwards Hughes was associated more and more closely with Lloyd George in the policy of a 'fight to a finish' against the Germans, becoming a member of the British War Cabinet and carrying on, in Australia, a bitter struggle not only against the Trade Union left wing but also against his former Labour Party colleagues who had refused to follow him on the conscription issue.

Even before 1914 a system of compulsory military training had been introduced in Australia by the Fisher Government ; but this did not carry with it any power to enforce service outside the Australian continent. The Australian contingents that served in Europe were made up of volunteers ; and, as the war dragged on and the demand for soldiers became ever greater, there were growing difficulties in filling up the ranks of these contingents. Hughes accordingly proposed, while he was still Labour Prime Minister, to apply compulsion for this purpose ; and he succeeded in persuading his colleagues to allow the question to be submitted to a referendum of the electors. The referendum, which sharply divided the Labour Party in the Commonwealth Parliament, resulted in a rather narrow defeat of the Prime Minister's proposal — by 1,060,033 votes against 1,087,557. Thereupon, in November 1916, Hughes and 25 of the 65 Labour M.P.s seceded from the Labour caucus ; and Hughes, instead of resigning office, induced his former anti-Labour opponents to join with his group in a Coalition Government. The Labour Party majority retaliated by expelling Hughes and his supporters, and reconstituted the Party as best as they could. The split put an end to Labour rule in the Commonwealth for a dozen years. Not until 1929 was the

Labour Party again in a position to form a Government —
under a new leader, James Henry Scullin (1877-1953), who
held office from that year to 1932, but was seriously handicapped
by the lack of a majority in the Senate. A year after the defeat
of 1916 Hughes attempted a second referendum on the same
issue, and was again defeated — this time by the larger majority
of 1,187,747 against 1,015,159. But he remained in office after
this renewed defeat, and was able to maintain his position
until 1923.

The struggle over conscription was fought with great bitterness on both sides. Hughes and his group did their best to
represent all who opposed it as anti-war 'disloyalists'; but, in
fact, many of the opponents were not against the war, but
regarded enforced war service as contrary to Australian liberties
or were simply unwilling to be sent, or to have their relatives
sent, to serve as soldiers at the other side of the world in a
struggle in which they felt Australia to have only a remote
share or interest. There was, however, among Hughes's opponents a vigorous group of anti-war militants; and against
these the new Government proceeded to take drastic action
both under the existing War Precautions Act of 1914 and under
the new Unlawful Associations Act, which proscribed the
I.W.W. as an unlawful body and was used to attack other
militant industrial and political groups. The I.W.W. was the
chief sufferer. Twelve of its best-known leaders were arrested
in November 1916 and charged with conspiracy to commit
arson and with sedition. Others, including Barker, were
already in gaol. Very severe sentences were pronounced on
most of the twelve: Peter Larkin, brother of the Irish leader,
James Larkin, was sent to prison for ten years, together with
Charles Reeve, who had been active in the I.W.W. since the
beginning. A number of others were committed to gaol for
five years; and the entire group remained in prison till 1920,
when the Labour Government then in office in New South
Wales was induced to appoint a judge as a Special Commissioner to investigate the affair. The Commissioner, Mr.
Justice Ewing, found that, although a few of the prisoners had
been rightly convicted, there were others who ought never to
have been convicted at all, and yet others whose sentences had
been grossly out of proportion to anything that had been

proved against them. Peter Larkin was among these last, and was set free after serving less than half of his sentence. This, however, happened only when the war had been over for nearly two years. In the meantime, before the war ended, Tom Barker had been deported in 1918 to Chile, whence he presently found his way to the Soviet Union.

The arrests and trials of the I.W.W. leaders, though they necessarily weakened the industrial left wing, did not prevent serious industrial troubles from breaking out the following year in New South Wales. These began in the railway workshops, over the introduction of a 'card' system which the workers resented as a step in the direction of industrial conscription and a device for unfair speeding-up of work. The trouble spread, first to other railway employees and then to the miners and to the waterfront ; and there was a bitter struggle, in the course of which the Government and the employers introduced blacklegs to replace the strikers and, when the latter were finally starved into submission, engaged in widespread victimisation of the Trade Union activists. In this case, too, the Story Labour Government of New South Wales at length, in 1921, ordered a special enquiry, which showed that many railwaymen were still being victimised for their part in the dispute. But the Story Government fell before it had had time to take action on the report ; and no redress was secured.

When the war ended, there were renewed outbreaks of industrial unrest ; and a number of small left-wing groups which had managed to survive the repression came back into the open. Several of these declared their solidarity with the Third International and applied for affiliation to it. In 1920 several of them came together to establish a Communist Party, which was accepted as a member-Party of the International and largely replaced the I.W.W. as the point of focus for extreme left-wing opinion. At first the new Communist Party had only a very small following, and did not attempt to challenge the Labour Party by putting up candidates for either federal or state elections ; but it gradually obtained a hold on a number of the Trade Unions, and, from 1925 onwards, began to run candidates of its own, who in a few cases polled largely but were unable to achieve any positive success. Meanwhile the Federal Government, under Hughes's leadership, while letting some of its special war-time powers run out, kept others in being under the War Precautions Act Repeal Act of 1920, and in the same year altered the provisions of the Arbitration Act so as to empower the courts to impose heavy fines on Trade Unions convicted of inciting to strikes in defiance of federal arbitration awards, which were, in general, very unfavourable to the workers' claims. Even before 1914 there had been a tendency for the Arbitration Court and for the wage-determining bodies in the States to award conditions substantially less favourable than the Court had set out to enforce at the time of the famous Harvester Judgment of 1907. The projects of Mr. Justice Higgins for the enforcement of high and rising minimum standards of living had been defeated, first by the decisions of the Supreme Court limiting the Arbitration Court's powers, and subsequently by the hostile attitude of his successors, who were mostly former anti-Labour politicians. In relation to the cost of living, wages had already begun to fall before 1914 ; and the fall continued during and after the war. Nevertheless a good many Trade Unions, fearful of the outcome of industrial conflict, clung to the arbitration system, which also received the continued support of most of the political leaders of Labour.

Feeling against the working of arbitration continued, however, to grow, and, in order to deal with the mounting unrest, the Commonwealth Government in 1926 secured the enactment of the Crimes Act, endowing it with additional repressive powers. Two years later, in 1928, began a new epidemic of strikes, which continued into 1930. The most serious of these occurred in 1928 on the waterfront, provoked by the introduction of a licensing system for employment, which was bitterly resented as an attempt to impose slave conditions, and the following year among the timber workers, who were faced by the Arbitration Court with wage-reductions and worsened conditions of employment at a time of economic prosperity and rising prices. In this latter case the timber workers in New South Wales and Victoria struck against acceptance of the Court's award. For this several leading Trade Unionists were arrested and fined ; and the Commonwealth Government invoked a provision of the Arbitration Act authorising it to order a secret ballot on the question of a return to work. Most of the workers refused to take part in the ballot, and, of the minority who did, all but a handful voted against accepting the award. The Government then ordered the arrest of the principal strike leaders — among them the old I.W.W. leader, Charles Reeve, not long out of prison after his ten years' sentence of 1916, and J. S. Garden, the Secretary of the New South Wales Labour Council. The jury acquitted them without calling on the defence counsel, Dr. H. V. Evatt (b. 1894), holding that there was no case against them. But a number of men arrested for picketing offences were less fortunate and were sent to goal for terms of from six to eighteen months for assaults on blacklegs. In the end, despite big financial contributions from other Trade Unions not involved in the dispute, the timber workers had to call off the strike just as a Commonwealth Labour Government was coming back to office after its long period of exile. During most of this same year — 1929 — the coal-miners of northern New South Wales were locked out, the owners demanding wage-reductions which they refused to accept. In this case the dispute continued well into the following year, and ended in the defeat of the workers after an affray with the police, sent to protect blacklegs, in which one miner was killed and seven were wounded by police fire.

While these struggles were in progress, the recently established Australian Council of Trade Unions — a belated attempt to unify the Trade Union forces throughout the Commonwealth — had screwed up its courage to denounce the arbitration system and to declare a boycott of the Arbitration Court. But the defeats encountered by the Unions on the waterfront, on the railways, and in the timber and coal-mining industries rendered this decision abortive ; and hard on the heels of these defeats came the great world depression of 1931 and the following years, involving heavy unemployment and a sharp decline in the Trade Unions' power. The Labour Government did what it could to protect working-class conditions in face of the depression ; but its power was very limited, especially as the anti-Labour Senate was in a position to block its legislative measures. In 1932 it lost its majority in the Lower House and fell from office, handing power back to the anti-Labour Coalition, which continued to govern the Commonwealth right up to and during the second world war.

In this account of Australian Socialism between 1914 and

the depression of the 1930s there is but little sign of new Socialist thinking. Australian Communism, which was new as a movement, in the main took over the pre-war following of the I.W.W. and the Trade Union left, replacing the semi-Anarchism, or Anarcho-Syndicalism, of the earlier period by the new creed of 'democratic centralism' with singularly little practical difference, despite the width of the theoretical gulf between them. Australia was too far away from the centre of the main conflict between Communism and Social Democracy and between the rival Internationals to be much affected by it; and there were significant differences between the Social Democratic and Labour Parties of Europe and the Australian Labour Party, which had played only a small part in the affairs of the pre-war Second International. It is true that the Australian Labour Party adopted in 1921 the socialisation objective, long urged upon it by its Queensland section and by other forward groups. Whereas it had previously demanded only the 'collective ownership of monopolies' and, in general terms, the 'extension of the industrial and economic functions of the State and municipality', it now, in 1921, declared in favour of 'the socialisation of industry, production, distribution and exchange' — a comprehensive project of public ownership which brought it into line with the declarations of the European Socialist Parties. This, however, in view of its exclusion from office in the Commonwealth and its loss of power in several of the States, could make little practical difference. Certain extensions of public enterprise did take place in Queensland and in New South Wales; but in the latter these had occurred mainly before the war, under the influence of W. A. Holman (1871–1934), and Holman, after breaking with the Labour Party on the conscription issue in 1916, retired from politics in 1920 and returned to the Bar.[1] Even in Queensland, where the Labour Party remained in power under E. G. Theodore (b. 1884), the developments of public enterprise did not greatly alter the general structure of the economy; and at the Commonwealth level the hopes excited by the setting up of the Commonwealth Bank in 1911 had been falsified even before 1914 and were put to a complete end by the changes made in its management in 1924, when control of its policy was virtually

[1] See Vol. III, Part II, p. 873.

handed over to the commercial banks. In practical politics the adoption of the socialisation objective as the A.L.P.'s long-term aim did not make much difference : it certainly did nothing to reconcile the antagonisms between the Labour politicians and the mainly industrial left wing, which passed in the 1920s increasingly under Communist influence.

Progress in the fields of social service and social reform legislation was also barred at the Commonwealth level by the Labour Party's fall from power. The Federal Land Tax Act of 1910, which had been intended as the first instalment of a great attack on the privileged position of the big landlords, was steadily whittled away by reduction in the scale of the taxes and by failure to adapt them to changing money values ; and the Act soon ceased to exert any noticeable effects on the distribution of landed property or on the returns accruing to its owners. At the state level, on the other hand, some progress was made in those States in which the Labour Party was able to exert a continuing influence. Queensland, where the Labour Party remained in office, first under T. J. Ryan and then under Theodore, from 1915 to 1929, introduced unemployment insurance in 1923 ; and New South Wales made a notable step forward with the Child Endowment Act of 1926. These, however, were no more than isolated successes achieved in an environment generally unfavourable even to moderate Labour claims ; and when at length, in 1929, the Labour Party did again win a Commonwealth election and J. H. Scullin took office as Prime Minister, little, as we saw, could be achieved in face of the continued control of the Senate by the Opposition and of the onset of the great industrial depression of the ensuing years. The forces of Labour in Australia remained deeply divided between the moderates, who, broadly speaking, accepted responsibility for making the Australian economic system work without fundamental social change, and an active left-wing minority which, while it largely accepted Communist leadership in the absence of any alternative point of focus, was in reality concerned much less with Communism as a world revolutionary movement than with immediate economic grievances arising out of the administration of the arbitration system and the repressive methods used by successive Governments against the more aggressive Trade Unions and their left-wing leaders. In effect, Australia contributed practically nothing during these years to socialist thinking, though in Queensland Theodore was responsible for a number of ventures into the field of state trading and production. Not a single Socialist book or pamphlet of any real significance was published during the period under review, unless we are to take account of occasional writing dealing with such matters as the controversy over conscription, or V. Gordon Childe's highly critical study, *How Labour Governs in Australia* (1923). H. V. Evatt's full-length biography of Holman, *Australian Labour Leader*, also a highly critical account, did not appear until 1940.

NEW ZEALAND

In New Zealand, as we saw in the preceding volume,[1] the Labour movement had suffered disastrous defeats during the years immediately before 1914. The power of the left-wing Federation of Labour had been utterly broken in a succession of strikes and disturbances in which extensive use had been made of blacklegs and of civil guards drawn largely from the farmers and from the middle classes ; and the arbitration system, which had originally been devised to protect and help the workers, had been converted into a weapon against them by the power given to the Arbitration Court to register 'moderate' or even blackleg Trade Unions and to make on their application awards that were binding on all workers in the trades concerned — even against the opposition of un-registered Trade Unions representing a majority of the workers concerned. The Trade Union movement had been split into contending groups, one accepting and the other repudiating the arbitration system ; and politically, too, the movement had split into rival factions. At the General Election of 1914 the rival parties — Social Democratic and United Labour — had both entered the lists, but had won only two victories apiece, *plus* one seat that went to a Labour candidate independent of either. The Conservatives seemed to be seated firmly in political power, the Trade Unions utterly in eclipse, and the Government sure of the support of a powerful Citizen's Defence Organisation ready at any moment to take a strong

[1] See Vol. III, Part II, p. 885.

line against any sign of a revival of industrial militancy. The old Liberal-Labour alliance, which under Ballance and Seddon had united the industrial workers with the small farmers and a large section of the middle classes, had entirely broken up ; and, in a predominantly agricultural country now dominated by small farmers rather than by great ranchers and absentee landlords, the weakness of the industrial workers, when they attempted to act alone, had been decisively demonstrated.

War conditions soon led to a coalition of the dominant Conservative, or Reform, Party with the Liberals, leaving the handful of Social Democratic and Labour representatives to form the Opposition. This situation soon led to a fusion of the rival Labour and Socialist groups, which came together in 1916 to form a single Labour Party, led mainly by the old left-wing groups, with H. E. Holland (1868–1923) as its outstanding personality.[1] The new Party declared its objective to be general socialisation ; but in practice it soon came to be concerned mainly with more immediate issues — first of all, with questions directly arising out of the war and later with the acute problems of post-war unemployment and the protection of wage-standards and development of social services to prevent the sharp sufferings inflicted on the workers during the years of depression. By 1918 the Labour Party, without withdrawing its long-term Socialist objectives, was proclaiming its immediate policy to be, not Socialism, but 'in the line of advance towards Socialism', and was announcing that its programme would be 'experimental rather than doctrinaire'. It was, indeed, beginning, despite the left-wing record of most of its leaders, to convert itself into the advocate of an advanced 'welfare state' policy in the hope of winning back the support of those large sections of public opinion which it had lost during the years of intense industrial militancy before the war.

On the left there was considerable opposition to the Government's war policy, and during the latter part of the war period, a growth of actual anti-war feeling, especially in what was left of the pre-war left-wing Federation of Labour. After the Russian Revolution there was a considerable circulation of Marxist and Bolshevik pamphlets and periodicals ; and from 1919 onwards, as in Australia, small groups in sympathy with

[1] For Holland's earlier career, see Vol. III, Part II, pp. 870 and 900.

the Comintern made their appearance. In 1915 the miners, formerly a leading unit of the Federation of Labour, seceded from it and became a section of the Australian Miners' Federation, leaving the Federation of Labour at its last gasp. War, however, brought full employment, and the Trade Unions got back some of their strength ; and in 1919 a new central body, called the Alliance of Labour, was set up to take the Federation's place. The scattered Communist groups came together in 1921 to form a Communist Party, at first attached to that of Australia, with which it remained in association until 1928, when it was at length admitted to affiliation to the Comintern as an independent section. It remained small throughout the period covered in this chapter.

In 1922 the post-war economic depression struck New Zealand. The Government cut the wages of public employees, and the Arbitration Court awarded a series of drastic reductions. Unemployment reappeared on a large scale among the industrial workers ; and, in the absence of any system of public provision for those out of work, severe distress became widespread in the towns. There were considerable strikes of seamen and of miners in 1923, and of railwaymen the following year, ending in defeat. Thereafter conditions improved for a while ; but serious unemployment set in again in 1926. Holland, the Labour Party leader, died in 1923, and his place was taken by Peter Fraser (1884–1950), who in 1926 introduced into Parliament an Unemployed Bill providing for the right to work or maintenance out of funds to be supplied partly from the budget and partly from a levy on employers of £2 for each worker employed ; but, of course, this Bill stood no chance of acceptance by the Parties in power.

From 1926 onwards the employment situation remained bad right up to and through the world economic depression of the early 'thirties, which, of course, made it a great deal worse. Farm prices fell off sharply, and serious balance of payments difficulties afflicted the New Zealand economy. In order to deal with the growing crisis, the Government resorted to stringent deflationary measures and set to work to cut down public expenditure to the lowest possible level. Industrial employers and farmers alike resorted to heavy wage-cuts, and both public and private relief payments were drastically reduced. Public works, too, were restricted to a bare minimum, despite the large numbers who had been thrown out of work. The employers, who had hitherto mostly supported the arbitration system, turned against it on the ground that it was failing to reduce wages to the levels at which the unemployed were prepared to accept work. They demanded the right to cut wages as they thought fit without any interference from the State ; and the Government yielded to them by making resort to the Arbitration Court voluntary instead of compulsory. Presently it became unavoidable to introduce a regular system of relief for the starving unemployed ; but the Government, now in the hands of the United Party which had emerged from the earlier Liberal Party, insisted on the principle that no payments should be made except in return for work done, and that even such payments should be at the barest subsistence level. One effect of this was that great numbers of workless persons were set to work on almost useless jobs, carried out with the minimum amount of capital equipment in order to set as many as possible to some sort of labour, no matter how unsuitable or uneconomic it might be. This led many employers, particularly on the farms, to discharge their regular workers in order to get back their services as 'relief' workers at very much lower rates. A sort of Speenhamland system of poor relief grew up, with devastating effects on wage-rates and morale. In 1928 the Government called together a National Industrial Conference, at which the employers pressed for the abolition of state arbitration, but also agreed that something must be done to organise a general system of relief for the unemployed. The Government also set up an Unemployment Committee, including a minority of Trade Unionists, to consider what should be done ; and this body, reporting in 1930, produced a scheme for financing relief mainly by means of a poll-tax on all adult men and women, supplemented by a tax of one penny in the £1 on all incomes above £200 and on undistributed profits and by a very small tax on land, to take account of the fact that farmers did not pay taxes on income. The Committee rejected the proposal to introduce contributory unemployment insurance, on the ground that it would impose too heavy a burden on industry if employers were required to contribute. The Government thereupon brought in a Bill providing for a poll-tax of 30/- on all males over twenty years of age, but omitting the other taxes recommended by the Committee and substituting for them a subsidy from general taxation. The fund was to be used mainly in providing work ; but subsistence allowances were to be paid, as far as funds allowed, to men for whom no jobs could be found. Women were excluded altogether, both from the poll-tax and from receiving benefits under the scheme.

This Bill became law just before the full impact of the world depression fell on New Zealand. In face of it, the Government intensified its deflationary measures, and the proposal to grant sustenance payments without work was dropped for the time being. It is to be doubted whether any advanced country treated its unemployed as badly as New Zealand during the years of acute depression. In 1931 the Alliance of Labour called together a general Trade Union Conference for the purpose of organising concerted resistance to wage-reductions, and at this meeting demands were put forward for a general refusal to pay rents and for a general strike ; but most of the Unions were too conscious of their weakness to consider such a plan, and nothing was achieved. The Trade Union movement was still split between the Alliance, representing the more militant groups, and the old local Trades and Labour Councils, the defenders of the arbitration system ; and all attempts to achieve unity between the two failed until some years later, when the worst of the depression was over. Then, in 1935, just after the Labour Party had won the General Election and taken over the Government, a formal unity was achieved in the shape of a new general Federation of Labour ; but there was a renewed left-wing split the following year.

The intense sufferings through which the people of New Zealand, including the small farmers and the blackcoats as well as the industrial workers, passed during these years of deflation and depression had a marked effect both on the Labour Party, which was forced to concentrate its attention on working out a general reform policy, and on the attitude of small farmers, traders, and black-coated workers towards the Party. The sharply deflationary policy of the Government and the inhuman treatment meted out to those who were forced to seek relief, even on the most humiliating terms, brought over a large body of middle opinion to support of the Labour Party, which moved a long way from its earlier standpoint to meet and to attract recruits. These shifts of opinion and policy carried the Labour Party to victory in the General Election of 1935, and set New Zealand, hitherto so backward in the field of social legislation, on the road to the creation of a Welfare State with a remarkably advanced programme of social security and state control over private enterprise in the interests of economic stability. These achievements, however, fall outside the period dealt with in this volume. From 1914 to 1935 the New Zealand Labour and Socialist movements had remained too badly dislocated by the defeats of the years immediately before the world war and by the isolation that was the penalty of their break with the predominant farming interests to be able to take any effective action for the protection of wages and conditions — much less, for any advance in a Socialist direction. Gradually, during this period of adversity, they had been reshaping and developing their forces ; and the recovery had been much greater in the political than in the industrial field. Under stress of unemployment and depression the Labour Party had been feeling its way towards the new policy which, from 1935 onwards, it proceeded to carry into effect. In this policy Socialism, or outright socialisation, was to play only a minor part, though the men who were chiefly responsible for it were largely those who had been on the eft wing in their younger days. In a sense, they had been chastened by experience ; they had become convinced that the first task was to put an end to the sharp suffering that the workers had been crushed under during the long period of reactionary rule. Accordingly, they shaped their policy to fit the immediate conditions and, if they gave no clearly Socialist lead, were able to effect a remarkable and rapid transformation in the condition of the people and to bring back, on a changed basis of Labour Party leadership, something like the old Radical alliance of which John Ballance had been the outstanding pioneer.

CHAPTER XXIX

SOCIALISM AND THE RIGHTS OF WOMEN, 1914–1931

URING the period covered in this volume a far-reaching transformation occurred in the political status of women. This change took place in many countries, and extended a long way outside the field in which it was manifested in the most spectacular way — that of the right to vote. Up to 1914 votes had been conceded to women in only a very few countries which practised parliamentary government. New Zealand had been the pioneer, in 1893, followed by Australia in 1902, by Finland in 1907, and by Norway in 1913. Finland had been the first country in which women had not only voted but had also been elected in substantial numbers to the successive Diets chosen between 1907 and 1914. In all the principal countries, however, women were still, up to 1914, denied the right to vote in parliamentary elections, despite the existence in some of them of large-scale agitations for women's suffrage with a long history behind them — especially in the United States and in Great Britain. The British movement for the emancipation of women, social as well as political, went back to the latter part of the eighteenth century, Mary Wollstonecraft having published her book, *A Vindication of the Rights of Women*, in 1792. From that time onwards the question of women's rights was continually under discussion, which spread to the United States early in the nineteenth century. In both Great Britain and the United States women played some part in early Radical and Socialist movements. In America the movement took shape in the Women's Rights Convention held at Seneca Falls, New York, in July 1848, and achieved its first success when, in 1869, the women of Wyoming received the vote on the same terms as men. Colorado followed Wyoming's lead in 1893, and Utah and Idaho in 1896 ; but the women of the United States were not enfranchised in federal elections until 1920. In Great Britain, when the Second Reform Act became law in 1867, it was claimed that the term 'men' used in the Act included women, and many women were actually registered as voters; but the following year the law courts disallowed the claim. When the franchise was further extended in 1884, women were still excluded, and remained so until 1918, when those over 30 years of age were at length given the vote. Ten years later voting rights were extended to all women on the same terms as men. The struggle for Votes for Women had reached its height in Great Britain during the years from 1906 to 1914, when Mrs. Emmeline Pankhurst (1858–1928) earlier a prominent figure in the I.L.P. in Manchester, was at the head of the militant suffrage movement organised by the Women's Social and Political Union. The W.S.P.U. had been founded in 1903, in opposition to the older movement led by Mrs. Millicent Garrett Fawcett, which was accused by Mrs. Pankhurst of giving exclusive attention to the claims of middle-class women and of being ineffective because it limited itself to strictly legal forms of pressure. Many Socialists attached themselves to the new militant movement; but before long Mrs. Pankhurst fell foul of the Labour Party, which, though solid in support of the women's claims to equal treatment, was not prepared as a body to endorse Mrs. Pankhurst's demand that the women's question should be given absolute priority over all others, or to support the violent methods adopted by the 'suffragettes'. The W.S.P.U., like its predecessor, became, in practice, mainly a middle-class movement; so much so that a section of it in East London broke away under the leadership of Sylvia Pankhurst, one of Mrs. Pankhurst's daughters, and became the East End Federation of Suffragettes, with a predominantly working-class following and appeal which led it, after changing its name to Workers' Socialist Federation, to become one of the constituents of the British Communist Party in 1920 and to incur Lenin's disapproval as guilty of 'infantile left deviation'. Long before this, the main body of the W.S.P.U. had suffered a number of other splits, provoked mainly by the autocratic leadership practised in it by Mrs. Pankhurst and her eldest daughter, Christabel. When war broke out in 1914, Mrs. Pankhurst and the W.S.P.U. gave vehement support to the war effort, and transferred their main efforts to recruiting women for the war services and for work on munitions, claiming the vote as a reward for the services rendered by women during the years of warfare. They received their reward in the Representation of the People Act, 1918, and women of 30 and upwards voted in the General Election of that year, and played their part in the immense victory of the Lloyd George Coalition over the Labour Party.[1] In the new Labour Party, however, membership was open to women on the same terms as men ; and the Party gave solid support to the enfranchisement of women, though the final enfranchisement Act of 1928, which removed the discrimination against the younger women, was passed by a Conservative Government.

In all the belligerent countries the war caused a great increase in the employment of women, above all in industrial occupations, and led to a great development of women's participation in many branches of social and economic activity. Many women replaced men who were called up for military service in Trade Union and Co-operative positions as well as in political party offices and in professional posts ; and by almost general consent the effects were satisfactory. Much was accomplished in the matter of breaking down irrational prejudices and thus preparing the way for an acceptance of equal citizenship. It would, however, be much too much to assert, as some have done, that women owed their enfranchisement in so many countries immediately after 1918 to the recognition of their war services, both because votes for women were won in neutral as well as in belligerent countries and because the movement for women's suffrage had been gaining ground very rapidly before the war. It may even be the case that in a number of countries conservative groups previously hostile to the extension of the franchise, finding themselves forced to give way to the claims of all adult males to be allowed to vote, acquiesced in the inclusion of women in the hope that they would provide, at any rate for some time to come, a preponderance of conservative voters, more susceptible than the men to religious influence. At all events, by the end of 1920 the number of States in which women had been granted the right to vote in parliamentary elections had risen from the four

[1] See p. 412.

of 1914 to 28, not including Russia, where the institutions established by the Revolution were based on complete sex equality in every sphere of life. The principal countries in which women were still denied the right to vote after 1920 were France, Italy, Spain, and Switzerland, and also Belgium, where women had the right to be elected, but not, save in a limited number of special cases, the right to vote. The German and Austrian Revolutions had established full equality of political rights ; and so had the Constitutions of the new States set up after the collapse of Austria-Hungary, e.g. Poland and Czechoslovakia, though in Hungary, as in Great Britain, only women over 30 years of age were allowed to vote. In France, Italy, and Belgium women had to wait for the concession of parliamentary voting rights until after the second world war ; but Switzerland is now the only important parliamentary country in which they are still excluded, unless one counts Spain, where parliamentarism has been destroyed, after a brief interlude of universal suffrage under the Republican Constitution in the 1930s.

The Socialist movement clearly cannot claim to have been exclusively or even mainly responsible for the great changes that have come about in the relations of men and women since 1914. It can, however, be fairly claimed that the women received strong Socialist support for their demands for equal citizenship, and that, wherever Socialism held power, the principle of equal rights was energetically affirmed — most of all in Russia, but hardly less in the Scandinavian countries. The first woman to become a Cabinet Minister was the Dane, Nina Bang, who became Minister of Education in 1924. Women held minor office in the British Labour Government of that year, and in 1929 Margaret Bondfield entered the Labour Cabinet as Minister of Labour. In the Soviet Union women did not, in fact, play a large part in political leadership, the outstanding figure being Alexandra Kollontai, who occupied several important diplomatic posts. The other outstanding woman in Russia, Marie Spiridonova, the leader of the Left Social Revolutionaries, did not hold office in the short-lived Bolshevik-Left S.R. Coalition Government of 1917–1918. In the United States, the first woman to hold high political office was Frances Perkins, who was at the head of the Labour Department for twelve years under Franklin Roosevelt.

The Second International, during the pre-war period, had held, in connection with its own Congress, a sequence of International Conferences made up of women delegates from its affiliated sections ; and at these gatherings resolutions had been passed constituting a programme of demands for sex equality, as well as pledging the women members of the International to active work in the cause of peace. We saw earlier how, after the abandonment of the projected Vienna Congress in 1914, Clara Zetkin, as secretary of the Women's section of the International, succeeded in carrying on the arrangements for an International Conference of Socialist Women, which met in Switzerland in 1915 and issued pronouncements against the war and in favour of an immediate negotiated peace. No further Conference proved possible during the war years, but when the new Labour and Socialist International held its constituent Congress at Hamburg, a special Women's Conference was held in association with it, and at this gathering an International Committee of Socialist Women was set up, and was subsequently given a representative on the Executive Committee of the L.S.I. A similar Women's Conference was held in connection with the Marseilles Congress of 1925, and the Congress adopted unanimously a resolution, moved by Adelheid Popp of Austria, for the constitution of an international consultative committee of Socialist women, to be elected by the affiliated national Parties and to take charge, under the Executive Committee, of the organisation of an international women's conference to be held in connection with each Congress, and to be generally responsible for dealing with women's questions on the International's behalf. It was strongly insisted that there was no question of the women differing in policy or principle from the men, and that the women's committee should be chosen, not by the women alone, but by the Parties as representing men and women together ; and this arrangement satisfied those who were inclined to be suspicious of any form of organisation representing women as a separate group. Thereafter, Women's Conferences continued to be held regularly in connection with the Congresses of the L.S.I., and the Women's Consultative Committee played a recognised part in its work. An International Women's Day was regularly celebrated by large recruiting meetings and demonstrations in many of the leading countries. By the end of 1930 the number of women members affiliated to the L.S.I. had risen to over one million, and 65 women were recorded as members of various national Parliaments. In 1929 the Belgian Socialists, despite the inclusion in the Party Programme of a declaration in favour of equal voting rights for men and women, voted in the Senate against a Catholic Party proposal to extend the suffrage to women. This led to a sharp controversy inside the Party, and in 1931 the Party Congress not only reaffirmed the equal suffrage provision in the Programme, but also instructed its representatives to vote in favour of the Catholic proposal when it was reintroduced. Nothing, however, was accomplished in either Belgium or France until the conclusion of the second world war.

There were a number of questions on which sharp differences arose among and between the women's Socialist groups in the various countries, both nationally and in the Conferences of the L.S.I. For example, the women in the Scandinavian countries were for the most part opposed to special legislation for the protection of women workers, holding that protective laws should apply equally to both sexes, whereas most of the other Parties supported special measures for women, on the lines of existing factory legislation. Another hotly debated issue was that of birth control, which was strongly opposed by Catholics and by others who feared that support of it might split the working-class movement. In this matter, the British women took up a middle position, favouring the supply of birth control information by official medical and welfare agencies to those who wanted it, but refusing to pledge the Labour movement as a whole to either support of or opposition to birth control as a social policy. In general, however, these differences were not pushed to extremes ; and the Women's Section of the L.S.I. was able to adopt a common line on most of the questions debated at its Conferences. The Austrians and the Germans played a specially active part in this sphere of the International's activity, which was hampered by the weakness of the women's organisation in a number of countries, particularly in France and Italy. Adelheid Popp and Emmy

Freundlich, who was also President of the International Women's Co-operative Guild, were outstanding Austrian representatives ; from France the leading figure in the women's movement was Louise Saumonneau and from Great Britain Marion Phillips and A. Susan Lawrence, who held office in the Labour Government from 1929 to 1931.

CHAPTER XXX

CONCLUSION: COMMUNISM AND SOCIAL DEMOCRACY FROM 1914 TO 1931

I N my original plan for the fourth volume of my *History of Socialist Thought* I intended to cover the entire period from the outbreak of world war in 1914 to the renewed outbreak of 1939. Surely, I said to myself, a period of a quarter of a century is not too long, considering that both my first volume and my second had spans of more than forty years — broadly, from 1789 to 1850, and from 1850 to 1889. True, for the ensuing period of twenty-five years, from 1889 to 1914, I had needed to swell my third volume out to upwards of a thousand pages. As soon as I set to work to develop my plan in detail I found that my original plan would not do, because I could not, without losing the essential unity of treatment, cover in a single study both the Revolutions that accompanied and ensued upon the first world war and the period of counter-revolution and increasing international tension that set in with the world depression of the early 'thirties and the victory of Nazism in Germany. I therefore altered my plan and decided, after some hesitation, to make a break round about 1931, so as to take in only the earlier phases of the great depression and to concentrate attention on the consequences of the great Russian Revolution of 1917 in dividing the world Socialist movement into two bitterly contending factions between which it was very difficult for any intermediate or deviant bodies of opinion to survive, or at any rate to exert any powerful influence on the course of events.

The Second International, which ran its course from 1889 to its collapse in August 1914, did stand, despite the sharp conflicts of policy that arose within it, for a conception of Socialism as a single and fundamentally united world force. This unity, broken in 1914 in the field of organisation, disappeared in the realm of thought as well as of action as a consequence of the Bolshevik Revolution in Russia and of the appearance of Communism with its gospel of World Revolution on the Russian model. For the Communism of the Third International from 1919 onwards involved a deliberate and world-wide attempt to split the Socialist and working-class movements of all countries into sharply opposed factions contending for the allegiance of the workers, and led to the co-existence not only of rival Communist and anti-Communist Labour and Socialist Parties, but also of contending Trade Union movements and to perpetual conflicts inside the Trade Unions in every country. In these circumstances there was no longer even the shadow of a single world Socialist movement animated by a common purpose of overthrowing capitalism and setting up Socialism in its place. Instead of uniting to destroy capitalism, the rival Socialist movements became intent on fighting each other ; and those who attempted to stress what they had in common, in the hope of reuniting them, found their efforts everywhere thwarted by the zealots on both sides. In Communist eyes, the reformists, and presently the revolutionary 'deviationists' as well — that is, the so-called 'Trotskyists' — stood branded as 'social traitors', while, on the other side, the main body of these alleged 'traitors' loudly asserted that there could be no Socialism without 'democracy' — meaning by democracy, parliamentary government based on a structure of contending Parties and majority rule under conditions of universal suffrage and 'free' elections.

Accordingly, anyone who sets out to write the history of Socialism, in either thought or action, after 1917 has to study no longer a single movement or tendency, but at least two — at any rate, unless he is prepared to narrow his conception of Socialism by excluding completely either the one or the other. Such exclusion would be, in practice, very difficult ; for, whatever view the writer might take concerning the claims of either group to be a true inheritor of the common Socialist tradition, he would have to deal, in practice, both with the conflict between them and with the numerous Socialist trends that cannot be fully identified with either. Even if he were prepared, as I am not, to regard the developments of thought and action in the one-Party Communist States as standing right apart from anything properly to be called Socialism, he would have to deal with developments in other countries in which Communism has been in direct competition with non-Communist Socialism for the allegiance of the working classes and of the peasantry ; and he could present no balanced or adequate account of events or theories without discussing the relations between the two. However sharply different Communism and Social Democracy, or democratic Socialism, may be in their philosophies and methods of action, it is undeniable that they do have certain common elements — for example, advocacy of public ownership and control of the essential resources and instruments of production and a belief in the historic mission of the working class in bringing about the transition from capitalism to public enterprise. The question whether this is to be done by revolutionary seizure of power by the workers, or by a Party purporting to represent them, or by a peaceable conquest of power by parliamentary action under universal suffrage, however important it may be, cannot present itself in the same form in all countries ; for, on the one hand, not all possess the parliamentary institutions of self-government which the second of these methods presupposes, and, on the other, in some that do possess these institutions there is no real question of revolution by violence or of the resort to one-party dictatorship. It would have been nonsense to tell the Russian Socialists at the beginning of 1917 that they ought to proceed only by constitutional parliamentary methods ; and it would be no less nonsensical to offer the same advice to-day to Socialists in Saudi Arabia, or Siam, or certain countries of Latin America — or to Negro Socialists in the Union of South Africa. Equally it would be nonsense to urge the Socialists of the Scandinavian countries or of Great Britain or the U.S.A to direct their efforts towards a revolution for setting up a 'one-party' dictatorship of the proletariat — though neither of these absurdities has failed to find advocates ; for no limit can be set to the follies of which individuals are capable when they start generalising on the foundation of special cases which they mistake for matters of universal principle.

The historian of Socialism, as soon as he advances into the period that began with the first world war and the Russian Revolutions of 1917, has, then, in my view, no way of escape from including in his survey both Communism and Social

Democracy, and therewith all the variant trends that cannot be subsumed entirely under either of these ideologies. For both, and all the variants, are heirs of the older Socialist tradition, just as both Protestantism and Romanism are heirs of a formerly united Christendom, within which heresies and schisms existed long before the Reformation.

When the general approach has been thus settled, in favour of comprehensive treatment, the historian is still in a considerable difficulty because he has to deal, not, in the main, with past quarrels on which he can hope to pass tolerably objective and dispassionate judgments or can leave his readers to judge for themselves in the light of a reasonably objective statement of the facts, but with disputes that are very much alive and will necessarily arouse both his own passions and those of his readers : so that he can hardly hope to be given the credit for stating fairly both or all sides of the questions he needs to discuss. The recent past is so entangled with the present and the future that we are all prone to look at it with our own actual and prospective attitudes and conduct very much in our minds, and to read back into it conclusions derived from these sources. Thus, our judgments of the Bolshevik Revolution and of Lenin's part in it are apt to be coloured by our view of the Soviet Union of to-day ; and, on the other side, the views we take about the behaviour of parliamentary Socialists after 1918 are affected by our current attitudes towards the Parties of the Socialist International.

In relation to these matters I flatter myself that I am in a better position than many of my fellow-Socialists to be fair as between the two extreme views because I have never found myself able to accept either. I am strongly opposed, on grounds of principle, to the Communist doctrine of 'democratic centralism', which I regard as leading fatally towards centralised bureaucracy and as destructive of personal liberty and freedom of thought and action. But I am no less opposed to capitalism and to the grave social and economic inequalities it involves, and am quite unable to accept the view that it is illegitimate to take action against these wrongs except by constitutional, parliamentary means, even where such means are either unavailable or evidently ineffective. I am against violent revolution, or even unconstitutional action, where the road to fundamental change by constitutional means is effectively open to the people ; but I am unable to agree that democracy is a necessary pre-requisite of Socialism, if by 'democracy' is meant the exclusive use of parliamentary methods in countries where no tradition of parliamentary government in fact exists and there are no parliamentary institutions capable of being used to bring about the change to Socialism. This attitude has ranged me, throughout my adult life, among the adherents of left-wing non-Communist Socialism — a position which, in my own country, I might have found it very difficult to sustain had I been an active instead of an 'armchair' or academic politician. I have never, even for a moment, considered the possibility of becoming a Communist — the whole idea revolts me ; but I have often been deeply exasperated by what have seemed to me plain departures from Socialist principle by the Labour and Socialist Parties and movements of the West, and I have been determined never to be led by my hostility to Communism into any sort of alliance against it with the declared enemies of Socialism. This has often placed me in a somewhat isolated position, which I have been able to endure the less uncomfort-ably because I have never allowed myself to become an active participant in politics, save as a writer fortunate enough to live in a country where I have been able to speak my mind freely. I have thus been in a position to watch, and within these self-imposed limits to take part in, the conflicts of opinion without becoming at all deeply involved in them as a spokesman of any particular party or faction, though I have been a member of the Labour Party for nearly fifty years and have held office first in the Guild Socialist movement and thereafter, for the past quarter of a century, in the reorganised Fabian Society and New Fabian Research Bureau. I am not suggesting that this need enable me to be impartial, or even objective, in reviewing the history of Socialism during the period studied in this volume ; but I do think it gives me some advantage over those who have been drawn entirely into the orbit of either Com-munism or parliamentary Social Democracy of the Western kind.

The epoch of Socialist history covered in the present volume is that in which, largely as an outcome of the first world war, Communism developed as a world-wide challenger, on the one hand, of capitalist imperialism and of the existing social order, and, on the other, of every sort of reformist or moderate evolutionary Socialism. This double challenge continues to-day ; but it assumed, in my view, a new and different form when Fascism, in its German shape as Nazism, came to power in Germany in the midst of the great world depression of the early 'thirties. Fascism, to be sure, had conquered Italy well before that, and Fascist tendencies had emerged in a number of other countries — for example, in Hungary and in the Balkans — not to mention China. It became, however, a world danger only with the rise of Hitler ; for only in his hands did it become a third force challenging on a world scale both Socialism and Communism on the one hand and capitalist parliamentarism on the other, and thus raise the issue whether it was properly to be regarded as a new, and perhaps final, form of imperialist capitalism or as an altogether different creed and way of life. My own view, from the first, was that the latter view was the more correct, and that the world of men was faced with an inescapable challenge against which it was need-ful to array every opponent who could be enlisted in the struggle : so that, for the time being, resistance to Fascism became an even more urgent matter than the attempt to over-turn capitalism. It was no doubt a foregone conclusion that many capitalists, above all in Germany, would take sides with the Nazis and would endeavour to use them to serve capitalist ends ; but this, to my mind, by no means proved that Nazism was simply a form of capitalism. It appeared to me as a thing fundamentally different and likely, if it prevailed, to sub-ordinate capitalism to its own gospel of militarism and racial superiority — a much worse enemy of human decency and progress in the art of living.

This conviction that Fascism was not, and is not, simply capitalism in its last stage of open war upon the workers, but was, and is, a third force in its own right, or rather its own wrong, played its part in my decision to stop short, in the present volume, of Hitler's assumption of power in Germany and to leave over for separate treatment both the anti-Fascist struggle of the 1930s and the repercussions of Fascism on the course of events and on modes of political thinking in the Soviet Union, so as to be able to concentrate attention on the development of Socialist thought between the Revolutions of

1917 and the next few years and the appearance of the Fascist challenge in a clearly recognisable form. I have therefore been mainly concerned in the present volume, first with these revolutionary upsets and with their effects in disrupting the unity of Socialism and of the working-class movement, and thereafter with the fortunes of Socialism, including for this purpose Communism and its allies, in the post-war world up to the onset of the great depression. This, I am well aware, involves breaking the record off, in relation to some countries, at an inconvenient point; but the countries to which this applies are not, for the most part, those to which attention needs to be mainly directed at the stage with which I am now concerned. The division between the 'twenties and the 'thirties serves well enough, not only for Germany and for most of Western Europe, including Great Britain, but also for the United States, where the depression and the Roosevelt New Deal sharply mark off the 1930s from the preceding decade, and also, I believe, for the Soviet Union, where Stalinism came to embody a radically different attitude from that of Lenin, or of Trotsky, even if this attitude was grafted upon Leninist roots.

I begin my story, then, after a preliminary chapter dealing with the impact of war on the Socialist movement in its international aspect, with the Russian Revolutions and with their impact on Socialism as a factor in world affairs. At this point, the essential point to grasp is that the Bolsheviks thought of their Revolution, not as a local or national substitution of a Socialist for a capitalist-imperialist régime, but as the first decisive step in a World Revolution to be made in its image by the workers in all other countries, and, above all, in the first instance, over the whole of Europe, with Germany as the key-point for its extension to the more advanced capitalist countries. They believed that the Revolution was destined by historic necessity to extend itself in this way, and that, unless it did so, their own local Revolution could not survive, though they were confident that, even if it were defeated for the time, it would rise again as it had done after the disasters of 1905-6. They therefore used every means in their power of fomenting revolution in other countries — above all in Germany — and of leading the revolutionary forces in Germany and elsewhere into compliance with their own conceptions, derived from what they themselves had achieved, of the correct way of making a revolution, with very little allowance either for the widely different situations in which Socialists and Trade Unionists were placed in other countries or for the different traditions that had developed in the various national working-class movements. Immensely proud of their own achievements — and prouder still when these had held firm against the interventions of the great capitalist powers — they called upon other countries to show their admiration for the Soviet example by following it as nearly as possible to the letter and by discarding utterly every tradition of working-class and Socialist behaviour that stood in the way of close imitation of the Bolshevik model. Had not they succeeded in making the Socialist Revolution while in other, far more advanced, countries the working class, that should have taken the lead, had lagged ignominiously behind and had allowed itself to be driven to internecine butchery by the capitalist war-makers? Surely the evident task of Socialists throughout the world was to make up for lost time and carry through their own Bolshevik Revolutions, or, where they could not, at any rate make as much trouble as possible for their own ruling classes and thus divert them from mobilising their resources for the overthrow of the Soviet Union. To the Russian Bolsheviks, such action seemed a plain matter of duty and loyalty to the country that had given so momentous and inspiring a lead. 'He that is not with us is against us', seemed the evident moral to be drawn.

This was the principle on which the Bolsheviks, face to face with the immense threat of counter-revolution at home, set to work deliberately to split the world Socialist movement. That, of course, is not how they put the matter to themselves. Their purpose, as they saw it, was not to split the workers but to detach them from their traitorous leaders who were betraying the revolutionary cause. In their view, every worker was a potential revolutionary, and could be prevented from becoming one actually only by being cajoled and led astray by false guides. The future, as they envisaged it, was one, not of rival revolutionary and reformist working-class movements contending for victory, but of a single revolutionary movement face to face only with a discredited handful of reformist leaders deserted by their former mass following. The Communists of the Soviet Union, and, under their influence, the Communist International, set out with a prodigious confidence in their power to convert the masses to their point of view. Historic necessity, they were sure, was on their side — and not only that, for the very success of their own Revolution showed that the time was ripe for others. Accordingly there could be no real question of a split that would weaken the working class by dividing it against itself. The right-wing leaders would speedily be left without followers, and would no longer matter. The real danger came from the Centrists — from those who opposed the right wing but refused to accept the Communist gospel — for they might for a time succeed in leading a section of the workers astray, though the 'contradictions' inherent in their attitude would prevent them from following any really constructive policy. In the long run they, too, were doomed to forfeit their influence; but in the short run they might attract enough support to check the spread of World Revolution. Therefore they must be fought against, even more bitterly than the right-wing leaders, by every device that could be used to undermine their influence upon the mainly well-meaning but muddle-headed workers who mistook their fine words for real revolutionary intentions.

In this spirit the Comintern drew up its Twenty-one Points, with the primary purpose of excluding all those groups which, moved by sympathy for the Bolshevik Revolution, were desirous of entering into fraternal relations with it without completely endorsing the Russian methods as applicable over all the world. In this spirit the leaders of the Comintern, urged on by Zinoviev and by the Russian Communist Party, set to work to destroy Longuet's Minoritaires (now become a majority) in France, Friedrich Adler and Otto Bauer in Austria with their Two-and-a-Half International, Serrati's all but completely Communist faction in Italy, the I.L.P. in Great Britain, and, most of all, the U.S.P.D. in Germany. What is more, they, for the most part, succeeded in this work of destruction. The U.S.P.D. was torn asunder, and its defeated minority driven into reunion with the right-wing S.P.D.; the Vienna International was forced into reunion with the revived Second International; the French Socialist Party was captured for Communism, and the Centrist group forced back into reunion with the right wing ; and in Italy the entire Socialist movement was so disrupted as to open the door to Fascism and to overwhelm both Communists and anti-Communists in a common disaster. As to the World Revolution, it failed to happen. The Soviet Republic in Hungary was speedily overthrown and gave place to the Horthy White Terror ; the Bavarian Soviet Republic barely existed long enough to be destroyed ; the German Communist Revolution proved a dismal failure ; and in Great Britain and most of the other countries of Western Europe — not to mention the United States — no revolutionary movement of any significance ever came into being at all. Judged by the standard of its early hopes and aspirations, the Communist International was an egregious failure. Instead of leaving the right wing isolated and shorn of followers, it presented them with a large part of the former Centrist groups. Instead of bringing about World Revolution, it helped, by dividing the Socialist and working-class forces, to bring about the triumph of Fascism, first in Italy and then in Germany and over most of Eastern Europe. It became evident even to the Russians that they had grossly miscalculated the revolutionary potentialities of the world working class and that it was necessary, not indeed to revise their fundamental doctrine, but to accept the need to wait until the still confidently expected crisis of world capitalism arrived and gave rise to a renewed outburst of revolutionary feeling.

Thus, Communist thinking about the future came to be dominated more and more by the idea that world capitalism, though it had somehow managed to reconstruct itself after the dislocations of war, *must* be rapidly approaching its 'final crisis', just as Marx and Engels had believed it to be forty years earlier, when the great depression of the 1870s was on the way. That crisis, indeed, had proved to be by no means 'final', and had given rise, not to any outburst of revolutionary action, but rather to the rise of a number of Social Democratic Parties which followed an increasingly unrevolutionary line. The 'next time', however, was bound to be quite different. In it, world capitalism would dissolve through sheer inability to keep the wheels turning ; and the masses would everywhere turn to revolution as the only way of escape. Hope and confidence were thus but deferred, and not abandoned ; and in the meantime the quintessential duty of all good Socialists was to protect the Soviet Union against its enemies, and of the rulers of the Soviet Union to demonstrate what had been previously regarded as impracticable — the establishment of 'Socialism in one country' as the model for the rest to imitate as soon as the next crisis made the time ripe.

This change of orientation, without any change in fundamental ideas, took place during the 1920s well ahead of the arrival of the crisis and, *a fortiori*, of the advent of the Nazis to power on the ruins of the Weimar Republic. It did not involve, at that stage, any fundamental revision of the Communist world outlook, though it did require an altered strategy for the Communists *in partibus infidelium*. These had to adapt themselves to a waiting policy, while standing constantly ready to rally to the Soviet Union's defence. Till the crisis came they had to do their best to combat right-wing or reformist tendencies in the Labour movements of their own countries, to win influence in the Trade Unions, and, where possible, to get themselves accepted as allies by the organisations whose leaders they intended to stab in the back at the first convenient chance. This was not an easy path to tread ; but in view of the necessary postponement of the World Revolution and of the primary obligation to defend the Soviet Union under all circumstances, no other was left open. The situation changed only when the onset of the world economic crisis and the conquest of Germany by the Nazis enforced a new line. For the crisis brought with it, not a wave of revolutionary fervour, but counter-revolution in Germany and elsewhere and, in the countries accustomed to parliamentary government, a serious temporary weakening of the working-class movement, especially in the Trade Union field, but also in that of politics. In Great Britain the eclipse of the Labour Government, though it resulted in a temporary leftward shift of working-class opinion, left the movement in a much weakened state from which it could make only a slow recovery ; and in the United States the New Deal, though followed by a great expansion of Trade Unionism into the hitherto unconquered fields of the mass-production industries, entirely failed to restore American Socialism even to the modest level it had reached in the first decade of the twentieth century.

CONCLUSION : COMMUNISM AND SOCIAL DEMOCRACY

Not only did the World Revolution, despite the widespread distress engendered by the depression, soon appear to be as far off as ever in the great capitalist countries : it had also now to face a new and plainly ruthless enemy who had no respect for the traditions of civilised behaviour that had served hitherto to modify the intensity of class conflict in the more advanced capitalist countries. It therefore became necessary for the Communists, if only in order to help in protecting the Soviet Union against the Fascist danger, to seek allies where they could, and, instead of repelling everyone who was not prepared to accept the entire Communist gospel, to call out loudly for the 'United Front' against Fascism. True, this was still a change only of 'party line', and not of basic attitude ; for the 'United Front' the Communists wanted was one that would enable them to take the lead and, as far as possible, to dominate the other groups with which they felt the need to co-operate in the anti-Fascist crusade. Where, however, as in Great Britain, they commanded only a tiny following of their own, and the achievement of the 'United Front' would have left them in a hopeless minority, their aim was in reality not so much to form a single front with their working-class opponents as to appeal to those very Centrist elements which they had previously denounced most of all, and also to win over as many as possible of the rootless intellectuals and students who were appalled by the irrationalism and brutality of the Nazi gospel. The 'thirties thus became the epoch of the 'fellow-travellers' who, eager to take part in the anti-Fascist struggle, rallied to the Communists as the most vocal and forthright enemies of Fascism without much regard for the niceties of Communist doctrine and in many cases without any real understanding of what it involved. Such recruits were the more easily gullible about what went on in the Soviet Union under Stalin because they had so little to go by in testing what they were told to believe and wished to believe, because belief seemed to rank them on the correct side in the contemporary struggle.

There is never, I know, a really good case for deceiving oneself or for allowing oneself to be deceived. There was, however, in the 1930s an eminently good case for putting the struggle against Fascism a long way ahead of all other issues. In the 1920s, on the other hand, it was a good deal harder to know what came first — at any rate after the immediate danger of armed intervention in Russia by the Western powers had disappeared. As the New Economic Policy began to yield evident results, many who were by no means Communists had high hopes of the Soviet Union, whose economic and social planning, in their earlier stages, seemed to be having remarkable success even before the launching of the first Five-Year Plan. There were many who looked forward to a relaxation of totalitarian control as the more desperate economic shortages were overcome, and hoped that the Soviet Union would settle down to a form of Socialism not too incompatible with Western notions of the value of personal freedom and political democracy. There was, especially among the younger people, in the West as well as elsewhere, a strong desire to admire the Soviet Union and to make the most of its really remarkable economic and educational achievements. There was even, in some un-expected quarters, a tendency to admire the Communist Party for the devoted service given by its members and to contrast the looseness of the bonds holding together the adherents of Western Socialist Parties with the rigorous discipline of the Communists — greatly to the disadvantage of the former. The Webbs, with their massive study, *Soviet Communism, a New Civilisation?* (1935), later became the most vocal spokesmen of this attitude. In the 'twenties and early 'thirties the Soviet Union was wide open to tourists from many countries, most of whom, even if they were critical of the totalitarian aspects, came back with strong praise of the economic and educational progress that was being made.

It is, no doubt, possible to argue that many Socialists who, in the 1920s, expressed admiration for the economic and social achievements of the Soviet Union were not really moved by admiration of these achievements, but were in a mood to admire whatever the Soviet Union achieved, irrespective of its real quality. It was, of course, bound to be evident to any visitor or to any student who really studied the facts that the Soviet Union was a very poor country and that its standards of living were immensely inferior to those of the capitalist West. What was admired was thus not the level of achievement actually reached either economically or socially, but rather the immense effort that was being made to improve the economy and to diffuse education widely among the people — or at any rate to develop advanced industrial techniques and to provide social services and education for the rapidly developing urban working class. To such admirers it was almost irrelevant how low the actual standards were : what counted was the effort to raise them, and, in doing so, to consolidate the Revolution and make the Soviet Union strong enough to stand up against the danger of capitalist encirclement and presently to rival and surpass the standards of the advanced capitalist countries. It is, of course, true that this was the spirit in which many Socialists deeply admired the Soviet Union — some of them even the more because life there seemed to offer the means of heroic living for an ideal which they failed to find in the Socialist movements of their own countries. The 'blood and sweat' of the Communist world, far from repelling such observers, stirred them to an admiration which the actual achievements did not then deserve in their own right. Only when the Soviet Union turned to mass collectivisation of the countryside, in an immense attempt to socialise the minds as well as the agricultural practices of the vast peasant population, did criticism spread from those who were actively hostile to the whole system and refused to see any good in it, to well-wishing observers who were appalled by the ruthlessness with which collectivisation was carried into effect, as well as upset by its consequences in the mass slaughter of animals and the evident mismanagement of many of the huge new state farming experiments. The great famine in the Ukraine and other areas, attributed to overhasty collectivisation as well as to harvest failure, did a good deal to alienate Western sympathy and to arouse a conflicting sympathy with the so-called *kulaks* who were the principal victims. Nevertheless, right up to 1939 much of the good-will created by the Revolutions of 1917 and the undoubted successes in industrial development remained in being among the working classes of the Western countries and among those who regarded the Soviet Union as the natural leader in the anti-Fascist struggle.

There were, however, by the later 'twenties, vigorous critics of the Soviet Union among Communists as well as among those who were offended by Russian ruthlessness in carrying policies into effect. From the moment when Trotsky was deposed from power, or at any rate from the moment when he was driven out of Russia, his views found support among minority groups in many countries. Not until later did 'Trotskyism' become an opprobrious label employed to blacken almost any dissident Communist who found himself opposed to Stalinist discipline on any ground; but the early Trotskyists, who mostly were followers of Trotsky rather than simply opponents of Stalin, soon began to exert some disruptive influence on the monolithic discipline required from foreign Communists by the Comintern. It was natural that in many cases these groups should make common cause with other dissidents who had fallen out yet earlier with the official policies — for example, with Industrial Unionists and other left-wingers who had been partisans of democratic workers' control. The Comintern at the beginning had set out to draw into its ranks the Industrial Unionist, Syndicalist, and shop stewards' movements that in various countries had been in rebellion against the established Socialist Parties; and it had succeeded in assimilating some of these elements and in getting them to accept the doctrine that the Trade Unions should be firmly subjected to Communist Party control. There were, however, among them not a few natural rebels against discipline who found the conception of 'democratic centralism' not at all to their taste. In the Soviet Union such rebels were speedily and ruthlessly liquidated or exiled; but in other countries they were beyond the reach of the Party and could be pursued only with virulent abuse. Some of them were Anarchists and carried on their propaganda in the little Anarchist groups that have continued to exist in almost every country. Others, for example in the United States, set up short-lived dissident Communist Parties or societies; and some of them were later active in the large-scale investigation of the Trotsky affair over which the educationist John Dewey presided. None, however, of these factions was able to establish itself on any considerable scale, though in the 'thirties Trotskyist Parties made their appearance even in some Asian countries. There was never really room for a rival Communist movement to build itself up in opposition to the disciplined influence of the Comintern with its Russian backing. There could be no more than 'splinters' quarrelling both with everyone else and among themselves and ineffective because they had no means of getting a hearing beyond quite narrow circles.

From the very moment when the great dispute between Stalin and Trotsky came to a head, it was exceedingly difficult to discover what the real substance of the quarrel was. It began largely, as we saw,[1] with Trotsky's well-merited attack on the bureaucratisation of the Communist Party under Stalin's influence. But it speedily ranged over a much wider field and became bewildering when Stalin appeared, within a few years of the breach, to be carrying into effect some of the policies of which Trotsky had been a leading advocate. It was Trotsky who had been among the first to stress the danger of yielding too much to the peasants and the imperative need to press on rapidly with industrialisation in order to strengthen the industrial working class. But it was Stalin who launched both the first Five-Year Plan, with its heavy stress on industrial development, and the policy of agricultural collectivisation, which aimed both at releasing surplus labour for industry and at converting the peasant into something analagous to an industrial worker. It is true that Trotsky, as the exponent of the doctrine of 'Permanent Revolution', had been foremost in urging that the Revolution could survive in Russia only if it could be expanded into World Revolution ; whereas Stalin soon made himself the leading exponent of the idea of 'Socialism in One Country'. This at any rate was a real difference, based in Stalin's case on a clearer recognition that the prospects of early revolution in the advanced capitalist countries had disappeared, if they had ever really existed. This difference, however, though of fundamental importance for the shaping of Soviet policy after the middle 'twenties, falls far short of explaining the ferocity with which the Soviet Communist Party and the Comintern pursued everyone who could be accused of taking Trotsky's side or of acting under his influence. It became more and more apparent that the real issue was between the monolithic conception of so-called 'democratic centralism', which meant in effect the domination of the entire Communist movement from a single centre by the ruling clique of the C.P.S.U., and the rival conception of a movement acting, no doubt, under severe central discipline, but arriving at its

[1] See p. 572.

policies by way of free discussion among the party activists —
free, that is to say, within the Party up to the moment when the
vital decisions were actually made. This continued to be the
really fundamental issue ; but it was largely hidden from view
beneath the mass of other controversial issues that had to be
faced, and even more beneath the weight of indiscriminate
abuse with which the Stalinists belaboured their critics and
befouled Trotsky's name — when they did not suppress it
altogether.

While these disputes were gathering force within the Communist movement, the Centrists, as we saw, were being ground
to powder between the upper and nether millstones of reformist
Socialism and of revolutionary Communism. The Centre, as
it existed in 1919, after the great war was over, was in a position
of growing difficulty. Its main strength was in the countries in
which Social Democracy had been a powerful force before the
war — above all in Germany, in Austria, and in Italy. In relation to other Socialist factions it was strongest of all in Austria,
no longer the capital of a multi-national empire, but a small,
almost wholly German State facing prodigious economic
difficulties and forbidden by its conquerors to seek a remedy
in reunion with the new German Republic. On the face of the
matter the most surprising fact about post-war Austria is the
failure of the Communists to make any substantial breach
in the unity of the Social Democratic Party. The Austrian
workers, entrenched in 'Red' Vienna and a few lesser industrial strongholds, remained almost solidly faithful to the old
Party and, during the first years of the Republic, were able to
dominate political affairs. But as soon as there had been
time for the anti-Socialists to reorganise their forces after the
upsets of the Austrian Revolution, it became plain that the
Socialists, however firm their control of Vienna, could not
command a majority in the whole country and had to choose
between coalition with their chief opponents, the Christian
Socials, at the cost of giving up their hopes of turning Austria
into a Socialist country, and renouncing their share in governmental power at the centre in order to preserve their independence and be able to carry on their propaganda unfettered by
any alliance with the political right. Nor was this merely a
choice for the moment ; for the little Austria of the post-war

settlement was, in fact, so made up as to institute a lasting conflict between the overgrown capital, Vienna, and the agricultural part of the country, on which the Socialists were unable to make any effective impression. At the outset there existed within the Christian Social Party a progressive peasant element with which the Socialists found it not too difficult to work. But the weight of the Catholic Church was thrown powerfully against this group ; and to the right of the Christian Socials there were frankly reactionary groups that hated the Republic and dreamed dreams of liquidating the traitorous Marxists and the Jews and of either restoring the Hapsburgs or setting up a kingdom without a king on the model of Horthy's Hungary.

In face of this political stalemate the Austrian Socialists, unable to win a majority so as to govern the country, found themselves compelled to concentrate on making the most of their unshaken control of Vienna. There, in spite of prodigious economic difficulties, they wrought wonders in the development of social services, in care for the unemployed, in building their famous blocks of working-class flats and in keeping rent levels very low, and not least in the encouragement of popular culture. They were able to maintain these policies, thereby earning high praise from many foreign visitors as well as at home, right up to the point at which Austria, never economically viable, was struck to the ground by the great economic depression. Thereafter, the position of the Socialists grew steadily weaker, especially after Hitler's advent to power in Germany. In face of the increasing violence of the reactionary Heimwehr and of the control of the central government by the reactionary wing of the Christian Social Party, the Socialists were continually having to choose between making concessions in order to avoid civil war and taking a stand which was certain to lead them into a civil war that would mean the starvation of Vienna. They gave ground again and again, until at length the Christian Social Führer, Engelbert Dollfuss, aided by the Heimwehr, trampled the Democratic Republic in the dust, only for his régime to be overthrown a short while afterwards by the invading Nazis, who annexed Austria to the Third Reich. The latter part of this tragic history, however, belongs not to this volume but to its successor. What concerns us here is the fact that of all the Social Democratic Parties of post-war Europe, the Austrian seemed for a time the most constructive and the best representative of the non-Communist left.

On this account it was naturally subjected to the fiercest attacks from the Comintern and from the theorists of Communist orthodoxy. 'Austro-Marxism' became a term of bitter reproach among those who had marked down the Centrists as their most dangerous antagonists. The writings of Otto Bauer and Karl Renner about Socialism and the problem of nationalities, with their insistence on cultural nationalism, were caricatured and held up to obloquy by Stalin and his disciples. The Austrians were accused of being the enemies of true Marxism and of betraying the materialist gospel and following after the strange gods of Kantian and Machian Idealism, of traitorous failure to go to the help of Béla Kun's Hungarian Soviet Republic, and later of failing to make a stand against the march of reaction led by Seipel and Starhemberg. They did indeed, when their attempt to build a bridge between the Second and Third Internationals had definitely failed, transfer their allegiance to the new Labour and Socialist International which reunited the revived Second and what was left of their own 'Two-and-a-Half', the Vienna Union.[1] But what else were they to do? There could be no home for them in the utterly unaccommodating Comintern; and they were in no position to stand out alone. The precariousness of Austria's international situation and the political stalemate on the home front alike compelled them to seek allies where they could.

The other main supports of Centrism were in Germany and in France, and, in a rather different sense, in Italy. In both Germany and France the factor that had counted for most in building up the Centrist position was the growth of anti-war feeling. The Minoritaires in France, headed by Marx's grandson, Jean Longuet, and the German Independent Socialists — Haase, Ledebour, Dittmann, and the Berlin shop stewards led by Richard Müller — developed as the antagonists of the 'social patriots', advocates of war to the bitter end, who dominated the majority Socialist Parties. Both of them included at the outset many who subsequently became stalwarts of the French and German Communist Parties; but

[1] See p. 683.

both were dominated at the beginning by 'middle-of-the-road' Socialists and even included some who, apart from their pacifism, belonged essentially to the right wing. An outstanding example of this right-wing pacifism was the veteran Revisionist leader Eduard Bernstein, who soon left the U.S.P.D., and returned to the S.P.D., when the post-war issues came to the fore. There were analogous figures in the Independent Labour Party in Great Britain and in the Socialist Party in the United States. In the main, however, the Centrist Parties and groups did stand well to the left of the 'social patriots', but were by no means at one with the Communists, and were hoping to reunite the world working-class movement round a policy allowing for wide differences of application from country to country, rather than to split it into two rival factions. The so-called 'Two-and-a-Half' International did not set out to be an 'International' on its own account, but to serve as an agency for reuniting the Second and the Third.

In Germany, as we saw,[1] the U.S.P.D., after breaking away from the S.P.D. during the war and then, for a short time, participating with it in the Government set up in the Revolution of 1918, withdrew its Ministers and resumed its independence only to fall into the hands of the Communists at the Halle Congress of 1920. A large fraction, however, thereupon seceded and attempted to carry on the U.S.P.D. as a non-Communist independent Party ; but before long this Party found its position untenable amid the conflicts between the Communists and the S.P.D., and in 1922 most of the remaining U.S.P.D. adherents agreed to return to the S.P.D., leaving only a small group, headed by the veteran, Georg Ledebour, which, rejecting both Communism and the S.P.D., ceased to exert any political influence. Thus, in Germany, Centrism went out of action as an organised force, leaving the German movement to be disastrously undermined by the continual conflict between the Communists and the predominant right wing. It is easy, because of this eclipse, to declare that the U.S.P.D. failed, and deserved to fail, because it never had any clear or really common policy or programme, but was made up of widely divergent elements united only by their dislike of the Majority Socialists. This accusation is, indeed, quite largely

[1] See p. 143.

justified. The U.S.P.D. of the years between 1918 and 1920 was a somewhat incoherent grouping of discontented parliamentarians, shop stewards, and Socialist intellectuals, who were united in disapproval of the policies of Ebert and Scheidemann and still more of Noske, but ranged in their positive attitudes from a faith in parliamentary methods and in the Weimar Republic to a belief that the Revolution of 1918 had been left less than half finished, and that it was necessary to press on with it further by revolutionary action. After the Halle Congress the partisans of this latter view mostly passed over to the Communist Party, while the parliamentarians attempted to carry on the U.S.P.D. as a mere rump. Of the large numbers who stood somewhere between these two attitudes a great many dropped out altogether : so that Centrism, though surviving as an attitude, ceased to be effective as an organised body of opinion. In the light of after events, it became, I think, plain that the U.S.P.D. committed a fatal error in entering the Government in 1918 without assuring itself of any effective share in controlling it. When the U.S.P.D. Ministers realised their error and withdrew, it was too late : governmental power was already firmly in the hands of their opponents, and the Communist challenge, rather than theirs, became the effective point of focus for left-wing opposition. This was shown at the Halle Congress, which finally destroyed the possibility of any effectual Centrist movement in the Weimar Republic.

In France the course of events was different, but the outcome in some respects the same. There the anti-war Minoritaires had become the majority before the war ended, and it looked for a time as if the French Socialist Party, under Longuet's leadership, would emerge as a Centrist Party, within which the defeated 'social patriots' would be compelled to toe the line. In France, however, the propaganda of the Comintern was much more successful than it was in Germany, largely because it continued to carry with it the main body of left-wing Trade Union, or Syndicalist, opinion. Aided by these elements, the Communists were able to capture the Socialist Party Congress and to take over the machinery of the old Party, though not the majority of its parliamentary deputies. The consequence was that the anti-Communist parliamentarians, supported by the defeated minority of the party membership, set up a new Socialist Party in which the predominant influence was gained, not by the Centrists, but by the old right wing they had defeated in 1918. As in Germany, there were again two Parties — Social Democratic and Communist ; but whereas in Germany the Social Democrats were on top and enjoyed the main body of Trade Union support, in France the position was largely reversed. The French Communists came to be, not only the major political force, backed by a high proportion of the manual workers, but also, in due course, the predominant force in the Trade Union movement. In both countries Centrism was almost wiped out as an effective movement.

Yet the French and German situations were radically different, because Germany did pass through a Revolution, of a sort, whereas in France revolution was never, in the 1920s, even a remote possibility. This was, of course, mainly for the reason that France, in 1918, was already a democratic Republic with an ancient revolutionary tradition behind it, whereas Germany, up to the end of the war, was an autocratic military State, needing to throw out its Hohenzollerns and its petty princes both for their misdeeds and in order to placate the victorious Allies and to accommodate itself to the conditions of the post-war world. The Germans had to have a Revolution, whether they liked it or not : the French, emerging victorious from the war, had no need for one — or at all events, even if some of them were in theory revolutionaries who regarded the bourgeois Republic as their class-enemy, these elements were not at all minded to attempt its overthrow by forcible means. Accordingly there arose in France a remarkable situation, in which a powerful revolutionary movement existed without any real will to make a revolution. The consequence, disastrous ever since for French political affairs, has been the existence within the Republic of a strong Communist Party unable either to play a constructive part in carrying on the Republic or to take action against it — a virtual disfranchisement of a large part of the working class save during the short interval of the United Front experiment in the 1930s and the still briefer episode of coalition Government, including the Communists, after 1945.

In Italy, there is yet another different story, culminating in the destruction by Fascism of the entire Socialist and working-class movement — left, right and centre — all overtaken by a common disaster. At the time when the war ended the Italian Socialist Party, as we saw,[1] stood well to the left of the Socialist Parties of the other Allied countries, having consistently opposed the war and taken a leading part in the war-time attempts to rally the forces of international Socialism against it. Indeed, it can almost be said that the Italian Socialists were without a right wing, except in some of the Trade Unions, the old right wing having been expelled before 1914. Turati, who thereafter led the more moderate and constitutional wing of the Party, was in essence a Centrist rather than a right-winger in any ordinary sense of the term. The Italian Socialist Party immediately gave evidence of its sympathy with the Bolshevik Revolution, and lost no time in applying for admission to the Comintern.

There, however, the trouble began ; for the Italians, though desirous of joining the new International, were not, for the most part, minded to accept the rigid discipline which that body demanded, or to receive its orders as determining their behaviour. In particular, having secured the endorsement of the Party for an advanced left-wing policy, Serrati and his fellow-leaders had no wish to promote a split by expelling the dissidents who stood for a less intransigent line. If Turati was prepared to stay inside the Party in the interests of unity, despite his disagreement with its current attitude, Serrati did not wish to turn him or his supporters out of it, at the cost of losing an important part of their parliamentary support. Turati's prestige was high, both in Italy and in Socialist circles in other countries, and his services to Italian Socialism had been outstanding. Accordingly, the Comintern's war *à outrance* against the Centrists, as embodied in the Twenty-one Points, was most unwelcome to the Italian leaders who were trying to hold the Party together ; and opposition on this score was reinforced by a traditional reluctance to accept any centralised discipline. Syndicalism, as well as Anarchism, was a real force in the Italian movement ; and there was a deep distrust of centralised authority and control. The Italian Party therefore refused to

[1] See p. 372.

accept the Twenty-one Points and became involved in a pro-
longed wrangle with the Comintern. Minorities on the extreme
left broke away and went over completely to Communism ; but
even they were apt to jib at Moscow's discipline. The Comintern, however, remained insistent ; and in consequence there
was a split, not on the right but on the left.

Meanwhile, the Italian Socialists were facing increasing
difficulties at home, as well as in their international relations.
Was there to be an Italian Revolution, or was there not ? The
Italian State was very weak in comparison with that of France,
or even of Germany ; and in the period after 1918 government
was largely paralysed. Yet, though the anti-Socialist Governments were too weak to govern effectively, there was no common
revolutionary will on the part of their opponents. Most of the
Socialists in Parliament were at most Centrists rather than
revolutionaries ; and the Trade Union movement was sharply
divided between activist and reformist factions. There were,
moreover, to be reckoned with both the romantic nationalists,
headed by d' Annunzio, and the still inchoate Fascist movement
of which the former Socialist, Mussolini, was the inspirer ;
and each of these could play on disappointed nationalist feelings
and on the frustrations arising out of economic dislocation and
distress. The consequence was that the Italian working-class
movement went only half-way towards revolution, and then
drew back. The occupation of the factories could not have
succeeded unless the leaders had been prepared to advance
beyond it to positive revolution ; and this most of them were
not confident enough to do. They attempted, instead, a kind
of guerrilla struggle which gave Mussolini, aided by the big
business interests, the maximum of opportunity to build up
against them his extra-legal army of thugs and ruffians, before
whose resort to force they were gradually compelled to give
way, until he became strong enough to destroy them altogether
and in due course to establish the first Fascist State, with its
façade of corporative organisation and popular nationalistic
fervour. In face of this theoretically contemptible but practically
effective demagogy the Socialists, of whatever wing or variety,
found themselves forced to beat an ignominious retreat. Italian
Socialism was extinguished for nearly a generation ; yet when
it came back, towards the close of the second world war,

something not unlike the old pattern was to reappear — a small Social Democratic right wing, under Saragat, a big Centrist Party, under Nenni, and a powerful Communist Party, led by Togliatti — this last much stronger than the out-and-out Communists had been in the period after the first world war. In Italy, unlike France or Germany, Centrism, though eclipsed during the long Fascist interlude, was to rise again.

There were indeed in the Italian situation factors which serve to explain this difference. Italy, much more than either France or Germany, is a divided country, with advanced industrial areas, chiefly in the north, but also with a deeply impoverished and backward countryside, above all in the south. It is also a country with only a weak and broken tradition of parliamentary government and with a very strong tradition of conflict both between Church and State and between the Church and the working-class movement. It is an area of strong local feeling, difficult to organise on a national scale in either political or Trade Union affairs. Much, no doubt, has changed in it since the 1920s; but these factors remain, and continue to prevent the Italian working classes from either accepting with any sort of unity the need to work constitutionally through the existing parliamentary machine or joining forces to overthrow it — for they hardly know what they wish to put in its place. Their policy — and this applies largely to the Communists as well as to the Nenni Socialists — is a sort of Centrism *faute de mieux*, different from the Centrisms I have been speaking of in France and Germany, but also poised between constitutionalism and Revolution, as Italy itself is poised between industrialism and primitivism — between the extremes of Turin and the uninformed and pitiably impoverished south.

Finally, in Great Britain the Centre, represented primarily in 1918 and the following years by the I.L.P., never became an effective power. There was, indeed, immediately after the war, a considerable left-wing ferment, especially in the leading Trade Unions; but it failed to win any large measure of political support. There were great strikes in 1919, 1920, and 1921, and then again in 1926, when the General Strike rallied again for a moment the left-wing forces that had been beaten back in the mining struggle of 1921. But only for a few months in 1919, while capitalism was being arraigned before the Sankey Coal Commission, did the left even appear to have the game in its hands. Even then it speedily became plain that control of the Trades Union Congress as well as of the Labour Party was securely in moderate hands. Nor was there, even at the height of the industrial troubles of 1919, even a hint of any revolutionary intention. The Labour Party had just been overwhelmed by the Lloyd George Coalition in the General Election of 1918 ; but that did not prevent it from accepting parliamentarism as its settled policy, in sure confidence that there existed in the country not even a single revolutionary group of which it was needful to take account. The Miners' Federation and some other big Trade Unions were no doubt pressing far-reaching demands for nationalisation and for 'workers' control' ; but even these were in no sense revolutionary demands, and, when the Miners called on the rest of the Trade Unions for industrial action in support of them, the demand was not at all for revolutionary action, but only for a purely constitutional strike — and even that demand found no backing from the rest of the movement. There were, indeed, a number of small groups, which presently organised themselves into a Communist Party ; but they were a tiny minority and knew, as well as others, that a British Revolution was quite off the cards. There was also a non-Communist left ; but it was not for the most part revolutionary in theory — much less in practice. It wanted a more aggressive and more Socialist Labour Party, and more militancy in the Trade Unions, but only in the hope of a speedier advance towards Socialism by non-violent means.

The I.L.P., during and after the war, had the reputation of standing well to the left of the Labour Party, to which it continued to be affiliated despite the differences over war policy. While the war lasted, the small group of M.P.s sponsored by the I.L.P. acted in effect as an almost distinct Party, though continuing to rank as Labour Party members. When the war was over, the I.L.P. found its position in the Labour Party profoundly altered as a consequence of the new Labour Party Constitution, which for the first time admitted individual members and provided for regular organisation in each parliamentary constituency, and also on account of the new Labour

Party Programme, *Labour and the New Social Order*, which committed the Party to a clear evolutionary Socialist objective. These changes deprived the I.L.P. both of its claim to be the main representative of Socialism within the Party and of its status as the only large-scale organisation open to individual Socialists. The I.L.P. had largely increased its membership during the war, the new recruits being a mixture of pacifists and leftish Socialists; and considerable disputes developed inside it when it attempted to define its attitude to post-war problems, both internally and in the international field. Its best-known leader, Ramsay MacDonald, had been closely associated with the changes made in the Labour Party; and from 1918 onwards he acted much more as a leading figure in the Labour Party than as an I.L.P. spokesman. Philip Snowden, who continued for some time to be active primarily as an I.L.P. leader, was strongly opposed both to the Comintern and all forms of Communist doctrine, and to the left-wing industrialist trend that was strongly influencing many of the younger members of the I.L.P. Regarded, and regarding itself as the representative of Centrist internationalism in the British working-class movement, the I.L.P. leadership speedily fell into an acrimonious dispute with the Comintern over 'dictatorship' and the 'Twenty-one Points'; and a smallish left-wing minority soon seceded from it and linked up with the Communist Party. The main body held together, despite sharp differences about workers' control and strike policy. When these issues became less immediate after the defeat of the Miners in 1921 the differences between the Labour Party and the I.L.P. became less marked. The Clydeside group, the strongest element in the I.L.P., was largely responsible for bringing MacDonald back to the leadership of the Labour Party in 1920, under the mistaken belief that this would strengthen the Labour Party's left wing. They were speedily disillusioned by the experience of the first MacDonald Labour Government of 1924 and by the attitude of the Labour Party during the next few years; and on the advent of the second MacDonald Government in 1929 they soon found themselves in sharp opposition to it, especially in connection with its handling of the unemployment problem. By 1931 the position had been reached in which the I.L.P. was refusing to accept the discipline of the Labour Party Executive, which retaliated by refusing to endorse the I.L.P.'s parliamentary candidates. These quarrels led up to the actual secession of the I.L.P. from the Labour Party in 1932, the few candidates elected in the preceding General Election under I.L.P. auspices thereafter sitting as an entirely separate Party. From that point onwards the I.L.P. had only a small following, except on Clydeside. It continued as a small Party in Parliament up to the second world war, and still remains in existence to-day as a small independent Socialist organisation, but has no longer any parliamentary following. Internationally, it adhered at the outset, in the early 1920s to the Vienna 'Two-and-a-Half' International, and when that body disappeared it became an adherent of the new Labour and Socialist International as an affiliated organisation of the Labour Party. As we saw,[1] it carried on in the 1920s a lively campaign in favour of 'Socialism in Our Time', with Clifford Allen as its chief inspiring influence. For a while this campaign looked like restoring its lost influence as a 'ginger' group attached to the Labour Party ; but when it quarrelled finally with the Labour Party in 1931 a substantial part of its membership refused to follow it in seceding from the Party and joined forces with other left-wing groups in the Labour Party to form a new body for advanced Socialist propaganda, the Socialist League.[2] The history of this body and of the groups that went to its making falls, however, outside the period covered in the present volume.

In Great Britain, right through the 1920s, Communism remained a negligible force. The C.P.G.B. was almost unrepresented in Parliament and was able to win only a very few seats in local government elections. Nor could it build up any substantial influence in the Trade Unions, despite its efforts to do so through the 'Minority Movement', whose very name served to emphasise the narrowness of its appeal. Not unnaturally, the Communists did least badly among the unemployed and in some coalfields among the miners, who were smarting under their repeated defeats. But even among these groups their influence was very limited. It became rather greater in the 1930s, as an outcome of the economic depression and of the rise of Fascism ; but even then they failed to achieve

[1] See p. 448.   [2] See Chapter XXI.

any mass following. Centrism, too, though it had more adherents, appeared in the 1920s rather as a tendency inside the Labour Party than as a separately organised movement ; for by no means the whole of the Labour Party's left wing had any connection with the I.L.P., nor was the I.L.P. itself by any means solidly either left or Centrist, despite the campaign for 'Socialism in Our Time'. Up to 1914 the British movement, though it belonged to the Second International, had played, apart from Keir Hardie, only a small and somewhat aloof part in international Socialist affairs ; and after 1918 this tendency towards relative isolation still kept some of its force, despite the larger part taken by the Labour Party and the Trades Union Congress in the post-war Internationals. Taking parliamentary action for granted as its essential political method and, at all events after 1926, reduced to a purely defensive policy in industrial affairs, British Labour ranked internationally among the most moderate and peaceable of the world's working-class and Socialist movements, together with the Scandinavians— save, for a time, the Norwegians — and with the Belgians and the Dutch. The defection of MacDonald and Snowden and of a few other leaders in the crisis of 1931 shifted it politically for a short time towards the left ; but its leadership never ceased to be in the hands of the moderates, among whom the out-standing figure, after MacDonald and Snowden had departed, was Arthur Henderson. Henderson, who had been the chief creator and organiser of the new Labour Party of 1918, turned more and more in the 'twenties to international affairs — above all, to the attempt to build up the League of Nations as an effective power for peace and for disarmament by international agreement. These preoccupations made him somewhat aloof from the day-to-day activities relating to domestic policy ; but his influence was great and was always thrown on the side of holding the Party together by combining moderateness in policy with a refusal to quarrel more than he was forced to with those who favoured a more militant line.

It would be tedious to pursue this analysis of Centrist tendencies in the leading countries any further by extending it over a wider field. I have tried only to show how and why the non-Communist Left and Centre, which seemed for a few years after 1917 to have a considerable body of support in many countries, fell to pieces and was mainly forced back into the organisations controlled predominantly by the reformist right wing, as occurred in both France and Germany, or was eclipsed altogether, along with its rivals, as in Italy and, later on, in Germany and Austria as well. On a world scale this meant that the contest continued between the Communists on the one side and the predominantly right-wing Social Democrats on the other, as represented by the rival Internationals, and that the intermediate views, if not silenced, in the main found expression only at a national level and could find no international rallying point.

Indeed, many of those who had been Centrists, as long as the Centre existed as an independent force, found themselves moving a good deal further rightwards than they really wished to move, when, rejected by the Communists, they were compelled to rejoin the Social Democratic Parties dominated by the parliamentary right wing. Even if they retained leftish sympathies they found it difficult to give any effect to them ; and constant denunciation by the Communists gradually wore away their leftish tendencies and drove them to accept the leadership of the Right and presently in many cases to go over to it altogether. It is not psychologically easy to maintain a comradely feeling for persons by whom one is continually denounced and abused ; and Communist abuse was usually of a particularly bitter and outrageous type. Thus, the right wing won the support of many Centrists even against their will ; and Centrism, though never wholly eliminated, became, even nationally, in most countries, no more than an ineffective current of minority opinion.

Throughout the period covered in this volume, Socialism, except in its Communist form, remained essentially European. The Communists did make great efforts to extend their influence to other continents, especially to Asia and to Latin America, appearing in both these regions primarily as the antagonists of capitalist imperialism and of open or concealed colonial rule. In Africa there was, at this stage, almost nothing for them to take hold of as a means even of making a start. In Australia and New Zealand they had some successes in the Trade Unions, but failed entirely to build up any effective political movements. On the Asian front, aided by the presence of the Soviet Union as an Asian as well as a European power, they appeared for a time to be making remarkable progress in China, on the basis of their alliance with the Kuomintang. But when, after Sun Yat Sen's death and the Northern March of the Kuomintang forces under Chiang Kai-shek, Chiang turned upon them, expelled the Russian advisers, and made short work of the Kuomintang's left wing, these gains were abruptly lost, and Communist influence was carried on only through the sustained guerrilla warfare of Mao-Tse-tung and his fellow-leaders, with peasants rather than industrial workers bearing the brunt of the struggle. Elsewhere in Asia the Communists managed to consolidate the Mongolian Republic under Sukebatur (1893–1923) and Choibalsung (1895–1951) as a satellite state and to win some support in Indonesia and in other areas of South-East Asia ; but these successes were very limited, and even in India, still under British rule after the Montagu-Chelmsford Reforms, Communism, with M. N. Roy as its principal theoretical exponent, made but little popular headway in face of the predominant influence of Gandhi and the Indian National Congress. True, in India in the 1920s non-Communist Socialism counted for even less — indeed it hardly existed until the Congress Socialist Party made its appearance in the following decade. By the late 'twenties Asian Communism appeared to be virtually a spent force : it began to recover a little under the impact of the world depression ; but it was not to grow formidable until the second world war created the conditions for a new uprising of Asian nationalism against imperialist control.

Nor did Communism achieve a great deal, despite the Comintern's efforts, in Latin America until the depression of the 1930s came to reinforce its appeal. Not only in Peru, but also elsewhere, the Aprista movement, basing itself on an appeal to the peasants and the lesser bourgeoisie as well as to the industrial workers, fitted in with the prevailing conditions a great deal better than the Comintern could hope to do except in Buenos Aires and a very few other developed industrial centres. Moreover, in Latin America, Syndicalist and Anarchist traditions had deep roots in many sections of the proletariat and offered powerful obstacles to the ideas of so-called 'democratic centralism' and party discipline such as the Communist philosophy required. Even in Mexico there was a long pause after the Revolution of the years just before the first world war, and Communist influence became substantial only after the period covered in the present volume ; while in the United States all the Communists were able to achieve was a proliferation of tiny sects, too busy fighting one another to spare much energy for the impossible task of converting any considerable section of the American working class. The Comintern could always muster at its gatherings a mixed bunch of delegates from countries outside Europe ; but these represented for the most part hardly more than themselves, though Moscow-trained exiles were indoctrinated in substantial numbers and sent back to act as missionaries in their own countries.

The Communists did, at any rate, make an attempt, in their efforts to make headway against the great capitalist powers, to build up Communism as a world influence, in other continents as well as in Europe : the Social Democratic and Labour Parties, on the other hand, hardly attempted at all to give their creed a world-wide meaning or application. No doubt, the British Labour Party gave rather lukewarm support to the Indian claim for self-government ; but its leaders had not got to the point of thinking about Indian independence — much less about India's severance from the British Empire. The French Socialists thought of Algeria as part of France, differing from the rest only in having a large, subject population of non-European stock, and of Morocco, Tunis, and Indo-China as territories to be ruled from France, with limited participation by a minority of native inhabitants thoroughly assimilated to French culture.

Nor were there, at the end of the first world war, any significant groups in colonial or other economically under-developed areas with whom the non-Communist Socialists could easily establish contacts. Their evolutionary Socialist philosophy led them to think in terms, not of revolutions or colonial uprisings, but at most of gradual advances towards limited forms of self-government that could be fitted into the framework of colonial rule or made compatible, in politically independent countries, with peaceful co-operation with foreign investors kept in some sort of order by their own Governments. Disliking revolution at home, they tended to disapprove of it in colonial or semi-colonial areas ; and even when they were theoretically against racial inequality and discrimination — as not quite all of them were — they thought rather of the gradual fading away of these evils than of their forcible removal. In addition, many Socialists felt a keen distaste for nationalism, which in their own countries was mainly a reactionary and militaristic influence, and drew no distinction between the nationalisms of the independent countries and those of the countries subject to foreign rule. They were not at all pre-pared, as the Communists were, to seize on almost any oppor-tunity of creating trouble for the great capitalist powers by taking the side of almost any nationalist movement that was resisting their domination. I say 'almost any' ; for even the Communists, especially after their experience with the Kuomin-tang, were wary of nationalist movements that put themselves into direct hostility to the working-class movement or set out to destroy it by demagogic Fascist, or semi-Fascist, appeals. There were many zigzags of Communist policy in dealing with the various nationalist movements, especially in Latin America ; and in predominantly agricultural countries it was never easy to find a way of reconciling insistence on strictly proletarian revolutionism with alliance with anti-foreign movements whose main support, or at any rate whose leadership, came from the middle classes. Reconciliation became easier in the 'thirties, when opposition to Fascism had become for a time the main-spring of Communist international policy ; but even then it was often difficult.

The Communists, however, according to their lights, did try to make an appeal on a world-wide scale ; whereas the Social Democrats and Labourites fought shy even of trying. The leaders of the revived Second International had begun by declaring unequivocally that Socialism and 'democracy' — by which they meant parliamentary government — were insepar-able and by emphasising a stark conflict between 'democracy' and 'dictatorship' as the very basis of their quarrel with the Comintern. This, even if it fitted sufficiently well the condi-tions of Western Europe after 1918, could hardly provide them with any satisfactory way of approach to peoples who were entirely unused to parliamentary government, even if such peoples were also much too under-developed industrially for the dictatorship of the proletariat to have any practical meaning for them. It made of Socialism something that could be aimed at in any practical way, at any rate for the time being, only in the advanced countries living under parliamentary systems of government, and left the Social Democrats with almost nothing to say to a large part of the world — and even of Europe. There were, indeed, in the Balkan countries and in certain countries of Eastern Europe newly emancipated from foreign rule — *e.g.* Poland — groups of Westernised Socialists — largely intellectuals — who could be appealed to in these terms ; but even in such countries the parliamentary democratic appeal could mean little to the masses, who were in most cases before long facing suppression under one form or another of autocratic rule enforced by means of violence. Social Democracy, or 'democratic' Socialism, thus came, in the 1920s, to be in the main a gospel limited to the more advanced parliamentary countries, and to lose the more comprehensive internationalism that the pre-war Second International had at any rate professed to endorse.

I am not saying that this was the main reason why non-Communist Socialism failed in the post-war years to make any effective impact outside Western and Central Europe. A more important reason was that, in the areas under imperialist rule, the rising nationalist movements were inevitably dominated in their earlier stages by the bourgeoisie and by intellectuals drawn mainly from its ranks, and that even those bourgeois or intellectuals who sympathised with the poorer classes mostly thought it a much more hopeful course to aim at building up a united nationalist movement than to break the national movement in pieces by leading a revolt of the poor against the rich. This would have been the prevailing attitude even if the anti-Communist Socialists had made any real effort to adapt their gospel to the needs of the subject and under-developed peoples — which, as we have seen, they did not. As they failed to do this, there was no impetus towards the establishment even of weak Social Democratic movements in most of the countries concerned ; and in these areas non-Communist Socialism began to have any history, apart from the thoughts of a few almost isolated individuals, only in the 1930s, under the impact of the world depression. That is why I have given so little space in this volume to the development of Socialism outside the advanced countries and the Soviet Union, but may yet seem to some readers to have given too much in relation to what there is to record.

In the preceding volume of this study,[1] I tried to show that in the one great advanced Western country outside Europe, the United States, the decline of the Socialist movement had begun even before 1914, after a period of rather rapid, but still only small-scale, growth during the first decade of the century. I linked this decline to the fact that American Socialism had been, throughout its period of growth, largely an imported doctrine, brought to the United States by successive waves of European immigrants, and to the further fact that the stream of immigration, while it continued to flow unchecked, tended to divide the American working class into two groups — those who had adopted the American 'way of life' and acquired the status of skilled workers, and the newer immigrants, largely from the less developed parts of Europe, who were engaged mainly in less skilled jobs at much lower standards of living. These factors stood strongly in the way of the establishment of a united Trade Union movement, and also of any rallying to Socialism on the part of the fully assimilated and relatively well-paid groups organised in the American Federation of Labor. Moreover, after the war the restrictions on immigration both slowed down the rate of arrivals from Europe and speeded up the assimilation of those already in the United States. The Americans who rallied to Communism in 1919 and 1920 included a high proportion of fairly recent immigrants from Eastern Europe — especially from Russia ; and the non-Communist part of American Socialism was increasingly dominated by immigrants, often of longer standing, from Western Europe — including a high proportion of Jews. Neither of these groups was equipped to make an effective appeal to the main body of American workers under the conditions of the 1920s ; and when, in the 1930s, the great depression did stimulate a larger body of anti-capitalist feeling, this still did not take, for the most part, a Socialist form, though it did for a time considerably swell the volume of Communist and near-Communist support. The non-Communist Socialist

[1] See Vol. III, Part II, p. 775.

Parties of Western Europe had, in effect, not much more to say to the American workers than to the Asians or Africans. Their gospel, conceived in terms of their own situation, did not fit the conditions of the United States.

To what extent this is regarded as a criticism of post-1918 Social Democracy will necessarily depend on the reader's conception of the essential character of Socialism as a creed. To the orthodox Social Democratic Marxists, such as Kautsky, it was an integral part of Socialist doctrine that Socialism could come about in practice only as the necessary successor of a developed capitalist structure. Capitalism and advanced industrialisation were treated as indispensable prerequisites to the growth of a powerful proletariat equipped to take the control of society into its own hands. The Bolshevik Revolution was felt to be all wrong because it had involved the seizure of power by a Party representing at most an immature proletariat in a still predominantly peasant country. It was bound, on this account, either to collapse in ruins or, if it maintained itself, to turn into an authoritarian tyranny utterly at variance with Socialist principles. Even if Kautsky had been correct in this view — even if he was in some degree correct — it would follow that Socialism properly so called could have no direct or immediate meaning except for the comparatively few countries which had already reached the required level of capitalist development. Kautskyite Socialism could not, of its very nature, be a world creed, or command a world following until the methods of advanced capitalism had been extended over all countries. No doubt Kautsky was convinced both that this was bound to happen in the long run — was he not continually predicting the inevitable decline of the peasantry and the increasing trustification of capitalist enterprise ? — and that the proletariats of the advanced countries could, by establishing Socialism within them, give a lead to the whole world and speed up very greatly the pace of industrialisation everywhere. Nevertheless, he had nothing much to say to the peoples, or to the workers, of the less-developed countries except that they would have to wait their turn and to pass through capitalist development as a necessary stage on the road to Socialist victory.

This view rested on a conception of the coming Socialist Revolution as destined to occur, country by country, as each arrived at the appropriate stage. Against this, the Communists, particularly at the outset, put forward the notion of the single and indivisible World Revolution, which would arrive, not country by country according to the economic stage which each had come to, but as soon as world capitalism, regarded as a single, though complex, structure, reached the point at which its inherent contradictions, as foreseen by Marx, rendered it unable to maintain itself or to achieve continuing economic advance. On this view, it was almost a historical accident that the Revolution had begun in Russia rather than in one or more of the countries of advanced capitalism. What had occurred was the snapping first of the weakest link in the capitalist chain ; and this had provided an opportunity of which it was the clear duty of the proletariat everywhere to take advantage by joining in the Revolution and converting it into a world-wide insurrection against capitalist rule. 'Workers of the world, unite !' was a slogan that meant not merely that the workers in each country should help those of other countries, but that there was in reality a single world-wide working class that was being called upon to take united action against a single and undivided capitalist world order.

This attitude was, as the event showed, unrealistic ; but it did, at any rate, provide the Communists with a gospel that could be preached, as a call to action, everywhere, and not only in the minority of advanced capitalist countries. Beside it, outside these countries, the Social Democratic gospel seemed unappealing, and even, in many cases, irrelevant to the local situation. When Stalin, disappointed of his hopes of speedy World Revolution, set to work to build up 'Socialism in One Country', he immediately forfeited part of the strength of the Communist world-wide appeal ; for he had then to call upon the workers of other countries to rally to the defence of the Soviet Union rather than to pursue the Revolution on their own account. But even when the Communist appeal had been thus weakened, the Social Democrats were still without any world-wide gospel of their own to set against it ; for they could hardly call on the workers of the less developed countries to rally to *their* defence, nor could the workers of those countries have done anything to defend them if the call had been made. In Germany Social Democracy had to wage its struggle against

Fascism, or to yield to it, with no help from the workers of other countries, backward or advanced ; for it was plainly fighting — or failing to fight — its own battle, and not that of the proletariat as a world-wide class.

This situation was indeed unavoidable. The creed of parliamentary Socialism necessarily involved carrying on the campaign for Socialism mainly on the national plane, on a basis of the independence of each national Socialist unit, so as to give each freedom to adapt itself to the electoral exigencies of its own state structure and climate of national opinion. Only if the League of Nations had been constituted as a super-State with a supreme legislative power over all its members, and the means of enforcing its authority, could this have ceased to be the case ; and, of course, no such super-League was even remotely practicable in face of the strength of national senti-ment and the relative weaknesses of international solidarity resting on either class or humanist feeling. Social Democracy involved not only diluting Socialist programmes to suit electoral prospects, but also framing them on national lines, to fit each country's conditions. It excluded any sort of unified inter-national programme of action such as the Communists accepted as a matter of world revolutionary principle.

This is not to say that the Communists were right and the Social Democrats wrong ; for the Communist gospel of World Revolution, however universal its appeal, was profoundly un-realistic. It rested on at least two quite false assumptions — the one that world capitalism had almost reached the end of its tether, and the other that the workers of the world, if not already ripe for revolutionary action, would become so almost to a man as soon as their traitorous misleaders had been exposed by the Communists and thus deprived of their following. Capitalism, after making a remarkable come-back in the 1920s, did indeed make a quite near approach to bringing the first of these prophecies to pass by its imbecile handling of the great depression — from which it nevertheless achieved a consider-able degree of recovery well before 1939. But the second prophecy was utterly falsified by events ; for instead of desert-ing the 'social traitors' a high proportion of the workers in the advanced countries rallied round them all the more firmly on account of the Communists' attacks and vilifications.

This, however, is not to say that the Social Democrats were in the right. Largely out of hostility to the Communists, they narrowed Socialism down so as to make it essentially a West European rather than a world-wide creed, and failed to offer any message to the masses in the colonial and under-developed countries, or indeed to anyone who was not in a position to tread securely along the parliamentary road. Social Democracy's chickens came home to roost in the 1930s, when the Nazis conquered Germany and set out to overrun Europe, and when the great depression turned unemployment into a cancer that rotted away the workers' strength. Only in a very few specially favoured countries, such as Sweden and Denmark, was it able to make continued headway at this time. In the great capitalist countries it lay, at best, fully reefed before the storm until the second world war came to afford it a means of escape.

In Scandinavia the Socialists fared a good deal better than in other Western countries during the post-war years. They were not indeed able until later to win clear majorities in the several Parliaments ; but they did make large electoral advances and were in a position to form several minority Governments with support from the more progressive elements either of the bourgeoisie or of the small farmers. In general, the Scandinavian Socialist Parties were moderate and made no attempt to introduce Socialism : their efforts were centred mainly on the enactment of progressive social legislation, on improving the tax system, and on pressing for effective measures to provide for the unemployed by means of public works. Only in Norway, under the influence of Martin Tranmael, did the Labour Party for a time adopt an aggressive left-wing policy, which led it into the Comintern — and then before long led it out again when it refused to accept the Comintern's dictation in the conduct of its affairs. In Sweden and in Denmark, though left-wing movements and Parties arose during or after the war, their followers were only a small minority, and the orthodox Social Democratic Parties retained their predominant influence. In Sweden the Social Democratic leader, Hjalmar Branting, became Minister of Finance in a coalition Cabinet as early as 1918, but resigned after a few months, returning to office in 1920 at the head of an all-Socialist Cabinet which, having no majority, lasted only for six months. Still without a clear majority, Branting took office again the following year, and this time retained his position, with one brief interval, until his death in 1925. His colleague, Richard Sandler (b. 1884), then took his place, but was defeated in 1926, mainly on the issue of the provision to be made for the unemployed. Thereafter the Socialists were in opposition until 1932, when the impact of the world depression brought them back to power under the skilful leadership of Per Albin Hansson (1880-1946), who stayed in office through the rest of the 1930s, and was able for the first time to put a substantial part of his Party's essentially moderate policy into effect.

Meanwhile, as early as 1916, the Danish Social Democrats, headed by Thorvald Stauning (1873-1942), had entered a Coalition under Radical leadership. The Social Democrats considerably increased their strength in the General Elections of 1920 and 1924 ; and in the latter year Stauning took office at the head of an entirely Social Democratic Cabinet, which, though it had no majority, stayed in office for the next two years. In 1926 the Socialists suffered a small electoral set-back, and a right-wing Coalition came back to power ; but in 1930 they were able to take office again, this time with the support of the Radicals. Thereafter Stauning remained in power as Prime Minister right up to the second world war.

In Norway, after the break with the Comintern, the Labour Party remained in opposition until 1928. It then, as the largest Party, but without a majority, formed an all-Socialist Government, which was defeated almost immediately when it brought forward a somewhat drastic proposal for the redistribution of wealth. Its defeat was confirmed at the General Election of 1930, during which its opponents accused it of wishing to introduce Bolshevism. J. L. Mowinckel, at the head of an anti-Socialist Coalition, then held power until 1932, when his Government was brought down mainly by its failure to take any effective action to deal with the unemployment problem. The Labour Party then took office under Johan Nygaardsvold (1879-1952), and thereafter stayed in power right through the 'thirties.

It will be seen from what has been said that the main positive achievements of Scandinavian Socialism belong to the 1930s and were largely an outcome of the world economic crisis, which intensified the demands for social security and for positive action to increase the volume of employment. The Scandinavian countries were indeed less hard hit than most others by the crisis, because their main exports were on the whole better maintained. They suffered enough, however, to bring many recruits to the Socialist Parties ; and these Parties were then in a position to take effective action because the difficulties were not overwhelming. The foundations for this successful action towards the establishment of the 'Welfare State' had, of course, been laid earlier ; but until the depression the Socialist Parties had had only very limited opportunities for carrying their policies into effect. They were, however, advancing almost steadily in influence during the 1920s. A fuller consideration of Scandinavian Social Democracy belongs therefore to the next rather than to the present volume of this history. In the 1930s not only many Socialists but also many non-Socialist progressives were to hold up Sweden in particular to admiration as the exponent of a 'middle way', and as showing how considerable advances could be made towards the 'Welfare State' without any great extension of socialised enterprise or frontal attack on capitalist institutions. Some of this praise was already being uttered before 1932, as the Social Democrats cautiously felt their way towards the conquest of political power, profiting meanwhile by the divisions among their opponents, and relatively unhampered by Communist movements which, after the Norwegian break with the Comintern, never commanded any large body of support. The Scandinavian situation was, however, *sui generis* ; for when these countries had once escaped from the undemocratic constitutions that had been used to hold back progress up to 1914, there existed in them a clear preponderance of democratic sentiment over aristocratic or sheerly reactionary claims, and it was difficult for the capitalist interests effectively to resist claims which had the backing not only of the industrial workers but also of most of the white-collar workers and in many respects of the smaller farmers. Scandinavian Socialism, most of all in Denmark but also largely in Sweden, developed along lines not of proletarian class-struggle against all other groups, but rather of reforms tending towards a lessening of social and economic inequality, without any strong emphasis on socialisation beyond the range of a few key monopolies. In both Denmark and Sweden the great strength of the Co-operative movement among both consumers and farmers powerfully re-inforced this tendency towards welfare legislation rather than socialisation ; while the close alliances between the Socialist Parties and the Trade Unions, as well as the closely knit organisation of the employers, tended to hold industrial militancy in check. No really similar conditions existed in the great capitalist States or indeed in the other small advanced countries of Western Europe. The Swedes, the Danes, and the Norwegians were in a position, mainly, to go their own way ; but in most other countries it was not open to the Socialist Parties to follow their example. In all these cases the Socialists had far more dangerous and implacable enemies to fight against ; and in most of them, though not in all, reformist Social Demo-cracy had also to confront much greater difficulties from the Socialist and Communist left wings.

For, throughout the 1920s, despite the domination of the Comintern by the Soviet Union, Communism was effectively, and not merely in declared intention, a left-wing force. Its aim was revolution, with the proletariat as represented by the Communist Parties at its head, and with the overthrow of 'bourgeois democracy', above all in the great capitalist countries, as its direct and as nearly as possible immediate object. The Communists were, no doubt, already doing their best to in-culcate the lesson that the proletarian's first duty was to defend the Soviet Union against its enemies ; but this was to be done, as far as opportunity allowed, by fomenting Communist Revolutions in further countries or, where this was clearly im-practicable, by relentless struggles against the Social Demo-cratic leaders, in the hope of wresting their followers from them. The United Fronts of which the Comintern spoke frequently in the 1920s were not meant to be United Fronts of the kind the Communists came to advocate in the following decade, when they had turned their attention to the attempt to build up common movements against Fascism and Nazism on a wider basis. Even then, they, of course, tried to establish such Fronts as far as they could under their own leadership ; but they were ready, if need arose, to co-operate with almost any-body who stood for united resistance to the Fascist dictators, whereas in the 1920s it was rank heresy to co-operate with Social Democrats except for the purpose of destroying their leaders' influence. Not until the world economic crisis had brought with it Nazism instead of the hoped-for final collapse of capitalism did the Communists' attitude change fundamentally ; and even then most of them remained unwilling to admit that Fascism could be, at bottom, anything other than the last throw of a capitalism doomed to speedy dissolution under pressure of its inescapable 'contradictions'.

At the point at which the present volume leaves the story of Socialism, world capitalism, no longer in operation in the Soviet Union — where it had never reached at all a high stage of development — seemed to superficial observers to have been at length reconstructed after the dislocations of war. There had been almost everywhere a return to the gold standard — the traditional basis of international exchange among the advanced countries — and, though this return had involved much deflationary hardship and unemployment, the defenders of capitalism felt entitled to congratulate themselves on having come through the period of the greatest danger without any spread of the Social Revolution beyond the Soviet Union ; for though Revolution had occurred in China, it had not turned out nearly so subversive as it had threatened to be and had not led to any linking of China with the Soviet Union — indeed, quite the reverse. There were, no doubt, ample signs of the precariousness of this recovery of capitalism from the moment of the first stock market collapse in New York in 1929 ; and the more prescient could see how little of real equilibrium lay at the back of the restored structure of international exchange. But at all events the danger of World Revolution and even of widespread working-class militancy appeared to have receded, if not to have entirely disappeared. The Soviet Union, embarked on its first attempts at comprehensive planning and industrial development and just plunging into its colossal scheme of agricultural collectivisation, appeared to have, for the time being, not much energy to spare for trouble-making beyond its frontiers ; and the idea of overthrowing it by foreign military intervention had been given up except by a few fanatics. Broadly speaking, most of the world did seem to be settling down under the rule of a capitalist system not fundamentally different from that of the years before 1914. There were fewer kings, and many more parliamentary electors, and there had been a considerable spread of at any rate formally democratic and responsible parliamentary government, only in part offset by the victory of Fascism in Italy and by the trend towards authoritarian and oppressive dictatorships in Eastern and South-Eastern Europe. In the economic field, save here and there, these political changes did not seem to have made a great deal of difference, though there had been a recrudescence of economic nationalism which the League of Nations had not been able to do more than hold in check by means of the none-too-successful 'Tariff Truce'. Negotiations were proceeding for some agreed measure of disarmament ; and these did not appear to be wholly without prospect of success. In the United States, which had become the key area in the determination of world economic prospects, there were still, despite the unstable condition of the stock markets, plenty of supposed experts [1] who prophesied a future of growing and uninterrupted prosperity, and argued vociferously that the American people needed no revolution because they had already had one that had solved the essential problems and had linked the well-being of the workers firmly to the prosperity of the employing class.

In these circumstances there were but few who, in 1929 or even in 1930, had any premonition of the magnitude of the impending storm. The Communists, of course, continued to prophesy that capitalism was destined quite soon to explode under the pressure of its internal contradictions, and that the World Revolution was only deferred for a while, and not defeated. But in the main these predictions were made *a priori*, and not on any basis of direct observation of the immediate facts and trends ; and the great depression, when it came, took the Communists hardly less by surprise than it took the capitalist world or the Social Democrats, who were busy projecting far-reaching improvements in the social services, in industrial legislation, and in the provision of public works for the unemployed. To a great extent, the great upheaval of 1917 seemed to have been successfully confined to backward Russia and to have been beaten back over the rest of Europe. The Labour

[1] *E.g.* Professor T. N. Carver.

Government that took office in Great Britain in 1929 had clearly no foreknowledge at all of the situation it would have to face, and found itself helpless and without a policy when the storm burst upon it in 1930 and 1931. Of course, having no majority of its own, the MacDonald Government was not in any case in a position to carry through a boldly Socialist policy ; but its record plainly shows that it had no will to do so, or even to follow the advice offered to it both by its own left-wing supporters and by an influential group of progressive Liberals headed by J. M. Keynes. Indeed, the Keynesian Liberals were allowed to make most of the running with their campaign for a bolder policy in dealing with unemployment. No Conservative Chancellor of the Exchequer could have been more orthodox an upholder of traditional capitalist financial policy that Philip Snowden ; no Prime Minister more dithering than Ramsay MacDonald ; no Cabinet more bewildered than the MacDonald Cabinet when it found itself confronted with a crisis the nature of which most of its members were entirely unable to understand. The British Labour Party, reputed the strongest and best equipped of all the Socialist or Labour Parties of the capitalist world, fell from office in 1931, with a resounding crash that cast grave doubts on the soundness of the Social Democratic approach, and might have given a strong impetus to Communist feeling had not the Communists at the same time been utterly mishandling the problem of Germany.

This mishandling was even more disastrous than the ignominious failure of the Labour Government in Great Britain. Badly misunderstanding the real nature of Nazism and bitterly hostile to the Social Democratic Party, with its policy of continual yielding to reactionary pressure, the German Communists and the Comintern made the fatal mistake of treating the Social Democrats as their principal enemies and even of joining forces against them on occasion with the Nazis. There were indeed good reasons for being highly critical of the Social Democratic line, which allowed the Weimar Republic to be more and more undermined by Hitler and by the reactionary militarists and nationalists without any real stand being made. But in a situation in which the only hope lay in united working-class action, it was unpardonable folly to take sides with by far the most dangerous of the reactionary forces. This folly was no doubt made easier by the fact that many Nazis were former Communists, who had passed over in despair and disillusion to the Nazi ranks. But it was none the less unforgivable folly, for which the workers of Germany had to pay a terrible price. For the driving force behind Nazism was not capitalism — though it, of course, obtained much capitalist help — it was aggressive nationalism and racialism raised to the point of lunacy by both material and spiritual distress ; and the only hope of combating it successfully lay in uniting in opposition to it everyone who could be enlisted in a crusade for decency and rationality, and not in opposing to it a counter-fanaticism that repelled and excluded the majority of potential recruits.

The German Revolution of 1918 was indeed, as we have seen,[1] a most complete example of the wrong way to make a revolution. Reformists who are aiming only at gradual and not too upsetting changes can to some extent afford to carry over into the new structure the major part of the old — to make use of the existing Civil Servants and courts of law, and even of the officers of the existing army, though the extent to which they can afford to do this must depend on the mental attitudes of these social groups. A real revolution, on the other hand, must, in order to succeed, make, if not a clean sweep, at least a decisive change in the composition of the higher ranks of the administration, the judiciary, and the armed forces, and must place at once in the key positions persons who can be relied upon to support the revolutionary cause. In view of the deeply reactionary outlook of most of the higher Civil Servants, of the judges, and of the officer class in Germany, it was imperative to take away their power. This was doubtless difficult in a country both defeated in war and badly dislocated by war conditions, and also under the threat of continued hostile intervention and even of sheer starvation. But, unless it were done, the Revolution was bound to fail and the disordered forces of reaction to regain strength and confidence. In the circumstances of Germany in 1918–19 it was disastrous to refuse to settle anything about the future until a Constituent Assembly had been elected by universal suffrage to debate and decide — the

[1] See p. 133.

more so because the Social Democrats themselves were without any clear vision of what they wanted and because such methods were almost certain to give rise to a leftist *putsch*, which would involve the revolutionary Government in shooting down an active section of the supporters of the Revolution, and would thus fatally divide the working class. The *putsch*-ists may have been quite wrong to let themselves be provoked into action that was certain to fail. I hold that they were wrong ; but that does not excuse the Social Democratic leaders whose disastrous errors brought the situation about.

Of course, as we have seen, the fact of the matter is that Ebert and Scheidemann and the rest of the Majority Socialist leaders — and a good many of the Independent Socialists as well — were 'revolutionaries', not of their own will, but because they could not help being so in the circumstances of November 1918. The Hohenzollern Reich dissolved in chaos, and they were compelled to attempt to put something in its place. This dissolution took place under conditions entirely different from those which the theorists of German Social Democracy had led their followers to expect. These theorists had looked forward to an onward march of parliamentary Socialist representation culminating in the winning of a majority in the Reichstag, which would thereupon call upon the Emperor to accept a new democratic Constitution and would take power into its hands in a constitutional way. The right-wing German Socialists had never really faced the question of what would happen if the Emperor, instead of accepting their demands, ordered the military to arrest the deputies and proceeded to shoot the democrats down. Such a possibility was too unpleasant to be considered seriously, especially as the German Trade Unions had shown themselves most unwelcoming to the idea of making themselves responsible for a general strike under any conditions. The Trade Union leaders had made it perfectly clear that responsibility for a general strike called for any political purpose would have to rest with the Party, and not with the Unions. In effect, the question of such a strike had been left unanswered though Kautsky, as well as Rosa Luxemburg, had made some attempt to face it ; and the question of what was to happen if the Empire collapsed and power passed into the hands of a Reichstag in which the Socialists were still in a minority had never been faced at all. This, however, was in 1918 the problem with which the German Social Democrats had actually to deal. The consequence was that they did not know what to do, and fell back on the attempt to construct a democratic Republic while leaving the old top Civil Servants and the judges in their places, the great landlords and capitalists in possession of their economic powers, and the officer corps in a position, while nominally coming to their assistance, to stab them in the back.

This does not mean that the Germans ought to have attempted in 1918 to make a Communist revolution on the Russian model, dictatorship of the proletariat, one-party system, and all the bag of tricks. In Germany such a Revolution would have divided, instead of uniting, the workers, and would have been doomed to failure, if only because, other factors apart, it would have resulted in military intervention by the Allied forces. There were, however, intermediate courses open to them. They could have used the power of the provisional Socialist Government to decree immediately the breaking up of the great estates, the socialisation of the great capitalist combines, and above all the replacement of the holders of key positions throughout the Reich by persons friendly to the Revolution and prepared to serve it in good faith. These things were not done, not only because the Social Democratic leaders were afraid to do them, but also because they did not want to. They feared the collapse of the existing society much more than they hoped for a really new social order ; and because of these fears they betrayed the Revolution and helped to bring the Republic to its dismal collapse.

Thus, in the great post-war emergency both Communists and Social Democrats followed wrong policies. The Social Democrats allowed themselves to become the slaves of parliamentarist dogma as much as the Communists became enslaved to the Russian myth. The Russians themselves, having made their Revolution by what were, most likely, in a broad sense, the only effective means open to them, not only mistook the situation in the outside world — especially in the advanced Western countries — but also turned the expedient of a disciplined party into the dogma of single-party government and allowed so-called 'democratic centralism' to degenerate, largely under Stalin's influence, into centralism without democracy. The worst effects of these perversions did not become manifest until the 'thirties ; but well before then the vendetta against Trotsky had given warning of what was all too likely to come about. The Socialist movement seemed to have become disastrously divided into Socialists who were no longer even aiming at Socialism and Socialists who refused to admit that there could be varying roads towards Socialism in countries differently placed, and would recognise only a single road — the sheer imitation of that which the Russians had been forced to tread. The few who fell into neither of these errors were left helpless under the united denunciations of the contending factions.

Yet the Russian Revolution, despite the evils that ensued upon it both internationally and at home, remains a great and a glorious achievement. The Czarism which it overthrew was a monstrous and utterly stupid tyranny which entirely barred the way to the good life for the Russian people — for the intellectuals as well as for the peasants and workers. It was an obsolete and revolting structure that needed to be overthrown and replaced, not by sheer chaos, but by a new power strong enough to lead the Russians into the contemporary world. Had the Bolsheviks failed to seize their chance when it came it seems most improbable that any other group would have been able to hold Russia together, to beat off the invaders, and to lay the foundations of an advanced economy and of a more democratic opening of opportunity for education and training in the arts of production. True, these things were achieved under the Bolsheviks only at the cost of immense immediate sufferings, of terrible inhumanities to alleged enemies of the Revolution, and of the growth of a stifling political structure of espionage and police control. Of these, the sufferings were largely unavoidable, whereas the inhumanities and the abuses of the police State could have been largely avoided by better leadership. For the faults of leadership Stalin must take a big share of the responsibility ; but it is absurd to attribute them to him exclusively, or to a small group of amoral 'realists' of whom he was the chief. The root of the trouble was not the so-called 'cult of personality', which was only a hateful excrescence. It was rather the cult of centralism and its accompaniment — a vast bureaucratic machine which was open to manipulation by men who, heirs to the evil traditions of the old Russia, identified strength with ruthlessness and discarded morality as a 'bourgeois prejudice'.

In spite of all this, I am sure the Russian Revolution did act as an immense liberating force. If it repressed free speech and political freedom, it was at the same time setting more and more of the Russians free from the brutalising social and economic repression of the old régime and creating not only a more skilled and mechanised working class but also one with immensely greater cultural and intellectual opportunities. That these achievements were badly marred by the abuse of political power does not make them of no value. There are more kinds of tyranny and oppression than the political, and more kinds of freedom than the liberal-democratic freedoms that are rightly valued in the countries of the West. It cannot be easy to strike the correct balance between good and evil ; but I, at any rate, can feel no doubt that the long-run balance will turn out to be on the right side.

BIBLIOGRAPHY

GENERAL

THE only considerable general accounts of Socialism after 1914 are contained in H. W. Laidler's *Social Economic Movements* (1944), based on his earlier *Socialism in Thought and Action*, and *History of Socialist Thought* (1920 and later editions), and in Édouard Dolléans's *Histoire du mouvement ouvrier*, vol. ii (Paris, 1939), and vol. iii (Paris, 1953). Of these, Laidler's work covers a very wide range, including sections dealing with almost every country in which an appreciable Socialist movement existed, and containing an account of Co-operative, but not of Trade Union, as well as of political developments. It is, however, rather pedestrian, and its accounts of the lesser countries contain little attempt at evaluation or explanation of the facts he recites. There is a considerable section dealing with Communism, but not much about Communist movements in particular countries. The book of Dolléans is much more selective : it does not attempt to deal with all countries and concentrates largely on French developments and on international developments closely related to the rise of Communism and to the struggle between the Communists and their opponents. It is, however, much more imaginative than Laidler's volume. Of other general histories, Élie Halévy's *Histoire du socialisme européen* (1948) is rather slight, but intelligent. Sir Alexander Gray's *The Socialist Tradition : Moses to Lenin* (1946) is entertaining and provocative, if hardly profound. Arthur Rosenberg's *Democracy and Socialism* (English translation, 1939) is good on the conflicts between Communism and Social Democracy. L. Valiani's *Histoire du socialisme au XXᵉ siècle* (1948) is also slight but interesting. His longer work on Socialist history has unfortunately not yet reached the modern period. Paul Louis's two volumes, *Cent Cinquante Ans de pensée socialiste* (Paris, 1947 and 1953), consist of a series of studies of particular Socialist thinkers, together with extracts from some of their principal writings. These are uneven, but valuable for their accounts of some writers whose works are none too easy to come by for the general reader. See also A. S. Rappoport's *Dictionary of Socialism* (1924) and A. C. A. Compère-Morel's *Grand Dictionnaire socialiste* (Paris, 1924), a sequel to his earlier *Encyclopédie socialiste* (1912-13), mentioned in the general bibliography to Volume III. Reference should again be made to Max Beer's *Fifty Years of International Socialism* (1935) and to his *Social Struggles and Modern Socialism* (1925) ; see also L. L. Lorwin, *Labour and Internationalism* (New York, 1929) ; A. Sergent and C. Harmel, *Histoire de l'anarchie* (Paris,

1949) ; Émile Vandervelde, *Souvenirs d'un militant socialiste* (Paris, 1934).

Works on Socialist theory and policy are listed under the chapters dealing with particular countries or with the conflict between the rival Internationals. Apart from works written by leading Communists, or in direct opposition to them, the post-war period up to the 1930s was not very productive in the field of Socialist theory. In Germany there were no major successors to Kautsky or Bernstein ; in France none to Jaurès. Émile Vandervelde had done most of his best work before 1914, and so had Louis de Brouckère. In Great Britain the Webbs produced their *Constitution for the Socialist Commonwealth of Great Britain* in 1920, and their massive work on *Soviet Communism* in 1935. My own *Self-Government in Industry* appeared in 1917, and *Social Theory* in 1920. Ramsay MacDonald's *Socialism : Critical and Constructive* was published in 1921. Neither the Italians nor the Spaniards produced any outstanding works. In Austria Otto Bauer's brief *Der Weg zum Sozialismus* appeared in 1919. Henri de Man's important *Psychology of Socialism* dates from 1928 : his *Plan du travail* belongs to the following decade. H. J. Laski's *Authority in the Modern State* (1919), *A Grammar of Politics* (1925), *Communism* (1927), and *Liberty in the Modern State* (1930) belong to the period covered in this volume. John Strachey's widely read left-wing writings were issued in the 1930s, as were the works of Herbert Morrison and Hugh Dalton mentioned in connection with Chapter XII.

CHAPTER II

Two volumes published in 1915 contained studies of the attitudes of the various Socialist Parties and movements on the outbreak of war in 1914. These are W. English Walling, *The Socialists and the War* (New York, 1915), and A. W. Humphrey, *Socialism and the War* (1915). For a later study see M. Fainsod, *International Socialism and the World War* (Harvard, 1935) ; and A. Van der Slice, *International Labour, Diplomacy and Peace, 1914–1919* (Philadelphia, 1941). The proceedings of the Zimmerwald Conference of 1915 were reported in *Conférence Socialiste Internationale à Zimmerwald, rapport officiel pour la presse* (Berne, 1915), and those of the Kienthal Conference of 1916 in *Seconde Conférence Socialiste Internationale du Zimmerwald* (Paris, 1916). There were also reports in German and in other languages. On the abortive Stockholm Conference of 1917 a long report on the proceedings of the organising committee was issued by that body in French, under the title *Stockholm* (Stockholm, 1918). It was presumably issued in other languages as well, but I have seen only the French version.

The proceedings of the International Socialist Women's Conference held at Berne in March 1915 were published in a supplement to the *Berner Tagwacht* on April 3rd, 1915.

BIBLIOGRAPHY

Works dealing with the breakdown of the Second International include Lenin's pamphlet, *La Débâcle de la Seconde Internationale* (Switzerland, 1915), Trotsky's *Der Krieg und die Internationale* (1914), K. Kautsky's *Die Internationale und der Krieg* (Berlin, 1915), C. Rakovsky's *Les Socialistes et la guerre* (Paris, 1915), O. Boulanger, *L'Internationale a vécu* (Paris, 1915); C. Huysmans, *The Policy of the International* (speech and interview) (London and elsewhere, 1916); Rosa Luxemburg's (as 'Junius'), *Die Krise der Sozialdemokratie* (1916), E. Bernstein, *Die Internationale der Arbeiterklasse und der europäische Krieg* (Tübingen, 1916); C. Grünberg, *Die Internationale und der Weltkrieg* (Leipzig, 1916); J. Destrée, *Les Socialistes et la guerre européenne* (Brussels, 1916); A. Rosmer, *Le Mouvement ouvrier pendant la guerre* (Paris, 1936); G. V. Plekhanov, *La Sociale-démocratie et la guerre* (Paris, 1916); C. Rappoport, *Le Socialisme et la guerre* (Paris, 1915).

For the Zimmerwaldian movement see also Angelica Balabanova, *Memoirs of a Zimmerwaldian* (Leningrad, 1925), and *My Life as a Rebel* (1938); N. Krupskaia's *Memoirs of Lenin*, 2 vols. (New York, 1930 and 1933); S. Grumbach, *L'Erreur de Zimmerwald-Kienthal* (Paris, 1917); F. Loriot, *Les Socialistes de Zimmerwald et la guerre* (Paris, 1917).

For the International Socialist movement in general see R. W. Postgate, *The Workers' International* (1921); L. L. Lorwin, *Labour and Internationalism* (New York, 1929).

See also the *Labour International Handbook* (ed. R. Palme Dutt) (1921) and the *Year-book of the International Socialist Labour Movement* (ed. J. Braunthal) (1956).

CHAPTER III

The writings about the Russian Revolutions of 1917 are so numerous that only a very few can be mentioned here. For a vivid eyewitness's account of the Bolshevik Revolution see John Reed, *Ten Days that Shook the World* (1919). L. Trotsky's *History of the Russian Revolution* (English translation, 1932) is a masterly study by a leading participant. Another remarkable first-hand account is N. N. Sukhanov's *The Russian Revolution, 1917* (1955), abridged by J. Carmichael from the original Russian version, *Zapiski o Revolutsii*, published in Russian in six volumes in 1922–3. These three are outstanding. Other important works include the opening part of E. H. Carr's *The Bolshevik Revolution, 1917–1923* (3 vols. 1950–3); I. Deutscher's first volume of the life of Trotsky, *The Prophet Armed : Trotsky, 1879–1921* (1954), and the same writer's *Stalin : a Political Biography* (1949); B. D. Wolfe's *Three Who Made a Revolution* (New York, 1948); Rosa Luxemburg, *Die russische Revolution : eine kritische Würdigung* (Berlin, 1922); N. Krupskaia's *Memoirs of Lenin* (New York, 1930–3); Trotsky's *Lenin* (English translation, 1925);

V. Marcu's *Lenin* (in German, 1927 — English translation, 1928);
M. Philips Price, *War and Revolution in Asiatic Russia* (1918) and
Reminiscences of the Russian Revolution (1921); A. L. Strong, *The
First Time in History* (New York, 1924); Louise Bryant, *Six Red
Months in Russia* (1918). For an Anarchist account see Voline (V. N.
Eichenbaum) *Nineteen Seventeen : The Revolution Betrayed* (English
translation, 1954).

For the antecedents of the Revolution see John Maynard, *Russia in
Flux* (1941) and *The Russian Peasant*, 2 vols. (1942); L. Shapiro,
The Origins of the Communist Autocracy (1955); D. W. Treadgold,
Lenin and his Rivals (1955); H. Seton-Watson, *The Decline of Imperial
Russia* (1952); F. Venturi, *Il popolismo russo*, 2 vols. (Turin, 1952);
M. Pianzola, *Lenin en Suisse* (Geneva, 1952).

Reference should also be made to Bernard Pares, *A History of
Russia* (1926), *My Russian Memoirs* (1931), and *The Fall of the Russian
Monarchy* (1939); D. S. Mirsky's *Russia, a Social History* (1931) and
History of Russian Literature (1927); M. N. Pokrovsky's *Brief History
of Russia*, 2 vols. (English translation, 1933); A. F. Meyendorff,
The Background of the Russian Revolution (1929); N. Berdyaev, *The
Origin of Russian Communism* (English translation, 1937), and *The
Russian Idea* (1947); L. Owen, *The Russian Peasant Movement*
(1937); E. T. Robinson, *Rural Russia under the Old Régime* (New
York, 1949); E. Wilson, *To the Finland Station* (1940); A. F. Keren-
sky, *The Prelude to Bolshevism* (1919), *The Catastrophe* (1927) and
The Crucifixion of Liberty (1934); P. B. Axelrod, *Die russische Revolu-
tion und die sozialistische Internationale* (1932); V. Chernov, *The
Great Russian Revolution* (New Haven, 1936). H. Ganken and H. H.
Fisher, *The Bolsheviks and the World War* (Stanford, 1940); A. R.
Williams, *Through the Russian Revolution* (New York, 1921); É. Van-
dervelde, *Three Aspects of the Russian Revolution* (1918); W. H.
Chamberlin, *The Russian Revolution, 1917–1921*, 2 vols. (1935);
J. Bunyan and H. Fisher, *The Bolshevik Revolution, 1917–1918,
Documents and Materials* (1934), and *International Communism and
Civil War in Russia, April-December 1918, Documents and Materials*
(1936); W. Hard, *Raymond Robbins's Own Story* (1920); R. H.
Bruce Lockhart, *Memoirs of a British Agent* (1932); H. Rollin,
La Révolution russe, 3 vols. (Paris, 1931); Boris Savinkov, *Memoirs of a
Terrorist* (New York, 1931).

CHAPTER IV

For the war attitude of German Social Democracy see Edwyn Bevan,
German Social Democracy during the War (1918); C. Andler, *Le
Socialisme impérialiste dans l'Allemagne contemporaine* (Paris, 1918),
and *La Décomposition politique du socialisme allemand, 1914–1919*
(Paris, 1919); A. J. Berlau, *The German Social Democratic Party,
1914–1921* (New York, 1949); E. David, *Die Sozialdemokratie im*

BIBLIOGRAPHY

Weltkrieg (Berlin, 1915); M. M. Drachkovitch, *Les Socialismes français et allemand et le problème de la guerre, 1870–1914* (Geneva, 1953); P. Gay, *The Dilemma of Democratic Socialism* (New York, 1952); K. Hainisch, *Die deutsche Sozialdemokratie in und nach dem Weltkriege* (Berlin, 1919); P. Lensch, *Die deutsche Sozialdemokratie und der Weltkrieg* (Berlin, 1915) and *Drei Jahre Weltrevolution* (Berlin, 1918); Max Schippel, *England und wir* (Berlin, 1917); Wolfgang Heine, *Zu Deutschlands Erneuerung* (Jena, 1916); K. Kautsky, *Sozialisten und Krieg* (Vienna, 1937); P. G. La Chesnais, *The Socialist Party in the Reichstag and the Declaration of War* (1915); Ernst Meyer, *Spartakus im Krieg* (Berlin, 1927); P. Scheidemann, *Memoirs of a Social Democrat*, 2 vols. (English translation, 1929); É. Vandervelde, *La Belgique envahie et le socialisme international* (Paris, 1917); J. Bourdeau, *La Minorité socialiste allemande* (Paris, 1916); L. Bergstrasser, *Geschichte der politischen Parteien in Deutschland* (1924); E. Haase, *Hugo Haase, sein Leben und Werke* (Berlin, 1930); F. Thimms and K. Legien, *Die Arbeitsgemeinschaft im neuen Deutschland* (Leipzig, 1915).

For the Spartacus movement see *Spartakusbriefe* (published occasionally during the war) and *Spartakus im Kriege* (issued by the German Communist Party after the War, 1927); *The German Spartacists : their Aims and Objects* (n.d. ?1920); Karl Liebknecht, *Reden und Aufsätze* (Hamburg, 1921) and *Ausgewählte Reden, Briefe und Schriften* (Berlin, 1952); Paul Frölich, *Rosa Luxemburg* (English translation, 1940).

For the Shop Stewards see R. Müller, *Vom Kaiserreich zu Republik*, 3 vols. (Berlin).

CHAPTER V

A number of the works cited under Chapter III are relevant here as well — *e.g.* those on the Spartacus movement and the Shop Stewards.

For the German Revolution of 1918 and its aftermath see especially M. Philips Price, *Germany in Transition* (1923); G. Young, *The New Germany* (1920); Arthur Rosenberg, *The Birth of the German Republic* (1931); H. Stroebel, *The German Revolution and After* (1923); R. H. Lutz, *The German Revolution, 1918–1919* (Stanford, 1922); P. Scheidemann, *Memoirs of a German Social Democrat*, 2 vols. (English translation, 1929) and *Der Zusammenbruch* (Berlin, 1921); E. Bernstein, *Völkerrecht und Völkerpolitik* (Berlin, 1919) and *Die deutsche Revolution* (1921.)

Refer also to Kurt Eisner, *Gesammelte Schriften* (Berlin, 1919); E. Eichhorn, *Eichhorn über die Januarereignisse* (Berlin, 1919); A. Fischer, *Die Revolutionskommandantur Berlin* (Berlin, 1922); K. Haenisch, *Die deutsche Sozialdemokratie in und nach dem Weltkrieg* (Berlin, 1919); Georg Ledebour, *Der Ledebour Prozess* (Berlin, 1919); R. Müller, *Der Bürgerkrieg in Deutschland* (Berlin, 1925);

R. Wissell, *Praktische Wirtschaftspolitik* (Berlin, 1919) ; K. Bycher, *Die Sozialisierung* (Tübingen, 1919).

For later developments see R. T. Clark, *The Decline of the German Republic* (1935) ; A. Rosenberg, *The History of the German Republic* (1936) ; E. Prager, *Geschichte der U.S.P.D.* (Berlin, 1922) ; H. Müller, *Die November Revolution* (Berlin, 1928) ; Emil Barth, *Aus der Werkstaat der Revolution* (Berlin, 1919) ; Anon., *Taktik und Organisation der revolutionären Offensive* (Berlin, 1921) ; Paul Levi, *Unser Weg* (Berlin, 1921) ; Toni Sender, *Autobiography of a German Rebel* (1940).

CHAPTER VI

The chief authority is E. H. Carr, *The Bolshevik Revolution, 1917–1923*, 3 vols. (1950–3). See also a number of the works referred to in the bibliography under Chapter II, especially those of Trotsky, Sukhanov, and Deutscher. Other important sources include A. Rosmer, *Moscou sous Lénine* (Paris, 1953) ; L. Trotsky, *Ma Vie*, with appendix by A. Rosmer (Paris, 1953) ; L. Voline, pen-name of V. M. Eichenbaum — *La Révolution inconnue 1917–1921* (Paris, n.d. — partly translated as *Nineteen Seventeen* (1954) and *1917 : The Russian Revolution Betrayed* (1954) ; I. N. Steinberg, *In the Workshop of the Revolution* (1955) ; Victor Serge, *Vie et mort de Trotsky* (Paris, 1951) ; V. M. Chernov, *Pered Burey* (New York, 1953) — in Russian ; F. Dzerzhynski, *Ausgewählte Artikeln und Reden, 1908–1926* (Berlin, 1953) ; R. Piper, *The Formation of the Soviet Union, 1917–1923* (1954) ; John Reed, *Red Russia* (1919).

Of Lenin's writings see especially *The State and Revolution* (1917) ; *The Proletarian Revolution* (1918), *The Land Revolution in Russia* (1918) ; *The Soviets at Work, April 1918* (Glasgow, 1919) ; *Will the Bolsheviks Maintain Power ?* (1922). See also many other writings in *The Essentials of Lenin* — two volumes of Selected Works (1947) — and also the complete works, issued in English with annotations, but later replaced by twelve volumes of *Selected Works* (various dates). See also *The Letters of Lenin* (1937). Refer also to L. Trotsky, *The Defence of Terrorism* (1921).

Among foreign studies see W. H. Chamberlin, *The Russian Revolution, 1917–1921* (New York, 1935) ; Bernard Pares, *Russia* (1941) ; Helen Pratt, *Russia : from Czarist Empire to Socialism* (New York, 1937) ; Arthur Rosenberg, *History of Bolshevism* (1939). See also N. Popov, *Outline History of the Communist Party of the Soviet Union*, 2 vols. (1935), and the official *History of the Communist Party of the Soviet-Union, edited by a Commission of the Central Committee, 1938* (Moscow, 1939) — both highly disingenuous ; A. Monkhouse, *Moscow, 1911–1933* (1933) ; A. Ransome, *Six Weeks in Russia in 1919* (1919) ; Victor Serge, *L'An I de la révolution russe* (Paris, 1930).

For the Anarchists and the Kronstadt Rising and for the Social Revolutionaries see A. Ciliga, *The Kronstadt Revolt* (pamphlet, 1935 ;

BIBLIOGRAPHY

English translation, 1942) ; and *The Russian Enigma* (1940) ; Alex. Berkman, *Die Kronstadt Rebellion* (1922) and *The Bolshevik Myth* (1925) ; Emma Goldman, *My Disillusionment in Russia* (1925) ; Ida Milt, *La Commune de Kronstadt* (Paris, 1949) ; I. Z. Steinberg, *Spiridonova, Revolutionary Terrorist* (1935) ; É. Vandervelde and E. Wauters, *Le Procès des social-révolutionnaires à Moscou* (Brussels, 1922) ; B. Bazhanov, *Avec Staline dans la Kremlin* (Paris, 1930).

Of the numberless books on the general theory of Communism I can mention only a few.

See N. Bukharin and E. Preobrazhensky, *The A.B.C. of Communism* (1922) ; N. Bukharin, *Imperialism and World Economy* (1930) ; R. W. Postgate, *The Bolshevik Theory* (1920) and *How to Make a Revolution* (1934) ; Bertrand Russell, *Bolshevism : Practice and Theory* (1920) ; Max Eastman, *Marx, Lenin and the Science of Revolution* (1926) ; W. Gurian, *Bolshevism : Theory and Practice* (New York, 1932) ; J. Macmurray, *The Philosophy of Communism* (1933) ; E. and C. Paul, *Creative Revolution* (1920) ; W. H. Chamberlin, *Russia's Iron Age* (Boston, 1934) ; S. and B. Webb, *Soviet Communism : a New Civilisation?*, 2 vols. (1936) ; René Marchand, *Why I Support Bolshevism* (English translation, n.d. ?1919) ; R. N. Carew Hunt, *The Theory and Practice of Communism* (1950) ; W. Z. Foster, *The Revolutionary Crisis of 1918–1921 in Germany, England, Italy and France* (Chicago, 1922) ; J. Stalin, *Leninism*, 2 vols. (1929 and 1933) ; H. Seton-Watson, *The Pattern of Communist Revolution* (1953) ; H. Marcuse, *Reason and Revolution* (1941) ; J. Plamenatz, *German Marxism and Russian Communism* (1954) ; B. Souvarine, *Stalin* (1939) ; M. Hillquit, *From Marx to Lenin* (New York, 1922) ; Karl Kautsky, *The Dictatorship of the Proletariat* (1919) and *Communism and Socialism* (New York, 1932) ; L. Trotsky, *Dictatorship or Democracy?* (New York, 1922), and *The Revolution Betrayed* (1937).

CHAPTER VII

For the eclipse of the Austrian-Hungarian empire see O. Jászi, *The Dissolution of the Hapsburg Monarchy* (1929) ; A. J. P. Taylor, *The Hapsburg Monarchy* (1948) ; and for post-war developments, R. Schlesinger, *Federalism in Central and Eastern Europe* (1945).

For post-war Austria, there is a vast mass of information in C. H. Gulick's *Austria from Hapsburg to Hitler*, 2 vols. (Berkeley, 1948), which should have been acknowledged, had I known of it sooner, in the bibliography to Volume III of this work. It is unfortunately too detailed — and too highly priced — for most readers ; but it is the indispensable work for the serious student. A most important original source is Otto Bauer, *The Austrian Revolution* (1923 ; English translation — unfortunately abridged — 1925). See also Julius Braunthal's *In Search of the Millennium* (1945) and *The Tragedy of Austria* (1948) ; and F. Borkenau's *Austria and After* (1938) ; J. Hannak, *Im Sturm eines Jahrhunderts* — on the history of Austrian Socialism — (Vienna, 1952); K. Renner, *Österreich von dem Ersten zur Zweiten Republik* (Vienna, 1953); F. Klenner, *Die österreichische Gewerkschaftsbewegung* (Brussels, 1955); J. Deutsch, *The Civil War in Austria* (New York, 1934); J. Böhm, *Erinnerungen* (Vienna, 1953).

On Hungary see Oskar Jászi, *Revolution and Counter-Revolution in Hungary* (1924); Count Karolyi's *Memoirs : Faith without Illusion* (1956); W. Boehm, *Im Kreuzfeuer zweier Revolutionen* (Munich, 1924); E. Horvath, *Modern Hungary, 1660–1920* (1923); C. A. Macartney, *Hungary* (1934) and *Hungary and her Successors* (1937); C. H. Schmitt, *The Hungarian Revolution* (English translation, n.d. ?1919); Béla Kun, *Revolutionary Essays* (n.d. ?1919); Alice Riggs Hunt, *The Facts about Communist Hungary* (1919); Béla Szanto, *Klassenkampfe und Diktatur des Proletariats in Ungarn* (1920); E. Varga, *Die ökonomischen Probleme der proletarischen Diktats* (?); A. Kaas and F. De Lazaruvics, *Bolshevism in Hungary : the Béla Kun Period* (1931) — useful for its appendix of characters. See also Hugh Seton-Watson, *Eastern Europe between the Wars, 1918–1941* (1945), *The East European Revolution* (1950), and *The Pattern of Communist Revolution* (1953); F. Borkenau, *The Communist International* (1938); F. Fejto, *Histoire des démocraties populaires* (Paris, 1953).

On Czechoslovakia see *The Evolution of Socialism in Czechoslovakia* (Prague, 1924); W. P. Warren, *Masaryk's Democracy* (Chapel Hill, 1941); E. P. Young, *Czechoslovakia* (1938); E. Beneš, *My War Memoirs* (1929); M. Mercier, *La Formation de l'état tchéchoslovaque* (1923); R. W. Seton-Watson, *A History of the Czechs and Slovaks* (1943); J. Chmeler, *The Political Parties in Czechoslovakia* (1936).

CHAPTER VIII

Particularly useful are Hugh Seton-Watson's two books already cited — *Eastern Europe between the Wars* (1945) and *The East European Revolution* (1950). For the separate countries there is not a great deal, apart from works dealing mainly with the years after 1945.

See also F. W. L. Kovacs, *The Untamed Balkans* (1941); D. Warriner, *The Economics of Peasant Farming* (1939).

For Yugoslavia consult Jules Moch, *Yugoslavia—terre d'expérience* (Monaco, 1953) and, in Serbo-Croat, N. Crulović (ed.) *Sotzialistichka Shtampa u Srbiji de xx Schweitz*, 2 vols. (Zürich, 1952). See also Tito's autobiography, written in collaboration with V. Dedijer, *Tito Speaks* (1953); and Hallam Tennyson, *Tito Lifts the Curtain* (1955). The Yugoslav Government has published a number of pamphlets in English describing its constructive work in various fields, and several periodicals are also issued in French and English, notably *Questions actuelles du socialisme* (Paris, monthly), and *Review of International Affairs* (Belgrade, fortnightly); but all these relate mainly to the period after 1945.

BIBLIOGRAPHY

See also H. Baerlein, *The Birth of Yugoslavia* (1922).

For Bulgaria see Ivan Karnivanov, *Ljudi i Pigmeji* (Belgrade, 1953), written by a dissident Communist; T. Tchitchovsky, *The Socialist Movement in Bulgaria* (1931); G. C. Logio, *Bulgaria Past and Present* (1936); K. G. Popoff, *La Bulgarie coopérative* (1927); I. Sakasov, *Bulgarische Wirtschafts-Geschichte* (1929).

For Rumania see D. Mitrany, *The Land and the Peasant Reform in Rumania* (1930); V. Bercam, *La Réforme agraire en Roumanie* (1928); J. L. Evans, *The Agrarian Revolution in Rumania* (1924); R. W. Seton-Watson, *A History of the Roumanians* (1934); T. W. Riker, *The Making of Roumania* (1934); G. C. Logio, *Roumania : its History, Politics and Economics* (1933); H. L. Roberts, *Roumania : Political Problems of an Agrarian State* (1951).

For Albania see H. C. Woods, *Albania Yesterday and Tomorrow* (pamphlet, 1927); J. Godart, *L'Albanie en 1921* (1922).

For Greece see J. Mavrogordato, *Modern Greece* (1931); A. R. Burn, *The Modern Greeks* (1945); G. N. Cafinas, *La Grèce économique* (1939); E. S. Forster, *A Short History of Modern Greece* (revised, 1946); K. Gibberd, *Greece* (1944); A. W. Gomme, *Greece* (1945); W. Miller, *Greece* (1928).

For Turkey see H. Kohn, *Nationalism in the Near East* (1929); T. L. Jameson, *Turkey* (1935); H. Luke, *The Making of Modern Turkey* (1936); J. Parker and A. Smith, *Modern Turkey* (1940); A. J. Toynbee and K. P. Kirkwood, *Turkey* (1926); B. Ward, *Turkey* (1942); E. G. Mears, *Modern Turkey* (1925).

CHAPTER IX

Main sources are the Reports of the various International Socialist and Communist Congresses, of the Berne (Second) and Labour and Socialist International, of the Communist International, and of the Vienna Union ('Two-and-a-Half'). It does not seem necessary to list these separately. The Reports of the L.S.I. contain special reports on the Socialist movements in the affiliated countries. See especially the Reports of the Marseilles Congress of 1925, of the Brussels Congress of 1928, and of the Vienna Congress of 1931.

The Reports of the Comintern Congress are simply more or less verbatim accounts of the Congress debates — often badly translated into English, together with some account of some of the proceedings of the Executive Committee. For most years — perhaps for all — there are separate volumes recording theses and resolutions adopted. The main mass of detailed information about the various Communist Parties has to be extracted from the files of *International Press Correspondence* (from 1922), the official organ of the Comintern, and from *The Communist International* from 1919. The best Report of the Opening Congress — that of 1919 — is in a special issue of *Inprecor* for March 1924. See also the special volume of Reports, *Le Mouve-ment communiste international*, submitted to the Second Congress (1920) and B. Lazitch, *Les Partis communistes d'Europe, 1919–1955* (Paris, 1956), which include a very brief history of the Comintern as well as of its constituent Parties.

There is no general history of the non-Communist Internationals after 1914. See, however, John Price, *The International Labour Move-ment* (1945) and L. L. Lorwin's *Labour and Internationalism* (New York, 1929); Max Beer, *Fifty Years of International Socialism* (1935); F. Borkenau, *Socialism, National and International* (1942); H. W. Laidler, *Social-Economic Movements* (1944), a revised version of *Socialism in Thought and Action* (1920), and *A History of Socialist Thought* (various editions); Arthur Rosenberg, *Democracy and Socialism* (1939); A. Sturmtal, *The Tragedy of European Labour* (1943); S. F. Markham, *A History of Socialism* (1930); W. E. Walling and others, *Socialism of To-day* (New York, 1916).

The opening phases of the struggle between the rival Internationals can be followed in R. Palme Dutt's *The Two Internationals* (1920) and in the *Labour International Handbook*, edited by Dutt (1921). See also the *Official Report of the Conference between the Second and Third Internationals and the Vienna Union*, held at Berlin in April 1922. The following should also be studied, L. R. C. James, *World Revolution, 1917–1936* (1937) from a Trotskyist standpoint; F. Borkenau, *The Communist International* (1933) and *Der europäische Kommunismus* (Berne, 1952; English translation, 1953); H. Seton-Watson, *The Pattern of Communist Revolution* (1953); L. Trotsky, *The First Five Years of the Communist International*, 2 vols. (New York, 1945); C. Kabakchiev, *Geschichte der Kommunistischen Inter-nationale* (Berlin, 1929); V. Serge, *From Lenin to Stalin* (New York, 1937); H. Gorter, *Offener Brief an Genossen Lenin* (1919); Lenin, *Left-wing Communism : an Infantile Disorder* (1920); Maria Sokolova, *L'Internationale socialiste entre les deux guerres mondiales* (Paris, 1954); Victor Serge, *Mémoires d'un révolutionnaire de 1901 à 1941* (Paris, 1951); Rudolf Rocker, *En la borrasca* (Buenos Aires, 1942) and *Revolución y regresión* (Buenos Aires, 1949); O. H. Gankin and H. H. Fisher, *The Bolsheviks and the World War : the Origins of the Third International* (Stanford, 1940); B. Lazitch, *Lénine et la Troisième Internationale* (Paris, 1950); A. Nin, *Las organisaciones obreros inter-nacionales* (Madrid, 1933).

For international Trade Union movements see the Reports of the rival Internationals — the Amsterdam International Federation of Trade Unions and the Red International of Labour Unions. See also L. Lorwin, *Labor and Internationalism* (1929). For the R.I.L.U. see A. Losovsky, *Marx and the Trade Unions* (1942) and *The Inter-national Council of Trade and Industrial Unions* (1920); J. T. Murphy, *The Reds in Congress* (1921); *The Constitution of the Red International of Labour Unions* (1921); *Resolutions and Decisions adopted at the First International Congress of Revolutionary Trade and International Unions,*

July 1921 (Glasgow, 1922) ; G. Zinoviev, *Towards Trade Union Unity* (n.d. ?1926).

CHAPTER X

See L. Lorwin, *Labour and Internationalism* (New York, 1929) ; L. S. Woolf, *Empire and Commerce in Africa* (1920) ; Norman Leys, *Kenya* (1924) ; Labour and Socialist International, *Reports* (see under Chapter IX), especially Report of Brussels Congress, 1928, vol. ii, *The Colonial Problem* ; Labour Party, *Memorandum on War Aims* (1917, and later versions) ; *Memorandum on Allied War Aims* (1918) ; *Memoranda on International Affairs* (1918-19) and *The Labour Party and the Peace Treaty : A Handbook for Speakers* (1918) ; *Stockholm : Rapport du comité d'organisation de la Conférence Internationale de Stockholm* (Stockholm, 1918) ; Labour Research Department, *The Labour International Handbook* (1921) ; M. A. Hamilton, *Arthur Henderson* (1938).

See also, for the background, H. N. Brailsford, *The War of Steel and Gold* (1914) ; E. D. Morel, *Ten Years of Secret Diplomacy* (1915 and later editions) and *The Black Man's Burden* (1920) ; Norman Angell, *The Great Illusion* (1910) ; J. A. Hobson, *Imperialism* (1900). See also references for Chapter IX.

CHAPTER XI

The best study from a Socialist point of view of the rise of Italian Fascism is A. Rossi, *The Rise of Italian Fascism* (English translation, 1938). The French version has some material that is omitted in the English version. See also E. Ferrari, *Le Régime fasciste italien* (Paris, 1928) and A. Rosenstock-Frank, *L'Économie corporative fasciste en doctrine et en fait* (Paris, 1934). A valuable, more specialised introductory study is W. Hilton Young, *The Italian Left* (1949). Reference should also be made to H. Finer, *Mussolini's Italy* (1935), and to G. Salvemini's *The Fascist Dictatorship in Italy* (1927) and *Under the Axe of Fascism* (1936). For Mussolini, see his *My Autobiography* (English translation, n.d.) ; G. Megaro, *Mussolini in the Making* (1938) ; and his own writings and speeches, *e.g. Le Fascisme : doctrine, institutions* (Paris, no date, several editions — there is a partial English translation) — and *Mussolini parle* (Paris, n.d. ?1929) ; also L. Roya, *Vie de Mussolini* (Paris, 1926) ; P. Nenni, *Storia di quattro anni* (1946).

Antonio Gramschi's *Lettere del carcere* and also his *Passato e presente* were reprinted at Turin in 1953, and his contributions to *L' ordine nuovo* (1919-20) the following year. M. M. Ferrara's *Palmiro Togliatti* appeared in Paris in 1954. See also F. Bellini and G. Galli, *Storia del partito comunista italiano* (Milan, 1953).

A selection of Giacomo Matteotti's writings, *Matteotti contro il fascismo*, edited by Anna Pagliaca, appeared at Rome and Milan in 1954, as did Gino Castagno's *Bruno Bozzi* in 1955.

For Italian Anarchism, see A. Borghi, *Mezzo secolo di anarchia 1898–1945* (Naples, 1954). For the Trade Unions, see G. di Vittorio and others, *I sindicati in Italia* (Bari, 1955). For the peasants, see A. Caracciolo, *Il movimento contadino nel Lazio, 1870–1922* (Rome, 1952).

For Socialist development, see L. Valiani, *Storia del socialismo nel secolo XX⁰* (Florence, 1945), and for a general bibliography and chronology, A. Leonetti, *L'Italie, des origines à 1922* (Paris, 1952, in the series *Mouvements ouvriers et socialistes (chronologie et bibliographie)*. See also F. Meda, *I congressi socialisti italiani dalla Prima alla Terza Internationale* (Milan, 1920) and *Il partito socialista italiano* (Milan, 1921) ; P. Gentile, *Cinquant' anni di socialismo in Italia* (Ancona, 1946) ; R. Rigola, *Cento anni di movimento operaio* (Milan, 1935), and *Storia del movimento operaio italiano* (1946) ; G. Zibordi, *Saggio sulla storia del movimento operaio in Italia* (1930) ; E. Vercesi, *Il movimento cattolico in Italia, 1870–1922* (Florence, 1923) ; L. R. Sanseverino, *Il movimento sindacale cristiano* (Rome, 1950); G. Spadolini, *La lotta sociale in Italia, 1848–1925* (Florence, 1948).

See also F. Turati, *Trent' anni di 'Critica sociale'* (Bologna, 1921) ; *Attraverso le lettere di corrispondenti, 1880–1925*, ed. A. Schiavi (Bari, 1947) ; and *Le vie maestre del socialismo* (Bologna, 1921) ; and also A. Levy, *Filippo Turati* (Rome, 1924) ; A. Schiavi, *Esilio e morte di Filippo Turati* (Rome, 1956), and *Filippo Turati* (Rome, 1955), and the same author's *Anna Kuliscioff* (Rome, 1955). Add Schiavi's *Andrea Costa* (Rome, 1955) to the book-list in Volume III.

CHAPTER XII

Reference should be made to the Annual Reports of the Labour Party, the Independent Labour Party, the Fabian Society, and other bodies, to the *Labour Year Books* of 1916, 1919, and later years, and to the *Encyclopaedia of the Labour Movement* (1928), and *The Book of the Labour Party*, 3 vols. (1925). See also the successive Labour Party *Programmes*, from *Labour and the New Social Order* (1918).

For the outline history of the working-class movement see G. D. H. Cole, *Short History of the British Working-class Movement, 1789–1947* (revised edition, 1948) ; G. D. H. Cole and R. Postgate, *The Common People, 1746–1946* (1938, revised edition, 1954) ; see also G. D. H. Cole, *History of the Labour Party from 1914* (1948) ; Max Beer, *History of British Socialism* (1919, new edition 1929) ; Francis Williams, *Fifty Years' March* (1950), and *The Rise of the Trade Unions* (1954) ; K. Hutchison, *Labour in Politics* (1925) ; G. A. Hutt, *The Post-war Condition of the British Working Class* (1937) ; G. D. H. and M. Cole, *The Condition of Britain* (1937).

See further *Beatrice Webb's Diaries*, ed. Margaret Cole, *1912–1924*

(1952), *1924–1932* (1956), and Margaret Cole, *Beatrice Webb* (1945) and (ed.) *The Webbs and their Work* (1949) ; J. Clayton, *The Rise and Decline of Socialism in England* (1926).

Outstanding biographies and autobiographies include M. A. Hamilton, *Arthur Henderson* (1938) ; R. Postgate, *Life of George Lansbury* (1951) ; Tom Mann, *Memoirs* (1923) ; Philip Snowden, *Autobiography*, 2 vols. (1934) ; H. G. Wells, *Experiment in Autobiography* (1934) ; F. Williams, *Ernest Bevin* (1952) ; M. A. Hamilton, *Beatrice and Sidney Webb* (1932).

See also Hugh Dalton, *Call Back Yesterday, Memoirs, 1887–1931* (1953) ; T. A. Jackson, *Solo Trumpet : Some Memoirs of Socialist Agitation and Propaganda* (1953) ; H. Pollitt, *Serving My Time* (1940), and *Select Articles and Speeches, 1919–1936* (1953) ; J. Clunie, *Labour is My Faith* (Dunfermline, 1954) ; D. Kirkwood, *My Life of Revolt* (1935) ; John McNair, *The Beloved Rebel* (1955) — a biography of James Maxton ; *Don Roberto* (R. B. Cunninghame Graham), by A. F. Tschiffely (1937) ; J. Hodge, *Workman's Cottage to Windsor Castle* (1931) ; Ben Tillett, *Memories and Reflections* (1931) ; S. G. Hobson, *Pilgrim to the Left* (1938) ; Lord Elton, *Life of Ramsay MacDonald* (1939), of which only vol. i has appeared ; L. MacNeill Weir, *The Tragedy of Ramsay MacDonald* (1938) ; J. R. Clynes, *Memoirs*, 2 vols. (1937) ; M. A. Hamilton, *Mary Macarthur* (1925) ; E. Sylvia Pankhurst, *The Home Front* (1933) ; John Paton, *Proletarian Pilgrimage* (1935) and *Left Turn* (1936) ; A. Fenner Brockway, *Inside the Left* (1942) and *Socialism over Sixty Years : the Life of Jowett of Bradford* (1946) ; F. J. Gould, *H. M. Hyndman, Prophet of Democracy* (1928) ; R. T. Hyndman, *The Last Years of H. M. Hyndman* (1923) ; R. Smillie, *My Life for Labour* (1924) ; C. R. Attlee, *As It Happened* (1954).

On the war years, see G. D. H. Cole, *Labour in Wartime* (1915) ; *Trade Unionism and Munitions* (1923) ; *Workshop Organisation* (1923) ; *Labour in the Coal-mining Industry* (1923) ; W. A. Orton, *Labour in Transition* (1921) ; Paul Kellogg and Arthur Gleason, *British Labour and the War* (1919) ; A. Gleason, *What the Workers Want* (1920).

For MacDonald's attitude during and after the war see J. R. MacDonald, *Parliament and Revolution* (1919) and *Socialism : Critical and Constructive* (1921).

For the General Strike of 1926 see R. Postgate, J. F. Horrabin, and Ellen Wilkinson, *A Workers' History of the Great Strike* (1927) ; R. Page Arnot, *The General Strike* (1926) ; W. H. Crook, *The General Strike* (Chapel Hill, 1931) ; Scott Nearing, *The British General Strike* (New York, 1926) ; J. Symons, *The General Strike* (1957).

For Socialist theory and policy, see S. and B. Webb, *A Constitution for the Socialist Commonwealth of Great Britain* (1920) and *The Decay of Capitalist Civilisation* (1923) ; Bernard Shaw, *The Intelligent Woman's Guide to Socialism and Capitalism* (1928) ; H. G. Wells, *The Work, Wealth and Happiness of Mankind* (1932), and *The Shape of Things to Come* (1933) ; G. D. H. Cole, *The Next Ten Years in*

British Social and Economic Policy (1929) ; and *The Principles of Economic Planning* (1935) ; H. Morrison, *Socialisation and Transport* (1935) ; Hugh Dalton, *Practicable Socialism for Britain* (1935) ; Douglas Jay, *The Socialist Case* (1937) ; W. S. Jevons, *Economic Equality in the Co-operative Commonwealth* (1933) ; C. R. Attlee, *The Labour Party in Perspective* (1937) ; Barbara Wootton, *Plan or No Plan ?* (1934) ; A. W. Humphrey, *The Modern Case for Socialism* (1928) ; E. R. Pease, *History of the Fabian Society* (revised, 1925).

For Guild Socialism, see S. G. Hobson and A. R. Orage, *National Guilds* (1914) ; A. J. Penty, *Old Worlds for New* (1917) ; R. H. Tawney, *The Acquisitive Society* (1920) ; G. D. H. Cole, *Self-Government in Industry* (1917), *Labour in the Commonwealth* (1918), *Chaos and Order in Industry* (1920), *Guild Socialism Restated* (1920), *Social Theory* (1920) ; Bertrand Russell, *Roads to Freedom* (1918) ; M. B. Reckitt and C. E. Beckhofer, *The Meaning of National Guilds* (1920) ; S. G. Hobson, *National Guilds and the State* (1917) ; A. R. Orage, *An Alphabet of Economics* (1917) ; G. R. S. Taylor, *The Guild State* (1919) ; N. Carpenter, *Guild Socialism* (1922) ; G. C. Field, *Guild Socialism* (1920). Consult also the files of the *New Age* and of the *Guildsman*, which became the *Guild Socialist* in 1921, and was merged into *New Standards* (1923–4).

For the Trade Unions, see also W. M. Citrine, *The Trade Union Movement of Great Britain* (Amsterdam, 1926) ; A. Creech Jones, *Trade Unions* (1928) ; G. D. H. Cole, *Organised Labour* (1924).

CHAPTER XIII

The handiest general study is in the third volume of E. Dolléans, *Histoire du mouvement ouvrier*. Of the modern part of this work there are at least two variant editions (vol. ii, *1871–1936* (1939), and vol. iii, *1921 à nos jours* (1953). For general background, see D. W. Brogan, *France under the Republic* (1940). See also M. R. Clark, *A History of the French Labour Movement, 1910–1928* (Stanford, 1930) ; F. Gaucher, *Contributions à l'histoire du socialisme français, 1905–1933* (Paris, 1934) ; Paul Louis, *Histoire du socialisme en France* (last edition, Paris, 1950) and R. Bothereau, *Histoire du syndicalisme français* (Paris, 1945) ; A. Zévaès, *Le Socialisme en France depuis 1904* (Paris, 1934) ; also G. Thorel, *Chronologie du mouvement syndical ouvrier en France, 1791–1946* (Paris, 1947) ; R. Garmy, *Histoire du mouvement ouvrier*, 2 vols. (Paris, 1936) ; G. Lefranc, *Histoire du syndicalisme français* (1937) ; J. Montreuil, *Histoire du mouvement syndical en France* (1947) ; P. Vignaud, *Traditionalisme et syndicalisme, 1884–1941* (1943).

Add to the biographies of Jaurès listed in the bibliography to Volume III, Marcelle Auclair, *Vie de Jaurès* (Paris, 1954) and for the pre-first-war relations between French and German Socialism, M. Lair, *Jaurès et l'Allemagne* (Paris, 1935) and M. M. Druchkevitch,

BIBLIOGRAPHY

Les Socialismes français et allemand et le problème de la guerre, 1870–1914 (Geneva, 1953). A collection of the writings of Léon Blum is now in course of publication.

See also R. Humphrey, *Georges Sorel* (Harvard and London, 1951); É. Vandervelde, *Jean Jaurès* (Paris, 1929); H. R. Weinstein, *Jean Jaurès* (New York, 1936); H. Bourgin, *De Jaurès à Léon Blum* (Paris, 1938); R. Millet, *Jouhaux et le C.G.T.* (Paris, 1937); D. J. Saposs, *The Labour Movement in Post-war France* (New York, 1931); M. Thorez, *Son of the People* (1938); O. Frossard, *De Jaurès à Lénin* (Paris, 1930).

See also the French Communist Party's *Open Letter to Lenin* (1918).

CHAPTER XIV

For Belgian Socialism, see É. Vandervelde, *Le Parti ouvrier belge 1885–1925* (1925); J. Devalte, *Histoire du mouvement socialiste belge* (1931); M. Antoine Pierson, *Histoire du socialisme en Belgique* (Brussels, 1953); J. Bondas, *Histoire anecdotique du mouvement ouvrier en Pays de Liège* (Liège, 1955); C. Mertens, *The Trade Union Movement in Belgium* (1925); L. Delsinne, *Le Mouvement syndical en Belgique* (1936); Centrale d'Éducation Ouvrière, *Évolution et structure du mouvement ouvrier socialiste en Belgique* (1953); N. Masson, *Histoire du mouvement ouvrier belge*.

Add to the book-list in Volume III, Léon Delsinne, *Le Parti ouvrier belge des origines à 1894* (Brussels, 1955) and the new edition of *Œuvres choisis* of L. de Brouckère, of which vols. i and ii appeared in Brussels in 1954 and 1955. Also J. Messinne, *Émile Vandervelde* (Brussels, 195?). See also L. Pieraud, *Belgian Problems since the War* (New Haven, 1929).

For the theoretical writings of de Brouckère, Vandervelde, and others, see the bibliography to Chapter XVI of Volume III.

For Switzerland, see Jacques Smid, *Unterwegs, 1900–1950* (Olten, 1953); W. Kups, *Hermann Greulich and Charles Fourier* (Zürich, 1949); Heinz Egger, *Die Entstehung der Kommunistichen Partei der Schweiz* (Zürich, 1952); H. Gridazzi, *Die Entwicklung der sozialistischen Ideen in der Schweiz bis zum Ausbruch des Weltkrieges* (Zürich, 1935).

CHAPTER XV

For Holland, see P. J. Troelstra, *Gedankschriften*, 4 vols. (Amsterdam, 1927–31). See also A. J. Barnouw, *The Making of Modern Holland* (1944); J. E. Morris, *Holland* (1936); B. Landheer (ed.), *The Netherlands* (1942).

For Scandinavia in general, see G. B. Nelson (ed.), *Freedom and Welfare* (1953) — a volume sponsored jointly by the Ministries of Social Affairs of Denmark, Finland, Iceland, Norway, and Sweden;

The Northern Countries in World Economy (1937) ; R. Kerney, *The Northern Tangle* (1946) ; B. J. Houde, *The Scandinavian Countries* (1948).

For Denmark, see C. Holland, *Denmark* (1927) ; E. Jensen, *Danish Agriculture : its Economic Development* (1937) ; P. Manniche, *Danmark : a Social Laboratory* (1939) ; E. C. Williams, *Denmark and the Danes* (1932) ; F. C. Howe, *Denmark, the Land of Co-operation* (1936) ; H. Jones, *Modern Denmark : its Social, Economic and Agricultural Life* (1927) ; J. Goldmark, *Democracy in Denmark* (Washington, 1936) ; E. Wünblad and A. Anderson, *Det Danska Demokraties Historie, 1871–1921* (Copenhagen, 1921).

For Sweden, see N. Bohman, *Present Day Sweden* (Stockholm, 1937) ; B. Braatoy, *The New Sweden* (New York, 1939) ; R. Heberle, *Zur Geschichte der Arbeiterbewegung in Schweden* (Jena, 1925) ; Z. Höglund, *Frau Branting till Lenin* (Stockholm, 1953) ; Ernst Wigforss, *Minnen*, 3 vols. (Stockholm, 1951 and 1954) ; W. Galenson, *Comparative Labour Movements* (1952) ; M. W. Childs, *Sweden : the Middle Way* (1936) ; S. Hanssen, *The Trade Union Movement in Sweden* (1927) ; J. J. Robbins, *The Government of Labour Relations in Sweden* (1942) ; P. Norgren, *The Swedish Collective Bargaining System* (1941) ; H. Tingsten, *Den Svenska Socialdemokratiens Identvecklung* (1941) ; N. Lamming, *Sweden's Co-operative Enterprise* (1940) ; A. Montgomery, *The Rise of Modern Industry in Sweden* (1939) ; E. Nylander (ed.), *Modern Sweden* (1937) ; R. Svanström and C. Palmstierna, *A Short History of Sweden* (1934).

For Norway, see *The Trade Union Movement in Norway*, a report by the Lands Organisation — the central Trade Union body (London, 1955) ; W. Galenson, *Labour in Norway* (1949) ; K. Gjerset, *History of the Norwegian People* (1932) ; G. Gathorne Hardy, *Norway* (1925) ; O. Grinley, *The New Norway* (Oslo, 1937) ; J. E. Nordskog, *Social Reform in Norway* (Los Angeles, 1935) ; J. Vidnes, *Norway* (Oslo, 1935).

For Finland, see J. Hampden Jackson, *Finland* (1938) ; T. Ohda, *Finland : a Nation of Co-operators* (1931) ; A. Rothery, *Finland : the New Nation* (1936) ; A. M. Scott, *Suomi : the Land of the Finns* (1926) ; J. H. Wuorinen, *Nationalism in Modern Finland* (1931) ; K. Gilmour, *Finland* (1931) ; E. van Kleet, *Finland : the Republic Furthest North* (1929) ; T. W. Atchley, *Finland* (1931) ; J. V. Hannela, *La Guerre d'indépendance de Finlande, 1918* (1938) ; E. Kuusi, *L'Œuvre de protection sociale en Finlande* (1928) ; J. L. Perret, *La Finlande* (1931) ; V. Tanner, *Die Oberflächengestaltung Finlands* (1938) ; O. W. Kuusinen, *The Finnish Revolution : a Self-Criticism* (1919).

CHAPTER XVI

The best book by far is Gerald Brenan, *The Spanish Labyrinth* (1943). See also F. Borkenau, *The Spanish Cockpit* (1937) ; S. de Madariaga, *Spain* (1942).

BIBLIOGRAPHY

V. Richards, *Lessons of the Spanish Revolution, 1936-9* (1953) — by an Anarchist and dealing mainly with a period subsequent to that covered in this volume. The same applies to A. Soudrey, *Nacht über Spanien* and to J. Hernández, *La Grande Trahison* (Paris, 1953) — by a former Communist — and also to G. Orwell, *Homage to Catalonia* (1938) and G. Jellinek, *The Civil War in Spain* (1938).

CHAPTER XVII

Many of the works listed under Chapters II and V are relevant for this Chapter as well. For the New Economic Policy, see especially the accounts in Carr's *The Bolshevik Revolution*, already cited, and in his *The Interregnum, 1923-1924* (1954), and in M. H. Dobb, *Soviet Economic Development since 1917* (1948) ; A. Baykov, *The Development of the Soviet Economic System* (1946) ; C. B. Hoover, *The Economic Life of Soviet Russia* (1931) ; A. Rothstein, *A History of the U.S.S.R.* (1950).

For the conflict between Stalin and Trotsky, see L. Trotsky, *The Lessons of October, 1917* (1925), *Cours Nouveau* (French edition, with commentary by Boris Souvarine, Paris, 1924) ; and *The Revolution Betrayed* (1937) ; Max Eastman, *Since Lenin Died* (1925) and *Trotsky, the Portrait of a Youth* (1926) ; M. S. Farbman, *Bolshevism in Retreat* (1923) and *After Lenin* (1924) ; V. Chernov, *Mes Tribulations en Russie soviétique* (Paris, 1921) and *The Great Russian Revolution* (Yale, 1936).

D. J. Dallin, *The Rise of Russia in Asia* (1950) ; H. Kohn, *Nationalism in the Soviet Union* (1933) ; D. Gramick, *The Management of the Industrial Firm in the U.S.S.R.* (New York, 1954).

For Soviet planning and policy up to the early 1930s, see V. V. Obelenski and others, *Socialist Planned Economy in the Soviet Union* (New York, 1932) ; Margaret Cole (ed.), *Twelve Studies in Soviet Russia* (1933) ; Maurice Hindus, *Humanity Uprooted* (1922), *Red Bread* (1931), and *The Great Offensive* (1933) ; M. Ilin, *New Russia's Primer* (Boston, 1931) ; W. B. Reddaway, *The Russian Financial System* (1935) ; Victor Serge, *Russia Twenty Years After* (New York, 1937) ; Anna Louise Strong, *The Soviet World* (New York, 1936) ; Louis Fischer, *The Soviets in World Affairs*, 2 vols. (1930), and *Soviet Journey* (New York, 1935) ; Beatrice King, *Changing Man : the Educational System in the U.S.S.R.* (1937).

CHAPTER XVIII

For the Ukraine, see Voline (V. M. Eichenbaum), *The Unknown Revolution* (1955) ; J. S. Reshetar, *The Ukrainian Revolution, 1917-1920* (Princeton, 1952) ; C. A. Manning, *Ukraine under the Soviets* (New York, 1953) ; Panas Fedenko, *Isaac Mezcpa* (1954) ; E. Yaroslavsky, *History of Anarchism in Russia* (n.d.) — useful mainly for a Bolshevik view of Makhno.

SOCIALIST THOUGHT

CHAPTER XIX

See R. Machray, *Poland, 1914–1931* (1932) ; P. Frölich, *Rosa Luxemburg* (1940) ; W. J. Rose, *The Rise of the Polish Democracy* (1940) ; O. Halecki, *History of Poland* (1942) ; G. Humphrey, *Pilsudski* (1936) ; E. Y. Patterson, *Pilsudski* (1935) ; R. Landau, *Pilsudski and Poland* (1929) ; K. Radek, *Rosa Luxemburg, Karl Liebknecht, Leo Jogiches* (1921).

CHAPTER XX

See H. G. Daniels, *The Rise of the German Republic* (New York, 1928) ; R. T. Clark, *The Fall of the German Republic* (1935) ; A. Rosenberg, *The History of the German Republic* (1936) ; F. Stampfer, *Die vierzehn Jahre der ersten deutschen Republik* (1936 ; revised, 1953) ; G. Ledebour, *Mensch und Kämpfer* (Zürich, 1954) ; Carl Ulrich's Autobiography ; M. Peters, *Friedrich Ebert* (Berlin, 1954) ; J. Dentz, *Artur Stegerwald* (Cologne, 1952) ; Paul Loebe, *Der Weg war lang* (Berlin, 1949 and 1954) ; W. G. Ochilevski, *Gustav Dahrendorf* (Berlin, 1955) ; W. Abendroth, *Die deutschen Gewerkschaften* (Heidelberg, 1954) ; Gustav Mayer, *Erinnerungen* (Zürich and Vienna, 1949) ; T. Cassau, *Die Genossenschaftsbewegung* (1925) ; J. Kuczynski, *Löhne und Konjunctur in Deutschland, 1887–1932* (Berlin, 1933) ; T. Leipart, *Karl Legien* (1929) ; S. Neumann, *Die deutschen Parteien* (Berlin, 1932) ; F. Ebert, *Schriften, Aufzeichnungen, Reden* (Dresden, 1926) ; G. Noske, *Von Kiel bis Kapp* (Berlin, 1920) ; H. Cunow, *Allgemeine Wirtschaftsgeschichte*, 4 vols. (Stuttgart, 1926–1931) ; P. Weidmann, *Die Programme der S.P.D. von Gotha bis Görlitz* (1926).

C. W. Guillebaud, *The Works Council : A German Experiment in Industrial Democracy* (1928) ; O. Hué, *Die Sozialisierung der deutschen Kohlenwirtschaft* (Berlin, 1921) ; P. Umbreit and O. Lorenz, *Der Krieg und die Arbeitsverhältnisse* (Stuttgart, 1928).

CHAPTER XXI

See references to Chapter XI.

CHAPTER XXII

See references to Chapter IX.

CHAPTER XXIII

For the United States there is an unwieldly mass of information scattered through the two immense volumes of D. D. Egbert and S. Persons, *Socialism and American Life* (Princeton, 1952). See also

the *American Labor Year Book* (Rand School, New York, 1916–32) ;
S. De Leon (ed.), *The American Labor Who's Who* (New York, 1915).
For the history of the American Socialist Party, see D. A. Shannon,
The Socialist Party of America (New York, 1955). Consult also
Maurice Hillquit, *Loose Leaves from a Busy Life* (New York, 1934);
H. W. Laidler, *Social Economic Movements* (1944); H. W. Laidler
and N. Thomas, *New Tactics in Social Conflict* (New York, 1926) ;
N. Thomas, *As I see It* (New York, 1932), and *America's Way Out*
(New York, 1932) ; J. Oneal, *Socialism versus Bolshevism* (New York,
1935), and *American Communism* (New York, 1927 ; revised edition,
1947) ; L. Corey, *The Unfinished Task* (New York, 1934) ; W. Z.
Foster, *Towards Soviet America* (New York, 1932), and *From Bryan
to Stalin* (New York, 1937) ; Earl Browder, *The Communist Party
of the United States : its History, Role and Organisation* (New York,
1941) and *What is Communism?* (New York, 1936) ; J. H. Maurer,
It Can be Done (New York, 1938) ; N. Fine, *Labor and Farm Parties
in the United States, 1828–1928* (New York, 1928) ; S. Perlman,
History of Trade Unionism in the United States (New York, 1922),
and *A Theory of the Labor Movement* (New York, 1928) ; M. R.
Clark and S. F. Simon, *The Labor Movement in America* (New York,
1938) ; P. S. Finer, *History of the Labor Movement in the United
States* (New York, 1947) ; S. Gompers, *Seventy Years of Life and
Labour* (New York, 1943) ; L. L. Lorwin, *The American Federation
of Labor* (Washington, 1933) ; S. Perlman and P. Taft, *A History of
Labor in the United States* (New York, 1935) — a continuation of the
standard work of J. R. Commons ; S. Yellen, *American Labor Struggles*
(New York, 1936) ; D. J. Saposs, *Left Wing Unionism* (New York,
1926) ; A. Bimba, *History of the American Working Class* (New York,
1927) ; L. Symes and T. Clement, *Rebel America : the Story of Social
Revolt in the United States* (New York, 1934) ; Joseph Freeman, *An
American Testament* (New York, 1936) ; E. G. Flynn, *Debs, Haywood,
Ruthenberg* (New York, 1939) ; H. U. Faulkner and Mark Starr,
Labor in America (New York, 1944 ; revised, 1955).
See also the bibliography to Volume III, Chapter XXI.
For Canada, see M. J. Coldwell, *Left Turn, Canada* (1945) ;
F. R. Scott and others, *Social Planning in Canada* (1935).

CHAPTER XXIV

Much the best study of Latin-American Labour Movements is
V. Alba, *Le Mouvement ouvrier en Amérique latine* (Paris, 1953). See
also R. J. Alexander, *Labour Movements in Latin America* (1947).
For Mexico, see the works listed in the bibliography to Volume
III, Chapter XXII, and add Marjorie Clark, *Organised Labor in
Mexico* (Chapel Hill, 1934).
For the Argentine, add J. Oddone, *Historia de socialismo argentino*
(Buenos Aires, 1934).

CHAPTER XXV

There is a wealth of important material in C. Brandt, B. Schwartz, and J. K. Fairland, *Documentary History of Chinese Communism* (1952); See also G. F. Hudson, *The Far East in World Politics* (1937); E. R. Hughes, *The Invasion of China by the Western World* (1937); Sir John Pratt, *War and Politics in China* (1943). Reference should also be made to K. S. Latourette, *History of Modern China* (1954); A. S. Whiting, *Soviet Policies in China 1917–1924* (New York, 1924); Peter Townsend, *China Phoenix* (1955); Liao Kai-lung, *From Yunan to Peking : the Chinese People's War for Liberation* (Pekin, 1954); H. G. Crick, *Chinese Thought from Confucius to Mao Tse-tung* (1954); R. C. North, *Moscow and the Chinese Communists* (Stanford, California, 1953); A. Malraux, *Storm over Shanghai* (?); E. Snow, *Red Star over China* (1937); M. N. Roy, *Revolution and Counter-revolution in China* (Calcutta, 1946 — original edition in German) — and *La Libération nationale des Indes* (Paris, 1927); H. Isaacs, *The Tragedy of the Chinese Revolution* (1938); L. Trotsky, *Problems of the Chinese Revolution* (New York, 1932); V. A. Yakhontoff, *The Chinese Soviets* (New York, 1934); I. Epstein, *The Unfinished Revolution in China* (Boston, 1947); G. Stein, *The Challenge of Red China* (New York, 1945); B. L. Schwartz, *Chinese Communism and the Rise of Mao* (Harvard, 1956).

CHAPTER XXVI

See E. S. Colbert, *The Left Wing in Japanese Politics* (New York, 1952), B. Swearingen and P. Langer, *Red Flag in Japan, 1919–1950* (Harvard, 1952); G. F. Hudson, *The Far East in World Politics* (1937); Isaö Abe, *Shakai-shugi-sha to Narimada* (Tokyo, 1947); Eijiro Kawai, *Watakushi No Shakaishugi* (Tokyo, 1950); Tetsu Katayama, *Minshu-seiji No Kaiko To Tombo* (Tokyo, 1954).

CHAPTER XXVII

See E. Thompson and G. T. Garrett, *The Rise and Fulfilment of British Rule in India* (1934); M. N. Roy and A. Mukherji, *India in Transition* (1922); M. R. Masani, *The Communist Party of India : a Short History* (1954); K. M. Panikkar, *Caste and Democracy* (1933), and *Asia and Western Dominance* (1953); A. Nevett, *India Going Red?* (Poona, 1954); M. K. Gandhi, *Autobiography* — best in the Adyar (Indian) edition, 1930, and other works, including *Towards Non-violent Socialism* (Ahmedabad, 1951); Jawaharlal Nehru, *Autobiography* (1936); S. C. Bose, *The Indian National Struggle,*

BIBLIOGRAPHY

1920–1934; Acharga Narendra Deva, *Socialism and the National Revolution* (Bombay, 1946) ; Asoka Mehta, *The Political Mind of India* (Bombay, 1952), and *Democratic Socialism* (Bombay, 1954).

CHAPTER XXVIII

For Australia the most useful source is B. Fitzpatrick's *Short History of the Australian Labour Movement* (revised, 1944) ; and see also his *The British Empire in Australia, 1834–1939* (1941). Refer also to E. W. Campbell, *History of the Australian Labour Movement : a Marxist Interpretation* (1945). For the background, see W. K. Hancock's *Australia* (1930 ; revised, 1945) ; E. O. G. Shann, *Economic History of Australia* (1938) ; A. G. L. Shaw, *The Economic Development of Australia* (1944) ; A. N. Smith, *Thirty Years : the Commonwealth of Australia, 1901–1931* (1933).

See also Lloyd Ross's valuable chapter in C. Hartley-Grattan (ed.), *Australia* (1947) ; H. V. Evatt, *Australian Labour Leader* (1945) — a large biography of W. A. Holman ; F. W. Eggleston, *State Socialism in Victoria* (1933) ; V. G. Childe, *How Labour Governs in Australia* (1923) ; W. G. K. Duncan (ed.), *Social Services in Australia* (1939) ; A. Brady, *Democracy in the Dominions* (1947) ; G. Anderson, *The Fixation of Wages in Australia* (1929).

For New Zealand, see S. Scott's very brief *Outline History of the New Zealand Labour Movement* (1941) ; J. C. Beaglehole, *New Zealand : a Short History* (1936) ; J. B. Condliffe, *New Zealand in the Making* (1930), and *Short History of New Zealand* (1935) ; W. B. Sutch, *Poverty and Progress in New Zealand* (1941), and *The Quest for Security in New Zealand* (1942) ; J. A. Lee, *Socialism in New Zealand* (1938).

INDEX OF NAMES

INDEX OF NAMES

INDEX OF NAMES

GENERAL INDEX

END OF VOL. IV